BACK EAST

BACK EAST

HOW WESTERNERS INVENTED A REGION

FLANNERY BURKE

University of Washington Press
Seattle

Back East was supported by a grant from the McLellan Endowment, established through the generosity of Martha McCleary McLellan and Mary McLellan Williams.

Copyright © 2025 by the University of Washington Press

Portions of chapter 3 were published in "Exploits against the Effete: Wallace Stegner and Bernard DeVoto, Men of Western Letters," in *Wallace Stegner's Unsettled Country: Ruin, Realism, and Possibility in the American West*, edited by Mark Fiege, Michael J. Lansing, and Leisl Carr Childers (Lincoln: University of Nebraska Press, 2024), and "Get Farther East Than You Are," in *Reconsidering Regions in an Era of New Nationalism*, edited by Alexander Finkelstein and Anne F. Hyde (Lincoln: University of Nebraska Press, 2023).

Design by Ani Rucki

Composed in Minion Pro, typeface designed by Robert Slimbach

All rights reserved. No part of this publication may be reproduced or transmitted in any form or by any means, electronic or mechanical, including photocopy, recording, or any information storage or retrieval system, without permission in writing from the publisher.

UNIVERSITY OF WASHINGTON PRESS
uwapress.uw.edu

LIBRARY OF CONGRESS CATALOGING-IN-PUBLICATION DATA
Names: Burke, Flannery author
Title: Back East : how westerners invented a region / Flannery Burke.
Description: Seattle : University of Washington Press, 2025. | Includes bibliographical references and index.
Identifiers: LCCN 2024056852 | ISBN 9780295753850 hardcover | ISBN 9780295753867 paperback | ISBN 9780295753874 ebook
Subjects: LCSH: American literature—20th century—History and criticism | Regionalism in literature | East (U.S.)—In literature | West (U.S.)—In literature | LCGFT: Literary criticism
Classification: LCC PS228.R4 B87 2025 | DDC 810.9005—dc23/eng/20250411
LC record available at https://lccn.loc.gov/2024056852

∞ This paper meets the requirements of ANSI/NISO z39.48-1992 (Permanence of Paper).

CONTENTS

Preface: My Brother's Stoop   vii

Introduction: Out West, Back East   1

PART 1 | SECOND CITY, FIRST DRAFT   11

Chapter 1: At the Other End of the Tracks   17

Chicago Interlude: The Crossroads   41

Chapter 2: The Marginal Man and the Marginal Midwest   55

PART 2 | THE EDUCATED OUTDOORSMAN   81

Chapter 3: Exploits against the Effete   85

California Interlude: The Marginal Woman   113

Chapter 4: When Nature Became Culture   127

PART 3 | THE AXES   155

Texas Interlude: Alienating as Hell   161

Chapter 5: The Primrose Path   178

Chapter 6: Back Here, Back Home   204

Conclusion: Eastward I Go Only by Force 232

Acknowledgments 239

Notes 245

Bibliography 279

Index 307

PREFACE
MY BROTHER'S STOOP

"We should get a stoop," announced my brother at dinner when he was twelve or thirteen. We lived fifteen miles from the city center of Santa Fe, New Mexico, in a one-story, ranch-style house on two and a half acres, off of a dirt road that a neighbor periodically graded himself because it fell within a no-man's-land of county jurisdiction. We had no basement, no gradient to the yard. I imagined a set of stone steps in the middle of the driveway, a drop from the edge to the gravel below. At nineteen I knew a lot, and I knew that we didn't need a stoop.

"What would we possibly do with a stoop?" I asked.

"Sit on it!" insisted my brother. "Shoot the breeze with people passing by!"

I smiled at the western expression, looked out the window at the sunset. A banner Halloween constituted as many as two trick-or-treaters.

"Where did you learn about stoops?" asked my father. He didn't like city crowds, but he did approve of *Sesame Street*. It's possible that he was agnostic on stoops.

"Stoopdude," answered my brother. "He's on a show. He wants to win a comics contest, and he calls himself 'Stoopdude,' who is one of his comic characters."[1]

"He must be from New York," asserted my mother. She was fond of New York, although I think she only visited twice. She read the *New Yorker*, even the lists of art show openings and film premiers that she could not attend.

"Maybe," said my brother. "Somewhere back East."

My brother was trying to include me. I attended college outside Philadelphia. A stack of *Seventeen* magazines under my bed paid tribute to the

East that I thought that I would discover upon arriving in Philadelphia's suburbs. For more knowledgeable readers, the maple leaf–strewn paths and plaid skirts advertised in the magazine's pages every September connoted New England. New England was back East too. In fact, a lot of places were back East. If my family met tourists visiting Santa Fe from Indiana, we said that they were from back East. Some people got jobs back East in Chicago. A lot of people I knew had gone to school back East in Vermont and Ohio and Massachusetts and Pennsylvania and Virginia.

For years I thought that I was simply ignorant. How was I to know there were different parts of the East? Or that Pennsylvanians thought Ohio was the Midwest? Or that the east coast of Virginia was in the South? By the time I was nineteen, I had visited New York with a family friend, and my brother and I had accompanied my dad to conferences in Washington, DC, but there was still a lot back East that intimidated me: toll roads and subway systems, the fast-paced accents that I had only heard in the movies and on television, the Ivy League schools, the halls of Congress, the New England summer camps that so many of my college classmates seemed to have attended. Even the snow was different, icier and less powdery than that of western slopes. As I started college, I realized that if the East was a place I was to understand, I would need to study.

My studies (and the sympathetic ministrations of a professor from California) took me out West. The discomfort that I felt in eastern environments was less my ignorance and more my upbringing, I concluded. I knew frontage roads and tribal police and Texas drawls and friends at Stanford and employees at Los Alamos National Laboratory and summer holidays on my grandparents' Kansas farm. If I felt out of place in Philadelphia, I was just a westerner back East. Easterners did not know that their myths about cowboys and dusty trails and untouched natural beauty were exaggerations or made up altogether. In much the same spirit that I had asked my brother why we would need a stoop, I decided that I would teach benighted easterners. I would be a western historian.

It did not take long for me to discover that I had plenty of company. I learned that the frontier—the idea of civilization moving westward across the continent from the East to the West—has deep roots in English colonization of North America, the colonial ambitions of the nascent United States, and the desire of white settlers and their descendants to claim their endeavors as a success. I learned how these pernicious fictions had led my textbook authors to avoid significant mention of French and Spanish colonial endeavors in North America. I learned how the US government had ignored and belittled Indigenous nations and their governments. I learned how those who had seized land in the West abused it. I learned that a lot of people in the past had used the words *frontier* and *West* synonymously. I learned that the frontier was a subjective presentation, shaped by the time and place of its creation. I learned that historians of the American West have spent considerable time debunking the misunderstandings that have adhered to the West and its residents as a result. I learned that the idea of the frontier is perhaps the most explored regionalist idea in US historiography. I learned that a fiction like the frontier can do a lot of harm.[2]

I learned about other western fictions too.[3] Westerns and anti-westerns occupied one semester, nineteenth-century artists seeking the sublime in the American wilderness another.[4] Rodeos and their antecedents fascinated me.[5] Many scholars took interest in tourist towns like Santa Fe, where I grew up, and revealed how everyday people spent their working lives building fantasies for visitors.[6] National Park employees told me about requests to see the "lost tribes" of the Grand Canyon.[7] At conferences, I encountered very-much-not-lost Indigenous scholars. They gave presentations about the narratives of disappearance and the labor of persisting.[8] I drove past "Spanish" red-tiled roofs in Southern California and thought about the white midwesterners who loved them.[9] The titles of the books and articles that I read and the museum exhibitions that I attended were filled with the words *magic, style, play,* and *imagination*.[10] But in all my studies of the fictional West, no one ever mentioned the fictional East.[11]

So many people had imagined a place that they called "out West" that their imagination had a history. I wanted to know: Where was the history of westerners' imagination? If I told it, could I escape the frontier? If westerners were the subjects instead of the objects of the story, might the ending change? Was back East a region? Was it a region that mattered?

This book is my best effort to build my brother's stoop.

Stop by. Shoot the breeze.

BACK EAST

INTRODUCTION
OUT WEST, BACK EAST

This book is about twentieth-century western writers and what happened when they imagined the East in the pages of their work. Just like easterners imagining the West, western writers usually thought that they had it right and usually got it wrong. Just like the fictions that easterners made up about the West, the fictions that westerners created had impact in the real world. The ideas of "out West" and "back East" worked in tandem. Together they contributed to income inequality and land degradation and women's disempowerment and antidemocratic violence and Native silencing. Together they also contributed to the founding of modern social science and the making of western universities and the formation of the National Endowments for the Arts and Humanities and amplification of Native voices. *Back East* shows what happens when Americans acted in real life on the basis of regional fictions. It encourages readers to think more deeply when we use our imaginations.[1]

THE WRITERS

I arrived organically in the diverse company of the particular writers and artists who appear in this book: John Hicks, Meridel Le Sueur, Max Big Man, Era Bell Thompson, Horace Cayton, S. Frank Miyamoto, Charles Kikuchi, Bernard DeVoto, Wallace Stegner, Edith Mirrielees, Stewart Udall, Lee Udall, Ricardo Sánchez, Roderick Elliott, Calvin Trillin, Leslie Marmon Silko, Deborah Taffa, and Louise Erdrich. I sought a diverse cast in the rich institutional archives of the American West that serve as testament to the region's long-standing literary traditions.[2] I began my research at Stanford after following a piece of correspondence suggesting that the school had formed in the image of eastern universities.[3] My early research introduced me to westerners at two crucial institutions that flourished in the years following World War II: the Bread Loaf Writers' Conference and the Pacific Coast Committee for the Humanities. Those institutions took me to the Department of the Interior in Washington, DC, and eventually to the Institute of American Indian Arts. Much as one might discover the works of an author or a new magazine by picking up a discarded book on a subway car or when passing along a misdelivered package to a neighbor, one work almost always led to another and opened the door to yet another archive.

The writers I examine were not born or raised in the East, and they did not come home to the East, not even when they used the word *back* to describe it. The writers who appear here heard about the East from family and friends, and they met newcomers and visitors from the East, and they consumed books and magazines written and published in the East. They constructed their East from borrowed memories and first impressions and the printed word.[4]

They also created their East from the work of western regionalists. Western regionalists writing in the 1930s did not always look to the narrative of the frontier to tell them what to say. Writing a generation after those who called themselves "pioneers," these writers found their inspiration elsewhere. They sought to describe their sense of place and belonging in the West by drawing on their local, natural surroundings. They followed models set by the little magazine enthusiasm of the 1910s and 1920s, and they often received funding from the federal government's New Deal programs in the 1930s to pursue their questions about the meaning of regions.[5]

World War II cast their questions in sharp relief. So many people moved to new parts of the country during and after the war that Americans rethought their origins and what places they considered local.[6] Federal military funding carried increasing numbers of Americans to the South and to the West, a mobility that inspired many of the writers in this book to wonder where those newcomers (and that funding) originated. The years between 1946 and 1949 constituted a watershed for regionalist thinking.[7]

Americans reconsidered their assumptions about their own regions and the regions they imagined. They questioned the norms of the places that they called the North and the South. In American literature, the Midwest emerged as a region of its own, rather than a proto-West that prepared its residents for settlement in the Rocky Mountains and along the Pacific coast.[8] Easterners and midwesterners moved westward in increasing numbers, thereby raising the frequency of the term *back East* in popular culture. Westerners built their visions of the East from such references and the government programs that facilitated or mandated their own journeys eastward. As the United States prospered, Americans reflected on how depression and war had changed them and the meaning of the places they had come from and moved to.[9]

As writers reflected, they participated as much in constructing a regional *imaginary* as they did a regional *identity*.[10] Although regionalism generally brings to mind writers describing their own local territory, the writers whom I consider thought more expansively about place, and they imagined regions other than the West.[11] In outlining the East as a region, the people at the center of this book announced themselves as writers, a challenge in and of itself to the typically cited source of American literature: the East. When they wrote of the East as a region, they did so to buttress their own regional credentials as well as to further understanding of issues of political and aesthetic significance to them. Attending closely to exemplary work from diverse authors within the genre of "the eastern" allows readers to acknowledge the multiple ways that writers may present regions and regional difference and to chart the impact of those presentations.

The impacts resounded. Associations of urbanity, power, and cosmopolitanism with the East—where the nation's stock market, its federal government, and its best-endowed universities were located—contributed to western suspicion, envy, and imitation among writers of the Midwest. In the 1930s, that suspicion took the form of economic critique of the railroads among writers of the Great Plains such as John Hicks and Meridel Le Sueur, who lamented western workers' exploitation alongside that of western land. Max Big Man (Apsáalooke) of the Crow Nation advertised western attractions for the railroad with the intention of undoing settler dominance.

Introduction 3

Western writers of color like Horace Cayton and Frank Miyamoto struggled to join the conversation as federal policies and regional narratives excerpted them from the West where they were born. As postwar prosperity spread across the West and persecution of leftist writers increased during the late 1940s and 1950s, the opportunity for a multiracial, regional radicalism alongside a consideration of the Midwest's literary contributions was lost. That is the story of part 1, "Second City, First Draft."

White western writers then moved their attention away from economic exploitation toward a western regional identity grounded in leisure and outdoor recreation. Their vision of back East shifted from Wall Street toward Washington, DC. They compared themselves with the East to prove that the West was better. Drawing on associations of rurality and wilderness with the West, dominant western writers from the 1940s to the 1960s presented themselves as educated outdoorsmen: emissaries of the natural world in the nation's cultural centers back East. Figures such as Bernard DeVoto, Wallace Stegner, and Stewart and Lee Udall contributed to national legislation that shaped nature and culture both, including the National Endowments for the Arts and Humanities. That is the story of part 2, "The Educated Outdoorsman."

And then back East faded away. Western writers who followed in the wake of the educated outdoorsman from the 1970s to the turn of the twenty-first century stepped from the West-East axis that had preoccupied earlier generations. Instead, they charted their own paths and opened new axes of inquiry.[12] Poet Ricardo Sánchez called attention to those narratives that carried his attention northward and southward. White supremacists of the Midwest and Rocky Mountains such as Roderick Elliott resented what they perceived as the abandonment of their region. They cynically used the rhetoric of the cowboy and a westward-moving frontier to criticize the federal government back East and to cover over their travels across the Great Plains, southward to Texas and northward to North Dakota. Native writers and artists such as Louise Erdrich and Deborah Taffa, who had been silenced by narratives that moved from West to East as much as they had by narratives that moved from East to West, worked along a web of stories stretching in all directions from Native homelands. Their journeys changed the meaning of regions in North America. That is the story of part 3, "The Axes."

Western writers whom readers might expect to see in these pages, such as Willa Cather, Hamlin Garland, and Laura Ingalls Wilder, appear only briefly. Their work celebrated settlers like themselves and their families who arrived from the East and colonized portions of what is today called Wisconsin, Minnesota, Iowa, Nebraska, and Kansas. Their writing led many readers from east of the Mississippi River to see those states as the West in the 1930s and states like Ohio, Indiana, Illinois and Michigan as the Midwest. For those writers born farther west, however, places like Minnesota and the plains states could be the Midwest or even the East, not the West.

Drawing clean lines around the Midwest and West matters less to this story than does ascertaining the perspectives of western and midwestern writers who identified regions in their work.[13] Moreover, arguing over definitions of what constitutes the Midwest can easily reproduce frontier, settler colonial narratives that privilege eastern perspectives.[14] Marking the East serves to unsettle commonsense assumptions about regional differences in the United States and reminds readers to query settler colonialism.[15] Not everyone in the United States formed their regional perspectives by moving from east to west or recalling ancestors who followed that path. Regardless of where these writers' journeys took them or whether they first identified themselves as westerners or midwesterners, each writer in this book imagined a place that they called "back East."[16] Theirs is the perspective I share.

Lots of westerners imagine, not just writers. Filmmakers and television producers and musicians and artists imagine too. They created their own visions of what back East was like. Artists, like writers, worked under the shadow of the frontier narrative, but the impact of their work followed a different timeline than that of writers.[17] Hollywood's location in California and its founders' ties to New York and New Jersey film studios create a different chronology for the fictional East in film. Moreover, the internet has so changed how people read, watch, and listen to media that the image of back East transformed dramatically in the last decade of the twentieth century and the early twenty-first century. The regional imaginaries in film, television, music, and art that portrayed a place called "back East" are worthy of investigation, and I return to some of them in the final chapter and in the conclusion to address what form back East may take next.

I center writers in this book because, among creative workers, writers are the most mobile, and mobility is crucial to the regional imaginary. Writers do not require extensive equipment or studio space. The writers I describe in these pages grew up in a place that they and others called "the West." They traveled first in books and then in person. Most of them saw travel as necessary for becoming a writer, some saw connections to the East as necessary for becoming a writer, and all were writers deeply imprinted by a place who looked for the imprints of place everywhere they went. They wrote during years of high mobility for most Americans and therefore regularly returned to the question of what constituted an American region.

How writers imagined regions had material impact. The East of the imagination reflected and transformed the West of the imagination. More important, back East changed the actual people and land of both the West and the East. Back East shaped rural and urban life, racial identity, literary communities, public lands policy, higher education, white supremacist movements, and creative expression. The nation's twentieth-century landscape comes into focus if we look through westerners' eyes. If we can see that the East is a region and if we can see that westerners invented it, we can see the culture of the twentieth-century United States.

THE INTERLUDES

In three places—Chicago, California, and Texas—writers found their sense of place and formed their images of back East in dialogue with, but independent of, the wider West.[18] I address each of these places in each part of the book in an interlude dedicated to just one writer. Because these are storied places in American culture broadly, not just the regional imaginary, mine is hardly the first commentary about these locales nor even about the writers whose work I read to understand them.[19] Each interlude acts as a bridge between back East and, respectively, the Midwest, the coastal West, and the Southwest.[20] By showing how ties and tensions between rural and urban, wealthy and poor, white and non-white, Black and non-Black, nature and culture, and Native and settler shifted regional designations, the interludes demonstrate how regionalism extends beyond identity and location to include imagination.

Chicago could be west in the eyes of eastern observers, east in the eyes of western ones, north in the eyes of southern ones, and south for Canadians and those who entered the city from the northern reaches of Wisconsin and Michigan. North Dakotan Era Bell Thompson considered it a crossroads. By the 1940s, western writers presented it as a place of its own, usually independent of its midwestern hinterland. The city had its own nationally known publishers, magazines, and universities as well as a growing and thriving literary culture.[21] The city met Thompson's expectations for a Black writer's home following World War II. She believed Chicago encouraged the nation to overcome inequalities frequently expressed as difference between the North and South. Drawing on her western upbringing, Thompson offered a form of pioneer respectability politics as a model for the nation as a whole.[22] That model ignored the colonialism, the extractive economies, and their attendant racial assumptions that barred Indigenous and most non-white people, including Thompson herself, from enjoying the full benefits of democracy.

California, identified as "west of the West" by President Theodore Roosevelt and "an island on the land" by writer Carey McWilliams, can act as both the pinnacle of the frontier experience and a place unto itself in the regional imaginary.[23] In the second interlude, I tell the story of Montanan Edith Mirrielees, a teacher, writer, and editor working at Stanford University and the Bread Loaf Writers' Conference, to illustrate how California could be both peak and unique. Among Stanford's earliest graduates and longest-serving faculty members, Mirrielees was a modest, private person. In this interlude, I respect the boundaries she drew around herself while acknowledging the ways that she built them on assumptions that shortchanged both her and her fellow westerners.

Like Chicago, Texas is simultaneously of multiple regions: too western to be South, too southern to be *el Norte*. Scholars and residents both struggle to explain just what Texas is. Like California, many of its promoters champion the state and its qualities, especially its size and independence, as unique. Poet Ricardo Sánchez loved Texas not because of its residents' boasting or its regional image but because of its unfulfilled promise. His stance put him in opposition to the white power advocates who claimed the cowboy as their preferred symbol, and he helped open the door to a new regional perspective, one that could follow diverse paths in partnership with Indigenous peoples and other scholars of color. Following insights he gained from eastern African Americans and Afro-Latines, Sánchez used his poetry and activism from the 1960s through the 1980s to advocate for a new orientation that placed Texas in the middle of America instead of putting America under the heel of Texas.[24]

THE MARGINS

In the physical books and magazines that writers, editors, and publishers produced and that fascinated me in the archives, a lot happened in the margins. These margins varied from the traditional blank space of a standard book to the layouts that formed headers, footers, and space for comics and illustrations. Researching in the internet age, I found the opportunities to hold and handle scrapbooks, first editions, and magazines, especially those decades old, a refreshing and emotional experience. After years of writing commentary for my students and colleagues in the (electronic) margins of their drafts, I realized that sometimes the margins are where writers and editors do their best thinking.[25]

When I began this book and wrote the word *marginalization* or *marginalized*, I imagined the people whom I studied shoved to the edges of the crumbling pages that I was reading. I endeavored to "center" a diverse cast of westerners under their own bylines. At the same time, I was curious about the work that they had accomplished in the margins. How were they able to write effectively in a compromised space?[26] And why did so many of the westerners who interested me find themselves relegated to the margins just when other westerners arrived at centers of power back East?

I learned that flipping the script to look back East does not automatically bring marginalized westerners into view. Regardless of when one begins the chronology, tell the story of the frontier in reverse, and most westerners are always just trying to catch up. They can never be urban enough, wealthy enough, educated enough, white enough, or civilized enough to satisfy the demands of the frontier narrative back East. The frontier is a fiction, among the most powerful fictions that Americans have told themselves. This book offers clues for how to break from its hold.

This book demonstrates how an ascendent economic and racial liberalism elevated the educated outdoorsman and left other westerners in the margins. The liberalism of the mid-twentieth century promised prosperity and individual fulfillment so long as rural people of all races moved to cities or suburbs and non-white people of all classes adopted the norms of middle-class whites. In the same years, racial liberalism promised non-white people that they need only aspire to white, middle-class life to attain it.[27] Liberal ideology transcended standard political divisions between Democrats and Republicans and does not serve here as a synonym for the thinking of the US Democratic Party. Rather, liberal postwar western writers and politicians put great faith in individual inquiry and democratic decision-making but gave less attention to the compromises and sacrifices that liberal democracy entails.[28] Midcentury western writers assured westerners who had been left in the margins that with time, patience, and access to economic, political, and cultural power back East, they would achieve equality and independence, but those rewards, including their ecological benefits, were always deferred.[29] Liberalism's western proponents asked for unending patience as they marginalized others in the name of inclusion, and they inscribed their ideology in their presentations of American regions.

THE MESSAGE

The chapters and interludes in this book rest on three premises well established by other scholars of the mythic West: regions are imaginary; the regional imaginary is part of regionalism; and the regional imaginary has material impact.[30] On the basis of these premises, I make three arguments: the years after World War II, especially in the period 1946–49, were rich years for the development of the regional imaginary; the regional imaginary contributed to mid-twentieth-century liberalism into the 1990s; and the western liberal regional imaginary produced both a rightwing backlash and new, less fettered axes for regionalist inquiry among people of color and Indigenous communities at the end of the twentieth century. Those new axes did not make regions less influential in the literary imagination or among policymakers. Rather, their creators broke with the frontier myth to recast what regions were and why they mattered. Along the way, Americans reset the boundaries of the Midwest repeatedly, imagining new regions such as the Sunbelt and the Pacific Rim and reimagining old ones, including the Appalachians and the Ozarks. More often than not, rural residents suffered when such designations emerged. Throughout, whether they produced or erased regions and homelands, the stories that Americans told about out West and back East reinforced one another. Together they made twentieth-century US culture.

They began in motion, on the train.

PART 1
SECOND CITY, FIRST DRAFT

GOING HOME
(BURLINGTON ROUTE)

How smoothly the trains run beyond the Missouri;
Even in my sleep I know when I have crossed the river.
The wheels turn as if they were glad to go;
The sharp curves and windings left behind,
The roadway wide open,
The crooked straight
And the rough places plain.

They run smoothly, they run softly, too.
There is not noise enough to trouble the lightest sleeper.
Nor jolting to wake the weary-hearted.
I open my window and let the air blow in,
The air of morning,
That smells of grass and earth—
Earth, the grain-giver.

> How smoothly the trains run beyond the Missouri;
> Even in my sleep I know when I have crossed the river.
> The wheels turn as if they were glad to go;
> They run like running water,
> Like Youth, running away . . .
> They spin bright along the bright rails,
> Singing and humming,
> Singing and humming,
> They run remembering,
> They run rejoicing,
> As if they, too, were going home.

Passengers boarding the Aristocrat, an air-conditioned car that ran on the Chicago, Burlington Quincy line in 1932, may have picked up a copy of "Going Home" in the station as they waited for their departure. The poem advertised the very car and the very line on which they rode.[1] For passengers who boarded the car in Chicago, "beyond the Missouri" likely connoted the West: the open, grain-giving prairies of Kansas, Nebraska, and the Dakotas, perhaps even the smell of morning dew in the mountain ranches of Montana (although attentive passengers would note that the Missouri River ran from west to east there). If Chicagoans hesitated at the notion of "going home" to the West, the smooth ride and peaceful, productive landscape may have tempted them to consider the great West an extension of their city, maybe even a place to settle.[2]

But what of those passengers who boarded in Denver? Did they also imagine themselves going home? And if so, were they glad to go like the wheels that carried them? Did troubles in Denver leave them weary hearted? Did they know in their sleep when they crossed the river? (The Missouri River ran from west to east in the state of Missouri too.) Did they feel their youth running away, maturity awaiting them? Did they rejoice as they remembered their first adventures upon their arrival back East? Did they consider Chicago maybe even a place to settle?

Much depended on the words *beyond* and *home*. Much also depended on the poem's author: Willa Cather. Perhaps no writer was more closely identified with the West than she in 1932. Born in Virginia in 1873, Cather moved with her family to Red Cloud, Nebraska, at age nine. Her father farmed briefly and then turned to real estate and insurance. The train station at Red Cloud fascinated a young Cather, and she often waited there to catch a glimpse of performers arriving for work at the Red Cloud Opera House. In *Song of the Lark* (1915), the second novel of her "prairie trilogy" (*O Pioneers!* was published in 1913 and *My Ántonia* in 1918), she fictionalized her own departure from the train station for creative, artistic endeavors in her depiction of Thea Kronberg. Kronberg, a Coloradan and aspiring singer, settles first in Chicago, where the Chicago Art Institute houses the painting by Jules Breton that gave the novel its name. And then she moves farther east. Drawing on her inspiration from the mountains, canyons, and Indigenous and Mexican populations of Colorado, she eventually triumphs in New York City.

Cather, like her fictional heroine, progressively moved eastward, first to Lincoln, Nebraska, to attend university, then to Pittsburgh at age twenty-three to work for *Home Monthly*, a women's magazine, and then to New York City to work for *McClure's* in 1906. She lived in New York and vacationed in New England and New Brunswick with her partner, Edith Lewis, for the rest of her life. In addition to her prairie trilogy, she returned to the West's history for inspiration in *The Professor's House* (1925) and *Death Comes for the Archbishop* (1927), which both described the Southwest and its Indigenous and Spanish-speaking inhabitants. She began writing novels full-time in 1912 and reached her peak popularity in the 1920s. She won the Pulitzer Prize for her 1922 war novel, *One of Ours*; taught at the inaugural Bread Loaf Writers' Conference; and gave several hundred public lectures. When "Going Home" appeared in the Burlington's advertising materials in 1932, Cather had completed her last trip back to Nebraska. She died in New York City in 1947, having made her career and her home back East.

For those western writers who followed in Cather's footsteps, her example offered both guidance and caution. The West was a rich vein for aesthetic inspiration but a more fragile one for reflection on the nation's economy and its inequalities. The West could inspire creativity, but that inspiration came from the West's past and conscribed the West's Indigenous and Mexican inhabitants to the past too. One could leave the West a local but might return from the East a tourist. One could cross the Mississippi and approach prestige, but crossing the Missouri, especially where it ran west to east, brought no change in status. The rural West could be home in fiction, but artists must seek their fortune in the cities of the East. And the farther east the better.[3]

The writers who appear in part 1—historian John Hicks, writer Meridel Le Sueur, advertiser Max Big Man, journalist Era Bell Thompson, scholars Horace Cayton and S. Frank Miyamoto, and social worker Charles Kikuchi—followed Cather's tracks. They often arrived in Chicago. Hicks and Le Sueur attributed economic exploitation of Great Plains farmers to railroads and Chicago financiers. Max Big Man went to Chicago to drum up eastern tourists for Montana attractions. Era Bell Thompson made her career in Chicago by drawing a contrast between its urban rhythms and her upbringing on North Dakota's rural prairies. Horace Cayton and S. Frank Miyamoto went east to Chicago to attain an elite education. Charles Kikuchi arrived in Chicago believing his presence would undo eastern racial norms. Each attempted to challenge frontier assumptions: that prosperity naturally moved westward for all, that only white men settled the West, that settlers set the terms of tourism, that erudition existed only in the metropole, and that racism would dissipate on its own. Each, for a while at least, saw Chicago as the East.

Writers who trod the frontier in reverse only wore its groove deeper. In the generation after Cather, western writers and readers imagined the East and the West in relationship with one another. While the easterner might have envisioned an untamed wilderness, a pastoral breadbasket, or a recreational wonderland at the other end of the tracks, the westerner was more likely to see the politician, the financier, the tourist, or the graduate advisor. The retorts from western writers that highlighted eastern urban centers, eastern finance, eastern tourists, eastern universities, and eastern race relations cast western cities, western economic development, western tourists, western universities, and western racial hierarchies entirely in the East's shadow. Even Thompson, who presented Chicago as a place unto itself, used the frontier's logic to advance her career via her family's pioneer past. The frontier promised a westward-moving, ever whiter and more prosperous nation, but going back east to Chicago did not deliver on the frontier's promises.

Cather wrote "Going Home" so that passengers could imagine themselves going west *or* east. Whatever direction they were facing, she left later western writers to work the line. By the time of her death, in 1947, western writers had begun presenting new boundaries of the East and West. They excluded the Midwest from conversations of western nature and eastern culture. They gave less attention to economics and more attention to aesthetics. They resisted confrontations with the racial and regional norms that segregated African Americans and forcibly moved and incarcerated Japanese Americans. They abandoned the promise of a multiracial regional radicalism for a white, western liberalism. The efforts of western writers to cast the Midwest as the East had failed.

Seen from the West, the East approaches. Sometimes the East makes it as far as Chicago, but the promises of the frontier's East—recognition, respect, and equality—never fully arrive for everyone. Absent eastern *or* western acknowledgment of its residents' diverse regional perspectives, the Midwest and its own economic and racial complexity became marginal to writers' representation of regions.[4] Even for those readers with the wealth to head east on the Aristocrat, Chicago could be no more than a first draft.[5]

CHAPTER 1
AT THE OTHER END OF THE TRACKS

Early in his career as a professor of history at the University of Nebraska, John Hicks joined the Nebraska Society of Mayflower Descendants. The organization, with its attachment to European colonization of the Eastern Seaboard, stood to raise Hicks's standing in social circles. He didn't care. His "fondest recollection of the Nebraska Mayflowers" was when "one lady genealogist after an animated recital of her 'line' to a bored male guest, inquired brightly: 'And what is your line?' To which he replied with greater accuracy than relevance: 'The Union Pacific.'"[1] Like many a western writer of the 1930s, Hicks turned to the railroad to explain where the East began.[2]

Himself a self-described westerner, Hicks grew up in Missouri and Wyoming as the son of a Methodist minister. He received his doctorate in history from the University of Wisconsin–Madison. He arrived there just a few years after the historian Frederick Jackson Turner—famous for his theory of a westward-moving frontier—left the Wisconsin faculty for a position at Harvard University.[3] Not surprisingly, Hicks noted in his autobiography that he was "determined to work on something pertaining to the West," but his reasoning was unexpected. "Probably," Hicks speculated, "this interest was due less to Frederick Jackson Turner's hypothesis than to the fact that my Wyoming experience had made me feel terribly western."[4] A "prairie historian," Hicks served as dean of the College of Arts and Sciences while he was at the University of Nebraska between 1931 and 1942, when he left for a position still farther westward at the University of California, Berkeley.[5]

Hicks made his career on the findings of his first book, published in 1931, *The Populist Revolt: The Farmers' Alliance and the People's Party.* He began the book with the sentence "The rôle of the farmer in American history has always been prominent, but it was only as the West wore out and cheap lands were no longer abundant that well-developed agrarian movements began to appear."[6] Hicks's history was a settler one. European American colonization and the origin of those "cheap" lands did not draw his interest. The rise of a political party in the West and its challenges to the railroad did. His research effectively began the field of agrarian populist studies and its attendant research in the political organization of rural people in the United States. In outlining western farmers' experiences, Hicks criticized eastern industrialists and the federal government who let them hold sway.

When Hicks wrote *The Populist Revolt*, those farmers who had participated in agrarian populist movements in the late nineteenth century had a reputation as a bumbling rabble, easily excited and without sophistication. In *O Pioneers!* Cather imagined the character Lou Bergson as sympathetic to populism and given to "bluster." He insists that "the West is going to make itself heard" and tells a visitor from New York: "You fellows back there must be a tame lot. If you had any nerve you'd get together and march down to Wall Street and blow it up." The visitor, a former neighbor who has moved to the East, laughs and explains that "the same business would go on in another street. The street doesn't matter."[7] Cather presented agrarian populists as sullen children inclined to a politics of grievance.

Hicks endeavored to reclaim agrarian populists as modest, sober citizens who contributed to democracy by advocating for federal oversight over railroads, grain elevators, and commodities market traders. He located their political movement—and the figure of the farmer—in the West and, to a much lesser extent, in the South. States west of the Mississippi that are indexed in *The Populist Revolt* include Colorado, Idaho, Iowa, Kansas, Minnesota, Montana, Nebraska, Nevada, North Dakota, Oklahoma, Oregon, South Dakota, Texas, and Wyoming. In addition to Texas, Hicks indexed four southern states: Alabama, Georgia, Louisiana, and South Carolina. No states east of the Mississippi, other than those located in the South, appeared in the index. If there were eastern farmers, Hicks did not make them the subject of study. Of western states, he gave the greatest attention to the Dakotas, Kansas, and Nebraska, an unsurprising focus given that he was working at the University of Nebraska at the time of the book's publication and during Depression years of intense farmer and labor activism.[8] Nonetheless, as "the rôle of the farmer" became less prominent in the work of professional historians, the effect of Hicks's work and fiction, like Cather's prairie trilogy, was to place "the farmer" in the western plains states.

Hicks acknowledged the existence of eastern farmers and the rural East. He just assumed that it was a westward-moving line of productive agrarian activity that was worthy of academic study. His prejudice was deeply rooted. Before his birth, his mother traveled to Vermont by train to visit family and described the region in letters that Hicks retained. "'Most of the farms,' she wrote her father, 'are old tumbled down looking places. I tell you, Pa, old Nodaway with its broad fields rich with grain will look good to me when I get back.'" Her uncle's farm yields in Vermont paled in comparison with what her father produced in Missouri.[9] His mother's and Hicks's own recollections created a narrative of ever-westward agrarian bounty.

Hicks's recollection of his western upbringing rested on an eastern foil, a technique he used in *The Populist Revolt* as well. Among those sources informing his book were "A Bundle of Western Letters," compiled by the *Review of Reviews* in July 1894.[10] The magazine's editors asked "several men of the West who are good observers and patriotic citizens to contribute letters which would help the East to a clearer view of Western economic conditions and movements." Such sentiments, the editors hoped, would allow greater understanding of the "so-called 'new sectionalism' that is arraying the West against the East."[11] The writers Hicks cited— professors, journalists, and authors from Kansas, Nebraska, Iowa, South Dakota, and Montana—spoke for the West. Hicks described the letters in his annotated bibliography as "a good cross section of western opinion on the Populist demands."[12]

The writers expressed western opinions but knew that their audience was the East. Their letters reveal the mirror image of the "new sectionalism." Among them was James Willis Gleed, a Kansas journalist whose work Hicks consulted repeatedly, including the 1894 *Forum* article "Is New York More Civilized than Kansas?" Hicks summarized Gleed's piece: "Finds the greater possibilities in Kansas."[13]

Hicks's description suggested a staid accounting of the two states' resources and perhaps a celebration of the railroad. (Gleed's brother, Charles, was a prominent lawyer who defended the Atchison, Topeka and Santa Fe Railway and had written a guide to western settlement for Rand McNally.)[14] Gleed actually chose a livelier tone, beginning with a quote from the *New York Evening Post* that asserted, "We do not want any more States until we can civilize Kansas." Gleed shot back, "The 'Evening Post' and New York do not care at all what is said of them—certainly not if it be said anywhere west of London."[15] The opening salvo indicated that the article would be as much about New York as it would Kansas.

Gleed, as Hicks would, took white westward settlement for granted, but eastern presumption of the same movement irked him. "The West knows the East; the East does not know the West." When rare eastern visitors arrived, they did not pay close attention, insisted Gleed. "In a very real sense the people are provincial. They ask the visitor from Kansas City if he knows their friends in St. Paul. They ask the visitor from Denver whether he enjoys any religious privileges in that city of churches."[16] For Gleed and his latter-day interpreter, Hicks, back East was a distant outpost by 1894 that sent few observers westward and did not notice much of the West's urban features when they arrived.

Having appointed himself the keener observer, Gleed revealed his sources: eastern newspapers. Farmers necessarily had to follow the news of eastern markets, while easterners rarely concerned themselves with western agricultural working conditions or burgeoning western urban centers. Therefore, Gleed concluded, "if Mr. Gould and Mr. Most monopolize the column of New York news, the Western farmer dependent on that column for information is gradually led to think of New Yorkers as either 'capitalists' or anarchists."[17] It was not roiling farmers that threatened to destabilize the national economy, said Gleed; it was eastern businessmen.

Hicks echoed Gleed when he concluded that the western farmers of the populist movement proposed modest reforms that tempered eastern profligacy. "The loan companies that have done the most mischief have been owned in the East. The unnecessary railroads have been built by the East. If those railroads have been foolishly or dishonestly managed, it has been by Eastern boards of directors," wrote Gleed.[18] In reclaiming the farmer, Hicks, following Gleed, created the persona of an even-tempered, observant farmer who contributed to the nation's democracy, not by bombing Wall Street but by moderating the excesses of eastern capitalist railroad barons at the ballot box.[19]

Gleed looked more favorably on New England than he did New York, but Hicks extended his views to the East as a whole. By the time of his research for *The Populist Revolt*, Hicks had decided that no part of the East was the right locale for him or his career, even though he had never lived there. When offered a job at Harvard, to which other midwestern historians had followed Turner, he turned it down, explaining that he "could never fit comfortably into an Eastern environment."[20]

Hicks chose instead to go farther West. He wrote his memoirs in California, where he ended his career as a historian at the University of California, Berkeley. Hicks arrived in the Bay Area in 1942 and embraced his new state as the apotheosis of not just western but national culture. He attributed his success to his settlement in the West, that part of the country that he saw leading the nation in the postwar period. As he recalled: "It is easy to pinpoint the beginning of this book. Early in December, 1962, five years after my retirement, William N. Davis, Jr., State Archivist and a former member of the University of California history department had me up to his house in Sacramento for a dinner in my honor. . . . After dinner Bill asked me to speak to the group but said he would like also to play a record by Samuel Eliot Morison, 'The Faith of an Historian.' . . . The contrast between Morison's eastern and urban background and my western and rural origin became the basis for my remarks."[21] By the time Hicks wrote his memoirs, he attributed the tumult that he had described in *The Populist Revolt* to an earlier age. The inequities that troubled him appeared to be largely a thing of his parents' West, not a postwar California where scholars celebrated their achievements over genteel parties listening to lectures on record players. One no longer had to be an easterner to be a respected professor. One could also be a Californian.

Hicks's work reflected three overlapping views that westerners increasingly held of the East following World War II that pushed Chicago eastward in the western imagination. By the early 1960s, when westerners looked eastward, they barely saw the South; they rarely acknowledged non-western farmers; and they rarely presented Wall Street financiers as plutocrats. Hicks's mentors, many of whom had studied with Turner, viewed the West as comprising those states north of the Ohio River, west of Pennsylvania, and east of the Rockies. By centering the agrarian populists of the Dakotas, Kansas, and Nebraska, who relied on railroads headquartered in Chicago, Hicks largely ignored the South. Midwesterners who felt marginalized were as likely to trace their relationship to the Union Pacific as they were the *Mayflower* to understand their status. In such presentations, Chicago formed a part of the East.

Hicks succeeded only briefly in reclaiming the role of the farmer as a symbol of democratic citizenship. His critics faulted him for ignoring those southern farmers who played a central role in challenging eastern and northern financiers.[22] Later observers cast his prairie farmers as reactionary racists, and still later historians have emphasized that the People's Party actually had its start among a diverse group of men and women farmers in Texas, including Black and Mexican members.[23] The whitening of Populist remembrance and historiography, however, stuck a reactionary, racist label on the term populism that remained into the twenty-first century.[24] Hicks's emphasis on *agrarian* populism also dovetailed with that of the Southern Agrarian literary critics, who championed the South's white, rural culture in the 1930s.[25] The effect was to make the West appear more rural and the East more urban than either actually was, erase farmers of color, and lump all white farmers of the United States together as reactionary.

Moreover, Hicks presented agrarian populism as a thing of the past that had done its work for the United States. The efforts of farmers in the 1930s to form cooperatives to manage their production, the continued challenges of farming an arid land evidenced by the Dust Bowl, and the industrialization of farming that accelerated in the 1940s and 1950s did not figure into Hicks's calculus of farmers' politics.[26] The West moved westward, and observers of the nation's regions were more inclined to forget the Midwest altogether. Mainstream audiences, including those at professors' parties in California, were less and less likely to see their contemporaries farming the prairies as the leaders of liberal democracy. Instead, they located democratic governance in the East, informed and funded by the energetic westward movement of the nation.

In the same years that Hicks endeavored to hold the nineteenth-century plains farmer in the role of moderate, democratic citizen, the author Meridel Le Sueur, writing in Minnesota, struggled to keep alive a "regional proletarianism" that she attributed to her parents' agrarian radicalism.[27] Born in Iowa in 1900, Le Sueur grew up with her mother, Marian Lucy, and her stepfather, Arthur Le Sueur, radical activists who supported the Populists and the Nonpartisan League (NPL) in Kansas, North Dakota, and Minnesota. Although the Populists and the NPL took a more moderate course, the Le Sueurs supported such movements from the far left and from the Midwest.[28]

Like Cather and Cather's fictional heroine Kronberg, Le Sueur moved progressively eastward, but unlike Cather and Kronberg, Le Sueur did not stay. She studied dance in Chicago and then drama in New York City, where she lived with fellow radicals in a commune headed by revolutionary anarchist Emma Goldman. She moved to California, as Hicks had. She briefly pursued an acting career and performed stunts in Hollywood films until the mid-1920s, then returned to the middle of the country. By 1926 she was a member of the Communist Party living in Minneapolis and writing full-time. She worked to protect the regional proletarianism of the West from the East.

In the mid- to late 1930s, regionalist enthusiasm found support from the New Deal's Works Progress Administration, while a series of independent, regionalist little magazines sprouted from the prairies and plains. This style of regionalism celebrated writers' connections to the places where they grew up, not to where they settled. The writing was less likely to celebrate pioneers and more attuned to the everyday lives of contemporaries. Much regionalism, but not all, focused on rural spaces.[29] Le Sueur championed how working people connected the rural and the urban in the Midwest during years when farmer-labor partnerships flourished.[30] Her regionalist advocacy allowed her a position with the Federal Writers'

Project in Minnesota working on the state guide. She recalled that "it was the first time in my life I had rent and food paid and could write." In 1945 she published *North Star Country*, a "history of the people of the Midwest, told from their dimension in their language." The book formed a part of the American Folkways volumes edited by Erskine Caldwell, a series that supported local understandings of American places in the regionalist style popular during the Depression and early 1940s.[31]

Just as the outline of a plow against the horizon functions as a motif in Cather's work, so does an image of Le Sueur or her protagonist in a cornfield.[32] Introducing her place in her family line, she chose to explain: "My people did not leave me land, or wealth, or great empires. I have on my desk a small inheritance, an instrument to estimate the prairie curve which my grandfather used."[33] Le Sueur repeatedly turned to the land as an actual place that had generated value for the nation. The railroad carried that value away from her beloved prairies, and she made it her most consistent symbol of eastern capital.

In her memoir of her parents' activism, the railroad served as their spur to protest. She dated their story's beginnings to 1900, when "Jim Hill and Pierpont Morgan agreed to combine the Great Northern and the Northern Pacific railways, despite the Populist laws against cartels. The manipulation and exploitation roused the farmers to form the Nonpartisan League in North Dakota which for one year, 1919, governed the state, building a mill and a bank, taking over the coal fields to protect the striking miners."[34] While Hicks saw the People's Party and groups like the Nonpartisan League as a brief florescence sufficient to meet the material needs of farmers and the democratic needs of the country, Le Sueur considered their activism a practice that required continual renewal in the land where it had begun.

Otherwise, Le Sueur argued, eastern capital exploited midwestern farmers. In *North Star Country* she described "speculators and railroads" who "grabbed one-eighth of Illinois, Wisconsin, Iowa and Missouri and Minnesota, and one-third of Arkansas. . . . Farmers who later bought back this land paid fifty million dollars for it, and then lost it again to the mortgage holders who accumulated millions of unearned wealth, in what the Populists called 'the multiplication of nothing.'"[35] While Cather depicted the

Midwest as a pioneer heartland and Hicks saw it as a democratic way station to an ascending and triumphant United States, for leftist agrarian radicals like Le Sueur, the land of the Midwest acted not just as metaphor but as a real place where people worked hard.

Recalling the late nineteenth century, Le Sueur lamented the systems by which farmers lost the value of their labor: "In Minnesota alone, in a deed of night, the Territorial Government gave the Northwest Railroad land grants which covered an area larger than four eastern states. . . . Organized in three centers of power, the Chicago Board of Trade, the Duluth Board and the Minneapolis Chamber of Commerce, they catapulted great fortunes with only the stroke of a pencil. . . . There was dockage for dirt, false balances, and phantom switching costs, and there were hives of commission men, speculators and elevator managers."[36] It was such practices that led farmers to resent the more immediate agent of their betrayal—the speculators in the region's cities and the elevator managers in the nearest small town—but for Le Sueur, the real path always led along the railroad tracks eastward.

Easterners may have owned the railroad, but in Le Sueur's pages, western working people laid the tracks and raised the crops that formed the freight. Describing the completion of the transcontinental railroad in *North Star Country*, Le Sueur imagined the road moving "by human muscle, by the clang of the sledge, the laying of rails weighing four hundred pounds—each stroke the work of a living man who has a past, who dreams of his life, wishes he was someplace East where the Indians didn't drop the man next to you." Le Sueur alluded to American Indian opposition to the railroad and described the road's completion and its aftermath: "The thousands of workers moved on, walked west, rode the freights back east, went south with the birds, were chased by the bulls off the trains." She ended the chapter on the railroad's construction with the songs of hoboes and migrant laborers. One song described a workingman's labor moving from East to West:

I've juggled a tray in a bowery café
Hopped bells for a hotel in Chi
Carried a pack along the B. & O. track
Glommed red-ball freights on the fly.

Another began with a westerner's perspective: "The lingering sunset across the plain / Kissed the rear end of an eastbound train."[37]

Le Sueur put her faith in the promise of a plains radicalism. Writing in the journal *Midwest* at the height of the Depression, she declared, "The regionalism which can now be effective is one not of isolation but of contact. In the middle west the historical movement of pioneering, of the Populist movement, the great agrarian revolts against the piracy of eastern capital, against the looting of the prairies, and the forests . . . these things must come alive."[38] Le Sueur's lyrical impressionistic style, so at odds with socialist writing conventions of the Depression era, made it difficult for readers and fellow writers to follow just what course of action she was proposing, but the path inevitably required connection across the people of the Midwest and followed the railroad tracks to "eastern capital."

Le Sueur's tendency to trace the origins of economic power eastward led her to a consideration of westward-moving conquest. Hicks had envisioned the frontier as westward-moving progress, but Le Sueur saw it as westward-moving extraction. "New York tenements were built from the wealth of the beaver, the buffalo, the bear, otter, mink and fox of the North Star Country," she told her readers. That wealth then appeared on display in the homes and on the bodies of eastern financiers as well as in the museums, universities, and other institutions that they funded. The last of the passenger pigeons, Le Sueur lamented, "died in an Eastern zoo many years ago."[39]

She acknowledged that previous nations had claimed the land of the plains and prairies and argued that the United States had benefited from their conquest. In her book *Crusaders*, in which she described her parents' political activism, she emphasized, "Empires were built by the seizures of Indian lands—nineteen million acres in Minnesota, three million in Iowa and as many from the Pottowatamies, of the Illini—and by the seizure of timber, and timber land." The figures of John Jacob Astor's account books, insisted Le Sueur, "were history. Those figures show the death of great nations—the Sioux and Chippewas, the extinction of millions of animals, the robbing of hunters of traders, destruction by famine, disease, and firewater."[40] Le Sueur's writing in the 1930s and 1940s depicted conquest as advancing westward, first in Michigan, Illinois, and Minnesota and then progressing farther westward into the Dakotas. Her narrative suggested that Indigenous nations such as the Oceti Sakowin and Anishinaabe (whom she called the Sioux and Chippewas) had died out, but unlike Hicks and Cather, she managed to acknowledge the existence of Indigenous people and their landholdings as well as the role that Native lands and peoples had played in building the wealth of white, eastern Americans.

Later in life, Le Sueur extended the connections she wanted to build among people of the plains to Indigenous communities. She lived for a while in the Pine Ridge Reservation and ran a radio show in Minneapolis, with support from folk singer Pete Seeger, which included interviews with Native women, discussion of Native education, and conversation with lawyers who defended those arrested at the 1973 Wounded Knee Uprising.[41] Her work was a continuation of the kind of education and community building that her parents had practiced. Writing about them in *Crusaders*, she recounted: "Arthur traveled all over the Dakotas with the huge map he unrolled in schoolhouses, ringing the bell and telling how the wheat exchange by the stroke of a pencil was robbing them of millions. . . . Farmers, mechanics, ranchers, hoboes, wanderers, itinerant workers mounted soapboxes, shouted in wheat fields, passed out leaflets at factory gates."[42] Although Hicks and later scholars of agrarian populism generally found otherwise, Le Sueur recalled miners, urban laborers, and farmers of the Midwest seeking common cause. That she also included hoboes, who challenged railroad barons' dominance by riding the rails for free, suggests how central the railroad was in her understanding of the position of the Midwest vis-à-vis eastern capital.

Her recollection also showed how deeply invested she was in honoring and educating a broad swath of midwestern working people. She cared as much about what passengers riding the train read as who rode it. She drew this inspiration from her parents as well. Her stepfather had led the People's College in Fort Scott, Kansas, and her mother had met him there in 1914, when she took a job running the school's publicity department and writing its English textbook. The People's College, founded in 1911, had its roots in a cooperative effort with the socialist newspaper *Appeal to Reason*, published in Girard, Kansas, by Emanuel and Marcet Haldeman-Julius.[43]

Supported by Socialist Party member contributions, the school had a brick-and-mortar center in Fort Scott and provided correspondence education to student farmers and machinists in Canada and, with the exception of the Southeast, much of the United States. Students received a copy of the writing textbook that Le Sueur's mother wrote, *Plain English*. Each installment of the book was signed, "Yours for Education, The People's College."[44]

There was a hint of nostalgia when, in 1955, Le Sueur credited her mother with suggesting the idea for the Little Blue Books, designed "to fit in the overall pocket, sell for a nickel, and contain excerpts from Jefferson, Lincoln, and Tom Paine, and later poetry and jokes and satire. You could carry them anywhere, whip them out while riding a freight or resting from plowing in the wheat fields."[45] Published between 1919 and 1978, the series enjoyed widespread popularity from the 1920s through the 1940s and provided an introduction to the kind of education that more prosperous students, such as Hicks, received at small regional, religious colleges or at western state universities. Emanuel and Marcet Haldeman-Julius intended the books for the hands of all classes. The small, stapled paperbacks were a key part of a campaign "for the common man to educate himself."[46] Le Sueur was not alone in her lingering affection for the Little Blue Books. In his memoir, *Education of a Wandering Man*, the popular western fiction author Louis L'Amour recalled reading his first when "another hobo was reading one, and when he was finished he gave it to me."[47] Like Le Sueur, L'Amour remembered the range of authors reproduced in the little books, from Shakespeare and Voltaire to Thomas Paine and Charles Darwin. Like her, he associated the books with a western education.

Marcet and Emanuel Haldeman-Julius knew their audience. Many readers were immigrants or the children of immigrants who had bypassed the East Coast and Chicago to settle directly on the plains. Reading works such as Lloyd L. Smith's *How to Pronounce 4000 Proper Names* (1925), Arthur Shumway's *How Newspapers Deceive Their Readers* (1931), Maynard Shipley's *Origin of the Solar System* (1929), Julius Moritzen's *Literary Stars of the Scandinavian Firmament* (1923), and Leo Markun's *Your Intelligence and How to Test It* (1929), as well as *Great Dates in History* (1931), acquainted hoboes, farmers, and miners with the norms of US educational knowledge.

The books circulated throughout the country, largely by subscription. For readers standing alongside each other at the kiosks that sold them, the little paperbacks had the potential to act as equalizers between people of different classes and people of different regions.[48]

The Little Blue Books educated a western, train-riding public in how to exit the margins, whether marginalization emerged from an individual's race, class standing, language, or region of origin. Were westerners tucking into John Greenleaf Whittier's *Snow-Bound* to be blamed if they imagined a North Dakota winter instead of a New England one as they looked from the window of a Great Northern car? Upon reading a reprint of James Russell Lowell's 1869 essay "Condescension in Foreigners," did they imagine not an English tourist but an eastern one when Lowell complained that "we had been a desert, we became a museum. People came hither for scientific and not social ends. . . . The sociologists . . . were the hardest to bear. . . . I was not the fellow being of these exploiters: I was a curiosity; I was a specimen."[49] Le Sueur wanted no one to be a specimen. In her efforts to include everyone in the reading public, she prepared plains readers to think of the East as a foreign land, a place from which condescension flowed but could be overcome with education.

By the mid-1950s, Le Sueur may have begun to doubt whether farmers and hoboes carried their education in their overalls. The People's College had been destroyed by vigilantes during the First World War because the Le Sueurs and others affiliated with the college were anti-interventionists. Emanuel Haldeman-Julius continued to publish another paper, the *Debunker*, into the 1930s, and the Little Blue Books' popularity persisted among travelers and farmers and past the deaths of Marcet in 1941 and Emanuel ten years later. But in the 1950s, the Le Sueurs' brand of socialism and free thought was in dramatic decline. Leftists were not welcome in moderate liberal ranks. Le Sueur herself struggled against blacklisting during national campaigns directed at socialist authors. She turned to writing children's literature, including books on Johnny Appleseed, a hero of hers. Even when most constrained, she endeavored to contribute to a print culture of the plains that led its readers to look to the land and the people who worked it.

Above and opposite Readers of diverse classes found themselves standing alongside each other at the kiosks and vending machines that sold the Little Blue Books. Their reading furthered the goal of Kansas-based Haldeman-Julius Publications to educate the masses from the prairies. Leonard H. Axe Library, Special Collections and University Archives, Pittsburg State University; and "Books via Slot Machine," *Newsweek*, December 11, 1939; photo by Pat Terry.

Hicks progressively moved westward; Le Sueur deepened her roots on the plains. She never consigned farmers or their economic needs to the past, and with age she grew more attentive, though clumsily, to the histories, landholdings, and political will of the Midwest's Indigenous peoples. Nonetheless, she and Hicks had their similarities. Both were inclined to discount the southeastern United States when considering American regions. Both had a tendency to conflate urban areas with the East and condescension with its institutions. Both, to varying degrees, considered the East a site where economic power should be tempered by the political organizing of those to the west. And both traced those lines of power along the railroad tracks eastward to Chicago.

Neither writer was wrong. The railroads exercised significant power in shaping regional boundaries when they advertised themselves and attractions along their routes. The Burlington line placed Chicago in the East as the 1939 World's Fair in New York approached. A 1938 pamphlet suggested that potential customers "Go East This Year: See Washington DC, the nation's capital . . . the great cities of New York, Chicago, and Philadelphia . . . visit historic, picturesque New England . . . behold the thundering spectacle of Niagara Falls . . . join the gay throngs at the Atlantic Ocean beaches. Travel by train—the fast, safe, economical way to see the East."[50] Westerners could envision an eastern United States from such advertisements. The East was composed of great cities, including Chicago; national leadership; historic landscapes; and crowds.

More than other railroad advertising, dude ranch promotion separated the West from Chicago and put the city in the East. Dude ranches first seized on advertising possibilities with the "See America First" campaign of 1919–20, which sold the attractions of America's National Parks (and nearby dude ranches) over the sites of Europe.[51] But it was not until the late 1920s, when automobiles began competing for passengers, that railroads really recognized the potential of dude ranch advertising. The Northern Pacific and Burlington lines sold fifty-five hundred tickets at an average cost of twenty dollars per ticket to dude ranches during the 1927 season, which greatly increased railroad interest in advertising such destinations. Both lines began issuing thick, elaborate brochures and booklets advertising ranches, and both also sent representatives to meetings of the Dude Ranchers' Association, which had formed in 1926, and began publishing its newsletter, the *Dude Rancher*, as a magazine for dudes in 1933. The Union Pacific joined the field in 1931 and, by 1933, had helped form the Colorado Dude and Guest Ranch Association.[52] California dude ranches served a rotating roster of tourists and Hollywood actors.[53]

Representatives of the railroads drew a consistent portrait of the typical dude. Max Goodsill, general passenger agent for the Northern Pacific, presented this image to an audience of dude ranchers: "Dudes lived in a land of unreality in the East, surrounded by gilded palaces; when they went on vacation, they wanted to come down to earth and leave artificiality behind them."[54] Such a portrait created an urban, elite image of the East around the figure of the dude. For those westerners working at dude ranches, presentations from railroad representatives such as Goodsill were their insight into what the East was like. Like the railroad tracks, the advertisements ran both ways—in selling the West, they showed westerners a glimpse of the East.

Dude ranches themselves often had eastern roots. In a short essay in 1960, Dick Randall's son described his father, a charter member of the

Dude ranch wranglers and other westerners formed their image of the East from publications like *Metropolitan* magazine, as shown in this 1915 photo of wranglers at Valley Ranch in Wyoming. Dude rancher Larry Larom, *front right*. McCracken Research Library, P.5.1810, Buffalo Bill Center of the West, Cody, Wyoming.

Dude Ranchers' Association, as "the man who put the dude in dude ranching," whose first customers were "Eastern contacts" and "industrialists, bank presidents, and international sportsmen" who "had grown tired of the gilded spas in other sections of the country." These men, explained Randall, "were interested in the everyday phases of ranch work and they wanted to be a part of them to relax and forget the cares of high-tension business."[55] Many ranches emerged from personal contacts as ranch owners realized that livestock alone would not consistently support them.[56] Ranchers then relied on word of mouth to attract dudes and repeat visits. Particular Wyoming ranches became connected to particular cities and eastern regions: Eaton's Ranch with Pittsburgh, Horton's H F Bar Ranch with Chicago, Siggins Triangle X with Boston. According to dude ranch historian Lawrence Borne, "The strongholds of dude ranch visitors were New York, Boston, Philadelphia, and Chicago."[57] Ranchers sent Christmas cards to former visitors and would sometimes visit former guests, host a series a parties, and solicit customers for the following season. Some were

At the Other End of the Tracks 33

easterners themselves, like Larry Larom and Winthrop Brooks, of Wyoming's Valley Ranch, who had offices in the Brooks Brothers Building in New York City.[58]

Such contacts allowed dude ranchers to select their own customers, who then reproduced their eastern prejudices on western ranches. Larom, the longtime president of the Dude Ranchers' Association, wrote in frustration to his Wyoming representative in Congress, Paul Greever, in 1936 because a ranch in New Jersey had opened with a name similar to his own: Valley Dude Ranch. "It is seriously affecting our business and status here and in the East," Larom complained. "All spring we have been bothered by telephone calls from the cheapest people, including many Jews for accommodations and information."[59] Such sentiments, beyond exposing bigotry, underscored the efforts of dude ranchers generally to limit their customers to "white Christians."[60] As late as 1957, only four of forty-two dude ranches that responded to a Dude Ranchers' Association survey accepted Jewish customers.[61] Dude ranchers presented their ranches as free of social distinctions, but their overlay of eastern prejudice onto western regionalism made most dudes wealthy, white, Christian, and eastern.

Dude ranch advertising also allowed railroads to skip over associations between themselves and economic exploitation. As the *Dude Rancher* explained in a reprinted article from the 1934 *Sheridan Press*: "There is very little material wealth in the West. Most of the money that has been sweated from its mineral bearing rocks has gone east."[62] Hicks and Le Sueur had united western miners and midwestern farmers in shared political aims, but the *Dude Rancher* dismissed their agitation as a temporary imbalance. The West was free of the market, and to be free of the market meant that the West was also free of class conflict, immigrant job seekers, urban crowds, and even, according to some advertisements, midwestern small-town pettiness. As the *Dude Rancher* and *Sheridan Press* assured their readers: "'The West' isn't anything like the pictures painted of it by the radical intelligentsia. It isn't a mass of toiling and moiling beet field workers nor is it marching bands of IWW's. The West isn't anything like Sinclair Lewis' Main Street."[63] The article placed "the radical intelligentsia" in the East. Through such messages, dude ranches presented the East as a place of social inequality and class discord, problems that dudes could ignore while in the West. The equality that Cather attributed to settlers' labor on the plains and Hicks considered a product of political organizing in the West and Le Sueur identified in the plains' well-educated masses, the Burlington Railroad presented as a natural product of Wyoming and Montana.

In emphasizing the Rocky Mountains' dude ranches, railroads also skipped over the Midwest's Indigenous people (many of whom were farmers themselves) and located living American Indians as tourist attractions in the Intermountain West, not the Midwest. Visits to reservations and tribal ceremonies were a selling point for some ranches, and advertisers played on common tropes about Native people by emphasizing that American Indians lived outside the modern era. A 1937 Burlington advertisement for ranches in Montana promised readers that "dudes may visit the reservations at any time, and each year the wild days before the coming of the white man are re-lived in tribal ceremonies."[64] As in Le Sueur's early writing, Native people in dude ranch advertising moved westward until the West itself disappeared into the past, taking the region's Indigenous peoples with it. Had such reading material been the only source available to them, Native people providing the labor of tourist entertainment in Montana and Wyoming might well have concluded that the East was a fast-paced realm of the future devoid of people like themselves.

That made the cultural labor for the railroads that Indigenous people performed all the more important. Among such workers was Max Big Man (Apsáalooke), a member of the Crow Nation, who was paid by the Burlington Railroad and was an "honorary member of the Dude Ranchers' Association." In 1930–31 he traveled to Chicago, Cleveland, New York City, Philadelphia, and Washington, DC, to elicit eastern customers for the railroad and for Montana and Wyoming dude ranches. Dude ranch advertising may not have displayed western inequalities, but privately, Big Man acknowledged them. Moreover, like Le Sueur, he observed how inequality could overlay rural-urban relationships. In a letter to his boss, he observed that "a great many of my Crow people think that they are not treated right but . . . I learn[ed] out here in these cities that my people are treated as good as anyone. Here they have bread lines for poor people."[65] Big Man had also done his homework in familiarizing himself with Burlington promotional material, and his professional persona echoed its messages. When interviewed about his impressions of Chicago and New York, he asked: "What are you going to do about advertising for Chicago if you put Al Capone away in jail for six months?"[66] Big Man recognized the value of "atmosphere" to effective marketing, and he knew that the tracks that ran west could also carry western tourists east.

Big Man used that skill to advocate for the Crow Nation politically. When he visited Washington, DC, he met with the commissioner of Indian affairs and the secretary of the interior and successfully campaigned for several bison to be placed on his wife's land in Montana, as a tourist attraction. In a 1934 article in the *Dude Rancher*, he introduced himself as having "traveled extensively through the east and middle-west the past few years in interest of creation of travel west."[67] In the guise of the eastern tourist, Big Man saw another easterner that non-Native westerners generally did not acknowledge: the settler.

Big Man argued that the distance between the white settler members of the Dude Ranchers' Association and the dude was not as great as advertising suggested. He framed his one request to his readers as a prayer: "Oh, Great Spirit, you placed my ancestors, the Crow tribe, here. At one time all this land was theirs. But you have permitted another people to come from the far East whose homes are made of timber and rocks; they now occupy the land of my ancestors. Our ancestors never pointed their weapons at the white race. Put into their hearts a soft spot for the Indians of today that they may still treat them much better in the future."[68] In writing for the *Dude Rancher*, Big Man directed his article at "dudes," the people who came from the "far East" and who influenced, not just ranchers' bottom line but the politics impinging on Apsáalooke sovereignty both locally in Montana and back East in Washington, DC. As an honorary member of the Dude Ranchers' Association, Big Man recognized that white ranchers and white dudes were not so different. They were both easterners in Big Man's eyes.

Meanwhile, Native people from east of Montana disappeared in dude ranch and railroad advertising in the 1930s. Just a year after Max Big Man's article appeared, the Dude Ranchers' Association began including parts of the West in what it had previously presented as "The East." "The West with a capital 'W' doesn't start until you leave Nebraska on the east and doesn't end until you pull out of Nevada and Idaho on the west," opined a writer in the *Dude Rancher* in 1934. "The great and beautiful states of California, Washington, and Oregon are west but not 'The West.' The rolling corn belt country is far west of Albany but Iowa, Nebraska, and the Dakotas east of the Missouri river are not 'The West.'"[69] In excluding so much territory from the West, the *Dude Rancher* expanded the East as well as its customer base but also erased the Midwest and its Indigenous and settler residents. If they had the resources, anyone from Iowa to urban California could call themselves a dude, according to the *Dude Rancher*. The East had grown large and easterners more numerous.

The problem for railroads and guest ranches was that by the late 1930s, *dude* appeared to have taken on a negative connotation, one associated particularly with being eastern. A 1937 Burlington advertisement assured its audience: "By the way, let it be said right here that the term 'dude' is not used disparagingly. It is simply the western way of referring to any visitor or guest from 'back East' . . . which means almost anywhere east of the cattle country."[70] Dictionaries agree that the term *dude* emerged in the 1880s and by the turn of the century had acquired connotations of "tenderfoot" or "someone wearing outlandish clothing."[71] The frequent protests in advertisements suggested that *dude* meant "a feminine and affected man" or "effete."

A signature strength of dude ranch advertising then became assuaging dudes' anxiety over their masculinity, a quality imperiled by eastern cities and rescued in western vacations. A short article from 1936 called "A Dudin' I Did Go" relates a trip that did not start well. When greeted by a local cowboy legend on a rearing horse, the dude forgot to clear his throat, his "howdy" sounded "weak and ineffectual," and he "even blushed." Initially, the dude considered himself "rather giggly and out of character in the ten-gallon hat, the chaps and spurs and kerchief" and "felt that he fooled nobody." After a rough day on the trail, the author tried to conjure some "urgent business" that could tear him "out of this Rustic Paradise before the week was up," but by the third day he had adjusted. He joined the midnight ride and looked forward to the gathering around the campfire, where the woman he had admired earlier "smiled" at him. He was "glad now there was no urgent business back in the city. . . . The city! Those poor, slave-driven critters back there in the city!"[72] Shorter advertisements told a similar story. Dudes could be true men if freed of the emasculating environment of the eastern city.

Western women writers felt the ground shift under their feet as railroad advertising joined the chorus of critics defining gender roles during the Great Depression. By the late 1930s, male literary standard-bearers in the East focused on building an American canon of literature while enduring the Great Depression, and they judged Willa Cather harshly. They showed both regional and gendered prejudice when they diminished Cather's standing by calling her a "minor" and "feminine" writer.[73] Cather's work centered white, western women. Thea Kronberg is a western woman creative seeking her voice in *Song of the Lark, My Ántonia* celebrates the life-giving energy of the woman farmer, and the blustering populist in *O Pioneers!* has made his fortune by relying on his sister's agricultural acumen. Bergson's New York interlocuter has romantic interests in Bergson's sister in *O Pioneers!* not because he seeks to make her a farmer's wife but because he sees the advantages of becoming a prosperous farmer's husband. As he admires the fields she has built, he remarks: "You're all rich as barons."[74] While such sentiments pleased critical audiences of the 1910s, by the 1930s they struck critics as tone-deaf at best and threatening to a common people's literature at worst. Dismissing Cather as a minor woman writer served as a form of dismissing her more conservative politics. It had the added effect of erasing settler women and the western places that had inspired them.

If Le Sueur expected better treatment given her leftist views, she did not receive it. Le Sueur did not advertise for "The Aristocrat," as Cather did, nor did she celebrate local farmers—women or men—who had become "rich as barons." Indeed, she kept her focus on the prairies' most needy. In one of her better-known articles, "Women on the Breadlines," published in the *New Masses*, she called attention to rural women's unique circumstances of poverty when they moved to urban centers. "There is a great exodus of girls from the farms into the city now. Thousands of farms have been vacated completely in Minnesota," she wrote. Some found work as shopgirls, noted Le Sueur, but the older women, "the real peasants," had "a more difficult time," particularly because shelters for women and children were limited.[75] Like Big Man, Le Sueur did not turn away from want or inequality, whether she found it in the country or the city or among women. These observations earned Le Sueur a dismissal from the *New Masses* editors as "defeatist in attitude" and "lacking in revolutionary spirit and direction."[76] The education of the masses so desired by 1930s socialists evidently did not extend to an understanding of women's lives. Whether midwestern women writers cast women as rich barons or starving peasants, they risked the charge that they and their midwestern subject matter were lacking.

In western literature, the Midwest's investment in its lands, that region's Indigenous people, and the western woman writer were disappearing. Dude ranch advertising hardly reflected leftist views, but it reinforced leftist critics' messages regarding regions. Musing in 1924, Struthers Burt, a Princeton graduate who published extensively before writing a memoir about his own dude ranch, said that the very best wrangler was "an educated Eastern man with a great deal of Western experience, or—but this is a rare combination—an educated Western man with a great deal of Eastern experience."[77] The notion that westerners might have their own institutions of education and could write their own memoirs about the process of acquiring "Eastern experience" ran contrary to the image that railroad advertising had built of dude ranches. A white man played in the West and acquired education in the East, and whatever western women of any race did was minor.

That meant that the westerners meeting dudes at the train station accepted new boundaries of the East and West. By the late 1930s, in presentations of the dude, the East—dudes' point of origin—moved westward, incorporating fully the city of Chicago. The West moved westward to the Rocky Mountains but did not include the region's major cities nor its western coast. Unlike farmers and miners, dude ranchers worked hand in hand with railroads to bring easterners to the West and rejected any presentations of the West as radical or socialist. Into the 1940s, proponents of mid-twentieth-century democratic liberalism, such as Hicks, aided such regional views by presenting midwestern populism and sometimes even the Midwest itself as products of the past. Le Sueur sought to keep midwestern agrarian radicalism alive in the national memory, but she struggled against censorship, blacklisting, and critical prejudice against both western and women writers. Big Man subtly maneuvered to undermine railroad advertising that ignored inequalities between rich and poor and urban and rural, but he worked for an agent of colonization. When advocating for his own people, all he could do was plead his case with his dispossessors. By the middle of the twentieth century, westerners imagining Chicago might have conjured the city's crowds, frenetic pace of business, dapper dudes, or even land-hungry settlers. Only rarely did they look for the plutocrats of eastern capital.

And for some, Chicago became a destination all its own.

CHICAGO INTERLUDE
THE CROSSROADS

In her 1946 memoir, *American Daughter*, Era Bell Thompson described her arrival in the city that she would call home:

> Chicago!
> My eyes grew big and my heart pounded as the yellow cab weaved in and out of the maelstrom of traffic, turned into Michigan Avenue, and started south. . . . A colored woman, another colored man. The crowds and the traffic slowly decreased. All around me now were colored people, lots and lots of colored people, so many that I stared when I saw a white person.[1]

Thompson differed from many of her new neighbors. She arrived not from the South but from North Dakota in the West. To be surrounded by Black people was unusual for Thompson, and she delighted first in the novelty and eventually in the homecoming.

Born in Iowa in 1905, Thompson moved with her family to North Dakota in 1914, where her father became a farmer. The tragedy of her mother's early death combined with the departure of her brothers for urban work led her father to Bismarck, where he worked for the governor of North Dakota during the Nonpartisan League's brief political dominance in the state. Later he found work as a cook and ran a secondhand store in Mandan. Following a track career and a difficult bout of pleurisy while a student at the University of North Dakota, Thompson lost her father and then finished school at Morningside College in Sioux City, Iowa, in 1933. Shortly thereafter, she moved permanently to Chicago.

Work was scarce during the Great Depression, especially for Black women, but Thompson found it with the Illinois State Employment services offices. A Rockefeller Fellowship in Midwestern Studies from the Newberry Library allowed her to write her memoir. A year later, in 1947, she began working for *Ebony* magazine, a new enterprise of the Johnson Publishing Company, which became "the most widely read black magazine in the world."[2] She made her career with the magazine as an editor and journalist and reported from places around the world, including Liberia, Ghana, the Democratic Republic of the Congo, Zambia, Zimbabwe, South Africa, and Mozambique, a 1953 journey that formed the basis of her second book, *Africa: Land of My Fathers*.

For Thompson, Chicago was the fullest realization of what the Midwest could offer and a new gateway to the old country defined expansively as both Europe and Africa.[3] Chicago was not a precursor to opportunity farther East as it was for Cather, a way station in the nation's development westward as it was for Hicks, a source of capitalist exploitation as it was for Le Sueur, the origin of American settlers as it was for Big Man, nor even the home of clueless tourists as it was for dude ranch wranglers. By pulling the Midwest's rural residents into its fold, Chicago was a city as good as those of the East in Thompson's eyes. Because so many of Chicago's residents came from farming families, like hers, she presented the city as a kind of pioneer metropolis, the place where settlers of all races made their fortunes. Thompson did not place Chicago on the edge of a frontier between East and West, nor did she characterize it as a chimerical model of progress. She did not pine for New York City or encourage others to do so. Chicago satisfied.

As the story of a Black woman from the plains, Thompson's narrative challenges the idea that only white men settled the West and that African Americans understood the nation only by looking toward the North or South. Thompson did not substitute the East for the North, nor did she follow Cather's tracks all the way to New York City. She used the rhetoric of regionalism to claim the prairie city as her own and the nation's. "Three times I came down from the prairies to live with 'my people' and twice I returned to my plains," she explained in the proposal for her memoir.[4] She let her reader do the math. The last time, she stayed.

In *American Daughter* Thompson built her regional consciousness from her childhood sensory experiences of the plains and in contrast to another region that she had constructed in her imagination: the South.[5] As a teenager, Thompson, her father, and her brothers received newspaper clippings from her eldest brother about race riots in northern cities and lynchings in the South. Although her brother had been forced to seek refuge at his Chicago employers' during a riot in 1919, "he had a fine job chauffeuring, he said, making good money, living a bright, colorful life. 'How,' he asked, 'can you folks stay out there in that Godforsaken country away from civilization and our people?' The boys read his letters and laughed no more, for their scorn had turned to envy."[6] For Thompson's older brothers, the work and color of life in Chicago beckoned.

Thompson felt differently. Weaving together her brother Dick's reports of his experience in the city and the harrowing stories of the *Chicago Defender* articles, an adolescent Thompson concluded that her place was the prairies: "For a long time, I could see the lifeless body dangling from the tree. To me it became a symbol of the South, a place to hate and fear. And Dick's civilization was a riot, where black and white Americans fought each other and died. I wanted never to leave my prairies, with white clouds of peace and clean, blue heavens, for now I knew that beyond the purple hills prejudice rode hard on the heels of promise."[7] Throughout her career as a travel journalist, Thompson described the regions that she visited and asked readers to question the local premises that contributed to segregation and discrimination there, but the horrifying treatment that she and others suffered in the South led her to see it as a regime more than a region.[8] The Midwest, suggested Thompson in her early musings, offered more hope.

Prairies were her refuge, but they, just like Chicago, were not perfect. In *American Daughter* Thompson took care to portray the region as she and other settlers in the Midwest experienced it: as a place of hardship and diversity and, for people like herself, prejudice.[9] Her undated notes titled "Book Incidents" listed "Norwegians, Indians, Jews, Irish, German" alongside "piano lessons... brothers... farm under snow... flying turkeys, ghost stories... blacken face—teacher & school, Father... dude... cook ... threshers, rodeos... athletics" and, finally, "Chicago... adjustment, jobs, landladies."[10] Thompson's North Dakota contained a wide variety of migrants, including her family. She placed herself within the settler colonial narrative that had made Americans of her family and her neighbors and later in her career encouraged other Black Americans to settle in the rural Midwest too.[11]

As her listing of "blacken face" indicated (a reference to a schoolteacher who wanted her to wear blackface in a school play), Thompson's inclusion of her own family's story within that of western settlement met white resistance. Thompson underscored her own narrative in response: she and her family belonged on the North Dakota prairies. As her stories of her Jewish, Indigenous, and Norwegian friends suggested, she considered herself and her family a part of the multiculturalism that typified westward settlement and American character broadly. It was not she who needed to change to become western or American; it was those who refused to accept racial diversity.

Writing, believed Thompson, was the key to that change. Her scrapbooks suggest that she had long looked to her regional upbringing for inspiration, long considered writing for her future career, and long used her writing to advocate for Black people and for the region where she grew up. Throughout her life, she kept mementos—such as her father's business cards—to prepare for writing projects. She revived those dreams when she studied in Iowa and contributed to a college humor column, Lights and Shadows, in the *Chicago Defender*. Thompson wrote under the name "Dakota Dick" alongside other college students identified by regional monikers—"Creole Kid," "Nevada Ester," "Wyoming Bozo," and "Desert Avy," for example.[12] The *Chicago Defender* held promise for those like Thompson who harbored aspirations for a career in journalism. That their dispatches found publication in the *Defender* made Chicago the destination for both the writers and their writing.

Thompson's first stay in Chicago spurred her writing ambitions. Following her illness and while her father was still living and she had his financial support, she stayed in Chicago for several months and found work there at a small Black magazine. "For the first time," Thompson recalled, "I read books written by Negroes.... It was the height of the Negro renaissance in literature, in the late twenties, when Claude McKay, Langston Hughes, Rudolph Fisher, and others were at their creative best." When Thompson began writing features, she had an opportunity to explore the city's cultural institutions, such as the Newberry Library and the Field Museum, "priceless treasures to enjoy free for the asking" that left her "days full with discovery, ecstatic with the fruition of prose."[13] These adventures came to a halt with the illness and death of her father.

After he died, Thompson returned to North Dakota and struggled to find a landing spot for several years. She ultimately finished college in Iowa with help from a patron, the Morningside College president, Robert O'Brian (called Richard Riley in *American Daughter*). While living with the O'Brians, Thompson had new encounters with prejudice that shaped her writing ambitions. When a white summer school student visited the president's house in the O'Brian family's absence, he confessed to Thompson that "he used to hate Negroes." Thompson, alone in the house, nervously asked if he still did. He said that after playing football with a Black teammate, he didn't, then he asked if she'd ever considered marriage. Thompson, likely in an effort to change the subject, offered to move his car to the garage. He followed her. Thompson finally asked, "Have you ever been in a big city?" The "handsome boy, tall, blonde, friendly," said that he had visited New York and met porters on the train who were Black. Thompson patiently explained that their ranks might include a future spouse for her, but she shared a larger message too: "Well, a lot of those porters you saw on the train were college men, working to make money to finish their education, and a whole lot more you didn't see are educated, are professional people with jobs and offices like the people you know."[14] Years later, a Black porter remarked on Thompson's heavy typewriter case. Upon learning that she was a writer, he proudly walked away, raising "his voice so that the white passengers could hear," and compared her to the most famous travelers he had assisted, including Lena Horne, "the great Negro educator, Mrs. Bethune" and the "come-upper Mae West."[15] Thompson understood that train travel itself did not confer transformation. It was the labor of the porter and the writer that moved them toward a more satisfying future.

Such encounters meant that when Thompson returned to Chicago, she did so without the fairy-tale expectations of the city (or the railroad) that animated the heroine in Willa Cather's *Song of the Lark*. Like Cather, Thompson aspired to be a writer from a young age, and she took note of successful Black creatives who moved East to find success, including singers.[16] Indeed, after having achieved a successful writing career herself, Thompson publicly endorsed Cather's *My Ántonia* for a radio series aimed at young and general readers.[17] But Thompson's previous stays in the city, her limited resources, and her deeper and more astute understanding of American race relations meant that she did not shy away from sharing her own encounters with racist barriers in *American Daughter*. Perhaps she even presented her own midwestern experience alongside American Indian, Jewish, and other immigrant European friends as a counter to the brief, cartoonish, and belittling depiction of an African American musician who appears in *My Ántonia* as an idiot savant.[18] Whatever enthusiasm she had for Cather's writing, Thompson understood the persuasive work that a Black pioneer family could do in narratives of US development.

Thompson applied that nuance to Chicago. In Thompson's writing, Chicago is a place in transition. It is becoming the nation's heartland city, but its residents cannot realize the city's full potential without acknowledging all of their neighbors—whether the Midwest's country farmers, the South's Jim Crow refugees, or the Old World's immigrant aspirants—as equal citizens. The transformation of eastward train travel to the city that occurred in other midwestern writers' work, in which food and labor became commodities or creative young dreamers became artists, did not preoccupy Thompson. Instead, it was Chicago, as the multicultural Midwest's representative city, that had to change. That transformation required an embrace that encompassed the Midwest's multicultural settler population and the city's growing Black population. To achieve its full potential, Chicago, Thompson gently suggested, had to hold her.

It did. As *American Daughter* nears its conclusion, Thompson calls Chicago "the crossroads of America. From the East and West, the North and South, they come—rich man, poor man, black man, white; the foreigner, the old-timer, the young, the intellectual, the illiterate—restless, changing jobs, changings skills and locations, seeking new industries and higher salaries."[19] Rather than see the city as the origin of her beloved prairie's economic exploitation, as Le Sueur and Hicks had, or as a way station to greater success in New York, as Cather had, Thompson saw it as a gyre pulling the nation's and the world's people into its urban energy and cultured institutions. What people did once they arrived, Thompson urged, was what mattered.

Chicago, as the hinterland's metropole, served as a template for Thompson of what the nation as a whole could become. Following two extensive trips across the United States in the late 1930s and early 1940s, she returned to the city to take up her work again in the Illinois employment agency. She concluded with satisfaction after successfully placing a white job seeker: "I know there is still good in the world, that way down underneath, most Americans are fair; that my people and your people can work together and live together in peace and happiness, if they but have the opportunity to know and understand each other. The chasm is growing narrower. When it closes, my feet will rest on a united America."[20] In this final passage of her memoir, Thompson invoked not just herself but "my people" and "your people." As Thompson settled in Chicago, what she had told as her own coming-of-age story became a story of national maturation centered in the nation's heartland city.

Thompson found enthusiastic support for her book from Friends of the Middle Border, an organization formed in 1939 whose members were endeavoring to build a library and museum dedicated to pioneer life in 1946, when *American Daughter* was published. With aid from the Westerners, a group formed in 1944, they celebrated Thompson and the book's publication. The society column about the evening described the Westerners as "an offshoot of the Friends of the Middle Border" and "an exclusively masculine company, whose interest is in the history of the west." Both groups sought affirmation for their endeavors in the cultural institutions of Chicago. The column noted that "Dr. Stanley Pargellis of Newberry library will act as master of ceremonies," which "recalls that Miss Thompson wrote her story on a Newberry fellowship" and gave considerable attention to the group's collection of books and art. Such observations raised the status of the Newberry Library and the Friends of the Middle Border while presenting Chicago as both a product of the rural Midwest and a cultured city.

Friends of the Middle Border sought status but did not look eastward for affirmation. As the society columnist explained: "Friends of the Middle Border hold that America had two frontiers. As they write the story, 'One started along the Atlantic seaboard and surged westward on a tide of flatboats and covered wagons. The other began later in the west and southwest and backtrailed toward the east. . . . They met in the Missouri valley—Iowa, Nebraska, the Dakotas, Montana, and the bordering states. Here on the middle border, so named by the late Hamlin Garland, the homesteader, the prospector, the cattleman, and the immigrant dreamed the American dream.'"[21] Thompson fit her story seamlessly within that told by Friends of the Middle Border and the Westerners. A product of North Dakota, she was from the region they championed and where they believed pioneer grit and western independence had united. Her book title even recalled that of Garland's two-part autobiography, *A Son of the Middle Border* and the 1922 Pulitzer Prize–winning *A Daughter of the Middle Border*. Thompson, like Hicks and the nascent Friends of the Middle Border, linked the Midwest's culture with the fullest realization of democracy. While Garland and other regionalists such as Cather had gone East to prove themselves, Thompson sought to prove that the Midwest was a site of literary and cultural significance on its own.

That meant that when Thompson did go East for the first time, she did so without the intention of proving herself as a writer. In the final pages of *American Daughter*, she embarks on two extensive trips to Canada and throughout the United States. "By vacation time, I had saved a travel fund of fifty dollars—enough to go East, for I had to see more of America; rural and urban Midwest were not enough." Her separation of the Midwest into rural and urban suggested that *urban* did not connote "eastern" in her view. Nonetheless, she carried with her some western preconceptions. "New York is a wonderful city," Thompson told her readers. "New Yorkers, contrary to western propaganda, turned out to be very friendly people."[22]

Friendliness aside, Thompson understood associations that westerners held between the East and professional success. "Before I left New York, I had . . . found Sarah Cohn, my Bismarck friend, now a well-paid secretary who divided her evenings between a private pool, where she was a lifeguard, and an orchestra, where she was the only female musician," Thompson wrote. "Sarah had followed through." Sarah had achieved what she had envisioned when the two friends confided their youthful ambitions to one another back in Bismarck. Thompson was pleased for her friend but also satisfied with her own achievements in Chicago. Immediately after describing Sarah, Thompson wrote: "The last thing I did in New York was to visit a colored newspaper and apply for a job. I wanted to hear 'No,' and know it didn't matter."[23] Thompson did not engage in any kind of economic critique of the East as an agent of despoliation, nor did she try to move East to prove herself.

Notably, too, she did not present the East as free of the prejudice that she had encountered in North Dakota and Chicago. On Riverside Drive, she shared a joke with a Black doorman about renting an apartment in the luxurious (and likely segregated) building where he worked. She was delighted to turn back and find him "doubled up laughing."[24] Thompson expected to find a few pretentious New Yorkers, but she associated that pretension not with their easternness but with their whiteness.

Her commentary on later encounters with the East highlighted the impressions that she presented in *American Daughter*. In 1949 Thompson received a fellowship to attend the Bread Loaf Writers' Conference in Vermont. She described her experiences there for her column, Bell's Lettres, in *Negro Digest*, in December 1949 and January 1950. Although "fellows were supposed to be a select group of advanced writers," Thompson lamented that "as the only Negro Loafer, I became a walking race relations delegate." She sarcastically described the "most heartening" of these relentless responsibilities as "the confessions of a few racists who had been recently converted to total brotherhood, as well as two novelists who asked me to read portions of their unfinished manuscripts to check for possible offenses in the handling of Negro characters."[25] Like New York City, New England was not without prejudice. The East was no refuge.

The second article highlighted Thompson's western upbringing. It included descriptions of Bread Loaf's famous outdoor activities and her pleasure when she "managed to get in some good horseback riding." Although Thompson attended Bread Loaf at a time when many prominent western writers served on the faculty—including Bernard DeVoto, a *Harper's* columnist, conservationist, and historian of the American West—she concluded that "the lions of the literary world were as normal as other people and twice as human." Ever the travel writer, Thompson noted that the stay was her "first excursion into either Vermont or New England." She "loved the Green Mountains" but observed that "the state has all the rocky ruggedness of my North Dakota, with a similar abundance of snow and lack of Negroes."[26] Along with her observations of New York in *American Daughter*, Thompson portrayed the East for her largely Black readers as neither exclusively urban nor rural, neither a refuge for nor a barrier to Black visitors, and neither free of prejudice nor immune to positive change. The East was another place to visit, to live, and to navigate even when one visited as a western, Black writer.

Era Bell Thompson did not seek affirmation through eastern associations, but she did within the informal networks of women's support for one another. Among the friends she found at Bread Loaf was Avis DeVoto, culinary editor for chef Julia Child and wife to Bernard. The DeVotos met at Northwestern University just outside Chicago, and Thompson may have felt a connection to them as a result. Avis wrote Thompson in November 1949, following Thompson's summer fellowship, and showed sensitivity to her needs as a promising writer. "What I meant to write you about as long ago as September was B[ernard]'s remark when he got back from Bread Loaf that Era Belle [sic] Thompson was head and shoulders above all the fellows this year as far as brains went and a damn nice gal as well. I think things like that ought to be passed along to take out and look at during the inevitable moments when it looks like a hell of a world and nobody loves us and why not go out and cut our throat anyhow?"[27] Famous for her blunt manner, Avis well summarized the fears that writers, especially women writers, faced when sharing their work with established authors and prospective mentors. Thompson clipped memorials about Bernard when he died in 1955, but her relationship with the DeVotos came not from a shared interest in writing about the West but from the friendship she had formed with her teacher's wife, Avis, herself an active writer and editor and, in a way, a Chicagoan.

Thompson did not limit her travels to US shores. Her second book, *Africa: Land of My Fathers*, which she published in 1954, described a ten-week trip across the continent amid multiple germinating independence movements. Thompson acknowledged general American ignorance of Africa: "Until a few years before, my knowledge of the continent, like that of most Americans, both black and white, was geared to concepts handed down by Livingstone and Stanley nearly a hundred years ago." Thompson had to change her own preconceptions before she could begin addressing those of her readers. "Little by little I heard and read about another Africa, one that went beyond ignorance and savagery, an Africa pieced together by black historians from facts disregarded by white historians who said Africa had no past, its people no culture."[28] Thompson shaped the dispatches from her trip toward emphasizing this second message.

Her opposition to segregation extended Thompson's sympathies to those Africans seeking independence, but the parallels she drew with the United States stopped short of any analysis of colonialism. Any writing about decolonization was risky in the mid-twentieth century and exposed those who tried doing so to charges of Communist sympathies and anti-Americanism. *Ebony* and Thompson carefully, though deliberately, navigated the politics of exploring Black international life into the 1960s.[29] Thompson compared the colonial endeavors of the Belgians, English, and Portuguese in Africa. And she compared the independence movements of the Congolese, South Africans, and Mozambicans to English colonial settlers who formed the United States. She spent the Fourth of July in a newly independent Egypt and thrilled to the coincidence. Never did Thompson suggest that the United States was itself a colonial power, however. Thompson not only denied any overseas colonial endeavors on the part of the United States; she did not see settlement in North America as an act of colonialism. She drew no parallels between the political status of colonized people in Africa and colonized people in the Americas.

Indigenous people in the United States were visible to Thompson. In *American Daughter* she gently teases her younger self when upon moving from Iowa to North Dakota, she eagerly anticipated meeting American Indians to match the children's stories she had read and heard. It was not until her teen years, when she lived in Bismarck and Mandan, however, that Thompson met or befriended any Indigenous people. In Bismarck she visited "the Indian school for girls." She acknowledged her childish fantasies as well as a different relationship with them than that of her white neighbors. "There were no wigwams, no squaws, no warriors, only big wooden buildings with little girls in pale blue dresses, their faces stolid and sallow, not red; their bobbed hair straight and black. Some of them ran to blue eyes and blonde tresses, and I was glad they couldn't blame my father for that."[30] In contrasting her childish stereotypes with her adult awareness of Indigenous women's vulnerability, Thompson drew a more complex portrait of Indigenous people's racial experience that acknowledged its differences from her own.

Nonetheless, a shadow of Thompson's childish conclusions still remained when she later observed that "Mandan marks the beginning of the real West. It is here Mountain Time begins, here the Indians come from the reservation to greet the tourist trains and dance at the big rodeo; here, on this side of the river, live the rattlers; and farther to the west, in the Bad Lands, is the town of Medora, once the ranch home of Teddy Roosevelt and his fabulous friend, the French nobleman, the Marquis de Mores."[31] Thompson's sense of regional distinctiveness grows more precise in the remainder of *American Daughter*, but her presentation of Indigenous people was largely restricted to a few encounters in Bismarck and a day in Mandan when the grandmother of a "Sioux" friend visited Thompson's father's concession stand at the annual rodeo. Thompson included Native peoples in the multicultural mix that was the early-twentieth-century plains, but she did not include them in her vision of the nation's future or see them as citizens of independent, sovereign entities. There were American Indians in Thompson's West but not very many—none in her Midwest, none in her Chicago, and never any in her East.

For Thompson, American democracy was a product of the Midwest and found its fullest expression in the city of Chicago. In rolling Indigenous people into a story of assimilation through colonialism, she followed the model offered by Friends of the Middle Border. The model transformed the Midwest from a region into its own kind of regime, one that furthered Indigenous erasure. Nonetheless, Thompson added a significant addendum to the story that the Friends told. Chicago, having absorbed the people and democratic impulses of the Midwest, offered to serve as a model to other cities and regions and regimes, particularly the South, as the nation overcame what Thompson considered its most significant challenge: the full acceptance of African Americans.

Thompson's emphasis on racial liberalism emerged less from her blind spots regarding the experience of midwesterners who were neither Black nor white than from her steadfast faith that full inclusion in the US democratic experiment would right all wrongs. Writing amid the prosperity of the postwar era, she could see the potential for an accelerating civil rights movement. Throughout her career, she expressed support for those of African descent, including children of Black servicemen and Japanese women born in the years following World War II, in terms that championed US democracy.[32] For her, full inclusion in the city of Chicago meant full inclusion of its hinterland and its residents. To bring the prairies into the fold of American identity and to thrust Chicago to the fore as the nation's exemplar meant erasing the inequalities that Thompson perceived between city and country and Black and white. Those between colonist and colonized occupied her only when they overlapped neatly with anti-Black racism in decolonizing Africa.

Chicago, as Thompson saw it, was its own place, not the beginning of the East. Chicago had its own East, but for her it was a minor place. Thompson differed in this view from other western and midwestern writers. For those like Cather, Thompson's inclusion of Black people in pioneer narratives undermined presumptions of white supremacy. For those like Hicks, Thompson's vision fell a step behind what he considered the nation's inevitable progress westward. For those like Le Sueur, too much attention to the nation's democratic promise at the expense of its economic exploitation risked everyone's and the land's well-being. For those like Big Man, Thompson's settler roots and acceptance of Chicago's assimilative power ignored calls for Indigenous sovereignty. And for other non-white westerners arriving in Chicago, marginal roles proved surprisingly alluring. Those seeking a theory that explained their relegation to the sidelines as well as a way beyond them found their way to Chicago too. They went east to get there.

CHAPTER 2
THE MARGINAL MAN AND THE MARGINAL MIDWEST

One Christmas holiday in the 1930s, the aspiring sociologist Horace Cayton drove his mentor, Robert E. Park, to New York City in Park's car. The two men were colleagues at Fisk University and had first met at the University of Washington (UW) in Seattle, where Park, a white man, challenged Cayton, an African American, to prove the validity of "Negro History." Everything, Cayton replied, has a history. They reunited at the University of Chicago, where Park served as cocreator of the famed "Chicago School" of sociology. Intellectual wrangling attracted them both, and they argued vehemently on this frigid night between Tennessee and New York about "the capitalistic system." Eventually, tempers grew heated, and Park told Cayton to stop the car and get out. Cayton reminded Park that it was below freezing outside. He also noted that Park did not know how to drive. The two continued in silence for over an hour, after which Park began to lecture on his theory of the growth of the city, an address that Cayton found so engaging that in his recollection of the evening, he concluded, "He was again the great teacher and I his humble servant."[1]

Cayton's memory was a reflection of the high esteem in which Cayton held his mentor and the power that Park's theories held over Cayton's own sense of self. Born in 1903 to a Seattle newspaper publisher and the grandchild of the first African American senator, Hiram Revels, Cayton spent much of his life as an outsider. In childhood and young adulthood, like Era Bell Thompson, Cayton was frequently the lone African American in his classes and his workplace. As a child of Black elites, he felt distant from the small number of other African Americans in the Pacific Northwest. In

1916, when his father lost his newspaper after publishing a series of antilynching columns, the Cayton family's fortunes declined. Cayton spent time in a juvenile detention center and struggled to recover from his incarceration. When he married a white woman whom he met at the University of Washington, she lost her job, and he barely retained his as a police deputy. As a Black man, a westerner, a survivor of the criminal justice system, and an intellectual, Cayton arrived in Chicago with high hopes that studying sociology back East could explain his experiences out West.[2]

Cayton saw in Chicago first the promise and then the disappointment of African Americans' efforts to make an equitable urban society. Like Thompson, Cayton abhorred the Jim Crow South. He hoped for Chicago to offer new opportunities for Black refugees of white southern prejudice and violence and for isolated Black westerners like himself. The city failed him. As he concluded in his cowritten book, *Black Metropolis*, Chicago offered no respite from systemic discrimination for African Americans. Chicago and its region did not grant escape from marginalization whether one called Chicago's region the North, the Midwest, or, for far westerners such as Cayton, the East.[3]

Cayton spent considerable time reflecting on marginalization because his mentor, Park, had developed the "marginal man" thesis. Like other Chicago School sociologists, Park believed that the built environment and its inequities marked an individual far more so than biology or inheritance. Race and region intersected for the marginal man because so much of Park's theory rested on the ways in which individuals experienced and understood their origins and destinations when they moved from one place to another.[4] Born in 1864, Park observed the mobility of a different generation of largely white Americans, a group that had moved from rural to urban centers along both banks of the Mississippi River. Park theorized that some Americans—by virtue of their rural background, their race, or their immigrant status—never fully assimilated to American culture, meaning that they never absorbed or displayed the symbols of white middle-class life. Like Thompson, Park grew up in that region celebrated by Friends of the Middle Border. In characterizing the marginal man as an observant and cosmopolitan outsider, Park recalled his own upbringing in Red Wing, Minnesota, and his movement through a journalism career toward Chicago and an academic life in other intellectual centers in the South and East.[5] Park had achieved success as a writer and intellectual through movement; others he mentored did not. As Park puzzled over the reasons why, he displayed both his white privilege and his western orientation.

Park developed his theory with influence from Asian Americans on the West Coast.[6] His first article on the topic, "Human Migration and the Marginal Man," appeared shortly after he and a team of Chicago School sociologists completed the 1924 Survey of Race Relations. The Chicago School emphasized field experience and ethnographic research, and the survey reflected the school's approach. It endeavored to explain anti-Asian prejudice among whites of the western United States and also to facilitate Asian American assimilation.[7] The survey and its later iterations included input from West Coast Asian American scholars who, like Cayton, possessed a deep intellectual curiosity, had experienced discrimination, and also saw themselves as marginal men.

Among them was S. Frank Miyamoto. Like Cayton, Miyamoto grew up in Seattle. Miyamoto's parents, Issei, or first-generation immigrants to the United States, initially formed a part of the diverse migrant labor force that cycled in and out of Seattle and its hinterland for work.[8] When they settled in the city, they lived at a distance from other Japanese immigrants. As a result, Miyamoto, like Cayton, felt marginal to both white and Japanese communities in Seattle. When he encountered those UW instructors with tight ties to the Chicago School, he felt a similar draw to the field of sociology and to the theory of the marginal man. In 1939, almost ten years after Cayton had made the journey, Miyamoto headed east to Chicago to pursue a doctorate in sociology.

He returned to Seattle in 1941 to finish his dissertation but was almost immediately incarcerated in Northern California following the Japanese attack on Pearl Harbor. In Tule Lake he worked as one of the lead researchers for the Japanese Evacuation and Resettlement Study (JERS), a white-led, multiyear expansive project that followed the effects of incarceration and resettlement on Japanese Americans. Of the many social scientific studies about Japanese incarceration, scholars have called the JERS study "the most influential in shaping ideas about Japanese Americans, and by extension, the nation's racial order."[9] From Tule Lake, Miyamoto once again returned to Chicago, this time following federally relocated Japanese Americans who were allowed to leave the camps, provided they did not return to the West Coast. Although Miyamoto was once again headed back East, this time he understood that movement eastward did not bring release from marginalization.[10]

The Chicago School taught students to see race as a binary, not necessarily between Black and white but between non-white and white. Both Cayton and Miyamoto acknowledged Seattle's multiracial landscape in their early days as students of sociology, but they struggled in later years to squeeze their own experiences into the bounds of the marginal man. Although Park developed his ideas with his own background and that of West Coast sociologists in mind, the marginal man theory still exhibited a binary view of social relations: the marginalized and the assimilated. That theory mapped well onto historical divisions of the United States between North and South that divided the nation racially between Black and white but did not ring true among all westerners who found their way to Chicago a generation after Park came of age. The marginal man thesis flattened the multiracial experience of westerners and whitened the multiracial experience of midwesterners.

At least one relocated Japanese American observed the regional and racial flaws of the marginal man thesis. Charles Kikuchi began keeping a diary when he entered the Tanforan camp in California, maintained it when he was moved to the Gila River camp in Arizona, and continued writing daily for the remainder of his life. Like Miyamoto, Kikuchi worked for white sociologists at JERS, but he did not adopt a binary view of race as a result. He drew his conclusions regarding race from his multiracial community in Northern California and observed multiracial communities throughout his life. In Chicago he closely observed anti-Black prejudice among Japanese Americans as well as community building between Japanese Americans and African Americans working cooperatively to resist white racism. Years after wartime incarceration and relocation, when he had settled in New York, he was able to develop an outlook that did not lump all non-whites together, nor did it require non-whites to assimilate to a presumed white norm.

For Kikuchi, back East could offer the same multiracial landscape as the West Coast, but for Cayton and Miyamoto, it could not. They retained the marginal man's binary view of race. They each, respectively, fought hard against anti-Black and anti-Asian prejudice among whites, but they never adopted a multiracial perspective in their academic work. They argued forcefully that whites must change their racial perspective, but their arguments ran aground on the shortcomings of the marginal man thesis and the conjoined racial and regional prejudices of their mentors. As the Midwest grew whiter in the regional imaginary, it also grew less visible and less promising for far westerners. Back East, confined for most westerners to the East Coast by 1960, offered greater racial diversity in the western imagination.

Park had developed the marginal man theory with the "Middle Border" in mind. He described opportunities that he believed awaited migrants to Chicago. For white western writers in the same years, movement and regional distinctiveness offered opportunities and upward mobility. Westerners of color seeking to broaden discussions of race in the service of racial equality, however, struggled to escape the constraints of the marginal man. They increasingly rejected presentations of the Midwest as a region they could call their own and Chicago as a city that offered opportunity to westerners.

Park believed regional racist regimes such as in the Jim Crow South and on the anti-Asian West Coast could be undone by Black and Asian American mobility. He prescribed movement and assimilation rather than regional or national structural change. More than most of his peers, Park worked on behalf of immigrants and young people of color seeking a place in the academy. He believed opportunity was open to all. But push too hard on the regional and racial barriers that confined the marginal man, and he could threaten to leave his critic on a cold road back East, even when that critic knew better than he how to get where they were trying to go.

Cayton titled the first chapter of his memoir "Childhood in the West," and in it he described what he had learned of the South. Like a young Era Bell Thompson, he grew up in the shadow of his parents' memories and expectations, and he envisioned the South as a fearful place. Cayton's father was the child of an enslaved man and the white daughter of his father's enslaver. While a student at Alcorn College, he met Cayton's mother, the daughter of Hiram Revels, who was elected to the Senate from Mississippi during Reconstruction. Cayton's parents chafed against the restrictions that African Americans increasingly faced in the Jim Crow South. Cayton recalled that his paternal grandfather had provided his father "an education and the desire to escape the southland," and he speculated that his mother had married his father "to escape the South."[11] The couple moved with the hope that a "frontier" community would offer more opportunity and greater freedom.[12]

A formative event in Cayton's childhood was a 1909 visit to his family's home in Seattle from Booker T. Washington. Remembering his father's conversation with Washington in his memoir, *Long Old Road: Back to Black Metropolis*, Cayton imagined their discussion in terms likely more reflective of his 1963 readers than his six-year-old self. "The Negro is an insanity which exists in the mind of the white southerner," insisted his father. "There is no compromise with this attitude. The colored people of this country should make a bold strike for freedom, the freedom which is denied them in the South. Here in the Northwest we are striking out in every direction. . . . We are the new frontier, and thousands of Negroes come to this part of the country and stand up like men and compete with their white brothers. . . . We have an opportunity and a great challenge, not only for us but for all Negroes and for the American dream. We can prove that America is right."[13] Cayton's father understood racial discrimination regionally and saw promise for African Americans, not just up North but also out West.

His statements angered Washington, who replied coldly: "You speak of the insanity in the South with regard to the Negro. I sincerely hope, Mr. Cayton, that insanity does not overcome you here in the relative freedom of the Northwest. I hope that the infection of Negro prejudice does not spread to this part of the country." Washington had no patience for the argument that places out West promised more equality. He understood sites of power. "He had eaten with the President; he had been honored by Harvard and Dartmouth."[14] Washington's prestige, acquired back East, along with his conviction that racism existed everywhere, struck the young eavesdropper.

Cayton spent his career in the tension between the two positions. On the one hand, Cayton revered Washington's credentials, his access to power, his intellectual acumen, and his proximity to large Black communities. As he matured, Cayton also agreed with Washington that the "infection" of prejudice existed everywhere. On the other hand, Cayton abhorred compromise. He would not negotiate with injustice, he had great faith in his family's and his own capacity to succeed, and he believed that the civic promises of the United States hinged on the equal status of people like himself. In his memoir, he set the terms of his success. Like Washington, he achieved national recognition and respect but with the message articulated by his father: democratic prosperity hinged on racial equality, not accommodation of white expectations.

Nonetheless, one white expectation haunted him: that US culture moved from East to West. As a result, Cayton's upbringing on "the frontier" gave him a sense of foreboding that anti-Black racism was approaching. In *Long Old Road* Cayton offered multiple case studies that may have shaped his perception of his own status in the West. When Cayton's father began publishing anti-lynching stories, white men threatened him with violence. The newspaper failed. The Cayton family subsequently suffered a series of financial setbacks. They lost their house in Capitol Hill, their capacity to employ servants, and their elite social status. Cayton felt isolated and unsupported at high school. After he drove the getaway car for a robbery, he was incarcerated in a juvenile justice facility, where members of the staff physically abused him and sexually abused other incarcerated children. Along the way, he worked as "a longshoreman, a sailor, a common laborer in a gold mine, a porter, a waiter of three varieties (hotel, dining car, and steamboat)."¹⁵ After missing his ship in Alaska, he cleaned and cooked for a brothel, where he observed that "there were no other Negroes in town, and in Alaska the race problem was really between Indian and white."¹⁶ Once he finished high school, he became a sheriff's deputy to pay for his attendance at the University of Washington. He marveled at the authority he had over white men but felt increasingly uncomfortable subjecting others to state violence. He married a white woman despite disapproval from others. (Washington, unlike Oregon, did not have anti-miscegenation laws in the 1920s.) Any of these experiences may have led Cayton to see an approaching anti-Blackness on the eastern horizon as the source of his marginalization.

Cayton relayed these stories in his memoir almost as parables of US race relations. As he would later recall, "Perhaps my parents, in their fevered hope to escape the terrors of the plantation, had tried to escape the entire race problem by migrating to the Northwest. But the race problem had overtaken us and I was the first of my family to begin the back track to the main currents of Negro life, to find some satisfactions in group living which were denied me in my home."¹⁷ *Long Old Road* was less a faithful accounting of his life than it was an academic argument that weighed a series of causes for Cayton's experiences to conclude that racism most shaped social outcomes. Cayton left aside the colonialist message behind this reasoning. He did not linger on his observation that the "race problem was really between Indian and white" in Alaska. Rarely did he concern himself with the status of Indigenous people in Seattle, Alaska, or anywhere else. He focused instead on his conclusion that anti-Black prejudice moved from East to West. If he wanted to counter anti-Black racism, he would need to go back East to discover its origins.

With support from his first wife, Cayton began his journey. Cayton met Bonnie Branch at the University of Washington. Their early marriage was happy, though marred by disapproval of the union from their classmates, employers, and health care providers. They feared reprisal the first time they walked across campus together, and a white doctor insisted that Branch accept a tubal ligation after he met Cayton and saw he was Black. Branch managed to maintain optimism for their union. Cayton recalled that after they married, she planned to "save enough money to move east where there isn't so much prejudice." When she lost her job, after her employers learned that her husband was not white, she concluded: "We can save money by running the house more economically. It'll take us a little longer, but we can save enough in two years to move east. They're at least civilized back there."[18] Cayton's memories of Branch's words suggest the promise for their marriage and for racial equality that she saw back East.

In contrast, Cayton had doubts. Theresa McMahon, a University of Washington economics professor born in Tacoma, Washington, wrote him during his first summer studying at the University of Chicago. Her reply to a letter of his suggests that he struggled with his encounters with Black urban poverty in Chicago. She told him that his letter recalled the time she had spent in Chicago following her doctoral studies in sociology at the University of Wisconsin–Madison. "I do not think it was the big dirty city that got on my nerves, the heat (I arrived in July also), nor the fact I was far away from my relatives," she explained. "It was the 'dear people' who made me conscious of the fact I was not a part of them. Born and raised in the West, where people are cordial and more trusting of one's neighbor; where men scorned pennies and never missed the dimes they gave away—at least they were too proud to admit it if they did miss them—the Chicagoans were to me a heartless, mercenary, self-seeking bunch."[19] McMahon wrote as a mentor, and she directed her letter to encourage Cayton. She tried to convince him that it was their similarities as fellow westerners, including their aversion to hot, humid summers, that accounted for his frustrations and isolation, not race.

In addition to comparing notes with his undergraduate advisors, Cayton formed his sense of regional difference, class inequality, and racial prejudice in the early 1930s, in dialogue with the books and magazines that had influenced authors like Meridel Le Sueur. Either before leaving Seattle or immediately upon his arrival in Chicago, he began reading the *Debunker*, published and edited by Emanuel Haldeman-Julius, like the Little Blue Books. Like other Haldeman-Julius publications, the *Debunker* showed its Kansas roots by giving attention to all regions of the country, including the West. Like its predecessor, *Appeal to Reason*, the *Debunker* was aimed at readers working for wages in both rural and urban settings.

Young, impulsive, and curious, Cayton had much in common with the typical *Debunker* enthusiast. Like Little Blue Book readers, he sought to educate himself. Articles such as "What Times Square Reads," "How the New York Yokels Do Their Stuff," "Debunking Rural Virtue," and "Pasadena—A Charming City,—But" offered Cayton an opportunity to speak more knowledgably (and sometimes cynically) about the imperfections of other parts of the country.[20] His experiences working on the railroad and in shipping led him to favor greater rights and protections for workers—especially those who cycled in and out of urban areas and their rural hinterlands, as in Seattle and Chicago. He was sensitive to regional labor market gradations examined in articles such as "If You Don't Like It Here, Go Back Where You Came From" and "The Restaurant Racket."[21] Perhaps what most drew Cayton to the *Dubunker* were those articles that addressed racist violence. The issues that he retained contained articles such as "A Klown of the K. K. K. Invades Kanada," "Wherein Maryland Is Not a Free State," "Violence: A Novel of Today's South," and "When Thirteen Negroes Were Hanged in Texas."[22] Such reading may have reinforced his fear of the South and his reluctance to work there. With his move to Chicago, Cayton increasingly understood race as Black and white and region as North and South.

Cayton thrived professionally during his years in Chicago and in subsequent travels to New York City, Tennessee, and European countries, but he failed to find the justice he hungered for. When he explored teaching positions in the South, Branch could not accompany him because she was white. Unable to start a family, the two drifted apart, divorced, and Branch returned to Seattle. Ambivalent about a teaching career in the South, Cayton finished his coursework but not his dissertation. Instead, he became a research assistant for the Sociology Department at the University of Chicago. In 1934 and 1935 he worked for Harold Ickes in the Department of the Interior to investigate the effects of New Deal programs on African American populations. From that research, Cayton coauthored a book with University of North Carolina professor George S. Mitchell, entitled *Black Workers and the New Unions*.[23] He began writing a column for the *Pittsburgh Courier* during these years and taught between 1935 and 1936 at Fisk University (likely the period when he and Park drove together to New York City). At Fisk, Cayton met a Black woman, Irma Jackson, who married and divorced him twice over their almost decade-long relationship. Cayton returned to Chicago and secured funds from the Works Progress Administration and the Julius Rosenwald Fund. He and University of Chicago anthropologist St. Claire Drake then conducted the research for *Black Metropolis*, a hallmark publication of mid-twentieth-century Black life and culture in the United States.

The book, published in 1945, revealed Cayton's working relationships and his regional outlook. A combination of scholarly analysis, activist rhetoric, and literary reflection, *Black Metropolis* still shapes contemporary understanding of Black life in Chicago. Drake wrote the majority of the chapters. Cayton edited the book and secured an introduction for the volume from his friend, the acclaimed writer Richard Wright. They dedicated the book to "the Late Professor Robert E. Park of Tuskegee, the University of Chicago, and Fisk; American Scholar and Friend of the Negro People."[24] Like Cayton's, Drake's upbringing was not rural. He spent his childhood and adolescence moving among Harrisburg, Virginia; Pittsburgh, Pennsylvania; and Staunton, Virginia. He shared Cayton's skepticism of Booker T. Washington's theories and led a student strike at Hampton Institute to spur the school to hire African Americans as full professors.

Shaped by their respective backgrounds and Park's mentorship, *Black Metropolis* served as Drake's and Cayton's efforts to navigate the influence that the marginal man theory had had on their careers. The massive influx of Black southerners to Chicago during the Great Migration led them to emphasize northern racism against Black Chicagoans in contrast to the racism of the Jim Crow South. The differences they charted between northern and southern anti-Black racism overlay cleanly Park's theory of the marginal man. Migrate north, and Black Americans had a more likely chance of successful assimilation to American society. Cayton and Drake made the critical addition of showing that it was racism, not Black behavior, that stood in Black migrants' way. Indeed, they stressed the power of Black solidarity in efforts to overcome anti-Black prejudice in the North.

Although the book offered the potential to celebrate the thriving Black culture that Era Bell Thompson, Cayton, Drake, and so many others found upon their arrival in the city, in some ways Thompson had more to support her in Chicago than did Cayton and Drake. In building her own Black metropolis, Thompson could pull on the positive associations that white Chicagoans had with the rural Midwest. People like Park had followed a trajectory not entirely unlike her own as they moved from the Middle Border to the city. Thompson did not quite preach assimilation, but she could identify common experiences with some of Chicago's white residents and champion the rural Midwest without feeling compelled to renounce her rural upbringing. Rural life, however, did not interest Cayton and Drake. Neither mentioned the Black population of the rural Midwest and West, and like Thompson, neither held affection for the rural South. Theirs was an urban focus without sentimentality. Neither one, for example, described their sensual experience of Chicago's physical landscape — its variable seasons, its noise, its light. Those qualities were the province of the Midwest metropolis, to which the Black metropolis did not yet have equal access.[25]

Like the theory of the marginal man, the book suggested that rural people must assimilate to urban norms. Unlike the white marginal man, however, the Black newcomer to the city met violent intimidation, limited job opportunities, and discriminatory housing policies that crowded Black residents into substandard living conditions. Moreover, unlike Thompson, whose lodestone in the city was *Ebony* magazine, aspiring Black intellectuals such as Cayton and Drake relied on the white institution of the University of Chicago and on Park and other white men. The discrimination that Black newcomers to the city felt in their everyday efforts to secure housing and employment, Cayton and Drake felt in their experiences in the academy. Although they did not explicitly name it, Cayton and Drake had written the betrayal for Black people that lay at the heart of the marginal man thesis into their portrait of the city. Like Meridel Le Sueur and John Hicks, Cayton associated back East with urban life and, for a while, with the possibility of racial equality. He and Drake together then repositioned Chicago regionally as up North rather than back East. They concluded that movement, whether from country to city, up North, or back East, did not bring racial equality. Instead, the marginal man thesis whitened the

A 1968 photo of Era Bell Thompson and Horace Cayton, who both brought expectations of the East with them when they lived and worked in Chicago. Their expectations shaped their presentation of Chicago, of American regions, and of race relations. J. Paul Getty Trust and Smithsonian National Museum of African American History and Culture, Vivian Harsh Research Collection, Chicago Public Library.

experiences of people like Thompson and her diverse rural neighbors even as it turned away from the multiracial Midwest and West.

That multiracial West included Asian American sociologists who came of age in the 1930s and 1940s and for whom the marginal man thesis played an equally strong role. Among them was S. Frank Miyamoto. Born in 1912 to immigrant parents, Miyamoto grew up on Beacon Hill, away from the tight-knit community of Japanese immigrants and their children in Seattle.[26] Nonetheless, Miyamoto felt a connection to other Japanese. As a child, he attended Japanese-language school and delivered Japanese newspapers in downtown Seattle. In a 1984 introduction to his 1939 master's thesis, "Social Solidarity among the Japanese in Seattle," he explained the need to revisit his thesis themes: "Apart from my study there is not, to my knowledge, any other published study of a Japanese minority community before World War II—not of Los Angeles, San Francisco, Sacramento, Gardena, Florin, Hood River, or the dozens of other communities about which we knew

Marginal Man and Marginal Midwest   67

more—yet most Japanese minority members on the Pacific Coast before the war lived in or were in some fashion bound to a Japanese community and were significantly influenced by the affiliation."[27] Miyamoto's parents raised their children, the Nisei generation, at a distance from their fellow Issei, the immigrant generation. Nonetheless, as Miyamoto observed, most Japanese Seattleites were "in some fashion bound" to them.

Miyamoto credited his upbringing for his sociological stance. He noted in a University of Chicago seminar application essay, "There was the additional circumstance of the Japanese culture being superimposed upon the American culture. . . . I felt a step removed from both and no strong subjective attachment to either. In this way I was developing the attitude of detachment fundamental to the sociologist—I was becoming, in a sense, a 'marginal man.'"[28] Miyamoto attributed the marginal status of Japanese Americans to anti-Asian racism among whites just as Cayton had attributed the marginal status of African Americans to anti-Black racism among whites. Like Cayton, Miyamoto sought explanation for that marginalization in his coursework in sociology at the University of Washington.

Miyamoto also privileged his identity as a scholar over that as a writer. When he was a child, Miyamoto had "entertained a youthful dream of becoming a novelist." Nonetheless, he initially chose engineering over "the liberal studies" because his father favored "the more practical field fearing that I would suffer economic insecurities in the former, especially because of my racial background."[29] Following his father's death, Miyamoto was inspired by a friend at the University of Michigan and a visit to the UW campus from Japanese internationalist Inazo Nitobe to pursue his interest in sociology.[30] At UW he encountered professors trained in the Chicago School who took him under their wing. He once called his undergraduate mentor "a white angel."[31] Miyamoto's studies opened the door to a novelist's descriptive expression in the close observation of the Chicago school sociologist. He made his own journey to the city in 1939.

While Cayton anticipated his encounters with a large and growing Black community, Miyamoto appears to have focused on Chicago's educational environment without addressing its Black population. If he had a chance to record impressions of Chicago similar to those in *Black Metropolis*, he did not share them in his published writing. He did, however, reflect some of his thoughts in his application essay for Ernest Burgess's graduate seminar in sociology at the University of Chicago. He considered his "strongest criticism of American society" to be "the matter of race prejudice." Like Cayton's family, Miyamoto's had been among the few non-white homeowners in white neighborhoods, and he recalled that they "took the brunt of white-American disapproval." Miyamoto remembered that he "felt deeply the injustice of the whole affair, and naturally began searching for means by which these injustices might be removed. Thus, the problems of Japanese-American relations came to take on personal meaning for me, and the significance of the problem was doubly impressed on me by the barrage of literature upon the question that appeared in my childhood during the years when the Immigration Act of 1924 and the Anti-Alien Land Laws of the Western states were being passed."[32] Miyamoto did not raise the effects of racism against African Americans at all, nor did he examine the status of those few Asian Americans in Chicago, even though he attributed anti-Asian prejudice to regional difference via his reference to "Western states." Like Cayton, he may have been seeking racial equality back East.

Miyamoto did offer a western outlook on race relations. His application essay listed "areas of life" with which he was familiar and included: "Southeastern Alaska in the salmon canning industry. Some acquaintance with Indian life there" as well as "Union activities, The Alaska Salmon Cannery workers. Also the relations between Japanese and Filipinos."[33] If Ernest Burgess encouraged these interests or suggested that Miyamoto expand his outlook in Chicago to include a variety of Asian American communities, Indigenous peoples, or African Americans, his advice did not reach the historical record. Chicago School sociologists had an opportunity to bring the West's multiracial relationships into sociological discussion, but their theories left little room for life experience like Miyamoto's. He finished his coursework and returned home to the West. Like Cayton, he increasingly saw race as regional and binary, although he separated his racial analysis into West and East, Asian and white.

Shortly after his return to Seattle, the federal government forcibly evacuated Miyamoto from his home alongside over 110,000 Japanese Americans living on the West Coast. Japanese Americans living in the interior West and in cities like Chicago were not evacuated. The majority of evacuees were American citizens, members of the US-born generation called Nisei. Still, the United States government questioned their loyalty following the Japanese attack on Pearl Harbor.[34] The War Relocation Authority (WRA) first moved Miyamoto and his family to Puyallup, Washington, and then moved most Japanese American Seattleites to the Minidoka camp in Idaho. Miyamoto and his wife, however, went to Tule Lake in Northern California, an unusual placement that had its origins in his Chicago connections back East.

The movement and cultural pressures that evacuation and incarceration placed on Japanese Americans sparked anew an interest in Asian American experience by white sociologists. Japanese American students themselves began to wonder what sociological effect the outbreak of war would have on Japanese American communities. At the University of California, Berkeley, sociologist Dorothy Swaine Thomas, spouse to Park's former colleague William I. Thomas, listened to her students' concerns, anticipated the forced evacuation of Japanese Americans from the West Coast, and made Japanese American incarceration her field of study. She devised and for a time oversaw the Japanese Evacuation and Relocation Study, a mammoth endeavor to record thoroughly every aspect of incarceration and, later, resettlement, when the WRA endeavored to relocate Japanese American prisoners to non-western locations. Without the promise of a free, multiracial urban life, Chicago could no longer be back East in many Japanese Americans' eyes. Much as the Jim Crow South had influenced Cayton's casting of Chicago as the North, JERS and forced relocation would recast Chicago for many Japanese Americans as the Midwest.

Miyamoto's own movement traced the Midwest's and Chicago's departure from the East he had imagined. He and his wife were incarcerated at Tule Lake in Northern California, that camp closest to Berkeley, "for the convenience of Dorothy Thomas."[35] Miyamoto's job was to serve as a participant observer of incarceration. Like other incarcerated Japanese Americans, Miyamoto felt the loss of his civil liberties, his precarious financial status, and the indignities of imprisonment. Participant observers from the study also risked the accusation that they were government informers, a charge frequently leveled at members of the Japanese American Citizens League (JACL) who appeared too accommodating of WRA policy to some of the incarcerated. Those pressures lessened somewhat when Miyamoto and others in the JERS study moved to Chicago to study the "resettlement" of "so-called loyal Nisei" whom the WRA had allowed to leave the camps provided they swore a loyalty oath.[36] Approximately 36,000 Japanese Americans left the camps to begin life again. Of these, the largest number, 6,599, had moved to Chicago by 1944.[37] The forced migration colored Japanese Americans' experiences of the city and its surrounding region.

Aiding Japanese Americans in their resettlement in Chicago was the Parkway Community House, run by Horace Cayton. At Parkway, Cayton hired Setsuko Matsunaga Nishi, who edited and ghostwrote for the *Pittsburgh Courier*. Nishi had been a vocal opponent of incarceration of West Coast Japanese Americans while a student at the University of Southern California. Upon Franklin Roosevelt's issuance of Executive Order 9066, she sent a telegram to the White House that read, "THE PRESIDENT: WE NISEI AMERICANS LOYAL. PROTEST INTERNMENT AS UNDEMOCRATIC CURTAILMENT OF CONSTITUTIONAL RIGHTS AND CIVIL LIBERTIES."[38] She was among the first to accept the resettlement program that carried Japanese American students eastward, and she received a master's degree in sociology at Washington University in St. Louis before moving to Chicago, where her parents had relocated. There she began work for Cayton at Parkway.

Cayton held a position with the Committee on Minority Groups of Chicago's Council of Social Agencies, and he used it to advocate for resettled Japanese Americans. At Parkway he trained Nishi to navigate the city's social welfare services and to lead a series of People's Forum discussions on racism. She recalled that the position was her "first really close contact with Negroes, who knew so much better than Nisei the destructiveness of the fear and hatred of racial prejudice—which gave me the courage for facing what minorities must."[39] Together Cayton and Nishi argued that Japanese Americans needed solidarity.[40]

At Parkway, Nishi met Charles Kikuchi, another participant observer in JERS who had relocated from the Gila River camp. Born in Vallejo, California, Kikuchi lost his parents at an early age and grew up in a multiracial orphanage north of San Francisco.[41] He worked migrant labor jobs, as Cayton had, and then managed to begin training in social work at the University of California. He began his diary in 1941 and maintained it until his death in 1988. An early recruit to JERS, he arrived in Chicago with his two teenaged sisters so that all three of them could finish their education together.

There, working under the direction of Dorothy Thomas's husband, he collected sixty-five "life histories" of relocated Japanese Americans. Miyamoto credited Kikuchi with collecting the largest number and most thorough of the life histories from the study. Thomas published fifteen of his interviews in her second book about JERS, *The Salvage*.[42] Although flawed by Thomas's prejudices and the coercion of its participant observers, *The Salvage* offers insight into how forcibly relocated Japanese Americans perceived American regions and how their relocation led them to distinguish the Midwest from the East.[43]

Like Miyamoto, Nishi, and Kikuchi, other Japanese Americans accepted relocation because they wanted educational opportunities and to get out of the camps. Several had worked potato and sugar beet harvests in Oregon, Utah, and Idaho on "seasonal leaves" that allowed them to leave their camps temporarily prior to relocation. One recalled that he and other laborers "used to talk, and we all had the intention of going east to New York, Chicago, or Cleveland. All the guys said they were going east because jobs paid a lot more than farm work." Another looked eastward as his connections to the West diminished. "There is no restaurant for me to go back to, but we are still making payments on our house yet. That is our only root left in Seattle. . . . I follow the economic security reasons more than the geographical or sentimental choice of places. In my line of work I hope to end up eventually in New York City because the most chances for advertising work are there."[44] Incarceration and relocation had tainted the emotional attachment that relocated Japanese Americans could hold for regions.

For westerners like Cayton and Branch, the Midwest had once been part of the East and had meaning as a site of opportunity. For Japanese Ameri-

Western Japanese Americans incarcerated during World War II faced relocation under circumscribed conditions without their full civil liberties. They were not free to follow "the sentimental choice of places" in deciding where to settle. "Japanese Americans in a camp library, January 1944, Minidoka concentration camp, Idaho," *Densho Encyclopedia*, https://encyclopedia.densho.org/sources/en-ddr-densho-37-44-1.

cans of the West Coast, wartime-forced relocation cast any regional attachments under the cloud of federal aggressions against civil liberties. Some camp newspapers encouraged relocation by advocating that incarcerated Japanese Americans "take this pioneering step and get rehabilitated now. Go east, Nisei, bravely, proudly," but many of those who relocated conceded to low-paid agricultural, factory, or domestic labor in the Midwest and the East, a forced choice that gave them little more freedom than the camps had.[45] Figures such as Nishi, Kikuchi, and Miyamoto, who left to pursue education or urban office work, experienced different discrimination than did those Japanese Americans who worked for New Jersey's Seabrook Farm or for farmers surrounding Chicago or Philadelphia, but they experienced discrimination all the same.[46]

Local prejudice and oppressive policies also hindered incarcerated Japanese Americans from forming attachments in the interior West. Larry

Marginal Man and Marginal Midwest 73

Larom, a dude rancher in Wyoming, discouraged local officials from granting fishing licenses to Japanese Americans incarcerated at Heart Mountain in 1945. Although the camp was soon to close, Larom said that Japanese Americans had previously "cleaned our streams and lakes." Most fished to supplement meager camp diets, but Larom argued that the licenses should be denied to "eliminate friction between the Japanese and residents."[47] Japanese Americans who happened upon his dude ranch advertising in Chicago were unlikely to find a return to prejudices like Larom's appealing, but relocation to the Midwest revealed prejudice outside the West too.[48]

In Chicago, Kikuchi initially concluded that Japanese Americans were free of racism because they had left the anti-Asian prejudice of the West Coast. He concluded in his diary that organizations like Cayton's "discounts the fact that a new type of precedent is being established. . . . Cayton is a most sincere individual and quite a brilliant person. He is speaking from his own past experience[. H]e has found organization effective so that he thinks this is the only way for the Nisei to protect themselves. It would actually slow down any integration process because it assumes that the level of acceptance by the Caucasian for the Nisei starts on the same plane as the Negro groups. It overlooks certain facts that the Nisei as a group do not have the long tradition of non-acceptance over the country as a whole so that it is impossible for them to jump over certain barriers the Negroes face when they come to the Midwest area."[49] Kikuchi observed greater prejudice against African Americans, but in 1945 he did not see that as a barrier to Japanese American success. He concluded that the prejudice of the Midwest was a stubborn and pervasive anti-Blackness and thus would not affect him or other Japanese Americans; he saw anti-Blackness as nationwide but anti-Japanese sentiment as regional.

Later in life, when he was no longer working for JERS, Kikuchi embraced a different theory. Following the war, Kikuchi moved to New York City, married Martha Graham Company dancer Yuriko Amemiya, whom he had met at the Gila River camp, and became a psychiatric social worker. He counseled African American veterans, and his wife moved among the Black entertainment elite, including Ruth James, Duke Ellington, and Ada Jones. He spent a 1949 afternoon reading *Black Metropolis* and wrote in his diary: "I notice that [Brooklyn neighbor and Nisei artist] Bunji Tagawa downstairs did all of the illustrations for the book. The book poses a lot of dilemmas and it concludes that we are rapidly coming to an explosive situation more dangerous than the atomic developments if the race question is not somehow solved."[50] Kikuchi considered a broad swath of the US racial landscape, observed the shortcomings of US democracy to serve all its people fairly, and concluded that the status of African Americans constituted the nation's racial bellwether.

Kikuchi's intellectual journey paralleled his physical one. Reflecting decades later about his work for JERS, he recalled: "I believed the Nisei would be best served by rapidly integrating into American society. In time, I realized that the path to this goal was an individual choice; there was no mass solution to a 'melting pot.' I concluded that this process of integration could best be achieved by a move to the East Coast."[51] Kikuchi, even more than Miyamoto and Cayton, occupied the position of the marginal man. Although Kikuchi did not engage in agricultural labor during resettlement, his difficult upbringing, his rural labor, and his urban cosmopolitanism all conformed to the portrait that Park had sketched. Nonetheless, Kikuchi did not follow Park's path and seek to assimilate by conforming to a white, middle-class norm. As a social worker, rather than an academic sociologist, the marginal man theory had less of a hold on him. He sought to understand the multiracial experience that was characteristic of so much of the United States, and he sought to do so back East. His observations in Chicago and New York ultimately led him to conclude that the nation must prioritize African American equality to achieve a true democracy.

Kikuchi formed part of an eastern diaspora of Asian American scholars with roots in Northern California whom he had first met when studying at Berkeley. His closest friend at the university was Warren Tsuneishi who became head of the Asian Division at the Library of Congress. Their circle included Lillian Ota, who left the Tanforan camp to study history at Wellesley as an undergraduate and at Yale as a graduate student. She later became a professor at the University of Connecticut. Their story replicated that of western white writers in the 1930s and 1940s who went back East and found professional success. Rather than westerners, however, the moniker more often ascribed to such Japanese Americans was that of the model minority.[52]

The stereotype reinforced the anti-Blackness against which Cayton still struggled.[53] Cayton's work at Parkway with people like Kikuchi opened the door to a multiracial analysis more reflective of his Seattle upbringing, but he never walked through it. Instead, he increasingly grouped all non-whites together. That view was on display when his work with resettled Japanese Americans ended. He furthered a binary view of race more reflective of his and Miyamoto's Chicago School mentors.

Cayton reflected on the significance of region to race relations in a 1948 essay entitled "The Bitter Crop." The essay appeared in the volume *Northwest Harvest*, an edited collection organized by the Pacific Coast Committee for the Humanities, a postwar endeavor funded by the American Council of Learned Societies to elevate western humanist inquiry. Cayton's original journey back East, however, had been in pursuit of Black humanist inquiry, and he used his essay to instruct his fellow writers in the persistent racism that marked him as a Black person rather than as a westerner.[54]

Alongside other Pacific Northwesterners, Cayton recalled his upbringing and the future of the Northwest. He did not share the optimism that his father had expressed almost forty years earlier. He stated firmly, "I belong to the Northwest," but he expressed no desire to return to Seattle. "The cities of the Pacific Coast and the Pacific Northwest are now in the same position as were New York, Chicago, Philadelphia, Cleveland, and Detroit after the First World War," he concluded. "They, too, will have to deal with the problem of assimilating a large Negro population which has escaped the cruelties of the plantation system. Whether they can do it more intelligently, can exploit the experience of the Middle West and the East, remains to be seen," he observed.[55] Park's influence was much on display in Cayton's essay: white people must assimilate non-white people. Marginalization occurred when assimilation failed. Racism moved with the frontier westward. Race relations, a product of division between the North and the South, did not form in the West; they arrived there from the East.

Cayton was too good a scholar, however, to ignore racist antecedents in the Northwest. He cited an unnamed undergraduate advisor at UW who had studied "the race relations cycle on the Pacific Coast." Cayton and his advisor perceived this cycle as a product of the "need in a frontier for cheap labor." He charted the arrival to the Northwest of first the Chinese, then the Japanese, then Filipinos, then Mexicans, each of whom experienced discrimination when the desire for cheap labor faded. "All this I learned in my study as a sociologist, and in learning it I not only grew to know something of our own Pacific Northwest and the entire Pacific Coast, but I began to get some vague, dim notions about the real America." In recalling his early training as a sociologist, Cayton tentatively suggested that race relations could not be reduced to relationships between Blacks and whites. He added the thesis that he and Drake had presented in *Black Metropolis*: discrimination of any kind mitigated against the full realization of democracy. "I learned that democracy was a hope and not a reality," Cayton acknowledged, "that culturally we were torn between two traditions—the democratic ideal and racism." He drew on the Northwest's multiracial labor history in his essay as well as western writers such as Black Angeleno Chester Himes and Filipino Carlos Bulosan to conclude, "The Negro is the ultimate test as to whether democracy must always mean white supremacy."[56] In charting his own academic journey, Cayton, like Kikuchi, suggested that the West had insights to offer the rest of the nation regarding race relations.

Despite this glimmer of hope in his essay, Cayton never found the same solace in identifying multiracial alliances and tensions that Kikuchi did back East. Cayton's work for the Parkway Community House and the Chicago Council of Social Agencies as well as the racist reaction to a growing Black population in the West torpedoed any lingering faith he had in what he called "white liberalism." Although the officials responsible for wartime relocation of Japanese Americans curtailed civil liberties, they perceived themselves as liberals committed to the fundamental rights of all individuals, including the right to pursue individual freedom. Even white scholars who challenged Japanese American incarceration or endeavored to demonstrate its potentially negative impacts—such as Dorothy Thomas—were inclined to see racism as a temporary barrier to democracy's triumph. Cayton saw this view as hypocritical, whether applied to Blacks, Japanese

Americans, or both. If non-whites could not achieve individual freedom and fundamental rights, then democracy was a promise unfulfilled. In a 1944 column titled "Liberals?" he scorned the tendency of his white liberal friends to "talk the race problem away" and attribute discrimination to a "few undemocratic whites in key positions and a far too great sensitivity in the minds of all Negroes."[57] The contradictions wore on him.

Cayton felt increasingly alone, isolated from mentors, colleagues, and fellow thinkers. He later recalled that during these years he spoke "before many important groups in the Middle West. . . . It seemed to me I was wasting my efforts on prejudiced whites whose opinions on race simply couldn't be changed or a few white liberals who felt guilt at my criticism but who believed they had discharged their debt by coming to hear me speak." Cayton was at a party in New York when he learned that the United States had used atomic bombs in Hiroshima and Nagasaki. He remembered that "that entire bunch of white liberals was overjoyed."[58] They did not seem to share his concern for the power of the weapon and its use in a non-white country. Cayton felt increasingly panicked and fearful in the company of whites and increasingly unhappy in the Midwest, where white liberalism appeared to prevail.

Not long after the end of the war, Cayton experienced a descent into severe alcoholism. He was briefly married again. Eventually, he moved to New York, where he lived on the royalties from *Black Metropolis*, his *Pittsburgh Courier* column, press coverage of the United Nations, and the kindness of his friends. He formed a romantic attachment with the writer Lore Segal, whose flight from the Holocaust brought her to the United States. She fictionalized their romance in her novel *Her First American*, a study of her own assimilation to US race relations and her love for a dashing, alcoholic, middle-aged Black man. Cayton had finally found Park's ideal marginal man in the form of a younger Jewish woman, but as a Black person, he could not embody the role himself, not even back East in New York City.[59]

After living in New York, Cayton moved to Northern California, where friends and family helped him to moderate his drinking. As he recovered, Cayton renewed his friendship with his first wife, Bonnie Branch, corresponded with her as he finished his memoir, spoke at area universities as the civil rights movement crested in the 1960s, and began work on a biography of Richard Wright. He received one of the first grants from the newly created National Endowment for the Humanities to further the biography. He died in 1970 in Paris, where he traveled to conduct research in Wright's records. Cayton had returned West, begun to recover his health, and continued to serve the public with his insights on race, racism, and democracy. Nonetheless, he never attained either the comfort within a multiracial America that Kikuchi contributed to building in New York nor the equality he first went back East to seek.

Miyamoto did not suffer the same health consequences from his encounters with racism and his embrace of the marginal man thesis as did Cayton. Following the war and the conclusion of his work with JERS, he finished his dissertation and secured a full-time position at the University of Washington, where he taught for the entirety of his career. He served as chair of his department and as dean of the College of Arts and Sciences. Throughout his academic work, he reminded readers how the West had forced Japanese Americans eastward to a Midwest that they struggled to call their own.

By the close of the twentieth century, Miyamoto articulated the structures that he saw constraining Japanese Americans in much the same terms that Cayton had described those afflicting all non-white people in *Northwest Harvest*. In 1992, when interviewed for the documentary *Rabbit in the Moon*, Miyamoto repeatedly stressed that those Japanese Americans from places that harbored intense segregation and prejudice were the most resistant to relocation and to "the white population, the federal government, and the like."[60] Miyamoto and Cayton understood racism as a binary structure that extended from white dominance of US governance and its most prominent institutions, including universities. They learned that moving back East and all it conveyed to non-white, far western writers—influence in the halls of government, cosmopolitanism, a literary life—offered little respite from racism.

Cayton moved restlessly, seeking a region of racial equality. Miyamoto sought to educate from the West, Kikuchi to reform society from the East. All left the Midwest in the margins. Strip the Midwest of the economic analysis that Hicks and Le Sueur had offered, acknowledge the colonialist message at the heart of frontier stories that brought dude ranchers to Big Man's doorstep, divest yourself of the security that Thompson had built by connecting Chicago with its diverse hinterland, oppose Chicago's anti-Blackness with Cayton's vigor, visit as a forced migrant as did Miyamoto, Nishi, and Kikuchi, and the Midwest became a region difficult to call one's own. By the 1950s, white western writers could ignore the Midwest or, like Hicks, leave it behind for the far West. Black Chicagoans like Thompson could claim the city, but not its rural hinterland, as a place where they belonged. Kikuchi could celebrate a multiracial America in New York City but not in Chicago. Following the war, the Midwest dropped from far westerners' conception of their own region, and midwesterners' views of "back East" received scant attention among writers, filmmakers, and other artists.

The emergence of the Midwest as its own (albeit ignored) region shortchanged opportunities for western writers of color. Those from the Midwest, like Thompson, fell from view. Chicago functioned as a place unto itself, distinct from the East, the West, and its midwestern hinterland. Far western writers of color, even those from urban areas like Seattle, approached the Midwest within the constraints of theories such as the marginal man and wartime forced relocation. Cayton, Miyamoto, and Kikuchi continued to perceive themselves as westerners, but their racial identities eclipsed their regional ones in their daily interactions, their scholarship, and their activism wherever they went.

Whether navigating the Jim Crow South or the settler colonial Midwest, western writers of color encountered material barriers that sprang from how Americans imagined regions. Even for Kikuchi, a multiracial nation informed by a multiracial West could only take root in New York City, not in the Midwest. And even then, that vision was eclipsed by the model minority myth. Cayton, Miyamoto, and Kikuchi could not find the successes they sought through regional identification and movement. White western writers could. Their story moves this one from the margins to the center.

PART 2
THE EDUCATED OUTDOORSMAN

White westerners saw the racial landscape of the nation differently than did non-white westerners in the late 1940s. As World War II ended, the writer Wallace Stegner, in a lengthy essay for *Look* magazine, voiced the white liberal position that had so troubled Horace Cayton and that railroaded Charles Kikuchi and S. Frank Miyamoto into the model minority myth. Stegner began the essay in the West, with discussions of what he called "Pacific Races": Filipino, Japanese American, and Chinese populations on the West Coast. He treated "Mexicans" separately from the "Oldest Americans," whom he defined as American Indians and "the Hispanos of New Mexico." He then moved eastward to describe African American encounters with prejudice in the South and in northern urban centers.[1] *Look* never published the full essay, but with encouragement from his wife, Mary, Stegner himself did as a book titled *One Nation*.[2]

One Nation acknowledged the country's racism. Stegner criticized the government's wartime incarceration of Japanese Americans. Nonetheless, he echoed the Chicago School sociologists more than he did Charles Kikuchi when he argued that the "Pacific Races" could assimilate successfully to mainstream American culture because the success of Japanese Americans could be a model for others. "Their record during a great trial has been excellent," Stegner concluded, and if prejudice persisted in California, home for most Japanese Americans prior to incarceration, then, "with help" Japanese Americans could "outside the region of prejudice . . . turn the unhappy evacuation experience into an enduring good for themselves and their children."[3] He offered no advice for those Japanese Americans like Miyamoto within "the region of prejudice." Stegner did not see the flaws that Cayton, Kikuchi, and Miyamoto had identified in the marginal man's journey. One nation, Stegner argued, would preserve regional distinctiveness while eliminating any regions of prejudice.

One Nation encapsulated Stegner's vision: the West would lead the country if the East could just get over itself. Although he acknowledged outliers, Stegner's maps and text drew attention to concentrations of non-white people in particular parts of the country: Asian Americans in California, Mexicans in Southern California, Indigenous peoples in the Intermountain West and Southwest, and African Americans in the South and in northern urban centers. Such a discussion regionalized race for Stegner's readers such that the book erased the experiences of Asian Americans and Mexican Americans in the Midwest and East, African Americans in the West, and any Native people outside reservations. He concluded that "the suspicions aroused by these concentrations, which often seem purely local in their causes and effects, are all part of one large pattern," and Stegner prescribed one consistent solution: the federal government.[4] The federal government could solve the nation's racism if Washington, DC, policymakers listened to westerners like himself and his mentor, Bernard DeVoto.

No two writers were more strongly associated with the West in the mid-twentieth century. They made their careers as western writers in contradistinction to what they called "the eastern literary establishment." Via their connections to Stanford instructor Edith Mirrielees and Secretary of the Interior Stewart Udall, their legacy shaped both higher education and federal arts policy. Both had roots in Utah and a vexed relationship with the Church of Jesus Christ of Latter-day Saints that led them to embrace outsider identities wherever they went. Born in 1897, DeVoto was the child of a Catholic father and a Mormon mother. Although he aspired to be a novelist, DeVoto made his career as a pugnacious critic and as a writer of popular history. Stegner was twelve years DeVoto's junior. His parents were non-Mormon, itinerant westerners constantly seeking the next boom. They landed in Utah in Stegner's teens, and there he found the communal culture a balm to his father's independent recklessness. Stegner made his life the subject of much of his fiction and provided a model of regional writing for his many students at Stanford following World War II when the editor Edith Mirrielees hired Stegner as her successor as the director of the university's creative writing program.

Mirrielees's mentee performed well in the role that she had imagined for him. His association with Stanford contributed to its reputation as a pinnacle educational experience. As John D. Hicks had, and like Mirrielees, Stegner began to take California's dominance for granted. Describing a 1959 conference on the question "Has the West Coast an Identifiable Culture?" Stegner concluded: "Two days at Carmel convinced most of us that we felt pretty much like the rest of the United States, only more so.... Contribute regionally to the national culture? We are the national culture, at its most energetic end."[5]

With the platform provided by Mirrielees, Stanford, and California, Stegner and DeVoto celebrated the natural world of the Rocky Mountain West, circulated among its most ardent defenders, and brought a western conservationism to the very highest levels of government. Because both men played such prominent roles in defining public lands policy, western history, and western literature, the effects of their work extended well beyond their friendship. And their friendship, based on a cultivated vision of western masculinity, extended to their work. Their writing thrust the cowboy out of the spotlight and offered a new model of the ideal westerner in the form of the white, educated outdoorsman.[6]

That form was made flesh when Stewart Udall, secretary of the interior during the Kennedy and Johnson administrations, arrived in Washington, DC. With support from his wife, Lee, Udall represented the educated outdoorsman in the halls of government by presenting the West as the locus of the nation's nature and nature as the source of American humanist expression. Stewart and Lee saw appreciation of the natural world as a precondition for its stewardship and humanist training in the West's natural world as a precondition for appreciation. As a result, they cultivated humanist methods and support for the arts within the Interior Department while also championing the establishment of the National Endowment for the Arts and the National Endowment for the Humanities, which were created in 1965, during Udall's time as interior secretary.

While it was never their intention, the Udalls' public service back East inadvertently betrayed their western origins, both by severing examinations of nature from examinations of culture and by refusing the West a place in federal cultural programs established in Washington, DC. In the years following the Udalls' advocacy, western resentment of those back East would fester and rise. That resentment targeted those Interior Department and Environmental Protection Agency policies that appeared to ignore western understanding of nature as well as federal cultural programs that appeared to ignore western culture grounded in the natural world. Once again, back East became a place that many westerners resented.

When Stewart Udall left public service, he briefly took up a new position as adjunct professor of environmental humanism at Yale University's School of Forestry. "I don't know what it means," he told the twenty-six students in his first seminar as he referred to environmental humanism, "but we're going to find out." The western liberal union of nature and culture that the Udalls had carried to Washington, DC, they now offered to the Ivy League. "He bounced around the Yale campus like a freshman," reported the *New York Times*. Udall used eastern expectations to his advantage. "As an unwashed Westerner, I never attended any school that was not in Arizona," he told an audience of several hundred amused students and faculty. Like Stegner and DeVoto, Udall endeavored to speak for a union of regions as one nation. As the *Times* concluded, "The students seemed to respond to the former Secretary's style of delivery, which was one-third Government expert, one-third philosopher and one-third western posse."[7] The educated outdoorsman had proven an effective ambassador for the West back East, but his triad of traits could feel like betrayal to the westerners who followed in his wake.

CHAPTER 3
EXPLOITS AGAINST THE EFFETE

They laugh. Two men at the top of their game. Harvard boys. Well, almost. Close enough for one, never enough for the other. Maybe one has just arrived, still jittery from the road. The other awaits him on the porch, already surrounded by friends and admirers. One pockets his keys. The other spreads his arms. Undoubtedly, back slapping. Perhaps subtle jibes about a promised tennis match. Wallace Stegner and Bernard DeVoto. Wally and Benny, men of western letters, in their element at the Bread Loaf Writers' Conference back East in Vermont.

Under their hand, the educated outdoorsman rose to prominence as the western voice of environmental stewardship. Stegner's and DeVoto's imagined figure was white, male, and heterosexual. He hailed from the Rocky Mountains. (Both writers would make the occasional exception for a New Englander and maybe for a Princeton man but never for a New Yorker.) He worked for the National Park or National Forest Service, or he was a writer like themselves. He loved and understood the land. His enemies were New York's literary establishment, the West's provincial businessmen, and cowboys. He was tenacious.

But he had his weaknesses. Stegner's and DeVoto's fixation on the eastern literary elite and their vision of an ideal western man left them ignorant of western literary communities already in formation and the broader western public that they potentially represented. With the exception of an occasional kind word for someone like Era Bell Thompson, they excluded non-white westerners from both the ranks of the educated and the future of the West.[1] Ironically, the two men also contributed to western resentment of figures like themselves who had found professional success in the East. People of color in the West saw them as greater hindrances than help for western conservation measures like the return of Native land or traditional, communal management of forests. Moreover, the two men did little to open to western writers of color their own route to professional success via eastern educational and literary institutions. For their white western opponents, particularly men, their writing and their connections in the federal government ultimately made them no different than the New York literary communities back East whose members they had criticized as effete. Stegner and DeVoto made their writing careers as western men, but they could be painted with the same brush they wielded. They were men of letters at home in the eastern establishment.

DeVoto risked the charge from his adolescence. He steadfastly worked his way East. In 1915, after a year of study at the University of Utah, he left to attend Harvard University, took a hiatus from the university to serve in the US Army stateside during World War I, and returned to Utah only temporarily before teaching at Northwestern University in 1922. He regretted the departure from Harvard and the East. As he wrote to one of his mentors: "Do you think that . . . I can still catch on at Syracuse or some other place that far east? I'm not disposed to go anywhere else so long as there is a possibility of doing anything in Cambridge or Boston."[2] The East was good in DeVoto's view—Cambridge was better; Harvard was best.

DeVoto formed his view of Harvard in light of the university's reputation in Utah. As a non-Mormon, DeVoto had often felt excluded from circles of power and influence, and he sometimes expressed his resentment in regional terms. In 1922, describing Utahans' reaction to Harvard's president, Abbott Lawrence Lowell, DeVoto lamented, "His point of view is, needless to say, wholly incomprehensible to the local intelligentsia, who have the healthy business attitude. . . . a firm conviction that Harvard men are uncomfortable in trousers that reach below the knee, I am sorry to say, is the complete impression of Harvard in these enlightened parts."[3] Early in his career, DeVoto couched his presentation of a literary man in regional terms and defended the mature masculinity of Harvard men against perceived slights among his Utah neighbors.

Although DeVoto never succeeded in securing a full appointment at Harvard, he did make his home and career in Cambridge, where he returned from Northwestern University with his wife, Avis DeVoto, in 1927. DeVoto considered himself a "pro," by which he meant a professional writer.[4] Without a permanent academic appointment, he supported his spouse and two children by working at the Bread Loaf Writers' Conference, where he began teaching in 1932, and with his writing, which included short fiction and potboiler novels that he published under the pseudonym, John August. He wrote for eastern publications, including *Harper's*, where he authored The Easy Chair column beginning in 1935 and ending with his unexpected death from a heart attack in 1955. As he had in Utah, he resented but also emphasized and used strategically his semi-outsider role.

DeVoto cemented his reputation as a western writer when he published "The West: A Plundered Province" in *Harper's* in 1934. DeVoto presented himself as the West's champion, its native son who would speak truth to the metropole. For him, as for Meridel Le Sueur and John D. Hicks, the East was imperial, and in DeVoto's work, its western hinterland simmered with resentment. "Financial organization had not made the West wealthy. It has, to be brief, made the East wealthy," DeVoto proclaimed. Although years would pass before DeVoto fully emerged as a conservationist, he demonstrated his commitment to protection of the natural world in "The Plundered Province." Like Le Sueur and Hicks had done in their explorations of agrarian populism, he followed the money: "The Westerner has seen palaces rise on Fifth Avenue and the endowments of universities and foundations increase with a rapidity that establishes the social conscience of his despoilers. . . . Meanwhile, the few alpine forests of the West were leveled, its minerals were mined and smelted, all its resources were drained off through perfectly engineered gutters of a system designed to flow eastward. It may be empire-building. The Westerner may be excused if it has looked to him like simple plunder."[5] DeVoto prided himself on his own success in the East, but that was the East of New England. He reserved his frustrations with the East for New York.

Exploits against the Effete

Bernard and Avis DeVoto made their careers as writers back East. Courtesy of the Wallace Earle Stegner Photograph Collection, J. Willard Marriott Library, University of Utah.

And sometimes for Chicago. Throughout his life, DeVoto remained firm on the location of the West, but the East had a tendency to move around. As he put it: "Briefly..., the West is the Intermountain West, the land that is dominated by the Rocky Mountains."[6] Where did that leave the East? In New England when DeVoto referred to culture and literature, but somewhere between Chicago and New York City when he referred to industry and finance. As DeVoto's polemic continued, he took to task the *Chicago Tribune* as well as the *New York Times*, Illinois as well as Massachusetts, as the agents of the West's despoliation.[7]

DeVoto railed against the East in "The Plundered Province," but he ultimately revealed himself as an eastern transplant when he described whom he perceived as a real westerner. "He is a tough, tenacious, over-worked, and cynical person, with no more romance to him than the greasewood and alkali in which he labors. He is the first American who has worked out a communal adaptation to his country, abandoning the hope that any crossroads might become Chicago. The long pull may show—history has precedents—that the dispossessed have the laugh on their conquerors."[8] DeVoto, like many historians in the mid-twentieth century, confused the frontier with the West as a region. As a result, he engaged in a common, erroneous, and colonialist substitution among historians of the frontier. White settlers became "first Americans." DeVoto's eastern peers identified him as a western writer. He actually wrote about the frontier.

DeVoto's writing about the frontier led to his professional success. Two years before "The Plundered Province" appeared in *Harper's*, he published *Mark Twain's America*, a rejoinder to a biography of Twain by Van Wyck Brooks that had presented the Missourian as a stunted product of a provincial backwater. In contrast, DeVoto argued that it was Twain's most western adventures, particularly his time in Nevada and California, that made the writer an American original.[9] In 1946 he published the Pulitzer Prize–winning history *The Year of Decision: 1846*, the first of his frontier history trilogy, followed by *Across the Wide Missouri* (1947) and *The Course of Empire* (1952), which won the National Book Award for Nonfiction.[10] In 1953 he published, as editor, *The Journals of Lewis and Clark*, and between 1946 and his death in 1955, he wrote more than forty articles about the West, most addressing conservation on western public lands. DeVoto published novels and articles about topics other than the West, but it was his writing on Mark Twain, his editing of the Lewis and Clark journals, his trilogy on the history of the frontier, and his conservationist writing that sealed his reputation in the East as a frontier expert.[11]

Stegner's and DeVoto's regionalism grew with their friendship, in dialogue but toward different ends. Among the items in DeVoto's collection at Stanford is a letter he wrote to Stegner in 1937, early in their relationship, when Stegner was living in Wisconsin. "Teaching is an excellent vocation for [the young writer] if his mind is vigorous enough to resist the academic infection," De Voto began. "The turnover is large, and if your academic standing is satisfactory you can probably get farther east than you are. These days regional and provincial cultures are extremely promising, and I think will be more important in our literary future."[12] Regional and provincial cultures would be of significance to both men but in different ways. Although both had a tendency to blur the West with the frontier, they diverged in their ambitions. While DeVoto sought to establish himself as a writer by finding his own place in the literary establishment of the East, Stegner was interested in presenting the West's cultural cachet as equal or even superior to that of the East.

As a result, Stegner did not concede to eastern perceptions as easily as did his friend. He was younger than DeVoto and had greater freedom to choose what kind of writer he wanted to be, in part because of the ground that DeVoto had cleared and in part because he hit his stride in his career during the post–World War II economic boom. Stegner, too, worked at Bread Loaf, beginning in 1938, and taught at Harvard from 1939, but he made a clean break from the East when he left for his position at Stanford University in 1945.[13] (Although he returned to Bread Loaf in subsequent years, he was not present when Thompson was a fellow in 1949.) Philip Fradkin, in his biography of Stegner, asserts that "the acquaintances and friends that Stegner cultivated at Bread Loaf would lift him out of the boondocks of the Mountain West and the Middle West and launch him into the elevated ranks of East Coast teaching, writing, and publishing."[14] Stegner likely would have rejected the term *boondocks*, but he recognized

The Bread Loaf Writers' Conference allowed many western writers to network with eastern publishers. Bread Loaf Writers' Conference, 1938. *Top row*: Raymond Everitt, Robeson Bailey, Herbert Agar, Herschel Brickell, Wallace Stegner, Fletcher Pratt; *middle row*: Gorham Munson, Bernard DeVoto, Theodore Morrison, Robert Frost, John Gassner; *bottom row*: Mary Stegner, Helen Everitt, Kay Morrison, Eleanor Chilton (Mrs. Herbert Agar). Courtesy the Wallace Earle Stegner Photograph Collection, J. Willard Marriott Library, University of Utah.

those elevated ranks as much as DeVoto had. He, too, made his career writing about the West. Nonetheless, from 1945 he did so from a home base in California, a place with an ambiguous relationship to the West, to be sure, but hardly Cambridge, Massachusetts.

In the heady, rich days of post–World War II California, Stegner became a powerful supporter of the humanities from his teaching position at Stanford. There Stegner dedicated himself to creating the literary institutions—from public funding for the humanities to local bookstores—that would cultivate regional literature in the West. This had long been his goal. In 1939, in an article on western publishers, he praised Caxton Printers of

Caldwell, Idaho, which began operation in 1927 and published the Idaho state guide by the Works Progress Administration (WPA). In a subtle jibe at the preferred literary format of New York intellectuals, Stegner concluded that "far more than a little magazine could do, Caxtons are offering an outlet to the literary activity of a region formerly entirely dependent on Eastern sanction and condescension."[15] Although he expressed ambivalence about whether California fell within the West or not, Stanford proved to be an influential headquarters from which to make his case. Near the end of his career, and thirty-five years after DeVoto's death in 1955, Stegner celebrated in the *Los Angeles Times Book Review* what had been, in many respects, his life's work:

> It is exhilarating to me, 60 years after I graduated from a Western university and 45 years after I made the decision to come back West to live and work, to see the country beyond the 100th meridian finally taking its place as a respected and self-respecting part of the literary world. I used to yearn for the day when the West would have not only writers but all the infrastructure of the literary life—a book-publishing industry, a range of literary and critical magazines, good bookstores, a reviewing corps not enslaved by foreign and eastern opinion, support organizations such as PEN, an alert reading public, and all the rest.[16]

Stegner's image of the West and what he wanted for its literary culture had remained consistent from his 1939 articles on regionalism and regional publishing until the close of his own life. By the time he wrote DeVoto's biography in the 1970s, Stegner was well practiced in presenting himself as a western writer and the West as a region that produced writers and a literary culture.

That image was reflected in *The Uneasy Chair*, his 1974 biography of DeVoto. Stegner used DeVoto as a character to push against eastern notions of the West as backward, unsophisticated, and unlettered. The term *east* appears as the West's foil at least thirty times in the book. In Stegner's account of DeVoto's early years, the East functions as DeVoto's father's origin point. His Catholicism "was bound to seem eastern, exotic, aristocratic" to a boy from "the gopher hole of a Utah town," and DeVoto learned from his father "a sense that culture existed only farther east." Upon entering Harvard, DeVoto headed toward "the mysterious and intellectual and literary East from which his father had come. Never mind that his father had come from Indiana. To an Ogden boy, anything east of Cheyenne is back East." DeVoto's ambition stemmed from his perception of the East. "From early in his career he had mythologized his pilgrimage eastward as a quest or a trial, a journey designed to let him prove himself in the intellectual East from which his father had dropped out." DeVoto's years in the Midwest, when he taught at Northwestern University between 1922 and 1927, were merely "a way-station on the road East."[17]

In Stegner's presentation, DeVoto's eastward yearnings clarified his vision of the West and his identity as a western man. DeVoto's reflections on his hometown of Ogden "forced him to the perception that for all its advantages, the East was effete, that it lacked the continental view, that its assumptions and prejudices needed a little western fresh air. The literary needed to be told they were sissy." DeVoto's biography of Mark Twain was "a logical outgrowth of his study of the frontier and his irritation with some of the things Easterners had said about it." DeVoto's scorn for the literary elite of the 1920s stemmed from his vision of "the Young Intellectuals as the 'in' crowd, the aesthetes, the expatriates, the ambulance drivers, the effete Easterners." DeVoto's book *Mountain Time* "had also contained, in ways that he could not quite tie down, the West-East conflict, the problems of Westerners who came East toward enlargement and opportunity and were never quite satisfied, were always eaten by the desire to return."[18] That DeVoto never actually returned to live in the West did not stop Stegner from speculating that he wanted to. Stegner's drawing of DeVoto's character pointed toward provincialism, not the West's but the East's.

Stegner identified this eastern trait particularly in its treatment of himself. Premonitions of the sentiment had appeared in his swipe at the condescension of eastern publishers in 1939, but he grew more direct in later years. In a series of oft-quoted interviews with historian Richard Etulain, published in 1983 as *Stegner: Conversations on History and Literature*, Stegner complained that the *New York Times* called him the "Dean of Western Writers" and got his name wrong "all in the same instant."[19] As one of Stegner's students, the writer Wendell Berry, put it: "The adjective 'western,' as all regional writers will understand, would have been dismissive even if the name had been correctly given. This is the regionalism of New York, which will use the West, indeed depend on it, but not care for it."[20] Berry articulated the resentment that Stegner felt when the eastern press used the designation "western writer" as well as the frustration that Stegner and Berry alike felt when they were unable to stir concern in the East for conservation of western land.

Stegner did not find all of the East and its literary institutions provincial. New England, particularly the New England of the annual Bread Loaf Writers' Conference, was altogether a different East than New York City for him, just as it was for DeVoto. The conference had its roots in summer sessions at Middlebury College in the early 1920s, when both Robert Frost and Willa Cather served as instructors. The formal conference at Middlebury's Bread Loaf Inn began in 1926 under the direction of John Farrar, a poet, editor of the literary monthly the *Bookman*, and later cofounder of the publishing house Farrar, Straus & Giroux. Frost lectured in 1927 and returned regularly thereafter. Ted Morrison, a writing professor at Harvard and a former editor at *Atlantic Monthly*, became Bread Loaf's director in 1932 and hired DeVoto the same year. As director, Morrison managed, in DeVoto's words, "to make coherent what had been an amusing and sometimes brilliant but haphazard experiment."[21] In 1938 Morrison hired Stegner, and Morrison's wife, Kay, became Frost's personal secretary. She helped nurture the connection between the poet and the conference.[22] Stegner and DeVoto both adored it. DeVoto dedicated the occasional Easy Chair column to the conference, and Stegner described Bread Loaf as "frenziedly, manically literary.... It was argument, gossip, news ... hikes ... swims ... square dances ... furiously competitive tennis ... an annual softball game down at Robert Frost's Ripton farm ... and ... a lot of not-uncompetitive drinking."[23]

The camaraderie and dedication to writing that Stegner found at Bread Loaf and at Harvard led him to present New England in more positive terms than he did New York. As Stegner himself put it: "If I had gone to

New York looking for an entry into the literary establishment I could not have done a quarter as well as I did in the intimate atmosphere of Bread Loaf."[24] Later in life, he reflected: "Having left Harvard in 1945, I more or less withdrew from American literature. I was much more in it there, even though I didn't live in New York."[25] He followed DeVoto's example.

DeVoto called himself "an apprentice New Englander." When he left Harvard briefly in 1936 to edit the *Saturday Review*, he lamented in an Easy Chair column: "It was a long way, in 1915, from Utah to Harvard Square, but it's a longer one, in 1936, from Harvard Square to New York." In a letter to a confidante, he called Bread Loaf "the best club I've ever belonged to."[26] The DeVotos' home in Cambridge served as a headquarters for writers and literary Harvard students and professors. DeVoto memorialized their tradition of weekly cocktails in his book *The Hour*, and he cultivated students in his own image. "What do you do," he once asked a Harvard student upon learning that he neither drank nor smoked, "to smell like a man?"[27] DeVoto incorporated as much of the spirit of Bread Loaf into his daily life and work as he could, a spirit he found lacking in New York City. Like New York, Cambridge and New England may have been the East, but they were superior in Stegner's and DeVoto's eyes. New England better combined city and country, better nurtured intellectual communities, and had a longer hold on what the two men considered American literary tradition. If westerners had to go East to be writers, then they would go to New England.

Stegner emphasized DeVoto's preferences and prejudices in *The Uneasy Chair* in language that rested on racist stereotypes grounded in the two men's conception of the frontier. When DeVoto's biography of Mark Twain met more critical acclaim than had Brooks's, the triumph was not just DeVoto's, according to Stegner, but the West's.[28] Stegner proclaimed that DeVoto "was not simply a red Indian dancing the scalp dance and striking the pole and boasting of his exploits against the effete. He was a sort of champion of the West, a yea sayer where there had previously been a chorus of scornful nays. . . . *Mark Twain's America* was a hymn of praise, not only a corrective report on the West and the frontier, but a celebration."[29] Stegner presented DeVoto during his brief stint in New York City not as the anointed western writer of the literary elite but as the self-appointed critic of the East, and he used racist language to do so. His offensive and cartoonish invocation of the West and westerners dehumanized Native people, offended Native readers, and probably reinforced eastern expectations of westerners more than it satirized them.[30]

Significantly, Stegner also portrayed DeVoto as "boasting of his exploits against the effete," a framing of the West as masculine and the East as feminine that Stegner employed most often when decrying eastern, specifically New York's, provincialism. Stegner, moreover, did not stop with an allusion to the effete. He concluded graphically, "All the old whipping boys, all those whose ideas and ways of thinking [DeVoto] had been resisting since he was a schoolboy, were there before him in New York, stooped over, hands grasping ankles, backsides enticingly bared."[31] Stegner presented himself and DeVoto not just as western writers but as western men and claimed regional writing for the West as an aggressive, masculine gesture against a feminized eastern literary establishment headquartered in New York.[32] Stegner's ambition and aggression differed from DeVoto's. DeVoto wanted to prove that westerners could be writers and that writers could be manly. Stegner wanted to prove that western writers were more manly than eastern ones.

The two visions of masculinity fused when, together, DeVoto and Stegner became ardent conservationists. Opposition between western ranchers and the federal government had been growing since the passage of the Taylor Grazing Act in 1934.[33] Federal officials, including Secretary of the Interior Harold Ickes, saw the act's provision of grazing fees for use of common lands in the arid West as protection against both erosion and the dominance of large operations. DeVoto agreed, calling the larger landholders "western hogs."[34] Low-fee permits, according to Ickes, allowed experts in the federal government to determine the best places to protect from grazing and also gave smaller ranchers federal support in their inequitable competition with larger landholders. Taxpayers subsidized ranchers to allow federal oversight of land management and to balance small and large ranch holders' use of the land. This meant, in Ickes's view, that the land belonged to the federal government, and during his tenure as secretary, the Department of the Interior had "a keen sense of its possessing the land."[35]

Ickes first concentrated on moving the Forest Service, in the Department of Agriculture, into the Department of the Interior because the Forest Service oversaw grazing as well as logging, mining, and recreation in National Forests. In Wyoming dude rancher Larry Larom actively campaigned against the move, believing that it would imperil his and other dude ranchers' landholdings. His fellow Wyomingite Milward Simpson, who would later serve as governor and briefly as a US senator, responded to Larom's frustration in a letter in 1939: "If they ever have occasion to take the Forest Service into the Department, it will undoubtedly be under National Parks. That, in my mind, is the long range view of these people. They are unable to get hold of our lands by acquiescence of our people through enlargement of old or establishment of new Parks, so they skin the cat in a different way by taking over the Forest Service into the National Parks."[36] Neither Larom nor Simpson acknowledged that they did not own Forest Service land any more than they did National Park land. The multiple use that characterized the Forest Service, however, allowed them to see the land as more open to privatization—the same view that ranchers held of grazing lands. As a result of opposition like Larom's and Simpson's, the effort to move Forestry into the Interior Department failed, and ranchers continued to perceive National Forest land as their own.

Nonetheless, over 1946 and 1947, Ickes's successor in the Interior Department was able to propose fusing two other agencies, the Grazing Service and the General Land Office (which had overseen the Homestead Act), to create the Bureau of Land Management. Meanwhile, led by Senator Pat McCarren, a Democrat from Nevada, a Senate committee successfully argued that the Grazing Service must be self-sustaining and that its costs should be covered by reductions in staff rather than increases in grazing fees. The result was that the Bureau of Land Management had virtually no resources upon its inception because Congress had slashed the Grazing Service's budget.[37]

McCarren and Representative William Barrett, a Republican from Wyoming, led the charge to curb federal oversight of the lands and instead move to private control. They and the ranchers who supported them also cited the Taylor Grazing Act as their basis of support. They should own the land, they countered. In fact, they believed that they already did. They viewed their use of public lands for grazing as a right, not a privilege for which they paid with their grazing fees. They traced this right to the Taylor Grazing Act, which, they argued, had created vested rights for permit holders and established a pattern of shared use that they believed private owners could better execute in the future. Indeed, a trade in grazing permits by which permit holders profited had already begun, suggesting that the permits held value for individual ranchers even if they themselves did not use the land. The best way to acknowledge their property rights, these ranchers argued, was to privatize the land and take it out of the hands of the federal government altogether. Upon their formation from the American National Livestock Association and the National Wool Growers Association in 1946, the Joint Livestock Committee on Public Lands formalized this goal. "The purpose of the committee is to work for the ultimate goal of private ownership of public lands," the committee stated bluntly. Stegner later summarized the strategy: "They wanted to liquidate the Bureau of Land Management and emasculate the Forest Service and gain ownership of a princely but fragile domain that belonged to all Americans."[38]

DeVoto exploded. Having just returned from a 1946 trip west, he had fallen in love anew with the Rocky Mountains and was primed to present the region's public lands as exactly that: public. He launched his campaign with two articles in *Harper's*, "The Anxious West" (December 1946) and "The West against Itself" (January 1947). The land did not belong to ranchers, insisted DeVoto: "They do not own the public range now; mostly it belongs to you and me, and since the fees they pay for using public land are much smaller than those they pay for using private land, those fees are in effect one of a number of subsidies we pay them." The stock growers' plan amounted to simple theft in DeVoto's eyes, a theft from the American public. "They are to be permitted to buy the lands—the public lands, the West's lands, your lands—at a fraction of what they are worth. And the larger intention is to liquidate all the publicly held resources of the West."[39] In one phrase, the public's lands became the West's lands and then DeVoto's readers' lands: "your lands." It was effective advocacy that allowed DeVoto to enjoin his readers to resist the ploy.

As it had in "The Plundered Province," Wall Street, once again, played the role of the East. "The East has always held a mortgage on the permanent West," DeVoto asserted, "channeling its wealth eastward, maintaining it in a debtor status, and confining its economic function to that of a mercantilist province." Stock growers were not true westerners in DeVoto's view. They were sellouts. DeVoto drew on memories of his youthful frustrations with Utah's Chambers of Commerce as he pushed his point hard: "Westerners have always tended to hold themselves cheap and to hold one another cheaper. Western resentment of its Eastern enslavement has always tended to be less a dislike of the enslavement than a belief that it could be made to pay."[40] Whatever his rationale, DeVoto focused his anger on westerners, and it was their empty economic devotion to the East that drew his ire.

In what should westerners, the public, and DeVoto's readers invest instead? DeVoto proposed recreation of the kind he had enjoyed on his 1946 trip. "The great fact is the mountains," he proclaimed. "They put solitude and silence at the disposal of everyone. Western life has come to incorporate mountain living. . . . As a result most Westerners are hunters and fishermen and campers. Most of them are in some degree mountain climbers, naturalists, geologists. They know nature at first hand and intimately, are adept at outdoor skills, can maintain themselves comfortably in the wilderness."[41] When DeVoto imagined the public, he imagined it recreating in the West.

DeVoto saw himself at the helm of this public. He was informed by a western sensibility but understood eastern culture. Thus, he condemned eastern exploitation of western lands like he had in "The Plundered Province" but sympathized with the western intellectuals who fled the region in the face of an oppressive provincialism, as he himself had done. DeVoto thought that westerners had to be instructed in understanding the value of their own region. That instruction had to come from outside the region, ideally from people like himself.

The West's own economic and cultural elite would not do. "The two kinds of Westerners who are most obviously unhappy and most obviously out of harmony with Western culture" were, in DeVoto's view, "the intellectuals and the rich." Their frustration, moreover, was not "economic but cultural."

Exploits against the Effete

The rich merely served the plunderers. "In the overwhelming majority they are either local representatives and managers of, or else are necessarily allied with, the system of absentee exploitation that has drained the West's resources eastward and channeled its wealth in the same direction." Meanwhile, the intellectuals, at least those DeVoto respected, had left. "In the United States at large the professions—the learned professions—journalism, literature, and the arts contain a disproportionate number of men and women who grew up on Nine Mile over against Dead Man but whose address is now Westport or Winnetka or Palo Alto. They found the going too hard and so they got out. They refused to waste their strength fighting an unfavorable environment."[42] DeVoto clearly saw himself in that camp. That DeVoto included Winnetka, a suburb of Chicago, suggested that the Midwest's metropolis continued to drift in his regional portraits. That he included Palo Alto on his list indicated that he considered Stegner a fellow expatriate. He may have been in California, but Stegner had left the West.

According to DeVoto, cultural preservation of the West's best attributes—its cultivation of outdoor life, the solitude and silence its mountains offered its residents, and a legacy of cooperative settler communities who managed scarce resources for future generations—came not from the West and not from California but from the East. "Efforts to recover the Western past or to preserve its vestiges are the work of the federal government, and they are usually conceived and carried out by Easterners," DeVoto concluded.[43] Histories of the kind he had written and would write came not from the West but from the East. The key to the West's future, then, was not among westerners but in navigating eastern power. DeVoto's goal was to convince the West to resist Wall Street and embrace Washington, DC.

DeVoto expressed Wall Street's exploitation of the West in gendered and violent terms. He particularly took to task chambers of commerce that aided cattle companies that pursued the privatization of public grazing lands. They posed the greatest threat to the vision that DeVoto imagined of young westerners like himself growing up with the country instead of fleeing to the East. Those who cooperated with the stock growers made the West "an easier setup for absentee exploitation" and "only increased the West's historic willingness to hold itself cheap and its eagerness to sell out.

The West has certainly been raped by the East but its ads and its posture have always invited rape."[44] The metaphor showed how aggressively DeVoto defined masculinity and how readily he could imagine a region's victimization. If readers winced at the metaphor, that reaction does not appear to have bothered him. DeVoto presented an alternative to the independent cowboy and the Wall Street financiers who paid to advertise a way of life that was impossible to sustain. He insisted that the conservation-minded outdoorsman would be the West's masculine symbol.

Stegner remained DeVoto's steadfast ally and pursued conservation measures according to similar strategies, but he did so from California. He deplored the myth of the individualist cowboy possibly even more virulently than DeVoto did. In his 1990 celebration of western literary institutions, Stegner recalled, "Nothing could convince them in New York or Massachusetts that there was anything of literary interest in the West except cowboys," and of the mythic cowboy himself, he said that he was "a culture hero, given . . . by the novelist Owen Wister, an Eastern snob who saw in the common cowherd the lineaments of Lancelot."[45] After DeVoto leaped into the political fray on behalf of public lands, Stegner followed his lead, began publishing more on conservation themes, and dedicated himself to completing his biography of John Wesley Powell, *Beyond the Hundredth Meridian*, a study of the West's aridity. When he faltered at the challenge, it was DeVoto who spurred him on. Stegner dedicated the book to him.[46]

By the time it was published, in 1953, the effort to "emasculate" the Bureau of Land Management and privatize grazing lands had been temporarily defeated. In his joint biography of the men and their environmental activism, John L. Thomas concludes: "It came down, then, to a matter of values and the urgent need in a postwar age of environmental heedlessness to educate, organize, and activate national public opinion. This task, Stegner agreed with DeVoto, now fell to a new agent, the enlightened and energized public intellectual: novelist, short story writer, biographer but also environmental spokesman."[47] This new agent was the figure that Stegner and DeVoto chose as the West's masculine symbol, one that reflected their frustrations with the western tendency to dismiss writers as effete and the eastern tendency to dismiss westerners as provincial.

This agent, though, was usually not a westerner, at least not by the terms that DeVoto and Stegner had laid out in the 1930s. DeVoto himself was writing from Cambridge at the height of the grazing fees battle. Era Bell Thompson recalled in 1949 that he "would rather talk soil conservation any day than tell eager Loafers how to write for a living."[48] Stegner was in Palo Alto, progenitor to what later writers would call "coastal elites."[49] DeVoto's allies occupied similar positions. Of the three men whom Stegner praised most for cooperating with DeVoto in his 1946–48 campaign against stock growers—Struthers Burt, Chet Olsen, and A. B. Guthrie—only one, Olsen, had lived his entire life in the West. Each of them suggested the fault lines in DeVoto's and Stegner's strategy to ground conservation of western public lands in their vision of western masculinity.

In *The Uneasy Chair* Stegner identifies Burt as "of Jackson Hole."[50] Burt spent portions of each year near Jackson Hole at a ranch that he owned with his spouse, and he had briefly run a dude ranch in the 1920s. Burt, however, was originally from Philadelphia, attended Princeton University, spent most of his year outside the Rocky Mountains, and by the 1940s refused to call himself a dude rancher. In one of his first pieces of correspondence with Stegner, written in February 1948, he insisted, "No, I do not run a dude ranch." The Burts' ranch was more of a family retreat where friends and trusted associates paid enough rent to cover costs. In fact, Burt's letter to Stegner invited him for just such a stay. Stegner, however, misunderstood (though he accepted the invitation to the ranch) prompting another forceful explanation from Burt: "I beg you, do not call this a 'dude ranch' . . . much as I admire for his many virtues the dude-rancher, I want no part of it."[51] Stegner's presentation of Burt and Burt's alliance with DeVoto on conservation efforts made him appear a westerner, but by Burt's own measure, he was not.

In fact, it was Burt who had identified the ideal dude ranch wrangler as "an educated Eastern man with a great deal of Western experience, or—but this is a rare combination—an educated Western man with a great deal of Eastern experience" in his book *Diary of a Dude Wrangler*.[52] Like members of the Dude Ranchers' Association, Burt had contributed to changing perceptions of the railroads and their eastern financiers. He may have stepped away from his days as a dude rancher, but it was the West of recreation and its future that Burt and DeVoto were defending in their conservation battle. When that effort appeared successful in late 1948, Burt wrote Stegner from St. Croix, in the American Virgin Islands, and described their conservation efforts as "a very human story of certain men, poor and native Far Westerners, rich and from New York, trying to do a great and idealistic job over a period of years."[53] In Burt's eyes, his conservation activism was not uniquely western. It included both native westerners and rich people, like himself, from places back East. Westerners might have seen his efforts more as a defense of elite eastern tourists' recreation than as a defense of westerners' daily life.

If Burt was the educated eastern man with a great deal of western experience, Guthrie was the presumably more rare, educated westerner with a great deal of eastern experience. Born in Kentucky, Guthrie grew up in Montana and attended university there. At age twenty-five, he returned to Kentucky, where he wrote for the *Lexington Leader* for twenty years. By the time of DeVoto's conservation battle, he had begun to write novels and had come under the mentorship of Ted Morrison at Harvard, where he held a fellowship in 1944, and at Bread Loaf, where he began teaching. In 1950 Guthrie published the Pulitzer Prize–winning novel *The Way West*, and he wrote the screenplay for the western *Shane*, released in 1953. He returned to Montana in 1952 and wrote full-time there for the remainder of his life. Until his 1952 move, though, Guthrie could be subject to some of the same charges from westerners as DeVoto. He had left Montana, become a writer, and ingratiated himself at Harvard and Bread Loaf. Although he eventually returned, Guthrie was another intellectual who had fled the West.

That left Chet Olsen. Like DeVoto and Stegner, he was from Utah. Like Burt, he opposed the stock growers. Olsen worked for the National Forest Service. It was he who had alerted DeVoto to the efforts of some westerners to privatize public land. In 1955, following DeVoto's death, it would be Olsen who would scatter from an airplane DeVoto's ashes above the Lochsa River near the Idaho-Montana border, and he would be among those who would later establish a memorial to DeVoto at the same site honoring DeVoto's work as a conservationist. How exactly he conveyed his and the Forest Service's concerns to DeVoto is unknown. At Olsen's request, DeVoto's spouse, Avis, burned his correspondence with her husband.[54] Nonetheless, inklings of Olsen's views and of his employer's appeared in DeVoto's published work. In the opening paragraph of "The Anxious West," DeVoto observed that the West's "natural wealth is enormous and belongs mostly to the East and the national government."[55] In "The West against Itself" he argued that "federal intervention . . . alone was powerful enough to save Western natural resources from total control and quick liquidation by the absentee Eastern ownership."[56] DeVoto's opinion that the federal government owned public lands may have reflected Olsen's influence. Olsen had spent his entire life in the West, but in his way, he was similar to Guthrie and DeVoto in that he was a westerner with a great deal of eastern experience. He was a federal employee. He did not work in the East, but he worked for the East, an East that took the form of Washington, DC, instead of Wall Street.

In the most critical western eyes, Burt was a tourist, Guthrie was a sellout, and Olsen was a bureaucrat. For his detractors, DeVoto combined all three. In 1953, when DeVoto pursued a number of travel pieces, the editor of *Argosy: The Complete Man's Magazine* indirectly suggested that DeVoto wrote largely for an eastern audience. "We know that for quite a few years now Mr. DeVoto has been lashing out at the groups that are attempting a wholesale rob of what are the public's lands," the editor wrote to DeVoto's agent. "An awful lot of that material has reached the same hands, the readers of *Harper's*. It is a highly articulate audience to reach but also a somewhat restricted one. . . . The best thing about [our] audience is the fact that a huge percentage of these people are outdoors people and a big number of these are from the western states."[57] DeVoto considered himself a complete man, but like many of his readers, he made his living in the East. DeVoto relished the fight with his adversaries and successfully defended conservation measures in the Intermountain West, but he did so from the East by writing for eastern audiences about federal land policy created in the East.

In private correspondence, DeVoto both acknowledged such realities and incorporated them into his strategies. "An eastern vote for conservation in Congress counts just as much as a western vote and may sometimes be easier to obtain," he told one ally.[58] With another, he detailed his plans for just that outcome: "One of the ideas I have had is to get hold of some eastern Congressman . . . and to preach religion to him. There is a fine chance for some sophomore in the House to take hold of conservation . . . [and] get himself a national reputation without in any way, if he is an Easterner, treading on the toes of his constituents."[59] DeVoto wrote as a westerner, and his love for the protection of western lands was sincere, but he persisted in courting an eastern audience and eastern power in his defense of the West. For DeVoto and Stegner, the adversaries were always advocates for privatization of public land, and the educated outdoorsman proved an effective combatant.

Where the two men failed was in demonstrating with precision who the public was. Their image of the ideal western advocate excluded potential allies. Neither man sought common cause with midwestern conservation efforts or writers such as Hicks and Le Sueur because they did not see the land east of the hundredth meridian as part of the West. As DeVoto once angrily told his agent regarding a requested article: "Their original letter contemplated having the West begin at the Mississippi. It can't for it doesn't and it doesn't because it can't. It begins at the Missouri or thereabout. Nebraska is no more a Western state than Missouri, and Missouri no more than Pennsylvania."[60] Some ranchers and western outdoors enthusiasts supported continued federal management of public lands, but they were hardly visible in DeVoto's articles and were likely offended by his skewering of cowboys.[61] Referring to a conflict between locals and the Forest Service over an effort to diminish the Gila Wilderness, in New Mexico, the *Argosy*'s editor observed that DeVoto's draft presented the conflict as "a battle between the Forest Service and the Stockmen instead of between the readers as outdoorsmen and the stockmen."[62] The editor wanted DeVoto to represent "the people who actually live in and around the regions where the larceny is being planned."[63] Moreover, federal administrations changed with every election. DeVoto and Stegner found themselves at odds with politicians (sometimes even the very ones whom they had elected) who were amenable to privatization and government extraction of the West's natural resources.[64]

DeVoto and Stegner dramatically changed national perceptions of westerners to consider the outdoorsman alongside the cowboy, but their presentations of the outdoorsman had a tendency to equate the public with the federal government. Their opponents seized on the error and presented the federal government as the East, using exactly the image of the East that DeVoto and Stegner had built to discredit it. A more expansive view of the public and of lands meriting conservation, along with a clearer-eyed view of the nature of the federal government, would have made Stegner and DeVoto far more successful advocates, but it also would have eaten away at the identities as western writers that both men had cultivated for themselves.

DeVoto's and Stegner's narrow definitions of "the public" and their scorn for the effete East had its most material impact in the Southwest. The region was arid and west of the hundredth meridian, but neither man had ever defined it as a part of the West. In a 1939 article on regionalism, Stegner addressed the Southwest separately from the Rocky Mountains and parts of California and Nevada, arguing that "in the Southwest there was a strong Mexican and Indian influence that indelibly marked the region and still does," whereas "the dominant note" in the "Rocky Mountains and parts of California and Nevada" was mining.[65] Stegner did not acknowledge the existence of American Indian and Mexican miners in any other region. DeVoto reasoned similarly. In his early essay "Footnote on the West," when DeVoto spoke for westerners and defined the West as the Intermountain West, he lamented: "To our sorrow, Arizona and New Mexico are not West, for they are Southwest, and Spanish and Indian civilization separates them from us."[66] Both men considered the Indigenous and Spanish heritage of the Southwest the region's defining features and the justification for excluding the region from discussions of the "real" West.

DeVoto also had no patience for Anglo writers who had made the Southwest their home. In 1934 he wrote a scathing condemnation of the writer Mary Austin's *American Rhythm* in "How to Not Write History," an essay for *Harper's*, in which he took her to task for her "literary" approach to the past and her romanticized view of American Indians.[67] He mocked regional (Stegner would have said "provincial") literature as a "coterie manifesto," and in reference to the artists and writers surrounding the patron Mabel Dodge Luhan, such as D. H. Lawrence, he asserted that "fiction that wears a squash blossom in its hair or talks about the plumed serpent is just silly."[68] He repeated the charges in 1946 in "The Anxious West," arguing that the western writer had "fled into coterie literature, with the result that the little magazine is making its last stand in the sagebrush." "This escapism," he concluded, "is pathetic."[69]

A close friend to Stegner and DeVoto, Edith Mirrielees, echoed their views. Originally from Big Timber, Montana, Mirrielees became an English professor at Stanford University, her alma mater, in 1909. She worked for Bread Loaf from its inception and met Stegner and DeVoto there.[70] Mirrielees also worked for the Bureau of Indian Affairs in schools for Indian children. In 1940, when DeVoto took a trip west with historian Arthur Schlesinger Jr., Mirrielees was teaching at a school in Albuquerque, New Mexico, but the two men had not visited her. She wrote DeVoto in mock frustration that they had missed one another. "Oh dear, oh dear, oh dear!" she teased. "A human being of intelligence—of supposed intelligence—and he comes to see the West and goes to Santa Fe . . . and to Taos. . . . And he chooses to go to Taos, where once I saw a man, a full grown man, leading a lamb by a blue ribbon down the street in full daylight. Probably he even called on Mabel Luhan, but he does have the grace to conceal that."[71] That Taos and Santa Fe were precious and a little ridiculous seems to have been a running joke between them. Moreover, it was a joke expressed in gendered terms. Not just women of the arts community but men who did not follow traditional gender norms came in for their disapproval.

Mirrielees remained a sympathetic audience for DeVoto in 1947, just one year after the trip that had transformed him into a conservationist. He wrote to her that year about a correspondent from Santa Fe who had asked for DeVoto's attention to Pueblo Indian water rights along the Rio Grande. The letter came in the midst of the widespread western criticism that DeVoto endured between 1946 and 1948, when he threw himself into the conservationist cause. "It is being borne in on me that I'm being hanged and shot in many Western areas," began DeVoto as he introduced the letter that he had recently received. "The enclosure comes under this general heading, and I wish you'd read it and tell me if you think I'm right in thinking that she is to be classed as a Santa Fe mind and disregarded.

What she's talking about here comes under the Rio Grande project and it *is* full of inequities and injustices, and God knows I know how many assaults the Indians in general are getting these days. But I have quite a few things to do and, as I told her when I answered her first, only-three-page letter, I won't write about things I don't know about. Now this deep throb. She's Owen Wister's daughter."[72] DeVoto made clear that he would write only about that which he had knowledge, which did not include management of the Rio Grande River nor Native struggles. Further, while sympathetic to the water rights of New Mexico's Indigenous peoples, he would not extend his conservation activism to them. That Marina Wister, the wife of artist Andrew Dasburg, also of Mabel Dodge Luhan's circle, had written to solicit his support mattered little to DeVoto. Wister lived in Taos, but she was "to be classed as a Santa Fe mind and disregarded." Literally and figuratively, Wister was a daughter of the mythic cowboy and married to the "coterie manifesto." She was the cowboy's progeny "with a squash blossom in her hair" come to life.

DeVoto's snub is surprising given how much he prided himself on his research and his investment in understanding the ecological consequences of unrestricted grazing and dam building. Rivers, forests, and wildlife hardly acknowledged state and national boundaries, but DeVoto had never counted the Southwest as part of the West. Moreover, his prejudices against Mexicans and Mexican Americans and his preference for an Anglo-American frontier as an explanatory tool hamstrung his capacity to explain Spanish colonization and acknowledge Indigenous presence and sovereignty. The legacy of Spanish colonialism meant that Nuevomexicane and American Indian people could be at odds, but both groups also had grievances with the US federal government, ones driven by policy executed by local Forest Service rangers like Olsen and Indian School teachers like Mirrielees.[73] For both groups, the East was the source of colonialism. DeVoto's ongoing assumption that the public and the federal government were one and the same had the effect of excluding Nuevomexicane and Indigenous populations from the public, exactly the disempowerment that Wister had sought to bring to his attention.[74]

Given their influence and their standing as deans of western writing, the gaps in the two men's vision had consequences. As the educated outdoorsman rose in prominence, other models of western writers and western writers faded. Had DeVoto and Stegner embraced more comprehensive definitions of the West, the western writer, and the public during the years that DeVoto most dedicated his time to conservation advocacy, their success may have been more enduring. A wider definition of the West would have included the Great Plains as well as the Southwest and its Mexican, Spanish, and Indigenous histories. A wider definition of the western writer would have included women and people of color. The two men could have played a larger role in explaining the kind of local relationships to the land that some editors found lacking in DeVoto's work and that Stegner had always considered necessary for true regional writing. A wider definition of the public would have recast government as an institution of deliberation and decision-making rather than discipline and colonization. The two men could have been midwives to a diverse, communal, conservation-minded western literary culture, but neither man could bear such a description of themselves.

To see themselves as midwives would have required that they sacrifice their ideal image of the western writer. It was a sacrifice they never made readily or entirely. They clung too tightly to the outsider identities they had defensively embraced in Utah. They had invested too much in distancing themselves from New York City and its effete literati. They had embraced Cambridge and the image of the West that they built at Harvard and Bread Loaf too warmly. The educated outdoorsman, their preferred symbol of the western public intellectual and his allies, was too grounded in their attitudes toward the East—DeVoto because he had always wanted to belong to it and Stegner because he had always wanted to best it.

Writing in 1975, twenty years after De Voto's death, Stegner lamented that his friend had not lived to see the successful defeat of a dam at Dinosaur National Monument or to "hail the Wilderness Act or any of the major conservation legislation of the Kennedy and Johnson administrations under the leadership of Secretary of the Interior Stewart Udall."[75] In later years, Stegner might also have lamented that DeVoto did not live to witness other transformations too. DeVoto did not live to see his friend, ally, and fellow western writer revise his own views of the West and western writing. He did not live to see Stegner acknowledge Southwestern Native writers N. Scott Momaday or Leslie Marmon Silko for demonstrating that "literature comes out of deeply lived-in places, out of a long shared tradition" or to argue that such writers along with "James Welch ... Louise Erdrich and other Western Indians speak from the present, from the very battlefields of cultures."[76] He did not live to read Stegner condemn the "hoodlums who come to San Francisco to beat up gays" as "vigilantes, enforcing their prejudices with violence, just as surely as were the miners who used to hunt down Indians and hang Chinese in the mother lode."[77] He did not live to hear Stegner call Maxine Hong Kingston's character Wittman Ah Sing "as American as Huck Finn" or to hear her reflect, following a lecture that she delivered back East, that she shared his view that "there is a Western mind and reality—just by writing about the land and people we know, we are taking literature into a far out avant garde."[78] Stegner never praised Mexican American authors in the same tone, and he never called attention to Mexican American women's writing, which addressed many of the same themes of nostalgia, homemaking, and natural conservation that Stegner's writing did.[79] Nonetheless, he did come to see a western literature that "inevitably reflect[s] a different ... orientation: a different history, a different emphasis and expectation, a different ethnic mix, a different culture."[80] In establishing himself as a western writer and forging a western literary community, Stegner had helped readers acquire a new orientation, one that looked to the world from a literary base in the West, rather than the East.

Stegner's personal evolution came too late to push western writers off the path that he and DeVoto had built. Washington, DC, occupied westerners' minds far more than eastern capital in later years. Any efforts to acknowledge western culture had to pass through a federal filter that idealized western nature. Writers of color in the West had to struggle all the more to show the links between their own displacement and US federal action. By then, such writers were fighting a two-front war to enter the cultural elite on both coasts.

Among the figures who changed the cultural landscape of the West Coast was Stegner's and DeVoto's close collaborator Edith Mirrielees. With support from Stegner and the Pacific Coast Committee for the Humanities and the American Council of Learned Societies, she edited the *Pacific Spectator*, a journal that began in 1947, and provided a Californian basis of support for the later establishment of the National Endowment for the Humanities as well as US efforts to establish dominance in the Pacific.[81] A Montanan, a Bureau of Indian Affairs employee, and a friend to the two writers most closely associated with the West in the mid-twentieth century, she was no longer a westerner when she took the helm of the *Pacific Spectator*. By then, she had become a Californian.

CALIFORNIA INTERLUDE
THE MARGINAL WOMAN

"Oh, I wish I were a man!" exclaims a schoolteacher in Edith Mirrielees's 1912 short story "The Shooting at Raeder." The schoolteacher is aiding the local attorney. Just that day the town's bartender has shot and wounded himself after a Swedish immigrant confronted him for shorting him his change. A lynch mob pursues the Swede. The attorney recruits the schoolteacher to fool the mob into believing that schoolchildren are in the jail, just enough of a delay for the falsely accused man to escape on the afternoon train. Although Raeder's attorney assures the teacher that she "can help more as it is," she tells him again, "I wish I were a man, all the same; I'd be right there." When the attorney reveals their successful trick to the townspeople, his voice "cracks hysterically" as he shouts: "The only man in Raeder, she is! The only one that wasn't afraid—"[1] The hero of the hour is not there to hear her praises sung. She's taken the students on a picnic.

As a writing instructor, Mirrielees fashioned many of her stories as didactic models. "The Shooting at Raeder" may have taught her students at Stanford another lesson besides how to build suspense. In the rough-and-tumble world of publishing, she implied that however much women wanted to be "right there," the margins offered women the chance to "help more" and enjoy a picnic besides. As she sifted contributions and struck errant phrasing, Mirrielees justified the margins that contained her and other writers who challenged mid-twentieth-century literary norms.[2]

She found her way to the margins through Stanford University. Wallace Stegner recalled that in 1903 "Edith Mirrielees came to Stanford University from Big Timber, Montana, in much the same spirit that brought DeVoto to Harvard."[3] What Stegner did not relate was that Stanford had become Stanford in much of Harvard's spirit as well. Founded in 1885, the university looked eastward for inspiration. Writing in 1915, Harvard's president, Abbott Lawrence Lowell, advised a Stanford trustee that "a university more of the eastern type could do work which the State University, with its strongly vocational tendencies, would find it very hard to rival."[4] Lowell's letter came after Edith Mirrielees's time as a student at Stanford but during her early years as an instructor; she taught at Stanford for the entirety of her career. She had a thorough education in what a California university of the eastern type could be. Where DeVoto had used his associations with the East to raise his own standing as a western writer, Mirrielees used hers to raise California to an apex that separated it from the rest of the West.

Until then, Mirrielees concluded, Stanford felt its westernness. In *Stanford: The Story of a University*, published in 1959, Mirrielees related that David Starr Jordan, whom the Stanfords hired as president, had reported with frustration on his efforts at faculty recruitment: "In the Back Bay where I am now are men whom nothing would induce to go west of Springfield, and men the regret of whose lives is that they were born outside Boston." Mirrielees took care to note that "nonetheless, he made his attempts even in that benighted region.... Closer to the Brahmin center than his employers, he knew better than they how upstart to some eyes the Stanford venture must appear."[5] In the pages that followed, Mirrielees presented Stanford as shedding its early reputation as an upstart. Inspired by but distinct from "the eastern type," Stanford, and by extension California, outstripped eastern expectations. It was of the West but also beyond it.

Mirrielees herself arrived at Stanford at twenty-five years old as the university was still in the process of forming what kind of place it would be. Just one year after she began her studies, Edith's younger sister by eight years, Lucia, arrived at Stanford as well. Thereafter, the sisters walked similar paths. They both majored in English; they both taught in English Departments; they both published on the topic of writing and writing instruction;

and they both taught at the Bread Loaf Writers' Conference in its earliest years. The sisters survived a campus typhoid epidemic, the San Francisco Earthquake (which Edith observed was always spelled with a capital *E*) and World War I, when Edith served with the Red Cross. Lucia earned a doctorate and returned to teach at the University of Montana, but she moved to California upon her retirement and died there in 1957, five years before the death of her older sister. Neither ever married or had children.[6]

After completing their degrees at Stanford, the Mirrielees sisters continued to prepare women to teach and men to write. Lucia's dissertation was titled "American University Training in English of Prospective High School Teachers."[7] She arrived back home in 1924 and taught English at Montana State University in Missoula (now the University of Montana) until 1950. Most of her work focused on training middle and high school teachers of English. Such work was more readily available to women in the early twentieth century and composed one of the central features of university English programs.[8] Edith herself had taught high school for six years before attending Stanford, and Lucia's advice to teachers on appropriate dress and decorum assumed a female audience.

Their teaching expertise opened the door at Bread Loaf back East, DeVoto's treasured second home and Stegner's springboard to success. John Farrar, who founded the writers' conference, hired the Mirrielees sisters in 1926, Bread Loaf's inaugural year, and Edith returned every summer thereafter until 1950. The sisters referenced Bread Loaf in their acknowledgments and dedications, and memorials to both women cited their education at Stanford as well as their years at the writers' workshop.[9] By all accounts, the praise was deserved. In *The Uneasy Chair* Stegner described Edith as a "natural-born teacher ... and [an] acute critic of a manuscript."[10] She could, explained Stegner, "cut away literary gangrene, or put a deformed story out of its misery, so gently that the victim did not even know he bled, and kissed the knife that ventilated him."[11] When Edith wrote DeVoto to apologize for how little she had paid him for a piece, he replied: "I'd a damned sight rather write for you at $25 than for any editor besides you at any price. That you like the piece is velvet and, I think, more than it deserves, or I."[12] To the extent that Edith Mirrielees advertised herself, it was through the calling cards of Stanford and Bread Loaf.

Those cards worked well in recruiting Stegner to Stanford. The Depression proved challenging for the university, and the humanities departments felt increasingly marginalized and lost promising faculty members. Mirrielees never named herself in the telling of Stegner's hire, but she described it in her university history and concluded, "Compared with the whole, the appointments to the School of Humanities were not many, but their quality and placing made them of powerful effect. . . . even the most critical had to grant that Stanford had strengthened its weakest part, was now deserving of the name university."[13] Stegner, in a letter to Ted Morrison, put the situation in more colorful terms: "I look at a full professorship in a first-class university and I can't see turning it down. . . . Edith has apparently laid down some rules about her successor, and I must say her rules are good rules from my point of view. . . . Goddam. Life, it's wonderful."[14] Acquiring Stegner allowed Mirrielees to accomplish the goals that he attributed to her when she first arrived at Stanford as a student in 1903: to make in California a preeminent university.

Among their first joint efforts was the Pacific Coast Committee for the Humanities, established by the American Council of Learned Societies (ACLS) in 1944 "to advance the work of the humanities in the Far West by encouraging scholarship and research and by fostering interest and activity in literature and the fine arts."[15] The ACLS worried that the distance of the West from eastern institutions placed the region's humanists at a disadvantage; Stanford's provost, Frederick E. Terman, worried similarly about the region's scientists and engineers.[16] Mirrielees and Stegner worked closely with another Pacific Coast Committee member, Reginald "Rex" Arragon, a historian at Reed College and the chief architect of Reed's first-year humanities program, to support conferences and publish volumes about the region to create literary and cultural institutions in the West. The committee also published *Northwest Harvest*, which carried Horace Cayton's vision of

Edith Mirrielees and Theodore Morrison played important roles as mentors, editors, and friends to Wallace Stegner and Bernard DeVoto, 1940s. Courtesy the Wallace Earle Stegner Photograph Collection, J. Willard Marriott Library, University of Utah.

the West's racism and likely brought Cayton into Stegner's and Mirrielees's company just as Cayton was beginning to decry liberalism. Mirrielees, though not a member of the committee, which was composed entirely of men, brought their efforts into the purview of Stanford's vision for its future in 1947, when she took on the editorship of the *Pacific Spectator*, the center of the committee's efforts.

The opening issue of the *Pacific Spectator* read: "Edited and published in the West, *The Pacific Spectator* could not—even if it would—avoid the influence of its environment, but it will not be confined to Western topics. The sponsors propose that it shall serve as a spokesman for humanistic interests in the West and for similar interests everywhere."[17] As the voice of western humanities, the *Pacific Spectator* undergirded Stegner's efforts to make the West a literary center and tied him to institutions that facilitated later similar endeavors on a national scale. Under Mirrielees's hand at Stanford, the *Pacific Spectator* articulated these goals from California.

In fact, California tended to dominate the journal's offerings, even those that criticized just such dominance in the publishing industry. Oscar Lewis, author of *The Big Four*, was well published by 1947, but he still lamented, in one of the first of the *Pacific Spectator*'s issues, that the West Coast writer was at a disadvantage: "His publisher is several thousand miles away in an office in New York or some other Eastern city. Although he is quite sincere in his belief that he views all projects submitted to him impartially and without sectional bias . . . he finds the subject so remote from his knowledge that, lacking the background for an informed opinion of the book's interest, value, or sales possibilities, he ends by dispatching westward a polite letter of refusal and proceeds to draw up a contract for yet another book of *New Yorker* sketches."[18] Lewis may have been reflecting on his own experience. At the time he published his article, he was cooperating with Alfred A. Knopf for a multivolume series on western Americana. The series was a success, and the *New York Times* ran an obituary of Lewis at his death in 1992 identifying him as an "early writer" on the history of the American West. The obituary misstated the locations of Sebastapol and Red Bluff,

California, an indication that the *New York Times* had not quite escaped the provincialism that Lewis identified in 1947, but it suggested how eastern publishers took note of California's writers in the years immediately following the war and the role that editors such as Mirrielees had played in the reconfiguration of the nation's literary community.[19]

That reconfiguration included not just Stegner but DeVoto too. Mirrielees ran two of DeVoto's essays in the magazine's opening year and liked one so much that she published it again in 1955, when she edited *The Spectator Sampler*, a compendium of articles from the journal's first years. "Queen City of the Plains and Peaks" encapsulated DeVoto's views on regionalist writing and acted as a rejoinder to Robert Frost, who announced during a public lecture in Utah that DeVoto never should have left the West because it made him a lesser writer. DeVoto noted, first, that Frost himself had been born in San Francisco and, second, that "some writers who were born in the West but have never resisted it since they first raised the price of a ticket East are good writers." He referred to himself when he observed, "Of one I can say with certainty that he became a Western writer solely by living in the East," and to Stegner when he described "a friend of mine who is one of the best writers in the West and the United States at large" who had "a way of writing me a droll gratitude whenever I publicly say that he is just that. He is grateful, the joke runs, to be called a writer."[20] DeVoto said overtly what he had implied in other essays: "The vigilante state of mind" led to "the assumption that because writing is not male as maleness goes in the Western fantasy," the writer "must be a homosexual."[21] Mirrielees's own editorship could have feminized DeVoto in reader's eyes, but her hand was deft. In claiming DeVoto, the West's champion in New England, Mirrielees and the *Pacific Spectator* substituted California editing for that of the East.

Not everyone on the Pacific Coast Committee for the Humanities agreed with the new casting. Rex Arragon and others at the journal worried from its outset that they would have to advocate for the Pacific Northwest in "a journal that naturally has on it so much of the stamp of California."[22] Arragon and others eventually shifted their focus to publication of *Northwest*

Harvest, which Mirrielees advertised but otherwise did not support. In keeping with the prejudices Stegner and DeVoto held, the Southwest and even Southern California also received less and less coverage in the *Pacific Spectator*. Arragon's objections, however, were not just to the journal's focus on California and its exclusion of the Northwest and Southwest. He questioned the notion of regionalism altogether. "The regional character of the Pacific coast gives a ground for the establishment of such a periodical, and yet this should not confine it to a narrow consideration merely of regionalism," he wrote Mirrielees in 1946, as the journal was first taking shape. "The region is important, however, as a point of departure both in regard to subject matter and in regard to contributors." Nonetheless, Arragon concluded, "We might outgrow our regional origins."[23]

Arragon proved prescient. More and more of the *Pacific Spectator*'s numbers focused on Asia in later years. The magazine formally announced this focus in 1954 in an opening editorial: "One section of the quarterly, a small one, devotes itself with each issue to Asian writing."[24] The new focus followed California's rising importance in international affairs as well as Cold War politics, which shifted reading audiences' attention across the Pacific. The interest in Asia, however, also reproduced presentations of the American West as a frontier, a resonance that one of the *Spectator*'s contributors, Thomas Arthur Bisson, observed in his review of Henry Nash Smith's book *Virgin Land*. "It would seem clear that the 'wealth of the Indies' concept has been a persistent strain in American thought about the Far East," Bisson wrote. "And yet it has remained, in terms of actual historical development, peripheral rather than central to the United States, despite the growth of American influence and power in Asia. . . . It should perhaps be asked what relation exists between these American concepts and the problems that are of immediate and vital concern to Far Eastern peoples."[25] As the *Pacific Spectator* itself engaged in a fantasy of "the wealth of the Indies," Mirrielees's vision of the American West doubled back on itself. Her pursuit of Asian "material" mirrored an earlier generation's colonial ambitions in North America, ones over which Mirrielees demurred in the *Spectator*'s slight discussion of North America's Indigenous peoples and her celebration of "pioneer" spirit at Stanford. Mirrielees highlighted instead the new cultural metropole the *Pacific Spectator* had helped build. If the future was in the Pacific, then she, Stanford, and California were at the center.

The focus on Asia also gestured toward the *Spectator*'s chief constraint: the Red Scare. Articles protesting loyalty oaths, including those required by the State of California, and defending academic freedom ran in the journal in the spring and summer of 1949; winter, summer, and autumn of 1950; summer of 1951; winter of 1952; summer of 1953; and spring of 1954. In the same years, DeVoto defended himself against charges of Communist sympathy that rattled both him and his wife, Avis.[26] Bisson, who had reviewed Smith's *Virgin Land*, lost his position at UC Berkeley under suspicions that he was a Soviet spy and Chinese Communist sympathizer in 1952.[27] The articles defending freedom of thought within and outside the academy showed the important work that the *Pacific Spectator* and its allies did in creating room for open-minded writers on the Pacific coast in the 1950s. These were bold moves of national significance for a "maiden lady" editor past retirement age in California.

Nonetheless, they took space and energy from the magazine's initial experiments with discussions of race and articles by Californian writers of color. As (Northern) California became more worldly in the *Pacific Spectator*'s pages, it lost those articles that described the experiences of non-white people on the Pacific coast and in the West to favor instead a midcentury, consensus color blindness. The magazine published more articles by Asian authors than by Asian American ones, never published articles by Mexican American or Indigenous authors, and even stopped altogether publishing articles by white authors *about* Mexican American and Indigenous experiences.[28]

As Cayton had in his *Northwest Harvest* essay, Mirrielees endeavored to link questions of race and racism within the United States with international affairs, rather than with regional culture. In a rare editorial written above her own signature on the eve of the 1954 *Brown v. Board of Education* Supreme Court decision, she wrestled with what she called "the sharpest and most dangerous of America's many contradictions: On the one hand, collective gestures of amity toward that dark-skinned three fourths of the world whose support we desperately need; on the other, individual acts of insult and outrage leveled day by day and almost hour by hour at such of the dark-skinned as are within our reach." Mirrielees took to task "John Doe's father," who "does not originate the petition against allowing a Japanese family to enter his neighborhood—but he signs it," and "John Doe's mother," who "moves over companionably when a white shopper comes to share her seat in the bus" but "sits stony when the shopper is black." Mirrielees provided astute observations, but her real concern was the threat such behavior posed to US international ambitions. "Either of them would consider it the wildest romancing if they were told that, between them, they had brought their son one step nearer to fighting in Asian forests."[29] In 1954 Mirrielees questioned everyday racism, but she did not question who was included in the "we" that desperately needed dark-skinned allies nor the inherent inequalities implied by the phrase *our reach*. Mirrielees asserted that the *Pacific Spectator* had, indeed, begun to speak for the nation. California could stand for the whole of the public.

California, however, could not stand for the federal government. When Mirrielees began editing the *Pacific Spectator*, the national government reflected hers and Stegner's political views. They differed from federal leaders in their open criticism of Japanese American wartime incarceration, and they angled along with DeVoto to counter western politicians opposed to conservation efforts. Their vision of federally administered public housing, employment programs, and Indian health and education services aligned with those of the New Deal and the postwar Truman era. By the 1950s, however, they found themselves at odds with the federal government, particularly the federal Indian policies of termination and relocation, which endeavored to end the nation-to-nation relationship of the US government with that of Indigenous nations and, in a separate, parallel program, relocate rural Indigenous people to urban areas for jobs and housing.[30] In a 1955 article for the *Atlantic*, Mirrielees stepped from the margins to critique termination but proved herself an imperfect ally still beholden to the East.

Mirrielees observed that many Indigenous people considered relocation a program "aimed at their destruction." She noted that termination policy rested within a colonial framework. "Consultations have been frequent, but they are consultations where unhampered authority speaks on one side and the subjects of that authority on the other." She cited her allies in the National Congress of American Indians, the Friends Committee on National Legislation, and the Association on American Indian Affairs. She quoted an open letter from the Shoshone-Bannock Tribes to the commissioner of Indian Affairs, which took to task those justifying termination as part of American democratic tradition. "This may be in the American Way and the American Tradition of ignoring treaties," wrote the Shoshone-Bannock Tribes, "but it is not in the tradition of keeping treaties. . . . Are we to expect less of honor from our own government than is exhibited toward . . . foreign nations?"[31] Such observations set the stage for an acknowledgment of Indigenous sovereignty.

But Mirrielees would not spotlight Indigenous self-determination. Instead, she always came back to solutions that emanated from Washington, DC. She concluded that the government's most significant error was failing in its responsibilities to Native people as citizens of the United States. It was Indians' incomplete inclusion—not failed treaty obligations—that troubled Mirrielees. "The changes were made without that 'consent of the governed' which is supposed to be of primary importance in a democratic land," she protested. The "cloud of mistrust" that hung over the Bureau of Indian Affairs and the Department of the Interior as well as Congress and the president and, ultimately, "the American people" could be dissipated, she argued, if everyone "took the trouble" to pay attention to Indian people and listen to their concerns.[32] In Mirrielees's view, white eastern men just needed a western education to right wayward federal Indian policy. But the policy would remain that of the US government all the same. Teaching at Stanford and editing the *Pacific Spectator* had given Mirrielees a platform from which to exert what influence she had toward her favored national politics. Californians would lead and even champion the marginalized on occasion, but they would not challenge US colonization nor the margins themselves.

Even that compromised position became more difficult in 1956, when the *Pacific Spectator* ceased publication. The magazine had always subsisted on ACLS funding, and when that ended, it lacked sufficient subscribers to continue. Edith Mirrielees's sister Lucia died just one year after the magazine closed, and by then Edith was seventy-nine years old. Edith published her history of the university in 1959. An updated version of her book *Story Writing* appeared in 1962 with a preface by John Steinbeck, a former student and that writer probably most associated with California in the mid-twentieth century. That year Mirrielees finished editing a collection of alumni memories of the campus titled *Stanford Mosaic*, which was published just two weeks after her own death. Her final editorial work reflected her ambitions and their limitations for California.

Like her university history, *Stanford Mosaic* highlighted prominent early alumni, including Herbert Hoover, a member of the "Pioneer class," and Arizona senator Carl Hayden. Alumni described their experience from the university's earliest days to the study-abroad programs in France, Italy, and Germany that were thriving in the postwar era. Kenneth Cooperrider, who completed his undergraduate degree in 1931 and worked as *Sunset* magazine's managing editor in 1962, contributed an essay titled "No Longer a Minority," which referred to "those ... who came from the isolated parts of the West" and found at Stanford an intellectual freedom that Cooperrider felt unavailable to those like himself from small towns elsewhere in California.[33] Mirrielees had maintained her support for young white men from the rural West aspiring to enter her own profession, especially those who landed in writing and editing jobs in California. While other women and Mirrielees herself remained in the margins, students such as Cooperrider ensured that her message of California's preeminence remained "right there" and advertised picnics besides.[34]

Those who actually remained minorities in 1962 received less representation than did students like Cooperrider. The year *Stanford Mosaic* was published and Edith died, the university admitted the largest number of African Americans it had yet: seven. Sandra Drake, who was among those seven and who, like Mirrielees, was an undergraduate who became a faculty member at Stanford, recalled of her first year that "Stanford was a very insular world, a western, California white world that seemed to be made up of valedictorians from every high school in the state."[35] That world changed quickly. In 1969 Drake's father, St. Clair Drake, who had cowritten *Black Metropolis* with Horace Cayton, left Roosevelt University in Chicago and began Stanford's African and African American studies program, where he remained until his retirement.

In *Stanford Mosaic* Mirrielees took note of a greater variety of students than just the California valedictorians, but she did not anticipate the innovations that the Drakes would bring to the university. Echoing the editorial mandate of the *Pacific Spectator*, she included two reminiscences from Asian Stanford alumni: N. V. M. Gonzalez, a Filipino novelist, and Fuji Imamura, who returned to Japan after completing her degree to teach and engage in social service. Of the sixty-four contributors to the volume, Imamura was the only woman of color. Only eleven others were women, and only one, Najeeb E. Halaby, was a non-white American. (He described himself as "half Syrian, half-Scotch-Irish, and all Texan.")[36] The volume reflected Mirrielees's and Stanford's frontier outlook: non-whites in the West were incorporated via their pioneer efforts and their inclusion in beneficent education. With time, they, like she had done, could make room for themselves in the constrained space of the margins. As Arragon had predicted and Mirrielees had facilitated in her editing of the *Pacific Spectator*, region and regionalism were merely stepping stones to a national culture with California at its pinnacle.

Mirrielees's last publications and editing ventures were performed from a home in Stanford that claimed the entirety of California, the West, and the Pacific Rim as its domain. While well-meaning, she performed her work with a mid-twentieth-century liberal mindset that gave very little consideration to those communities, including communities of women, who would challenge the boundaries that she had used so ably on her own behalf. When those challenges came, the humanist-scientist partnership that had made Stanford a world-class university, helped form the Pacific Coast Committee for the Humanities, and served as the model for Mirrielees's career had gone national. The vision that Mirrielees and Stegner had nurtured of a federally financed, conservation-minded humanism, one inspired by Harvard and Bread Loaf, emergent from the pioneering West, triumphant in California, and executed by the educated outdoorsman had arrived back East with the Kennedy administration in Washington, DC.

CHAPTER 4
WHEN NATURE BECAME CULTURE

In expansive moments, Stewart Udall asserted that when he and his wife, Lee, arrived in the capital in 1955, "two young persons from the rural West brought the arts to Washington.'"[1] From Stewart's years as a representative between 1955 and 1960 to his tenure as secretary of the interior from 1961 to 1969, he and Lee both used the West and its close associations with nature as avenues to explore their interests in literature and the arts, even though they lacked established bona fides in the universities, museums, and concert halls of Boston, New York, and Philadelphia.

They worried. Both feared that the DC establishment would perceive them as rubes because they came from the West. Following their first reception at the White House, Lee confessed to her mother that "Stew" had an inappropriate tie clip; that she had rushed at the last minute to buy formal white gloves; and that rather than parking their own family car, they had driven right to the White House entrance, where a diaper from one of their children tumbled out of the passenger side door. Although all was fine and their attire acceptable, Lee asked: "Now Mother, we don't want the general public to know what hicks we are. . . . Keep this to yourself."[2] That Lee, albeit humorously, ruminated over their reception at the White House suggests that she and Stewart were conscious of the ways in which their rural, western upbringing shaped their reputation in the federal government and in the Washington, DC, press.

Lee's mother apparently did keep things to herself, and the Udalls built a reputation in Washington as regular hosts to writers and artists, particularly those who made nature their theme. The close associations that members of government and the eastern arts community drew between the West and the natural world served as the Udalls' entrée into DC culture. While it might have been surprising for Arizonans to have the refined manners and attire of their eastern hosts and Californian neighbors, it was not unusual to associate "hicks" with nature. The Udalls saw the connection between their regional background and the natural world as providing political and social opportunities to pursue their interests in the arts. From their arrival in DC, much of the Udalls' advocacy for humanist expression and inquiry included nature.

They followed the model that Edith Mirrielees had established at Stanford, but the Udalls were not Stanford graduates nor Californians. The prestige and influence accorded the senior senator from Arizona, Carl Hayden, who had published in Mirrielees's collection of Stanford alumni memories, did not flow as easily to the Udalls. Not only were they westerners; they were members of the Church of Jesus Christ of Latter-day Saints and had attended the University of Arizona, a public university. The Udalls had to prove themselves and their interest in the arts and humanities legitimate, and they knew it. Their son Tom, who later served in the US Senate, recalls of his parents that "both had an instinctive and abiding passion for music, literature, and art" but that "the best part of the story is that my parents—when they came to Washington from their small Mormon towns in the plain and rural West—were such unlikely ambassadors of culture."[3] Even for their son, a US senator, the Udalls' successful presentation of themselves as cultured national leaders back East appeared to be a surprise.

The Udalls knew how to use surprises to their advantage. When Stewart Udall arrived in Congress, Arizona's senators, Hayden and Barry Goldwater, showed no sign of loosening their hold on their positions. After his election as president in 1960, John F. Kennedy sought a westerner, preferably a Utahan, for the interior secretary position. With few opportunities for a position in the Senate, Udall jumped at the chance and served as secretary of the interior until Richard Nixon became president in 1969. Udall was loyal to Kennedy. The hostile *Arizona Republic* once called him the "darling of the East coast liberals."[4] Even after Kennedy's assassination in 1963 and Lyndon Johnson's assumption of the presidency, Udall presented himself as a "Kennedy man," intent on furthering the image of federal governance as a kind of Camelot, informed by refined passions and deliberate judgment. His success in the role relied on a similar strategy to the one his son Tom employed in his family reminiscences: juxtapose low expectations of westerners' sophistication with westerners' own mastery of cultured realms. That strategy drew on the western model of humanist expression that Edith Mirrielees, Bernard DeVoto, and Wallace Stegner had established and popularized in the 1940s.

The Udalls were not alone in thinking of nature and the humanities together, but their efforts had ironic and unintended consequences. As scholars have documented, their work provided cover for the worst of the Interior Department's extractive and exploitative mandate. From Stewart's first years as a US representative, the Udalls recognized the political power of aesthetic presentations of nature. Their enthusiasm for the formation of National Parks and Monuments during Stewart's term as interior secretary derived in part from their ongoing support for mining and forestry extraction on public lands and abroad in those nations where the United States held sway. They did not see these aims in contradiction to one another. Indeed, they thought they and other Americans could have both resources drawn from the land and aesthetically pleasing recreational opportunities.[5] They thought they could advance an American democratic culture and have other nations' natural resources too. They were wrong. Stewart experienced a rude awakening in 1969, when an oil spill resulted from continental shelf drilling that he had approved in his role as Interior Department secretary. The subsequent creation of the Environmental Protection Agency (EPA) served as a rebuke for his vision of a holistic Interior Department policy.[6]

Less studied has been a second consequence of the Udalls' enthusiasm for culture. The creation of the National Endowment for the Arts (NEA), the National Endowment for the Humanities (NEH), and the EPA splintered federal support for the arts, public lands, and the environment into distinct bureaucratic categories. The formation of the NEA and the NEH separated humanist inquiry from environmental protection efforts and made the Interior Department more vulnerable to the demands of corporate extraction on public lands, upsetting the Udalls' aims. Westerners, accustomed to seeing the land as of a piece with aesthetic expression, as the Udalls did, struggled to find representation in the new federal agencies overseeing the endowments and the environment, while the Interior Department only erratically supported their vision of a cultured appreciation of nature. Western victims of US colonialism particularly struggled to share their conceptions of the natural world. The Udalls had argued so insistently for the role of the Interior Department in protecting natural spaces that they failed to see how distinct federal agencies dedicated to culture, nature, and public lands could sequester humanities programming from environmental efforts. Back East became the place where bureaucrats drew the line between culture and nature.

That future was distant when Ermalee Webb helped her parents pack their belongings for their summer trip from the desert to Pinedale in the White Mountains of Arizona sometime in the early 1930s. Remembering the adventure decades later, after she had adopted a new name, Lee Udall described an outdoor playground in the cool mountain air. A day might include tending to a bevy of animals and a "thriving vegetable garden," pulling water "from a well with a rope and bucket" followed by "an all-day hike," watching a rodeo, or going on "a wild, bareback ride through the woods, holding for dear life the waist of an older cousin." Lee wrote her essay with the intention of convincing American parents to plan vacations that offered their children "a chance to explore mountains or deserts or seashores and develop an insight into the land and its quality of self-renewal." That opportunity rested not just on outdoor adventures. "Sometimes, too, we would hike five miles through the woods," Lee continued, "to our Grandmother's house to help her weed her garden and view her book-lined shelves with awe. Grandmother was a lover of poetry and literature."[7] The Udalls always nestled appreciation of the arts and literature within an expansive natural landscape. One could not have one, they insisted, without the other.

That union was not evident in their first years in Washington, DC. Stewart was appointed to two committees upon his election to the House of Representatives in 1955, the Committee on Interior and Insular Affairs (generally called the House Interior Committee) and the House Education and Labor Committee. Stewart began to develop his sense of what he would later call "environmental humanities" during his time in Congress, but when he first arrived in the House, he was, in the words of his biographer Thomas Smith, "not much of an earth steward."[8] Nonetheless, while studying and working in Tucson, he had become a fan of the naturalist writer Joseph Wood Krutch. Mirrielees had published an essay of Krutch's about the value of solitude; it ran right before DeVoto's "Queen City of the Peaks and Plains" in *The Spectator Sampler*, an indication of Krutch's standing among the western literary elite.[9] Krutch's *The Desert Year*, like other American naturalist writing of the mid-twentieth century, such as Aldo Leopold's *Sand County Almanac*, urged readers to see nature as more than a commodity and readers themselves as belonging to the land. "There is all the difference in the world," Krutch wrote, "between looking at something and living with it. In nature, one never really sees a thing for the first time until one has seen it for the fiftieth. It never means much until it has become not a 'view' or a 'sight' but an integrated world of which one is a part."[10] The Udalls' public service gave them multiple opportunities to consider what it meant to be part of an integrated world.

Such reflection occurred in direct correspondence with Krutch. He wrote Stewart during a hotly contested debate about the site for a key dam in the Colorado River Storage Project (CRSP). Some plans called for placing one of the CRSP dam sites within Dinosaur National Monument on the Green River. The Sierra Club, Krutch, and other prominent writers invested in protection of the natural world objected.[11] In 1950 DeVoto had declared that if the dam were built, "the tempestuous, pulse-stirring river of John Wesley Powell would become a mere millpond."[12] DeVoto evoked Powell, the adventurous nineteenth-century explorer and early conservationist as well as the subject of Stegner's book *Beyond the Hundredth Meridian*, in presenting the river as one of the nation's most robust arteries. Five years later, in an effort to raise public awareness of the dam's effects, the Sierra Club published a richly illustrated book about the monument entitled *This Is Dinosaur*, edited by Stegner himself. In *This Is Dinosaur* Stegner warned against creating a world "with every natural beautiful thing endangered by the raw engineering power of the twentieth century."[13] At this early point in his career, Udall may not yet have known the work of DeVoto and Stegner. Perhaps he considered only Krutch's work and letter as he weighed the decision about the CRSP. Whatever his reflection, his support for dams held.[14]

After Dinosaur, Udall and environmentalists shared an acute understanding of the political power of aesthetic and humanist arguments.[15] In subsequent years, the Sierra Club invested heavily in large, glossy coffee-table books, such as *This Is Dinosaur*, to support the preservation of land, particularly land that club members called "wilderness." Udall acknowledged the power of such arguments but did not follow their lead. Following the CRSP vote, he wrote to the Arizona congressional delegation and David Brinegar, of the Central Arizona Project Association, in reference to environmental advocates and advised that they avoid a "head-on collision with these people." He suggested instead that they "neutralize" groups like the Sierra Club by ensuring that reclamation projects such as the CRSP did not impinge on the Grand Canyon National Park itself.[16] Reading Krutch may have given Udall a poetic pause as he contemplated dam placement, but his desire for water reclamation projects overcame any interest he had in countering the engineering power of the twentieth century or decentering human needs in Arizona's deserts. Udall believed he and other Americans could have the dam and the "pulse-stirring" river both.

If the House Interior Committee taught Udall a lesson in congressional action, the Education and Labor Committee provided one of inaction. Udall supported federal aid for education and linked efforts that furthered racial desegregation of schools. In 1957 he joined with Frank Thompson Jr., Lee Metcalf, George McGovern, and Eugene McCarthy to form a collaboration that eventually became the Democratic Study Group and included over eighty members. Stewart Udall's biographers emphasize his frustration with the chair of the Education and Labor Committee, Graham Barden, a North Carolina Democrat who stalled any efforts to use the committee to reform American education, particularly vis-à-vis racial integration. Udall publicly, though indirectly, chastised Barden and secured changes to the committee but not in time to save the fate of the very first piece of legislation: a bill proposing a National Foundation for the Humanities.[17] Udall's ally Frank Thompson Jr., of New Jersey, introduced the bill, and it was referred to the Education and Labor Committee, where, like most legislation referred to that body, went nowhere. Side by side, the two committees, which Udall actively contrasted when calling Barden to task, demonstrated his tolerance for contradictions in governance. On the House Interior Committee, he enthusiastically pursued compromise if it "neutralized" protection of the natural world on behalf of Arizona agribusiness. On Education and Labor, Udall recognized how compromise could stall social and political change such as racial integration in schools.[18]

Those contradictions foreshadowed Stewart's third term as a representative, when he and Lee hosted the poet Robert Frost for dinner. In 1959 the position of poet laureate did not yet exist in the United States, and Frost was serving as poetry consultant to the Library of Congress. In addition to his frustration with the lack of federal attention to the arts, Frost publicly vented that while serving as poetry consultant, he had been called on only three times by the White House, only once by a Supreme Court justice, and never by Congress.[19] While four consultations with senior government officials generally marked an unusual career for a poet, especially in the years before the position of national poet laureate existed in the United States, these were not enough brushes with government power for Robert Frost. The Udalls' dinner invitation was an effort to right what he considered a grievous wrong.

The evening was a domestic affair—the Udalls' children served as the wait staff, and Lee was late in her pregnancy with their sixth child, Jay, who was born early the next morning. In his report to the *Arizona Daily Star* on the event, part of an ongoing series of articles that Stewart sent to the paper, he reported that Frost "looks and talks like the New England farmer that he is."[20] Guests included Representative John Brademas, a former Rhodes scholar from Indiana; Edith Green, a representative for the district including Portland, Oregon, and an ardent advocate for education; and Kay Morrison, spouse to Ted Morrison and Frost's frequent companion.[21] In the Udalls' remembrances, the dinner with Frost functioned as a sort of origin story for their involvement in national support for the arts and humanities. The hosts and guests both played important roles in the mid-twentieth-century articulation of environmental humanities in the United States.

These roles varied. Kay and Ted Morrison integrated the Udalls into a community that included not just Frost but also the Bread Loaf Writers' Conference as well as DeVoto, Stegner, and Mirrielees. Brademas wrote parts of the legislation creating the National Endowments for the Arts and Humanities. The Morrisons united Bread Loaf conversations about nature with Brademas's efforts. Green had played a pivotal role in the passage of the National Defense of Education Act (NDEA) in 1958. While commonly associated with the sciences and US efforts to compete with the Soviets in defense, Titles IV and VI of the NDEA provided fellowships for future teachers of the humanities, and Green regularly supported similar federal education measures into the 1960s.[22] Each of these figures continued to play a role in linking the Udalls' interests in (western) nature with humanist exploration and with the (eastern) creation of the NEA and the NEH.

Stewart and Lee occupied a central role in these conversations long after that first dinner. Stewart continued to cooperate with Frost, most famously by suggesting that Frost read at John Kennedy's inauguration. Lee and Stewart together compiled a list of visitors for a "Presidential Cabinet Artists Series" that brought prominent artists, writers, and musicians to DC, including contralto Marian Anderson, poet Carl Sandburg, composer Leonard Bernstein, writer Thornton Wilder, and repeat visits from Frost. Both Udalls, and Lee particularly, advocated for the arts and humanities within the Interior Department, work that frequently overlapped with their efforts in the Artists Series.

The Udalls recognized that they needed the imprimatur of the East. One scholar has speculated that Stewart cultivated a relationship with Frost because "Frost craved assurance, adulation, and public attention" and that Stewart, "ambitious and anxious to be accepted," sought to "enhance his reputation among the eastern elite" by associating with the poet."[23] The Udalls recognized Frost as an eastern cultural figure, and it's possible that

"Stewart and Lee Udall talk with poet Robert Frost in Udall's office." Frost recited a poem at John F. Kennedy's inauguration at Stewart's suggestion. Stewart L. Udall Papers (AZ 372), 1950–77, University of Arizona Special Collections.

their dinner party had also provided an opportunity to see Frost's relationship with western writers, Stanford, and California via his connections to Bread Loaf. Association with him could enhance their standing on the coasts while also bringing their cultural appreciation of the natural world to a national audience.

Whatever his motivation, it was Stewart who suggested that Frost present a poem at John Kennedy's inauguration. He made his proposal the same evening that Kennedy offered him the interior secretary position. Stewart had already shared the idea with a receptive Kay Morrison, and Frost had also already visited the Udalls' home in Arizona, where he met with Krutch among others.[24] The Udalls used their western origins to suggest a change in national cultural expression back East.

That message, though, underwent a predictable transformation when

When Nature Became Culture

Frost recited at Kennedy's inauguration. For the inauguration, Frost composed an original poem entitled "Dedication" that began:

> Summoning artists to participate
> in the august occasions of the state
> Seems something for us all to celebrate.[25]

At the event itself, however, the wind and glare prevented him from continuing much farther, and he recited from memory, instead, "The Gift Outright," a poem celebrating the white westward colonization of the United States. That unscripted change underscored the Udalls' western cultural promise but obscured the central role that they anticipated for artists in the Kennedy administration.

Rather than ground cultural exploration in an appreciation of the natural world, the poem instead celebrated white westward expansion, a story more familiar and more easily assimilated by white American audiences in 1961. In the poem, Frost described British colonists on the Eastern Seaboard at the eve of the American Revolution as "Possessing what we still were unpossessed by, / Possessed by what we now no more possessed."[26] Stewart Udall's article about the reading of the poem, "Frost's 'Unique Gift Outright," ran in the New York Times Magazine in March 1961 under a dramatic picture of the Grand Tetons in Jackson Hole, Wyoming, with a caption that began, "Robert Frost's America, West."[27] The article's presentation muted the idea that the arts acted as a balance to the sciences or a rejoinder to corporate business. Moreover, it reinforced the role that the Department of the Interior had played in white western settlement through its oversight of the Homestead Act as well as its economic development of land seized from Indigenous nations.[28] Rather than emphasize nature, Udall's sponsorship, the poem's content, and the photo and caption underscored Kennedy's "New Frontier" slogan as well as the Department of the Interior's facilitation of US settler colonialism.

In 1961, for white Americans, the distance from the idea of the frontier to the colonialism at the center of "The Gift Outright" to discussions of nature was not far. Udall described in his article how Frost had puckishly requested an appointment in the Interior Department as "Undersecretary of Trees" upon his arrival at Union Station for the inauguration. He also appears to have seen the article about the event as an opportunity to reflect on the relationship of poetry to politics. "For years Frost has believed that leaders who hold the levers of national power need the redeeming insights of men of art," he wrote.[29] The journalist Edward P. Morgan, in a kind note to Udall regarding the article, observed of Frost's reading that "poignant with embarrassment as it was. . . . It reminded us that there are still wonderfully fallible human beings in this mechanical age, and that from them comes the strength of inspiration."[30] Morgan's concern about "this mechanical age" echoed some of Udall's own as well as some of Stegner's writing in *This Is Dinosaur*. Framed by the Grand Tetons, "The Gift Outright," and the rhetorical power of the term *frontier*, however, Frost's, Stewart's, Stegner's, and Morgan's subtle critique of a government that catered too much to technology and business was lost. Instead, a more familiar story of white progress achieved through westward settlement became ascendent.

That story proved a powerful counter to Udall's efforts to appear cultured. The department that oversaw the Homestead Act, issued grazing permits, and facilitated summer camping trips in National Parks hardly appeared to be the department of cultivated cosmopolitanism. As a result, the press noted with wry amusement Udall's interest in the arts. Upon his appointment as secretary of the interior, the *New York Post* called him "a happy cross-breed of Western outdoorsman and Eastern-style intellectual."[31] The *New York World Telegram and Sun*, writing in 1962 of the Artists Series that Stewart and Lee coordinated, remarked that "oddly enough, much of the new cultural trend seems to swirl about a man whom you would not describe as the chic type at all — Secretary of the Interior Stewart Udall, a rugged, outdoor fellow with a crew cut and a brusque manner — he looks like a football player."[32] Stewart's approach was to capitalize on the juxtaposition. If his message was that nature was necessary for cultural expression, then he was the perfect illustration of that combination, however surprising it was to the eastern press.

Lee came in for a similar amount of scrutiny. She was always described as "attractive" and "blond" and engaged in some seemingly unorthodox activity such as overseeing her six children on trips from Tucson to Washington, DC.[33] One *Baltimore Sun* article described the Udalls' home as having "all the qualities of a small-scale zoo" because the Udall children "wander far afield" in the "heavily wooded area" and "return with assorted animals." The articles praised Lee's resourcefulness in providing a splint for a blackbird's broken leg and otherwise tending to "some refugee from the woodlands."[34] Other articles noted her preference for climbing mountains in Tucson rather than the 826 steps of the Washington Monument.

Often these articles implied a gendered judgment of Stewart Udall's position in the cabinet and the Kennedy administration more broadly. One described the Udall family's encounter with "a group of hillbillies" while camping in the Shenandoah National Park. Upon meeting a boy whose friends insisted that he did not know the name of the president, Lee encouraged him. "Of course, you know the name of our new President," she urged. The child then "blurted out belligerently: 'It's Jacqueline Kennedy.'"[35] At best, such articles suggested that women stood poised to further the First Lady's interest in federal support for the arts. At worst, they implied that female leadership was laughable and that so-called feminine interests like the arts were below consideration in serious matters of state. Similar prejudices had confined Mirrielees to the margins of literary work and blinded Stegner and DeVoto to the full promise of nature writing about the West. Lee had to navigate these preconceptions. The Washington press placed her family in the federal government's social hierarchy somewhere closer to climbing mountains in Tucson and camping with Virginia hillbillies than to cultural institutions.

Nonetheless, the Udalls held firm in their cultural vision. In a 1961 list of the cabinet members' favorite books, Stewart listed the *Collected Poems of Robert Frost*, the *Collected Poems of William B. Yeats*, and *This Is the American Earth* by Nancy Newhall and photographer Ansel Adams. The closest any other cabinet members came to listing books addressing cultural explorations of the natural world were the secretary of health, education, and welfare, Abraham Ribicoff, who included *The Adventures of Huckleberry Finn*; and Treasury secretary C. Douglas Dillon, who listed *Moby-Dick* as well as two histories: *Montcalm and Wolfe: France and England in North*

America, by Francis Parkman, and William H. Prescott's *Conquest of Mexico*. Not even the secretary of agriculture, Orville Freeman, a Minnesotan, listed anything related to the natural world, although Robert McNamara, a Californian, included *The Meeting of East and West* by F. S. C. Northrop, a text that had also been reviewed in the *Pacific Spectator*. Exploitation of natural resources and American influence in Asia occupied Kennedy's cabinet, not poetic ruminations nor the "redeeming insights" Udall had forecast during Frost's recitation.

Still, the Udalls' interest in the arts and the outdoors inspired western artists to form connections with them. The Californian photographer Ansel Adams persistently sought amplification of his views in the Interior Department. Adams first approached Stewart in December 1960 to recommend that David Brower, the head of the Sierra Club during the debates over Dinosaur and Glen Canyon, be granted a position within the Interior Department. Adams explained that his own work "has been largely in terms of images rather than words" and that he had sometimes fought within his "own group—against well-meaning but complacent and unimaginative people who are full almost to the brim with ideals, but never seem to have the creative force or conviction to achieve a spillway!" In combining natural and cultural creative force, Adams felt that Udall would bring "new blood" to the Interior Department and "wake up some of our dormant interests and talents."[36] Although Udall did not grant Brower a position, a proposal of which Brower himself was unaware, a friendship with Adams blossomed.

Adams's experience with the Sierra Club and his photography of National Parks and Monuments led him to see the Interior Department as the government agency best suited to foster aesthetic appreciation of the environment. Adams had provided the photographs for the Sierra Club's best-known coffee-table book, *This Is the American Earth* (1960), which Udall had publicly listed among his favorites. The book acted as a successor to *This Is Dinosaur* and served as a major influence in the wilderness movement as well as a source of debate among environmentalists over the future of conservation.[37] In correspondence, Adams sometimes adopted an elite tone of the kind that initially intimidated Lee. He recommended that Udall lean on Jaqueline Kennedy, "with her great interest in art," to encourage the preservation of northern New Mexican villages. "I bring this matter to your attention because I would assume in the end that the quality of these important buildings and their environment would assume a National Monument stature," he concluded.[38] Adams drew on his familiarity with National Monuments, which were not restricted to unsettled spaces, to advocate for the preservation of lands that he considered significant. Writing in the summer of 1962, he insisted that "we need all the impact that art and imagination can contribute to the large issues."[39]

Adams remained steadfast in presenting aesthetic appreciation of nature as a "large" issue. By January 1964, when Adams wrote Udall for the first time following John Kennedy's assassination, he addressed the secretary as "friend" but still leveraged this friendship to advocate for nature. He lamented the emphasis at the Seattle World's Fair on industry. "The Ford Building looks a little larger than the Federal Government building!" he railed. "Who is equating Who with What? Are the conservation organizations represented?" Even as he sought to console Stewart in a private letter, Adams continued to press his case that conservation should have a louder voice in the halls of government than that of corporate business and that creative expression was the best way to make such voices heard in the East.[40] He did so with examples that he drew from the West: his own photography in the Southwest and in California as well as the Seattle World's Fair.

Wallace Stegner took an approach similar to Adams's in his relationship with Udall and the Interior Department. Udall was an early fan of Stegner's famous "Wilderness Letter," published in 1960, and he invited Stegner to be a "writer-in-residence" upon his appointment as secretary.[41] Fresh from his experience in the Pacific Coast Committee for the Humanities, Stegner was eager to see the West represented in federal cultural programming. He spent a semester of 1961 in Washington, DC. On his way from California, Stegner prepared a report about the Four Corners area that contributed to the conversion of Arches and Capitol Reef National Monuments to national parks and supported the creation of Canyonlands National Park.[42] After his arrival, Stegner advised the department on films about Frost and about the American landscape and also conducted research for and contributed to the writing of *The Quiet Crisis*, a book that Interior Department staff wrote beginning in 1961 and published under Udall's name with an introduction from John F. Kennedy in 1963.

The Quiet Crisis echoed the conservationist themes that DeVoto and Stegner had emphasized in the 1940s and 1950s. The book warned Americans that "successes in space and our triumphs of technology hold a hidden danger: as modern man increasingly arrogates to himself dominion over the physical environment, there is the risk that his false pride will cause him to take the resources of the earth for granted—and to lose all reverence for the land."[43] In *The Quiet Crisis*, and throughout his work for the Interior Department, Stegner found opportunities to advocate for wilderness, conservation, and nature as an antidote for the ills of technology and the dominance of corporate industry. He drew on his experience in western lands, especially in Utah, to make his case.

Stegner, like Adams, was acutely aware of the pressures that industry placed on the department and on Stewart Udall, and he used his role at Interior to resist them. When he wrote to Udall regarding the conversion of National Monuments to parks in Utah, he observed "that local opinion in proposed park areas is pretty largely ignorant and indifferent. Where it is formed at all, it is likely to be formed by resource interests such as uranium, oil, and grazing, and by politicians subservient to these." Rather than present ecology as an alternative to economy, Stegner proposed instead that a conservation organization "should answer.... with economic arguments on the other side, pointing out with all the figures available, that a park is an eternally renewable resource and that its economic value over any extended time will surely be greater than that of all the uranium mines or oil wells in the area."[44] Stegner, like DeVoto had, served on the Advisory Board for the National Parks, Historical Sites, Buildings, and Monuments, and like Adams, he saw National Parks and Monuments as aesthetic arguments in favor of American national culture and as a counter to an industrialized economy driven by profit.

His arguments laid the groundwork for late-twentieth-century environmentalism via a holistic appreciation of nature in the arts and humanities. In notes on a film about the American land, Stegner explained that film could call attention to human destruction of the environment and ecological interdependence in ways that still photos and text could not. "We can treat the community of life of which we are a part, treat it at any level, and treat also the violence we do to it, the exterminations we threaten to commit, the steps we take to protect this life community against its worst enemy, ourselves. It is a miracle we live on, and we are part of it, and all parts of it depend on all other parts. We live, literally, by courtesy of the earthworm."[45] In their focus on cultural appreciation of nature, the Udalls realized many of Stegner's ambitions. Stegner recalled of Stewart in 1982 that "we sort of think alike, and we come out of the same kind of background."[46] Wendell Berry, one of Stegner's former students, spoke in similar terms following the memorial service for environmental activist Edward Abbey: "I left Utah thinking again what I have thought often before: that if we ever do develop a culture capable of taking care of the world, it will grow eastward out of the west, and that you and your work and example will be right at the center of it."[47] A holistic appreciation of nature had always been Stegner's aim. To see it growing eastward out of the West in the hands of Stewart Udall satisfied him.

Nonetheless, their friendship did not prevent him from sending a gentle gibe in 1962: "I hear that as a member of the Sierra Club and the Wilderness Society I am engaged in suing you. Well, anything to make you do your duty."[48] A duty to both use and save public land—land both rural and urban and of both cultural and natural significance consistently meant that nature and culture overlapped in Interior Department work, especially in its cultural programming.

Even as momentum built for the National Endowments for the Arts and Humanities, the Udalls continued to facilitate cultural expression from within the Interior Department and the cabinet. Contralto Marian Anderson, for example, agreed to perform for the Artists Series that the Udalls organized. She did so in part to recognize Harold Ickes, secretary of the interior in Franklin Roosevelt's administration. In 1939 Ickes had made available the steps of the Lincoln Memorial, a National Monument, so that Anderson could perform after the Daughters of the American Revolution denied her entrance to Constitution Hall because she was Black. Stewart and Stegner also unsuccessfully tried to turn Robert Frost's property in Vermont into a National Monument. Stegner particularly wanted to memorialize Frost as a poet, and Frost himself was supportive of the measure during his lifetime. As with many private lands targeted for public memorialization, however, locals (including the Morrisons) objected because a public memorial could not be taxed.[49] The Udalls did not advocate for nature and the arts together because they were innate conservationists. Indeed, they caved to the influence of business on more than one occasion.[50] Nonetheless, they could not ignore the overlap of nature and culture in the places that fell within the responsibility of the Interior Department. They had to view the environment and the humanities as two parts of a whole because they were both parts of the public.

Lee's work consisted of finding palatable ways to present the Interior Department's agenda. At the center of her efforts was a gallery in the Department of the Interior building first established by Ickes. Describing the endeavor to restore it in 1964, Lee wrote that "our guideposts dictated our decisions about the Gallery: we wanted our exhibitions to dramatize the work of the Indian Bureau and we wanted its appeal to be as great to children as to adults."[51] The gallery opened with an exhibition of art by children enrolled in Bureau of Indian Affairs schools as well as with work from a new school also funded by the Interior Department, the Institute of American Indian Arts in Santa Fe, New Mexico. Subsequent shows in the gallery included work by the famous potter Maria Martinez of San Ildefonso Pueblo and by Adams, who chose his famous *Moonrise over Hernandez, New Mexico* for the show after years of pressing the Udalls for greater "creative force" in the halls of government. Like those of many wives married to prominent politicians, Lee's responsibilities included managing her husband's image.

In some respects, Lee presented the gallery as a kind of trophy cabinet that showcased the bounty of US expansion without acknowledging its harms. She called American Indians the nation's "first conservationists" and argued that "those who prize the out-of-doors find themselves returning to what are essentially Indian ideas and Indian attitudes toward man and nature." Such sentiments might have surprised those Diné (Navajo) leaders who were, just as the gallery opened, signing leases with Peabody Coal to strip-mine at Black Mesa on Diné and Hopi land with impetus from her husband and other administrators in the Department of the Interior.[52]

Lee Udall showcased art by western Native artists in the Washington, DC, Department of the Interior gallery revived during her husband's tenure as secretary of the interior from 1961 to 1969. "Photo of Lee Udall and Jim McGrath making selections for first Interior Department Art Gallery exhibit," May 1964, Stewart L. Udall Papers (AZ 372), 1950–77, University of Arizona Special Collections.

That a third of the gallery showed Indian children's art also infantilized American Indian expression at a crucial moment when Diné educators were attaining greater autonomy and control of schools educating Diné children.[53] Moreover, Lee never appears to have extended her enthusiasm for Indigenous cultures to Native peoples with homelands in the Midwest and East.

Nonetheless, Indigenous artists of all ages proved capable of speaking for themselves and showed material unexpected by the Interior Department's largely white audience. Lee described a variety of art created by the children attending Bureau of Indian Affairs schools "from a tempera painting of a Hopi Katchina in the classic Indian style to a Navajo boy's portrait of the Beatles."[54] Both students likely felt obligated to produce certain images to show how well they had assimilated to white expectations. Perhaps, like

Lee, the young Diné artist feared that eastern audiences would perceive him as a hick and sought to shore up his reputation as cultured and current by painting the Beatles. Perhaps he was simply a fan. Whatever his intentions, such work not only proved surprising to the gallery's visitors, it required that Lee explain it in her publicity for the gallery and ask journalists and others to acknowledge Indigenous modernity.[55] The arts and humanities may have been a way to neutralize or dismiss dissenting voices among the Interior Department's critics, but they could provide unexpected amplification of those voices too.

The Udalls' support for the arts and humanities within the Interior Department contributed to the creation of the NEH and NEA. As early as 1961, Frost confided to Stewart that he had been trying "to get a secretary of arts into the President's cabinet but I am as good as in there now with you to talk to. I have been reaching the President through you for some time."[56] The press also took note, praising Stewart for using Interior's jurisdiction over historic sites to preserve parts of the DC landscape, calling the Udalls' revival of the Interior Department gallery "another . . . perhaps small but significant contribution to Washington's culture."[57] Stewart specifically sought out Stegner's opinion regarding a federal institute for the arts, and Stegner replied at length. "It *is* time for development of a cultural policy by the Federal Government," Stegner agreed. "We have a long national history of indifference to the arts, or even hostility, to live down. There is no better time to begin than now. . . . Eventually such a committee ought, I think, to be consolidated into a National Arts Foundation, parallel to the National Science Foundation, and it ought to have under its jurisdiction the specific activities which emerge as the proper interest of Government in the arts. . . . I would think the formation of such a committee a step in the right direction and I would hope that it would carry on the sort of thing that you started with your Night with Robert Frost and Night with Carl Sandburg."[58] Stegner drew a direct line from the Artists Series and the work of western artists and writers to the creation of the endowments.

The Udalls had built other connections that culminated in the formation of the endowments as well. In addition to his reading at the inauguration and the Artists Series, Robert Frost had toured the Dumbarton Oaks gardens with Stewart Udall in a well-publicized event that showed the two men deep in conversation under the garden's trees.[59] Although Lee Udall never used her leverage to advocate for Indigenous sovereignty, the Interior Department gallery did allow her to make a case for Indigenous modernity and Native arts. The gallery had also provided an opportunity to showcase the work of non-Native western artists—among them Ansel Adams. After almost a decade of steadily lobbying the Udalls, Adams finally achieved his aim: a National Foundation on the Arts and Humanities was established in 1965. When the Rose Garden signing ceremony took place honoring the endowments' creation, aside from President Johnson, Adams was the only westerner present.[60]

The emphasis that the Udalls, Stegner, Adams, and Frost had placed on both using and saving land, however, was at odds with the legislation that ultimately established the NEA and NEH. As the legislation made its way through Congress, the arts and humanities appeared as luxuries, extra activities that the nation had earned, through first industrial effort and then political acumen. The epigraph for the 1964 Commission Report calling for a National Endowment for the Arts and Humanities was a quotation from John Adams: "I must study politics and war that my sons may have liberty to study mathematics and philosophy. My sons ought to study mathematics and philosophy, geography, natural history and naval architecture, navigation, commerce, and agriculture, in order to give their children a right to study painting, poetry, music, architecture."[61] An unfortunate effect of such sentiments is that the arts and humanities were perceived as leisure that came only after the work of science, industry, and politics. Commerce became culture's progenitor rather than its companion or adversary.

To muster support for the legislation, proponents also increasingly emphasized the parallel and separate qualities of the sciences and humanities. Scientists and humanists alike regretted the outcome. Writing in 1966, the historian John Higham wondered if it were "possible that the 'humanists' have at last achieved official recognition in America at the very moment when the antagonistic confrontation of the two cultures is beginning to yield to new unities and new diversities." Leland Haworth, the director of the National Science Foundation and a supporter of the endowments, meanwhile lamented "the common habit of drawing a hard and fast line between the humanities and the sciences."[62] Environment and humanities moved farther apart in such divisions. The courtesy of the earthworm that Stegner had imagined was lost.

In addition, the vision of the humanities that the Udalls had fostered in the Interior Department consistently ran aground of interdepartmental territoriality in the federal government. Hints of such outcomes had started early. Following the publication of his article about Frost's reading at Kennedy's inauguration, Glenway Westcott, the president of the National Institute of Arts and Letters, wrote a kind but firm note to Stewart about the possibility of a National Academy for the Arts: "Writing to you upon official stationery, I have something else in mind. You refer to the Bill considered by a Senate Committee last year with the view in the creation of a National Academy in Washington. We felt that this created a serious overlapping with the American Academy of Arts and Letters and its parent organization, the National Institute of Arts and Letters previously constituted by Acts of Congress."[63] Although the American Academy of Arts and Letters was recognized only by charter and its members operated independently of Congress, resistance like Westcott's contributed to opposition to a National Foundation for the Arts. Humanities educators also recognized that including the arts in any national foundation for the humanities would be strategically beneficial because the House was unlikely to support two new agencies. When the bill was finally written, Brademas, who had been among the Udalls' guests at the dinner with Frost in 1959, wrote the language creating two endowments within one foundation.[64] The separation almost instantly caused a rivalry between the two and a confused perception among members of Congress that the NEA supported art whereas the NEH supported building an audience for the arts.

That rivalry mirrored one that had been present in Interior Department policy as well. Although Stegner's and, to a lesser extent, Adams's correspondence with Udall suggests a more nuanced understanding of nature that included culture too, their most famous work in support of nature was peopleless. Stegner's well-known "Wilderness Letter" repeated the celebrations of colonialism in Frost's "Gift Outright." The letter advocated for preserving wilderness that nobody saw. "The reminder and the reassurance that it is still there is good for our spiritual health even if we never once in ten years set foot in it," he wrote. Adams, in one of his many letters to Udall on Interior Department policy, insisted that "the sheer delight which the visitor derives from the Canyon de Chelly tour cannot be measured in *numbers* of participants. In other words, I believe it is more important for a relatively small number of people to gain an intense experience than for vast numbers to obtain a diluted experience."[65] The Interior Department was charged with supporting industrial and recreational uses of nature while also endorsing appreciation of nature that "nobody saw." Divided public aims led public land managers to see themselves as competitors, as they had during the conservation battles that preoccupied DeVoto; those competitions mirrored the ones that developed between the NEH and the NEA in the 1960s and 1970s.

Udall illustrated the effects of such divisions when he encouraged the renovation of Ford's Theatre, which was a National Historic Site, into a kind of museum, rather than a functioning theater. In fact, the only mention of Stewart Udall on any part of the National Endowment for the Humanities website is a recollection by Frankie Hewitt, the 2002 National Humanities Medal recipient, who recalled that she began running Ford's Theatre as a living theater with regular productions because Udall's initial plan was "like building a monument to John Wilkes Booth."[66] Udall had sought to preserve the theater, rather than make theater as an art form accessible to a wide audience. As with nature, it could be difficult to both use and preserve culture.

Edith Green, who, like Brademas, had been present for the dinner with Frost in 1959, foresaw just such problems based on her extensive experience in public education efforts. In later recollections, Stewart did not think that Green had even attended that dinner. He recalled, instead, Richard Neuberger, one of Oregon's senators in 1959. Stewart was serving in the House, not the Senate, at the time of the dinner, and although unknown to the public, Neuberger was suffering from cancer in 1959 and died in 1960, five years before the passage of the act establishing the NEA and NEH. Neuberger was a former journalist, and he did publish a brief essay in *Northwest Harvest*, the Pacific Coast Committee for the Humanities publication that included Horace Cayton's work and appeared at the same time as the *Pacific Spectator* began publishing. Perhaps Stewart's later cooperation with Stegner brought *Northwest Harvest* to Stewart's attention. Or perhaps Stewart was recalling Neuberger's wife, Maurine Neuberger, who served one term in the Senate following her husband's death, after she herself had served in the Oregon legislature. Nonetheless, given that Stewart was a seasoned politician, the confusion is surprising, unless one considers how gender overlapped with expectations about governance in the mid-twentieth-century United States. Stewart's memory reinforced the prejudices that afflicted his wife, whose interest in the arts appeared secondary and less substantial than the material policy decisions Stewart made governing western rivers and mining. Indeed, gender prejudice appears to have reinforced the separation between economic and aesthetic land management in the Interior Department since Lee provided the unpaid labor for the Artists Series, for reestablishing the Interior Department gallery, and even for the family recreational trips that served to advertise National Parks and their value.

As a woman and a public official, rather than a woman married to a public official, Green had to navigate gender prejudices differently than did Lee. Green was divorced during her years as a representative, and the press referred to her as "Mrs. Education." She had to make the connections among the arts, the humanities, and education, known through her own paid work. Lamenting the lack of focus in government on issues of education when delivering Harvard University's Burton Lecture in 1964, she used Interior Department agendas to observe that "we will have to invest in education as we now invest in dams and flood-control projects." Green did not have the support of a spouse who found fulfillment through complementing her efforts. Stewart could push for dams in western riverine system in his Interior Department office while Lee showed stunning pictures of rushing western rivers in the Department of the Interior gallery. As a woman and a member of Congress, rather than a member of the cabinet, Green did not have the same advantage. No husband advertised the value of public education in federal government buildings on her behalf. Although education combined the sciences and humanities, just as nature did, Green had to imagine her policy goals in dialogue with one another more strategically than did the Udalls.

As a result, Green saw that federal administration could determine the direction of the National Endowments for the Arts and Humanities. She noted that education was a field that permeated all aspects of government from the Department of Defense to the Interior Department. She advocated for greater coordination among congressional committees as well as more attention to those departments, like Defense, that provided much of the nation's education but were rarely held responsible for it. As she advocated for both more and better administration of federal funds for education, she used the example of a hypothetical university that decided to build a general library but then changed course because the federal government would provide matching funds for a science building. "Is the Federal Government (with a $50 billion Defense budget and a $20 million space program both necessarily dependent on the sciences) now contributing to an imbalance between the 'sciences and the humanities'—to use a shorthand phrase?" asked Green rhetorically. She then followed the example with another on how administration of funds favored research over teaching. The favor shown science research over humanities teaching and a perceived shortage of humanities teachers had been just the issues that spurred many in the House to support the creation of the NEH.[67] As Green's lecture and experience warned, however, restricting funding for the humanities to only certain realms—such as teaching—risked abandoning holistic support for the humanities in all realms of governance, from defense to space exploration to the environment.

Stegner may have been similarly concerned. Even when he wrote Stewart so passionately in favor of a National Foundation for the Arts, he warned that he thought "the introduction of cultural presentations into the National Park System other than the interpretive programs now in effect, a mistake."[68] Much depended on administration and just who was doing the administering. Stegner had faith in Stewart's administration but not necessarily that of others, including those who may have led the NEA and NEH. Stegner questioned if support for *environmental* humanities could persist if such tasks were taken from Interior. As Green well knew, the NEA and the NEH on their own did not guarantee a holistic view of the sciences and the humanities or of research and teaching or of culture and nature or of economy and ecology. The endowments' existence did not ensure the support of environmental humanities, even though the Udalls, the Department of the Interior, Stegner, Adams, and Frost had all stood enthusiastically behind the creation of the endowments themselves with environmental humanities in mind.

Indeed, as federal agencies, the NEA and NEH were slow to support what the Udalls and their allies envisioned. Between 1965 and 1969, the endowments' administrators showed a preference for traditional artistic expressions like concert music and major art exhibitions, ones with institutional support located primarily in the East and in California and that typically did not make nature their theme. Funding did go to opera houses in Denver and San Francisco; Adams (a Californian) was an early recipient of an NEH grant; and Stewart's brother Morris "Mo" Udall, who served in the House, proved adept at directing funding toward little-known Arizona artists.[69] Early NEH funding also supported Cayton's biography of Richard Wright, but Wright was not a westerner, and Cayton had never given significant attention to the natural world. Few audiences thought of nature or the West when enjoying early NEH or NEA programming.

By the early 1970s, many western members of Congress initially supportive of the endowments, including Green herself, had changed their mind. After criticizing what she perceived as financial excess on the part of the endowments, Green yielded sympathetically to William Steiger of Wisconsin on the floor of the House in 1973. He observed that "the kinds of programs which have received large sums take place in Boston and New York, and other large cities, where they are enjoyed by the people in those communities but they do not benefit to the same extent the people in the smaller areas."[70] Steiger pushed, instead, for more funding to go to regional and rural libraries, an early cause of Green's as well.

Their pressure contributed to the expansion of state humanities councils, which proved an exception to national programming. In an echo of Meridel Le Sueur, the North Dakota Humanities Council funded the making of *Northern Lights*, a 1978 film that told the story of the Nonpartisan League with striking black-and-white depictions of the North Dakota winter landscape.[71] Created by members of the Marxist film collective Cine Manifest, the film also represented a national turn toward a wider definition of culture that embraced everyday forms of expression, including that of North Dakota farmers. Although fractious and persistent, the culture wars of the 1980s and 1990s, along with the growing influence of the social sciences, further broadened national understandings of the humanities to include a greater variety of people, issues of social justice, and everyday forms of cultural expression.[72] That broader foundation upheld environmental humanities inquiry into global contexts, environmental justice, and vernacular landscapes, inquiry spurred by the pressures of climate change.[73] Until the 1980s, though, federal humanities funding appears to have favored coastal institutions and individuals in urban areas who rarely made the environment their theme. Montana did not receive a major NEH grant until 1992, when the Western Heritage Center secured one, an event of enough significance that the recipients asked Wallace Stegner to write a statement about it.[74]

Some attributed such regional and topical inequities in NEH and NEA funding to elitism on the part of NEH leaders, a sentiment to which Green was increasingly receptive. In 1964, as Congress debated the Wilderness Act, which protected lands in National Forests and National Parks from development, Thomas Youngblood, a constituent, wrote Green a nearly seven-page, single-spaced letter supporting the act but decrying both the civil rights movement and "a new category of left wingers" developing "mostly" in the states of "New York, New Jersey, and Massachusetts." Youngblood associated this category with elites. "In the Northeast you have a stratified pecking or social class order that—thank goodness—we don't have yet in the West. It is still no disgrace to work with your hands in the West." Youngblood advocated for a balanced education, which he believed would create moderate western politicians: "The things that make up a Northeastern left winger are as follows: In college he studied mostly journalism, Business Administration, and law. . . . lived in the city or suburban areas of the Northeast all his life, never worked on a farm or had farm living, or worked at a trade with his hands." "We Westerners," Youngblood concluded, "should be happy that our educational system is more balanced and we don't turn out people like the Northeastern stuffed shirts."[75] Significantly, Youngblood received a personalized letter from Green in reply, not a form response, and Green's staff did not place the letter in the "crackpot file," where other letters of similar length and focus resided.[76] Green's later frustration with arts and humanities funding suggests, in fact, that she was sympathetic to Youngblood's view. She had moved rightward of the Udalls, who continued to advocate a western liberalism in the East.

Those to the Udalls' political and geographic left and right would struggle to compromise with the western-inflected humanities culture that the couple had built in the nation's capital. Rather than follow the Udalls' footsteps, they turned to different axes, which stretched northward and southward as often as they did eastward and westward. They recalled their forebears and expressed their critiques of the East with a different orientation. Back East became less of a place and more of a tool for westerners of the late twentieth and early twenty-first centuries. Western and midwestern writers turned East not to seek status or influence or control but to articulate their own point of view, regardless of where they called home.

PART 3
THE AXES

mt. carmel cemetery, Ysleta, Tejas,
My father, ay,
Your smile comes back,
the quickness of your mind
regaling me
with stories
of an era/place
you once embraced
in youthful frenesí,

your 1920's to 1930's
Chicago, Saginaw,
Kellogg, Michigan, and
Kansas City outposts
I would come to know
within
a churning/embroiling
Chicano Movement,

you, Padre Mío, who never saw me
in Brown Beret,
bedecked
by militant angers,
responding
to social causes/issues, and
remonstrations . . .

Yes, mi Viejito Querido,
mi estimado padre sepultado,
I now travel
as you once did,
and after travels
I leave clues
around
for my progeny
to find,
such as you did,
stories of this or that,
hoping that their minds
will be sparked
to also question
and their souls
moved rapturously
to also quest . . .[1]

Writing on Father's Day of 1979, the poet Ricardo Sánchez recalled his "estimado padre sepultado [esteemed, buried father]" at Mt. Carmel Cemetery as well as his father's journeys from New Mexico northward to Kansas City, Chicago, and cities in Michigan. Although Sánchez's father may have traveled as a migrant laborer, Sánchez saw his own journey as a poet and an activist as equivalent. Together, their memories and stories of travel left a legacy to prompt another generation of curiosity.

Sánchez's untitled poem was typical of his work. He composed it when he taught prisoners at the Southeast Regional Correctional Institution at Lemon Creek Prison in Mendenhall Valley for the University of Alaska. Like so many writers, travel led him to reconsider his origins. He wrote autobiographically, referencing in a separate section of the poem his own imprisonment in Soledad Prison in California and at Ramsey Prison Farm in Texas as well as his later readings and lectures "from el paso to yale / harvard, stanford, / and amsterdam & other lands." The work mixed Spanish and English in a style practiced by Sánchez and other Chicane poets of the late 1960s and 1970s that drew from the caló dialect of El Paso's El Diablo barrio and from imprisoned and formerly imprisoned Chicanos who called themselves "pintos."

Sánchez gave attention to the marginalized, not just in the example he offered his students at Lemon Creek Prison but in his memories of his father's migrations and his own journeys for the sake of social causes. Both brought attention to the midwestern Great Plains, that region that DeVoto, Stegner, Mirrielees, and the Udalls had largely ignored. As he almost always did, he time-stamped the poem with a date and place in the upper right-hand corner of the page. Many of his time stamps functioned almost as poems themselves, as this one did when it described his location as "far away from aztlán, alaskanizing my world" and "far away from family" as "llovisna y sentimientos se mesclan, siento los latigazos de y por la distancia."[2] This technique of chronicling and locating his own creative process mirrored a persistent theme in Sánchez's work in which he understood chronology and geography together, referenced as "era/place" in his homage to his father, an idea that he also expressed as "timespace."[3]

The timespace of the late twentieth and early twenty-first centuries often brought the margins and the center of arts and literary production into vexed conversations that scrambled the West-East axis of western literary liberalism. Those conversation played out in arguments over the direction of the National Endowment for the Arts. Sánchez served on the Literature Advisory Panel for the National Endowment for the Arts between 1979 and 1982 alongside Black poet Audre Lorde, a New Yorker born to Caribbean parents. NEA administrators hoped that Lorde's service on the panel would diversify endowment programming, but Lorde did not feel that the federal agency acted fairly. She joined the panel, she explained, "in spite of many reservations concerning the future of public arts programs, and questions about the fairness of the panel process." She resigned from the panel in November 1980 due to health and financial concerns, but she noted her "vision of public arts programs still remains one where creative people of good will attempt to move within the severe limitations of a system which means none of us any good." Like Sánchez, she had doubts about the capacity of a liberal government to support "Minority and Women artists as architects of a future within which all our children may flourish and create."[4] Lorde and Sánchez had deep faith in the capacity of art to liberate people who felt oppression, and they acknowledged the endowment as a source of support for artists of color. Nonetheless, the grind of continually speaking up on behalf of their fellow marginalized writers in institutionalized settings wore on each of them.

Sánchez sometimes expressed that frustration as resentment of the East. In later years, Sánchez complained to the endowment in terms similar to Lorde's. "I've heard that no Tejanos (Chicanos, Anglos, Blacks, Women from Texas) qualified for fellowships for writers/poets the last go-around due to 'our being purely emotional people who cannot write,'" he wrote the Literature Panel administrators in 1984.[5] NEA administrators assured him that he had only heard rumors and encouraged him to recall his own service on the panel and how information could be misconstrued in the process. But Sánchez's complaint was a regional one. He wanted *Texas* perspectives to receive government support, but those perspectives did not always fall in line with federal expectations of Texas.

Sánchez began in Texas and looked northward. He did so not because the North was a destination or the Southwest a homeland for him but because his perspective began in Texas. His outlook developed in the margins of his poems, as in the time stamps. He endeavored to bring attention to marginal perspectives without sacrificing those aspects of marginal cultures that he believed offered the nation and the region a more humane approach to life. When his perspective was not acknowledged, he expressed frustration and resentment of eastern institutions.

Other late-twentieth-century westerners came to resent the East also.

They, too, used different axes, axes that described the orientation of their outlook and axes that fractured regional coherencies. In the early 1980s, western white supremacist organizations such as Posse Comitatus seized on the gap between the reality and perception of the East to further a hateful agenda. Their message found fertile ground on the Great Plains, that region that had fallen from white western writers' conception of their home territory. Championing the figure of the cowboy that DeVoto and Stegner reviled, they targeted, instead, the educated outdoorsman and the eastern federal bureaucrat—roles that Stewart Udall had ably and eagerly embodied. The West's grassroots print culture turned about-face, from the Little Blue Books designed for the overalls of the everyman of the plains to the Posse Comitatus broadsides modeled after the California-based John Birch Society's publication *The Blue Book*. Farmers and ranchers suffering from falling crop prices and the inevitable challenges of cultivating a dry land in the late 1970s and 1980s fell prey to pernicious anti-Semitic and racist theories pedaled by those traveling northward and southward along the interstates of the Midwest. While Sánchez memorialized an axis that ran northward and southward to honor the journeys of people like his father, the white supremacist group Posse Comitatus used the mythology of the frontier to cleave those who looked from East to West from those who looked North to South.

Such groups were not alone in their suspicions of the federal government or the educated outdoorsman or their use of a north-south orientation, but other westerners chose a different tack. Perceiving the eastern federal government not as an overzealous state but, instead, as a force of colonialism, Indigenous writers pushed the orientation of their literary communities away from the East-West axis that white liberal regionalism took for granted and that white supremacists exploited. They looked instead in all directions. Like Sánchez, they performed their work from inside the institutions that the Udalls, Mirrielees, Stegner, and DeVoto had built as well as those midwestern universities, publishers, and bookstores that western literary culture had abandoned. They worked within a western literary culture to build a new one as they "moved rapturously to also quest."

TEXAS INTERLUDE
ALIENATING AS HELL

Born in 1941 in El Paso, Ricardo Sánchez left high school after a teacher told him that Mexicans became janitors, not writers. He remembered later that he "could not accept that as my place; all my life I would revolt and rebel; and for a long time I wrote secretively."[1] He earned his GED and joined the military. He was stationed in California, and his work showed the influence of both beat poetry and *pachuquismo* throughout his career. The pachuco culture that Stegner and Mirrielees had dismissed as a temporary and marginal subculture in the *Pacific Spectator* gave Sánchez a language and a style to describe the sense of community that he found as a child in El Paso and as a young man in California.[2] His perspective emerged from his educational experiences, and his presentation of regions emerged from his perspective.

Sánchez resisted assimilation to the white, middle-class norms that Stegner and Mirrielees had suggested would follow job programs for Mexican Americans, but he struggled with the violence that accompanied his impoverished circumstances. At nineteen he was arrested with two others on charges of kidnapping, robbery, and assault. He was dishonorably discharged and sentenced to five years at Soledad State Prison. In 1963 he returned to Texas and met his wife, María Teresa Silva. As an ex-convict, Sánchez struggled to find work, and he committed armed robbery when Silva was expecting their first child. Released from prison in 1969, he published some of his poems, which brought him to the attention of the *Richmond Afro-American*'s Frederick Douglass Fellows program. The program launched an academic career for him that included a doctorate and teaching positions in Texas, Wisconsin, Utah, and Washington.

Sánchez perceived his art and his activism as of a piece.[3] He worked in the Texas Rio Grande Valley and in Denver on behalf of migrant workers. He started his own press to publish his first book, *Canto y Grito mi Liberación*. Between faculty positions at the University of Utah and Washington State University, he ran a bookstore with his family in San Antonio called Paperbacks . . . ¡y Más! The store functioned as a community center and brought writers, musicians, and artists from around the world to share their work. Sánchez drew no lines between art and life. He sought to build their union along his own autobiographical axis, which extended northward and southward from Texas.

By the close of his life, Texas was less a place for Sánchez than it was a perspective. Back East had been a model for Edith Mirrielees in California. It had been a stop on a traveling journalist's itinerary for Era Bell Thompson from her home base in Chicago. Sánchez saw it as a prickly resource. His own Texas experiences shaped that view. Denied a nurturing education as a child, he endeavored to create the institutions that could repair that damage for himself and others. Much of those efforts included travel: eastward to universities, government arts organizations, and Black activist communities, northward to midwestern Chicane strongholds, southward to Mexico, and west to California. More than home, Texas was where Sánchez was from. Back East was just another place that he regarded from a Texan's perspective.[4]

Sánchez began writing and publishing poetry in California when he was in the army and encountered beat poets in North Beach, but his artistic philosophy began to emerge upon his second release from prison in Texas. He left for his Frederick Douglass Fellowship in June 1969. In "Flight: San Antonio, Houston, Atlanta, Richmond from El Paso . . . . ." time-stamped only with the date, "6/18/69," Sánchez lamented his departure.

I question
    self-motives

and
one year journalist fellowship
relegates La Raza, causa, etc.,
to minor role
    (if only temporarily)
and
mi alma weeps out
    its paradox.[5]

Even before he departed, Sánchez saw his fellowship as a resource. Richmond was not a destination. Becoming a figure like his patrons was not his goal. The result was ambivalence. He wanted to continue to serve Chicanes, whom he called "La Raza," and the Chicane movement in El Paso, but he saw the networks and opportunities that he would achieve through the fellowship as necessary for his cause.

Sánchez's fellowship prompted regional reflections, and his experience in Virginia included culture shock. In "Sojourns in Virginny...," he reflected:

it is by way of definition that i
now write this short introduction of myself
    a chicano,
lost in the wilderness of the deep south, and
very perplexed am i about this place.[6]

Sánchez wrote with an honest naïveté. In "Slums of Richmond, El Paso the Same," which was published in the *Richmond Afro-American* in July 1969, he explained that "the question of relating to others entered my mind, for I had never been in a place where my people—La Raza—didn't predominate."[7] That Sánchez had by this point in his life served in the military and completed two terms in prison in two different states without losing contact with majority Chicane populations was an indication of how his race and class had penalized him in the West. Political analyst Kevin Phillips coined the term *Sunbelt*, the same year Sánchez began his fellowship, to describe the growing population and economy of the South and West in his book *The Emerging Republican Majority*, but Sánchez understood the region from a different perspective.[8] He saw the segregation and marginalization that Chicanes had endured in the Southwest as parallel to that experienced by African Americans in what he called "the wilderness of the deep south." He saw both as defining features of the Sunbelt.

Parallels, however, did not mean identical. Sánchez did not see Black and Chicane people as the same. "I was the only Chicano in the program," he would later remember. "The rest were black, but I saw them as fellow travelers who shared the same societal conditions—comrades also in need for a place in the sun. The streets of Richmond reeked with the same racism that Texas is noted for."[9] Sánchez saw Chicanes and African Americans as allies but distinct. After his Virginia and Massachusetts years, he was a lifelong supporter of Afro-Latines, especially Puerto Ricans, but he never identified Black Mexicans or Blackness as a part of a Chicane homeland in the Southwest. In fact, he rarely, if ever, made Black Texans the subjects of his writing. Unlike John Hicks and Meridel Le Sueur, he was capable of seeing the South as a region with influence on the West. Unlike Era Bell Thompson, he could see the South as more than a regime. But he did not see Texas itself as the South. He saw the state as Chicane and as part of the Southwest.

Like Horace Cayton, Sánchez struggled with the liberal contradictions and compromises that social justice work in the press, the academy, and the literary world entailed. He demanded a purity in his politics that few mentors or fellow poets provided to his satisfaction. The Douglass fellowships were sponsored by the *Richmond Afro-American* and the Virginia Council on Human Relations. Conceived by *Afro-American* editor Raymond H. Boone and Frank T. Adams Jr., the state coordinator of the Virginia Council, the program recruited "not only on campuses, but also in prisons, ghettos, military services, and Job Corps centers." Adams insisted former prisoners were vital to the program. "We want to show that inmates are humans," he stated in a press release. "If any citizen can tell about the raw underside of American life, it is the man who has spent time in any of the nation's grim prisons, especially if he is young, black or Chicano."[10] Although the Douglass fellowship launched his academic career, Sánchez found Adams insufficiently committed to the cause. The two clashed over the insurance and health care provided to fellows, and in a draft essay about his experience, Sánchez, complained that "for all his alleged liberal intentions towards us, Frankie, blob-minded boy, managed to mismanage everything."[11]

The clash with Adams may have led Sánchez to leave Richmond for Amherst for the remainder of his fellowship. He worked there as a lecturer.[12] A poem described his other journeys back East in the first months of the 1970s.

Ayer, ay, ayer
i read your letter, carnal,
while on way to protest meeting
farmworker rep at Yale
and MEChA students asked me
to read poetry.[13]

Sánchez had continued to use poetry to advance his political causes. He maintained contact with other poets and friends, participated in migrant activism, and supported organizations like MEChA, Movimiento Estudiantil Chicano de Aztlán, which had formed at a conference of Mexican American students in California and established a chapter at Yale in 1969.[14] The conference drew on the idea of the American Southwest as a Chicane homeland dubbed "Aztlán."[15] In 1969 Sánchez understood the Chicane movement as emanating from the Southwest and arriving in the East with student activists and students like himself.[16]

Sánchez visited New York City during his move between Virginia and Massachusetts and, like a latter-day DeVoto, found the city too commercial and effete. He time-stamped a poem about it:

> new york bistros/
> boroughs, when people
> stop to gawk
> even wind bristles with
> mood of hustle/
> bustle disruption,
> even street women and gayboys
> snicker
> at foreign-ness stiltedly
> walking/stumbling
> against the herded hordes.

Sánchez appreciated cities. He would later thrill to the inspiration he found at the One World Poetry Festival in Amsterdam, and he wrote multiple poems about the binational twin cities of El Paso, Texas, and Juárez, Mexico. Moreover, he recognized New York's racial diversity. His New York poem included

> garment district rican women
> working arduous hours
> for token fares
> or buxomy types
> displaying wares,

But as DeVoto had, he recognized how much of New York's energy sprang from an extractive economy.[17] It was a connection that his conscience could not bear.

Because Sánchez's fellowship prompted his move to Richmond and Amherst, the two places merged in his poetry as a single influential event in his life, an event located back East. He returned to the West for a job aiding migrant laborers first in the Texas Rio Grande Valley and briefly in Denver in the summer of 1970. "Six months was all I could take of Amherst," he recalled later. "Its placid and verdant beauty did not move like the rapid eternities of the Southwest. I hungered for earth that is bronze and burnt by a vibrant, loving sun."[18] The rural East satisfied Sánchez no more than the urban East did. Sánchez returned to New York, New Haven, and cities in Massachusetts for later readings and lectures. Back East had served a purpose, providing the opportunity he sought.

Denver meant a return to the Southwest for Sánchez. He considered the city, along with El Paso, San Antonio, and Albuquerque, "citadels of Aztlán." The term *Aztlán* received widespread circulation after a 1969 youth conference in Denver rallied around it to advocate for Chicano nationalism. In later years, Sánchez was critical of Corky Gonzalez, the poet who authored the well-known "I Am Joaquín" and organized the 1969 conference. Sánchez felt that others involved in the movement that began in Denver had become too self-serving in their politics. He labeled Gonzalez's organization "THE CRUSADE FOR JUST-THEM" and called Gonzalez specifically a "bailbondsman who used to rip off pintos and their families."[19] He also appeared to envy the attention and press that Gonzalez received. Many Chicane writers of the left recognized the early 1970s as a generative age for their politics, but differences and conflicts still marked their efforts. Those differences and his urban focus contributed to a transition in Sánchez's poetry.

Sánchez began to downplay places and instead highlight travel that moved from south to north in the autobiographical stories that his poems told. In "migrant lament . . . ," time-stamped "7/28/70," Sánchez honored the

> migrant
> tumbling offtowork
> saca llena de algodon
> from tejas to colorado
> michigan to oregón.[20]
>
> [migrant
> tumbling offtowork

sack full of cotton
from Texas to Colorado
Michigan to Oregon.]

His new approach emerged in tension with the frustrations of his job. Sánchez struggled to square the political and artistic movement there with his experiences in El Paso. In "Stream . . . ," time-stamped "tenth month, el año de Chicano," he called Denver, "abject city of chicanos who no longer pueden hablar nuestro idioma (mestizaje), y les digo, carnales, que duele al oír mi raza periquiár en inglés o que éllos pidan poesía chicana escrita en el idioma del gringo [abject city of chicanos who no longer are able to speak our language (mestizaje) and I tell them, friends, it hurts to hear my people mucking about in English or that they ask for Chicana poetry written in the gringo's language]."[21] As in Richmond, Sánchez was uncompromising. He felt that other Chicano and Chicana poets accepted the demands of Anglo audiences too readily. Because they failed to convey to the next generation the unique Spanish that Sánchez and others used, they did not transmit the notion of Chicane identity as a mixture (*mestizaje*) that combined aspects of colonial Spanish and Mexican influences with Indigenous cultures. When they accepted the demands of an Anglo-dominated literary community, Sánchez thought that they sold out. Any behavior that suggested assimilation or compromise was suspect in Sánchez's view.

He likely would have rejected the charge, but Sánchez also gave only glancing attention to Chicana poets and writers. He objectified women in his poetry, including flight attendants whom he encountered with greater frequency in the 1970s and 1980s, and he rarely acknowledged the combined discrimination that Chicanas and gender nonconforming Chicanx experienced. In his largest book, *Hechízospells*, published in 1976, he lamented that "at meetings, regrettably is María Teresa introduced as the wife of Ricardo Sánchez, the poet/writer. She should be introduced as María Teresa, for her worth comes from her life experience, just as I am Ricardo—a person, not a poet. To place value on role or relationship and not on the human vitality of any person is to depersonalize/dehumanize the person."[22] Sánchez sought the full realization of individuals, but in his homages to other writers, few women appeared, not even fellow Texans, like Gloria Anzaldúa, with whom he worked during the rich years of Chicane poetry in the early 1970s. While *writer* or *poet* did not fully describe Anzaldúa either, poetry was a critical part of Anzaldúa's self-realization and a part of the Chicane movement that Sánchez championed.[23] Moreover, while Sánchez recognized his own wife's individuality, her labor supported their family for much of his career, a part of her self-realization that he did not explore deeply in his published work.

Instead, in the early 1970s, Sánchez focused on movement as a defining feature of Chicane life, and his own travel, whether accompanied by his family or not, served as his object of investigation. With this philosophy germinating, Sánchez returned to El Paso to found Míctla Publishing as a home for Chicano and Chicana writers. In the essay "Míctla: Long Road Home," he remembered that the "Richmond Afro-American Newspaper and the Richmond Chronicle (underground paper), made me aware of the need for our own publishing industries." While at Amherst, Sánchez "spoke with several publishing houses, but they could not yet see the need for Chicano publications: WE WERE NOT CHARISMATIC ENOUGH." The name Míctla was a reference to the Aztec underworld, and Sánchez's intention was that "the publishing house would help put to death—once and for all—the comic stereotyping of my people."[24] Like Stegner and Mirrielees had, Sánchez saw a need for publishing ventures and literary communities in the West. His experiences in Virginia also led him to draw from the example of the activist Black press in the South. He saw Texas less as a place and more as an origin point for the perspectives that Chicanes held and the East less as a place and more as a means of bringing those perspectives to national audiences. He directed his own charisma toward those aims.

After Sánchez established Míctla, he engaged in extensive lecturing and reading that took him around the country, a process that intensified when he began his distance doctoral program at Union Graduate School with a Ford Foundation Fellowship. Although Sánchez had never been to college, he explained in a later interview that he was accepted to the doctoral program "due to publications and programs I created and developed throughout the country, serving migrants and urban people in areas of education, literature, culture and health."[25] Like Le Sueur, Sánchez formed his literary viewpoint in dialogue with working people who cycled in and out of urban and rural areas. He channeled those insights as he began his doctoral program in the autumn of 1973.

The years of his doctoral study challenged him to confront his attachments and frustrations with Texas. After completing his degree, he recalled his travels as an outline of the Chicano movement. "And from Wisconsin to Omaha to Illinois to Nevada to Oregon / Washington / Idaho down to Califas / Arizona / Colorado / New Mexico and Tejas up to Michigan / Wyoming / Harvard / Yale into the barrios and campos and pintas and a host of universidades, youths and older Raza are aware that history is created by those who take stands, and we have taken stands and will take more stands."[26] Travel (including travel back East) and political action together constituted the Chicano movement in his eyes. Universities back East such as Harvard and Yale were merely a means to an end: they were places where Chicane organizers and artists found one another and acquired the education needed to produce art and activism both. Often, Sánchez believed, students did so by challenging institutional norms, not by seeking to belong to the institution or the region.

Sánchez felt similarly about California and Stanford. Where others he met through the Union program—such as Stanford education professor Homero Galicia, artist and poet José Antonio Burciaga, and poet and musician Javier Pacheco—found some support at Stanford, Sánchez did not. He acknowledged in his reports to his committee that his trip to a retreat in Sonoma was the first time he had been in a swimming pool and that the place provoked culture shock for him. Stanford may have been the same. In "MAÑANA: Stanford U. Breakfast Blues," time-stamped "isolation dances & mocks, 4-5-72," he laments his distance from El Paso:

>   here one night
>   and already missing banter rap;
>   yesterday, during breakfast
>   or night before last
>   in Juárez restaurant
>   music played
>   & i saw people embrace . . .
>
> here
> i see people embrace
>   newspaper or napkin
> as if to hide from their reality.

The penultimate line of the poem observes that "the institution prevails."[27] A growing Chicane presence at Stanford would eventually lead the university to acquire Sánchez's papers, but he never appears to have felt entirely at home there and never appears to have formed a relationship with Wallace Stegner or others in the writing program. In his 1992 poem "urgencia," he called Stanford "the Harvard of the West" and lamented a movement

>   now only
> alive
> in books
> & rhetorical
> recollections.[28]

The relationship of self-realization to region acquired particular importance for Sánchez when he considered the "place" of Indigenous peoples within the political movements of which he was a part. Sánchez's own family claimed descent from New Mexico's Pueblo peoples, a connection that he explored repeatedly when reflecting on his own identity. In "Old Man," written in October 1972, he recalled his grandfather

>   when being shepherd
>   in utah, nevada, colorado and new mexico
>   was life lived freely.
>
> Sánchez remembered that his grandfather would
>
>   speak sometimes
>   of pueblos,
>   san juan, santa clara
>   and even santo domingo
>   and his family, he would say,
>   came from there:
>   some of our blood was here,
>   he would say,
>   before the coming of coronado.[29]

Sánchez acknowledged Spanish colonization as a threat to Indigenous people, and he considered his Indigenous heritage an important part of his sense of self, but he rarely implied that his heritage bound him to a particular place. As his studies progressed, Sánchez presented Indigeneity as a part of Chicane history and identity, but he did not see Indigenous places as belonging to Chicane people or the Chicane movement, nor did he see Chicane people absorbing the Indigenous, not even in the US-Mexico borderlands, where he distinguished among Tarahumaran, Pueblo, Diné, and Chicane peoples. He felt enthusiasm for the ways in which travel, even the kind of travel that had led his grandfather to follow his flocks northward, constituted living "freely."[30]

Sánchez had a similar relationship to Mexico and Mexican identity. While he recognized the history that tied the Southwest and Texas specifically to Mexico, he saw himself and other Chicanes as unique. He recognized both Spanish and Mexican colonial endeavors in Texas and did not begin his presentations of the state with US colonization. More than once he addressed the battle at the Alamo in his work and how white American memory erased Mexican claims to the site. In the time stamp for "San Antonio phantasmagoria," written in March 1971, he described himself and friends "on way to eat and hear mariachis, night is cool, mood brutamente vibrant, until álamo comes into view and midwestern tourists prance about in ya buey euphoria, yo'all, and truth is again absent."[31] Sánchez felt frustration when white narratives, especially false ones, reigned over those of Black and brown people. That frustration extended to the misrepresentation of colonization by Mexico and Spain that preceded that of the United States.

Sánchez sought to liberate Chicanes within the state regardless of which direction colonialism had followed. When visiting Odessa, he decried "texas rangers" who "galivant about, seeking heads to crack," and he insisted "this area is crying for liberation."[32] He was especially unnerved when a white police officer in Dallas was charged and convicted with the death of a twelve-year-old Mexican American child whom the officer had shot in the head when trying to elicit a confession.[33] Sánchez found the case and the pattern of white police brutality against Mexican Americans horrifying, but he could not bring himself to leave Texas or the Southwest. As he told his graduate committee: "Yes, it shall be said repeatedly that activists (like me) take things too personally, but ... the indignity of living in this nation is psychologically violent. No, I cannot leave this land—for the shreds of blood which cover it are the rivulets of my family, of my people. Can I forsake the Sangre de Cristo peaks or the sandias or the valles and plateaus? This sundrenched land is more than home for me, it is my nomenclature."[34]

Sánchez loved Texas, just as some of the Black journalists with whom he worked in Richmond loved Virginia. He struggled with some of the same tensions they did as he combatted the violent segregation and marginalization of Chicanes in Texas while working to retain Chicane culture. He did not want to lose the perspectives and creativity that he saw in the margins, but he did want to end the marginalization that he witnessed

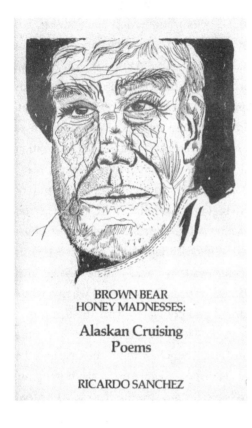

Artist José Antonio Burciaga used elements of the southwestern landscape to compose this portrait of Ricardo Sánchez for the cover of *Brown Bear Honey Madnesses: Alaskan Cruising Poems* (1982). Wisps of clouds above a mountain range sweep across Sánchez's forehead, yuccas dot the bridge of his nose, and a sun rises on his lips. Slough Press chose a yellow cover to indicate the Southwest and blue interior pages to evoke Alaska. Courtesy of Slough Press.

throughout the Sunbelt. The same Texas perspective that led him to look along a south-north axis also allowed him to look eastward from the Southwest and see the inequalities that marked the Southeast.

Sánchez felt a similar ambivalence about the academy. "Yale is alienating as hell for Chicanos from the barrio," he told his committee as he began to wrap up his degree, "yet it is an experience we must master if we are ever to liberate ourselves . . . we must understand the system in order to combat it. Some of our most brilliant minds are being hurt in Yale by the callous and methodical ways of an alien way of life and its concomitant demands."[35] Unlike Stewart Udall at Yale and Bernard DeVoto at Harvard and Horace Cayton and Frank Miyamoto at the University of Chicago, Sánchez did not seek entrance to an elite university to validate himself or other Chicanes. Neither did he attempt to reproduce the Ivy League in the West as Wallace Stegner and Edith Mirrielees had at Stanford. Rather, he recognized universities as sites of potential learning but also, for western, non-white scholars (especially those without Stanford connections), as sites of alienation. As a non-white, working-class writer and activist, he puzzled over how to navigate such spaces himself and how to aid others in doing so. Back East was a potential resource but also a potential minefield.

Sánchez arrived at the solution of greater Chicane presence in the academy. Along with other scholars of color, he pressed Union Graduate School to hire more non-white faculty and address inequality. Early in his graduate career, he queried his committee: "In conjunction with black peers . . . we explored the reality of social change within institutions that question racism, yet project racist attitudes; How can UGS speak of egalitarianism when it is obvious by the limited number of Chicanos, Borícuas, and other Spanish speaking students (and no faculty!) in the program? Where are the Asian Americans? Native Americans?"[36] Union subsequently offered jobs to Sánchez and another Chicano poet, but funding never materialized for the positions or for a permanent Union Graduate School–West.[37]

Sánchez returned to an emphasis on journeys in his poetry and turned away from representations of regions. He preferred his midwestern ventures in these years. After completing his degree, he took a position as a visiting instructor of creative writing at the University of Wisconsin–Milwaukee and then another visiting assistant position at the University of Utah in humanities. Sánchez felt enthusiasm for the Upper Midwest as a site for Chicane artistic expression. He helped establish the Canto al Pueblo, a poetry festival first held in Denver and California, and he later organized the first Midwest Canto al Pueblo. His poems written in Utah, however, often began with a time stamp that placed him in "(p)utah" or "(br)utah," editorial comment on the conformist culture that he felt marked the state. His overt hostility indicated that the West as a broader region did not hold him the way Texas had.

Following surgery for diverticulitis, he and his family returned to Texas in 1983 to establish Paperbacks . . . ¡y Más! in San Antonio. The store began receiving support from John and Marquetta Tilton in 1986 as part of the network of Paperbacks Plus stores the Tiltons supported. Like another Tilton-sponsored venture, Voltaire's in Austin, Paperbacks . . . ¡y Más! shared the cosmopolitanism of Texas's literary communities.[38] Together with María Teresa, Sánchez hosted a Poets of Texas series and conducted fundraisers for Central American refugees. If his work in Milwaukee reflected his perspective when he cast his gaze northward, at Paperbacks . . . ¡y Más! he looked southward for Latin American influence on Texas and the United States. One observer of his writing considered it "a specifically American idiom" from "a uniquely American experience" but underscored "that experience is hemispheric; his Americanness cannot be contained by either national borders or presumption's frontiers."[39] That aspect of Sánchez's work took center stage during his years in San Antonio.

María Teresa and Ricardo modeled the store in part after the Nuyorican Poets Café on Manhattan's Lower East Side, but Sánchez saw it as a Texan venture that reflected "the diversity of Texas cultures" and a means to channel the "strong urban orientation" and "country understanding" that allowed San Antonio to "project the diversity of humankind."[40] One of his collaborators, Rob Lewis, who later published a collection of Sánchez's poetry, recalled the store as an effort to "foster what we referred to as a Tejas/Texas fusion" and "expose the ways in which the differing communities of a genuinely multicultural society share in and are enriched by each other's conventions, histories, and presences."[41] The store was the Sánchez's family's effort to realize the creative promise of Texas's marginalized communities and their engagement with diverse national and international communities.

Sánchez supplemented his efforts with teaching at area jails and libraries, but when an offer for a position at Washington State University in Pullman presented itself in 1990, his family moved yet again. There his protests persisted but mellowed. In correspondence with his old friend Javier Pacheco, he accused the National Association of Chicano Studies of "simply perpetuating the problems as they strive to further assimilate a people who have historically shown that a goodly number do not care to play the game." Sánchez never gave up on his opposition to assimilation, but he expressed satisfaction at Washington State and felt respected by colleagues and students.

He still pulled on the inspiration that he gathered from his home too. Describing the Pullman campus, he realized that "sometimes I long to hear another idiom, music, or to simply wander about places where our people permeate everything with the aroma of raza . . . yet I recall that such an idyll was only a fantasy for me, that as a poet I never could have a people or place, unless I was to quell my disquietude and staunch the flow of words that questioned the lack of authenticity." Sánchez missed Texas and his home city of El Paso, a place he called a "city of marginal and wayward notes." He had always used those notes to feed his art and the communities of artists of which he formed a part.[42] When he was in the last stages of cancer, in 1995, he returned to El Paso to die.

El Paso had always been home, but for Sánchez, El Paso and Texas served even more as his education. He drew from the lessons he learned there in his poetry and as he responded to the changing landscape of arts and letters in the United States in the 1970s and 1980s. He recognized how the tensions between public and private, liberation and justice, rigor and delight, had shaped him. From Texas, he trod similar midwestern ground as Hicks and Le Sueur; longed for home, like Big Man; shared the frustrations of Cayton and DeVoto; established institutions such as those of Thompson, Mirrielees, and Stegner; and supported the arts, like the Udalls. But Sánchez did not advocate for the Midwest, the Southwest, the West, Texas, El Paso, San Antonio, or even Aztlán as places. Instead, he proposed a different narrative axis for westerners, one that looked north and south, rather than west and east, when recounting and planning Chicane journeys. He thrilled to wherever he and fellow writer activists used "marginal and wayward notes" to "question and also quest." Sánchez refused to be contained. Even in the margins—perhaps especially there—he made his mark. Texas showed him the way.

CHAPTER 5
THE PRIMROSE PATH

On June 18, 1984, the controversial radio show host Alan Berg drove to his Denver home in his VW bug. Remembering the evening, one commentator noted that "it was a sweet June night, the temperature is warm this time of year from winds that come down off the Rockies. In June, the sky literally is often turquoise blue with pink clouds at 9:30 p.m., just after sundown."[1] A tall man with haystack bangs, Berg was easily recognized around Denver. As he unfolded himself from the car, members of the white power group the Order fired a MAC-10 submachine gun into his body, lifting him from the ground and killing him.

The Order was a national white power organization committed to destroying the United States. Founded by an Arizonan born in Texas, the group attracted members from across the country, trained in paramilitary camps in Missouri, bought weapons from gun dealers in Alabama, produced false Costa Rican identification for its members, conducted armed robberies, produced counterfeit currencies, and endeavored to spark a race war so as to end the United States and create a white nation. The group consolidated at the July 1983 Aryan Nations World Congress meeting in remote Idaho and closely followed a racist utopian novel published five years before the Idaho meeting, *The Turner Diaries*, for guidance. Among the novel's scenes was the assassination of a Jewish journalist, which had contributed to the group's choice of Berg as a target. Money from their group's robberies funded additional cells of members in Arkansas, California, Idaho, Michigan, Missouri, Montana, North Carolina, Pennsylvania, and Virginia. Because the FBI never recovered all that the group had stolen, it is likely that additional members and cells existed elsewhere.[2]

Although the group was national in scope and took root in both urban and rural areas, initial narratives about it and Berg's murder associated the Order with the rural West and the group's targets with the East and California. The Order's own efforts to create a white homeland somewhere in the rural Northwest and its criminal activity in Idaho, Washington, and Colorado undergirded such impressions. So also did the contrast that the press drew between the rural West and the urban East. In *Armed and Dangerous*, one of the first comprehensive accounts of the Order and affiliated white power groups, journalist James Coates described the local impression of Berg as "the acid-tongued Chicagoan... just another Californicating liberal from the East." Subsequent memorials to Berg recalled his ski weekends at Vail and his support for environmental causes. Coates attributed the friction in Colorado as much to newcomers seeking to enjoy the natural world of Colorado as he did those who resented them. "If they were called Californicators," he wrote, "these glib intruders tweaked the establishment by calling the old guard, men and women alike, 'Cowboys.'"[3] Berg shared little with Bernard DeVoto, Wallace Stegner, and Stewart Udall, but those endeavoring to puzzle through the horrific violence and prejudice behind his murder put him in the same camp.

Regional perspectives both contributed to the white power movement and disguised its national scope. These perspectives were even more detailed and complex than the terms *Californicating* or *liberal from the East* or *Cowboys* captured. The emphasis in the press on Berg's Chicago origins denied the existence of long-standing Jewish communities in the Rocky Mountain West. It located American Jewish culture entirely in eastern cities and Hollywood. Colorado may have been enduring Californication, but in 1983, when Ronald Reagan had ridden his California governorship to the White House, *Californication* did not necessarily mean liberal. Reagan excoriated those he called "liberals" more than once. Moreover, the Order had no interest in arguing with Democrats about public land use, as Reagan and other Republicans did. The Order endeavored to destroy the United States, not work within established channels to lead it.

The specificity of regional perspectives becomes especially important in understanding Berg's murder because it intersected with another white power organization, Posse Comitatus. The Posse encouraged members to acknowledge no government official higher than a sheriff, file trivial lawsuits to overburden the court system, and refuse to pay taxes. In 1983 the organization used a North Carolina Ku Klux Klan poster that showed a lynched body in silhouette. In the 1980s Posse members clashed with local and federal police in North Dakota, Arizona, and Nebraska and contributed to violence in Oklahoma, Idaho, and Michigan. Among those peddling Posse ideas was Roderick Elliott, the former publisher of the *Primrose and Cattlemen's Gazette*, a weekly idiosyncratic mix of ranch news, antisemitism, and Republican politics published in Fort Lupton, Colorado, less than fifty miles northeast of Denver. Not long after Berg pilloried the *Primrose* on his radio show, David Lane, a member of the Order who had advertised antisemitic messages in the *Primrose* and worked for the newspaper, participated in killing the radio host.[4] The press and law enforcement typically called the Posse a midwestern organization and the Order a western one, but the *Primrose* suggests that they were united in their regional outlook: they both blamed the East.

The *Primrose* relied on the mythology of the frontier, and in the early 1980s, the frontier had failed farmers. Iowa, Nebraska, Kansas, North Dakota, South Dakota, and Minnesota farmers not only struggled with falling grain prices, rising equipment costs, and inflation; they also no longer felt included in the West despite the fact that the Great Plains were becoming more arid.[5] Aridity was a defining feature of the West according to Stegner and DeVoto, but far more of the Great Plains fell under the purview of the Department of Agriculture than under Udall's Interior Department. Most journalists perceived Colorado and Iowa, Nebraska and Idaho, as entirely different places. Those papers covering the farm crisis rarely included eastern farmers or migrant laborers, of the kind that Ricardo Sánchez memorialized, in their analysis. The frontier had passed the East by. According to its logic, farmers and farmworkers no longer existed there.

Elliott's criminal insight was not the use of the press, the targeting of economically imperiled farmers and ranchers, or the publication of antisemitic tracts. It was his recognition that frontier mythology led many Great Plains farmers and western ranchers to share a common resentment of the East. Most members of the national press and law enforcement were inclined to see the Midwest and the West as separate, a regional vision that delayed the insight that groups such as the Order and Posse Comitatus were linked and had attained a national following. Moreover, most journalists were inclined to see the frontier and the West as one and the same. West of the Mississippi, white power took root when the false promises of frontier logic hit the realities of midwestern and western life. Elliott wreaked havoc by stitching together the West's and the Midwest's regional visions into a rhetoric of resentment that targeted the East.

A growing frustration among farmers of the western plains marked the late twentieth century. After the relative prosperity of the 1950s, a greater reliance on technology, combined with the increasing cost of equipment and the comparatively low rise in prices for commodities, meant that grain farmers, dairy farmers, and cattle ranchers all struggled into the 1960s and 1970s. Reliance on technology, the market, subsidies, and government expertise meant that farmers felt increasingly dependent, a sensation that irritated those who prided themselves on their freedom. Agricultural economic experts encouraged farmers to use their land as collateral for loans, but credit became tighter as the land failed to pay in the late 1970s and 1980s. Moreover, farmers had other wage-earning options. Industry in rural and suburban areas had grown—from the factories that processed the meat that ranchers raised to those that produced the equipment farmers indebted themselves to buy. Military presence also grew on the plains following World War II, which both displaced farm families and provided another lure away from family farms.[6] Between 1960 and 1970, approximately one hundred thousand farmers sold their farms to seek out other work.[7] Small-scale production did not pay. Large-scale monoculture, wage labor, and military service sometimes did.

In the 1960s, farmers in Wisconsin and Iowa organized around the ideas that had motivated late-nineteenth-century agrarian populists: their own production. These were the same ideas that Meridel Le Sueur and, to a lesser extent, John Hicks had championed in their representations of agrarian populists in the 1930s. Mid-twentieth-century farmers coordinated with one another to form cooperatives and reduce production to improve prices for hogs and cattle. In the late 1960s, they began organizing "tractorcades" to Washington, DC, to protest Department of Agriculture policy. A brief uptick in grain and land prices in the mid-1970s cooled farmers' tempers, but a combination of declining prices along with farmers' indebtedness sparked the farm crisis anew in the late 1970s and early 1980s.

Not far from where the *Primrose* would publish a few years later, four farmers met in Campo, Colorado, in 1977 to form the American Agriculture Movement (AAM). The group spread rapidly, engaged in confrontations at farm foreclosures, and staged two tractorcades to Washington, DC, in 1978 and 1979. The incongruity of tractors on the National Mall was part of the AAM's rhetorical strategy. There were farmers in Maryland, Virginia, and Delaware too, but the contrast of rural farmers driving their tractors to the steps of the Washington Monument suggested the gulf that midwestern and western farmers perceived between their struggles and the federal policy designed to address it.

Into this moment of crisis stepped Roderick Elliott. Elliott's criminal record began in 1949, when he was arrested at age twenty-two for impersonating a federal officer. From early in his criminal career, he recognized the power that the eastern government conveyed. A serial con artist, he was later arrested for passing bad checks, perjury, and selling securities without a license. He was imprisoned in the Utah State Penitentiary in 1962 and again in 1965 for violating parole.[8] When he began publishing the *Primrose and Cattleman's Gazette* weekly with his wife, Karla, sometime in the mid-1970s, he did not mention his checkered past in the editorials that he posted on the front page.[9]

Instead, he fixated on the problems that he saw emanating from the East. A cowboy's profile gazing at a group of cattle graced every masthead. Below it, Elliott stirred the pot. Alongside an illustration of pioneer wagons, he took issue with "eastern college graduates with nothing but textbook experience, no practical experience within the framework of agriculture itself, being placed within the United States Department of Agriculture."[10]

Western farmers participated in the American Agriculture Movement's efforts to bring federal attention to farmers' needs. "Tractors, one flying the flag of the American Agriculture Movement, on their way to the US Capitol, Washington, DC, during the 'Tractorcade' protests of February 1979." *US News & World Report* Photograph Collection, Library of Congress. Photo by Warren K. Leffler.

In support of farmers, Elliott queried: "Why are so many families leaving the land? It is not that they want to; they are actually being forced off the land."[11] He lay the blame at the feet of "those pinstripers in Washington, D.C."[12] Elliott expressed common cause with the farmers he saw suffering in eastern Colorado and along the Great Plains by expressing resentment of the East.

Many of his editorials outlined pressures that farmers faced and that may have surprised those Colorado neighbors who were part of a burgeoning environmentalist movement in the late 1970s and early 1980s. He called corporations to task, especially in the oil industry. "When we realize that one third of all the oil that comes in the nation is used in the plastic business, I can't help but wonder why we need so much plastic." He concluded sarcastically, "You must remember, though, we can't hurt these huge oil conglomerates."[13] Elliott expressed particular concern for the effects of toxaphene, a pesticide banned for application on crops in 1982 but not

The Primrose Path 183

prohibited for use among livestock until the 1990s. Elliott drew on farmers' concerns that their own production might harm consumers. "These animals might have been dipped just four days ago, but instead of being put on quarantine, they are sold as hamburger for our kids and adults to consume as clean red meat."[14] Running alongside the many beef recipes on the paper's "Woman's Touch" page, such news could be unsettling.[15]

Audiences accustomed to the tricks of twenty-first-century media outrage likely recognize Elliott's approach. He sought to build a sense of belonging by printing a shared iconography and rhetoric in his paper. Although oil prices and toxic contamination were of genuine concern among farmers and other Americans, the *Primrose* gave little attention to details and accuracy when reporting on them. Elliott identified suffering people who felt alienated from existing institutions. He kept tempers high by reminding readers of perceived and genuine threats. He then exploited the imbalance he had perpetuated for political and personal financial gain.

This approach could look like mainstream political commentary, and many readers may not have noticed Elliott's excesses. In earlier issues of the *Primrose*, Elliott appeared to favor electoral politics that placed Republicans in local, state, and national leadership positions. The paper encouraged readers to join the "Senator's Club," which paid for "subscriptions" of the *Primrose* for US senators. S. I. Hayakawa presumably received a copy in California, as did Jesse Helms in North Carolina, whose canned column, Report from US Senator Jesse Helms, ran for several months in the *Primrose* and gave significant attention to questions of government spending, especially for social programs. The *Primrose* echoed Helms in numerous columns and in November 1981 ran a map that showed how much each state paid in taxes compared to how much it received in federal aid. The map's caption highlighted Texas ($1.40 paid for every dollar received), Vermont (45 cents for every dollar received), and Washington, DC (32 cents for every dollar received). The map did not provide a source and did not highlight states neighboring Colorado, like Utah and New Mexico, nor the ten southeastern states that all received more per dollar than they paid according to the map.[16] Western or rural solidarity did not appear to be the *Primrose*'s goal, but targeting the East, especially the federal government, did.

Initially, that goal dovetailed with western Republican goals. Until mid-1981, the paper ran Report from Washington, by Alan Simpson, a Wyoming senator and the son of Milward Simpson, who had corresponded with dude rancher Larry Larom about the Forest Service in the mid-1940s. In March 1980 the *Primrose* reported that "Simpson said he believes Reagan also has a solid grasp of the problems facing the West, adding, 'The present administration has not demonstrated a compassionate understanding of vital western issues. I believe Governor Reagan, as a westerner, does possess that understanding.'"[17] In his own column, Simpson advised readers on the best ways to write and contact their senators. Following the 1980 election, he celebrated what he saw as the West's ascendence: "The real impact of the changes that are about to occur in the Senate comes with the realization that nearly half of the Senate committee chairmen will represent the western United States, and they in turn will have direct access to a President of the United States who is also a westerner. That is 'powerful medicine' in Washington and it should be a great benefit to the citizens of the west."[18] In an article that celebrated the end of "Democratic domination of the Senate," Simpson equated the West with Republicans and celebrated the region's rise alongside his party's.

Bipartisan concerns, such as immigration, also received notice in the paper's pages. In May 1980 Simpson told readers that "America is no longer 'the frontier' with vast undeveloped areas and resources and a low population.... The new immigrants, coming mainly from non-European cultures, face greater adjustment problems than immigrants of the past."[19] In a subsequent column, Simpson questioned if "illegal immigrants" contributed enough to the nation economically to justify contemporary immigration policy.[20] In July 1981 the *Primrose* reprinted on its front page an article by Colorado governor Richard Lamm that had run in the *New York Times*. A Democrat, Lamm spoke in language strikingly similar to Simpson's. "Frontier America is gone," Lamm argued. Immigration limits, he asserted, would allow the nation to focus on economic problems like unemployment. Lamm drew particular attention to Mexico's growing population, expressed support for Simpson's legislation limiting immigration, and concluded, "The Lady in the Harbor symbolizes *Liberty* not immigration."[21] Although

Lamm and Simpson followed immigrants along paths that moved northward and southward, as Sánchez had done, they both attempted to garner western votes by restricting immigration. They laid their requests at the steps of the Capitol in Washington, DC, back East.

In the paper's political commentary, the Sagebrush Rebellion figured prominently. The "rebellion" attempted to move public lands into the hands of state government, where it could then be sold to private buyers. It was an effort akin to that DeVoto had battled in the 1940s and a repudiation of Stewart Udall's efforts to bring more of the West's lands under the stewardship of the federal government. Initiated in Nevada, the movement spread across Rocky Mountain and far western states resentful of their dependency on the federal government.[22] The Sagebrush Rebellion gained traction during Reagan's presidency under his secretary of the interior, James Watt. In May 1980 the *Primrose* highlighted Colorado legislators' efforts to join the movement and cited state senator Harold McCormick, a Republican from Canon City: "'If you look at the map and see how the eastern states have fared, many of them with less than 1 percent owned by the federal government and some of them a far smaller amount than that, and then look at the West and see what the federal government has done to us as they have become an increasingly aggressive, even hostile landlord, I think it's easy to understand why the 'Sagebrush Rebellion' was born."[23] Sagebrush rebels regularly relied on contrasts between the East and West to amplify their message of removing land from federal hands. That message fit neatly both with the *Primrose*'s target audience of western and midwestern rural residents as well as its target of resentment: the East.

Readers might have also been drawn to one of the *Primrose*'s strengths: its editor spoke "cow talk."[24] Alongside the articles in support of the Sagebrush Rebellion, limiting immigration to the United States, the dangers of plastics and toxaphene, and the high cost of oil ran a series of images, advertisements, and articles that may have attracted ranchers and farmers to the *Primrose*. The paper took advertisements for stock shows, calf roping services, farm trailers and elevators, concrete pouring, locksmiths, irrigation equipment, windmills, solar panels, Denver's Top of the Rockies Restaurant, liquor stores, the marines, and, on the Woman's Touch page, vacuum cleaners. It reported on the American Junior Hereford Association meeting in Kansas City, the appearance of the Texas Longhorn Queen at the Colorado State Fair, the appointment of a Youth and Education program manager to the American Simmental Association (which served both beef and dairy cattle ranchers), rodeo competitions, Nebraska county fair dates, and 4-H winners.[25] In September 1981 it reminded readers that the Colorado extension service offered "Citizen Effectiveness Training," which aided Coloradans in navigating county, state, and federal government bureaucracies.

Filler material in the margins may have drawn ranchers and farmers to the publication and disguised Elliott's loose commitment to truthful reporting. Next to a screed against Chase Manhattan Bank ran a poem by Lakenan Barnes titled "The Pleasures of Reading."[26] Barnes, a lawyer in Mexico, Missouri, published poetry on the side. The Woman's Touch page included a list of domestic violence shelters (likely placed by area social services) and praised an elementary school band. Elliott defended the *Primrose*'s antisemitism alongside a peaceful illustration of a cat gazing from a windowsill into a country kitchen.[27] An advertisement for Yellowstone National Park ran opposite one of Elliott's anxiety-inducing articles about toxaphene.[28] The column Riding along with Ranger Long decried the criminalization of marijuana and concluded: "My dad always called it bird seed. The birds ate it and were happy and sang and that made people happy."[29] Readers may have perceived the scenes of domestic harmony; the frustrations with eastern government and business; the longing for an imagined, past independence; and the elevation of local attractions and community as of a piece, conveniently gathered together in a single publication.

Those federal officials whose syndicated columns ran in the *Primrose* did not object to the paper's more extremist views. By foregrounding cow talk and bipartisan politics, Elliott may have dodged protest from elected officials. Simpson's column ran for the last time in the *Primrose* on July 20, 1981, although he continued to serve in the Senate until 1997. The paper's first prominent anti-Semitic article ran in November 1980. The paper continued to publish Jesse Helms's column for another year. In January 1984 it ran an article by Senator Nancy Landon Kassebaum, a Republican from

Kansas, titled "Railroads: A Key Link between Field and Table." Kassebaum reported on her service for the Surface Transportation Subcommittee of the Commerce Committee and its hearing in Hutchinson, Kansas. The hearing concluded that railroad contracts with grain elevators favored larger elevators, exactly the kind of issue that troubled agrarian Populists in the early twentieth century and Hicks and Le Sueur in the 1930s.[30] If federal officials did receive copies of the paper, perhaps they got filed, as similar materials did for Edith Green in Oregon, in a "crackpot file." In October 1983 Elliott claimed seventeen thousand subscribers, and in June 1984 there was a fourfold increase from the previous year.[31] He probably exaggerated these numbers, but the paper did an effective job of covering a wide range of issues in which rural midwesterners and their elected representatives likely had interest.

Until its last publication, the paper buried its most hateful messages in its idiosyncratic mix of local news and global distrust. A rant against global financiers of a "New World Order Trilateral Commission" appeared in the paper on page 8 of the November 19, 1980, issue from a hate organization called the Fund to Restore an Educated Electorate.[32] The second mention of the New World Order appeared in an almost full-page advertisement for a spring 1982 gathering in Denver sponsored by the John Birch Society that asked readers, "Are You Being Tricked into FINANCING COMMUNISM and Slavery?" The Economic Affairs Department of Rocky Mountain Orthodontics was listed as the funder of the advertisement.[33] Given the advertisement's size, some readers may have considered attending the John Birch Society gathering in the House of Lords Room at the Regency Hotel in Denver or picking up a copy of the society's *Blue Book*. Neither activity constituted the kind of criminal violence Elliott and Lane would later support.

By late 1982, Elliott consistently espoused an antigovernment line in his editorials. In October he authored an editorial titled, "I CAN'T ANSWER THAT!" decrying "that oil billionaire from Texas" who failed to understand "the average farmer or rancher" and took for granted "this so-called 'cheap food' that the rich and politicians go so merrily around boasting about." Elliott concluded that "as for political parties, at this point, we don't have any difference between either of them. They are both operated by the same scabs of the filthy rich who have no concern for the average persons of the land, not to mention concern in general for the farmers or ranchers of the country."[34] Earlier editorials in the paper had offered praise for Jimmy Carter and expressed support for corporations that took farmers seriously.[35] Almost two years into Reagan's presidency, neither the Department of the Interior nor the Department of Agriculture had won ranchers' and farmers' faith, a doubt that Elliott exploited.

Local community members, local press, and the local branch of the Anti-Defamation League shouldered the labor of combatting the *Primrose*'s prejudice and misinformation. Two weeks after Elliott abdicated any faith in electoral politics, he printed a letter to the publisher from "Zalmon Ber Tornek of the Z Bar H Organic Ranch," along with his own reply. Tornek's letter excoriated the *Primrose* for its hateful messages and noted that "many Jews came here to Colorado in the late 1800s to help settle the land as farmers and ranchers, many of whose descendants today are fine and respected citizens of the community working to make it better." In his reply, Elliott innocently proclaimed: "As for being an Orthodox Jew, good for you. I just happen to be an honest Christian." The comment was disingenuous. Elliott was likely aligning himself with the Christian Identity movement, whose theologians preached that non-white and Jewish people were children of Satan and asked adherents to rid the world of them.[36]

Elliott also questioned Tornek's masculinity. He continued: "I'm sure you're right about your clan coming out to the West in the late 1800s. All the Indian fighting and range wars had been fought by then and there wasn't much to worry about. This was during the time of the great migration of our Western women folks, it was safe to bring them here in numbers."[37] White Christian settlers colonizing the West through "Indian fighting" won the *Primrose*'s respect, not contemporary Jewish organic farmers who may have had many of the same concerns regarding mechanization and toxicity that the paper had previously published on its front page. Elliott may have been, in twenty-first-century parlance, trolling. He used the triumphant and gendered frontier myths of settler prosperity and Indigenous displacement to do so.

Elliott was fluent in the language of white supremacy. When introducing a staff member with a Spanish surname, he took pains to distinguish her from Mexican Americans or Mexican migrants like those for whom Sánchez had worked in Denver. The paper described the staff member as "Spanish in descent" and said other staff members had nicknamed her "The Contessa."[38] The *Primrose* never acknowledged connections or conflict between Spanish colonizers and Native people, as Sánchez did in his memory of his grandfather. A Philadelphia member of the Order who later turned informant, Tom Martinez, chose a similar approach to that of the *Primrose*. He insisted his surname came from white Castilian origins.[39] Elliott could show common cause with fellow colonists like the Spanish, provided he underscored their whiteness and masculinity.

Stegner and DeVoto had used similar gendered language, though not antisemitism, in their construction of the educated outdoorsman, but Elliott set about sabotaging any claims of the educated outdoorsman to western masculinity. In March 1980 the paper ran an article asserting that Robert B. Yegge, the former dean of the University of Denver College of Law, had propositioned an undercover male police officer posing as a prostitute. The article drew attention to the fact that Yegge had never married.[40] A Denver native and a Princeton graduate, Yegge had his similarities with the figure of the educated outdoorsman. He was a westerner who had gone East for college, and he was well respected for his career in law and his support for the arts. He also wrote for the *Rocky Mountain News* and was a consultant for the *Denver Post*. By playing on readers' homophobia, the article denigrated those organizations with which Yegge was affiliated, including organizations for the arts and outlets for respected local journalism.

Elliott also fought back when local journalists and politicians called out his prejudice. In April 1982 he used his front-page editorial to attack John Bromley, a Colorado journalist and professor. Bromley had criticized the paper for serializing *The Hidden Tyranny: The Issue That Dwarfs All Other Issues*, supposedly an interview with Harold Rosenthal, an assistant to US senator Jacob Javits of New York, in which Rosenthal presumably outlined a Jewish plan for world domination. The series first appeared two years after Rosenthal was killed by terrorists attempting to hijack an Israeli jetliner. As a result, the false text could spread without protest from its "interviewee." Titled "Fort Lupton Paper Anti-Semitism Sick," Bromley's article called *The Hidden Tyranny* "a study in hatemongering unlike anything I have ever seen in a Colorado newspaper." He asked the *Primrose*'s "readers, its advertisers, and all the rest of us who have had the misfortune to come across it" to condemn it. In his editorial, Elliott railed that the *Primrose* was protected under the First Amendment and that Bromley's own poor journalism should draw readers' ire.

Elliott reproduced Bromley's article in the same issue in which he criticized him. The article ran along with the illustration of Bromley that had appeared in the *Rocky Mountain News*. Born and raised in Colorado, Bromley attended the University of Colorado and the University of Michigan. He taught at Wayne State University, then returned to Colorado and became a Republican political speechwriter and then a columnist for the *Rocky Mountain News*. Three years after his tussle with the *Primrose*, he began teaching English at the University of Northern Colorado.[41] Bromley was not a Democrat nor a representative of the Department of the Interior, but he had gone eastward for his education, and he worked to improve public discourse in the press. Elliott's anger with Bromley demonstrated the *Primrose*'s abdication of standard journalistic ethics. Thoughtful consumers of journalism were a threat to the *Primrose*, even when their concerns were not overtly environmentalist or related to agriculture or penned by Democrats.

The *Primrose* likely acquired some of its readers a year and a half later, in December 1983, when the press wing of the American Agriculture Movement, the *AAM News*, shut down after six years. Farmers were still struggling. In 1981 the paper had begun to espouse right-wing conspiracy theories, but enough AAM members felt drawn to Jesse Jackson's Rainbow Coalition that the *AAM News* reported positively on Jackson's gatherings with Iowa farmers in the same year it shut down. But by the end of 1983, the *AAM News* editors, Alden and Micki Nellis, announced that their paper had only twenty-eight hundred subscribers and that subscriptions had declined over the past two years. When the *AAM News* closed, Micki Nellis asked readers to consider *Life in the Heart of Texas*, a magazine more focused on domestic life, which she and Alden published until 1986. Alden recommended the *Primrose*.[42]

As a result, the *Primrose* had a passing resemblance to publications like *Appeal to Reason* and the *Debunker*, which had inspired previous generations of farmers and of westerners who went east for education as Yegge and Bromley had done. To smear such figures as grifters or sellouts or of being effeminate provided cover for the *Primrose*'s hateful messaging and may have resonated with readers who felt ill served by public universities. On its surface, the *Primrose* appeared to have the same concern for rural working people and their relationship to urban consumers as did their agrarian populist antecedents. That the *AAM News* flirted with right-wing conspiracy theories and Jesse Jackson's Rainbow Coalition in the same year is not surprising when seen in light of the history of connection between people working for wages in rural and urban areas. The farm crisis brought those connections to light.[43]

A key difference between the *Primrose* and its predecessors is that these earlier publications had encouraged readers to educate themselves and to read widely. The Little Blue Books had endeavored to bring education to a mobile, working western population. They were a far cry from the John Birch Society's *Blue Book*. Movement east did not connote selling out for *Debunker* readers but, rather, curiosity. Le Sueur's enthusiasm for the Little Blue Books came from frustration with what she perceived as the exploitation of rural working people, not hatred for urban residents or urban centers. Indeed, like Cayton and Miyamoto, Le Sueur was closely attuned to the cycle of migrant workers moving between urban centers and rural hinterlands—cycles that paralleled the regions where the Order set up camp in Washington and Idaho and may have brought them into contact with migrant workers of Asian and Mexican descent in the 1970s and early 1980s.[44] Moreover, Le Sueur, Hicks, Cayton, and Miyamoto had all pursued further education. If they were frustrated with the offerings of universities, they sought to change them, not throw them out or shut them down. The *Primrose*'s regional outlook was not that of agrarian populists or western socialists or university students of the early twentieth century. Instead, the *Primrose* crafted a vision of the West as a vanished frontier and eastern government, not eastern business, as the agent of the West's loss. It was a politics of resentment, not of restitution.

If *Primrose* readers considered themselves familiar with the literary history of agrarian populism, they were unlikely to reference the *Debunker* or the Little Blue Books. Rather, most of them likely drew from a different literary source: the Little House on the Prairie series by Laura Ingalls Wilder and its television adaptation, which first aired in 1974 and concluded in 1984, the years of the farm crisis and the *Primrose*'s publication. Ranger Long, one of the *Primrose*'s columnists, made reference to the series when he described the *Primrose*'s move from Hudson to Fort Lupton, Colorado, in August 1982. He lamented that Hudson had failed to support the press and noted that "it has been a long ways from the little shack on the prairie to those fancy new offices now enjoyed by my publisher, Rick Elliott and his Cattleman's Gazette."[45] The newspaper relocated only thirteen miles west when it left Hudson for Fort Lupton, but the move marked the beginning of a very different newspaper, just as the television adaptation of Wilder's work marked the beginning of a very different series and "reinforced a powerfully simplistic reading of Wilder's work."[46]

As the writer Caroline Fraser has shown in her carefully wrought joint biography, Wilder published her books in the 1930s with significant editorial aid from her daughter, Rose Wilder Lane. Wilder's style was simple and nostalgic. The books chronicled the Ingalls family's move up and down the Midwest and emphasized Wilder's father's self-reliance and independent spirit. Children and adults alike took comfort in the scenes of familial domestic harmony as well as Wilder's close attention to the details of prairie nature. The books had millions of readers by the time of Wilder's death in 1957.

The Little House books told a pioneer story. Not until 1952 did a child write to object to the beginning of *Little House on the Prairie*, which read: "In the West the land was level, and there were no trees. The grass grew thick and high. There the wild animals wandered and fed as though they were in a pasture that stretched much farther than a man could see, and there were no people. Only Indians lived there." Wilder's editor, Ursula Nordstrom, apologized to the reader and suggested an edit that Wilder accepted. "Of course Indians are people and I did not mean to imply they were not," Wilder wrote in reply to her editor. The 1953 edition of the book read, "There were no settlers."[47] The exchange illustrated the context in which readers had received the books for two decades: as a story of white, westward-moving settlement and vanishing American Indians.[48]

The Ingalls family, however, had not really moved from east to west. In fact, the family never lived west of the 98th meridian and spent most of their years together circling Wisconsin, Iowa, and Minnesota along the 92nd meridian. To put their migration in the terms of DeVoto and Stegner, and even Wilder herself, the Ingalls lived in tallgrass prairie, not shortgrass. Most of their journeys were from north to south. Their two years in Kansas were in the southeastern corner of the state, and Wilder lived less than a total of ten years, between 1879 and 1894, in De Smet, South Dakota, the farthest west she ever lived.[49] After a bout of illness disabled Wilder's husband, the two sought out a better site for farming in the Ozarks with their only child, Rose. Wilder lived most of her life and wrote her books in Mansfield, Missouri. Mansfield, too, hugged the 92nd meridian. When Wilder famously described Osage forced migrants moving to "Indian Territory," the Osage were not filing past her Kansas home from east to west and vanishing into the sunset. Rather, they were moving from Kansas in the north to Oklahoma in the south, where they had purchased the land and its accompanying oil and mineral rights.[50]

Under the editorial hand of her daughter, Rose Wilder Lane, and in the hands of her readers, that story of northward and southward migration became a story of frontier pioneers who moved from east to west. Lane, too, was a writer, and she cut her teeth in San Francisco working for William Randolph Hearst in the field of yellow journalism. Lane encouraged her mother to present her own memories as "true" even when Wilder invented portions of the Little House series. Wilder's childhood nemesis, Nellie Oleson, for example, was a composite, but Wilder maintained the fiction that she was a real person and told inquiring readers "vaguely that she had moved back east."[51]

While Wilder remained in the Missouri Ozarks, Lane traveled widely. After an adventurous life and career that included work in California,

New York City, a home in Albania, wartime reporting in Europe, and the production of best-selling works, Lane settled in Connecticut.[52] There she gardened, canned vegetables, and continued to write. Lane had always been eccentric and contrarian, but she became more vocal and more strident in her politics, as well as more anti-Semitic, after she settled in the East.

By the close of the Second World War, Lane had become a fierce anti-tax advocate and is often identified as a "founding mother" of the libertarian movement in the United States. In 1943 she published *The Discovery of Freedom*, an anti-collectivist tract almost wholly derived from her mentor, Isabel Mary Paterson. In the book, Lane called the frontier "the god that created these United States and once made Americans strong and self-reliant."[53] She refused to accept Social Security assistance. Although she never learned to manage money well and became dependent on her mother's royalties following Wilder's death in 1957, Lane preached self-reliance. When her fellow libertarian Ayn Rand received widespread fame for her book *The Fountainhead*, Lane attributed it to the fact that Rand was Jewish.

When she died, in 1968, Lane bequeathed her politics and the rights to the Little House books to one of her mentees back East, Roger MacBride. Born in New Rochelle, New York, MacBride attended Phillips Exeter Academy, Princeton University, and then Harvard Law. Lane praised him for "combating socialism" at Princeton, and she wrote Phillips Exeter fundraisers that he would not donate unless they stopped "indoctrinating boys with socialism." While in law school, MacBride wrote a critique of the Electoral College, which was published by Caxton Printers in Idaho, one of those presses that Stegner had praised in his celebration of western literary community and which had begun publishing books that supported libertarianism. MacBride argued that the Electoral College should be retained and strengthened to empower electors further so as to elevate third-party candidates. In 1962 he won a seat in the Vermont state house of representatives. That year, too, the libertarian-leaning Freedom School near Colorado Springs named a building for Lane. MacBride campaigned for Vermont to ratify the "Liberty Amendment," a favored cause of the John Birch Society, which would have repealed the personal income tax, the estate tax, and gift taxes as well as eliminated subsidies to the Vermont state symphony, Middlebury College's forestry department, and several other popular programs that Bread Loaf attendees no doubt enjoyed. The amendment never passed, and MacBride's subsequent Vermont gubernatorial bid was unsuccessful. He went to work for the Republican Party in Virginia and in 1972 was a member of the Electoral College, where he cast his vote for the Libertarian candidate in defiance of his fellow Republicans, who supported Californian Richard Nixon. In 1975 he ran for president as a Libertarian himself. MacBride lost, as he expected, but he had support from the Koch brothers, Charles and David of Wichita, Kansas, near the 97th meridian, and enriched financial coffers from the television licensing proceeds for *Little House on the Prairie*.[54]

The TV show supported a politics resonant with that of the *Primrose*. Michael Landon, of the hit TV western *Bonanza*, quickly became the show's head writer and star, appearing as Laura's father, Charles Ingalls. With a father as the show's central character, the strict separation of gender roles that also appeared in the *Primrose* found reinforcement. Men chopped wood and supported their families entirely through their own individual farm labor; women canned vegetables and stood by their husbands. Both worked together to raise loyal children. As the *Primrose* began publication and the AAM was taking shape in 1977, its members may have watched Landon's Charles journey to Chicago and object to corruption in the collective farmers' rights organization, the Grange. Or they may have cheered Charles on when he put a neighbor's city cousin to work on the farm after the boy failed to "fit in."[55] The profits from such messages helped finance MacBride's failed campaign. A similar rhetoric—independent self-reliance, anti-collectivism, and conformity to heteronormative, gender-divided, nuclear families—propelled Ronald Reagan, a fan of the show, to the White House in 1980.[56]

By the mid-1980s, however, the show's and the *Primrose*'s messages also connected with extremists who diverged from mainstream politics. The *Primrose*'s emphasis on canning, rural living, and farmers' centrality for national success had always paralleled the survivalism that preoccupied white power groups, including Aryan Nations, the Order, and Posse Comitatus. For *Armed and Dangerous*, his book describing "Californicating liberals," James Coates chose the subtitle "The Rise of the Survivalist Right." For white power advocates, the purpose of such domestic tasks was not contentment but survival in the presumably inevitable demise of the United States. According to survivalists, that demise would follow an apocalyptic battle between Christian and non-Christians, whites and non-whites. A similar iconography marked closing episodes of *Little House on the Prairie* over the show's nine-year run. In 1983, the same year Berg was murdered outside his Denver home, Landon prepared the final installment of the series, a made-for-TV movie broadcast in 1984, in which the Ingalls and their neighbors rebel against the railroad by dynamiting their own town on Easter Sunday. They leave singing "Onward, Christian Soldiers."[57] The mild, homespun show that Ronald Reagan had publicly admired had met a different thread of the American political right halfway.

Just as pioneer mythology had covered over the Ingalls' family's migration northward and southward, so did the iconography of the *Primrose* obscure Elliott's organizing of white supremacist groups. Elliott looked from west to east when forming his rhetoric but, along with the Posse Comitatus organization, looked from north to south when forming strategy. Three Posse-related events between February 1983 and October 1984 trace the map of Elliott's influence. In February 1983 a self-identified racist and World War II veteran, Gordon Kahl, killed two federal marshals and wounded three others in a shoot-out in Medina, North Dakota, where Kahl had been organizing a Posse Comitatus group. Several weeks later, in April, a smattering of Posse supporters gathered along with members of the AAM to listen to the left-wing rural advocate Merle Hansen in Hico, Texas. Hico was not far from Iredell, where the struggling *AAM News* would soon close its doors. And in October 1984, near Cairo, Nebraska, Arthur Kirk, a struggling farmer, fired on a Nebraska State Patrol SWAT team that had surrounded his house after Kirk threatened a local law enforcement officer with one of his dozens of guns. The team returned fire, and Kirk died. Kirk had been an avid reader and supporter of the *Primrose and Cattlemen's Gazette*. Head south from Medina to Cairo to Hico, and one is never more than a degree away from the 99th meridian.

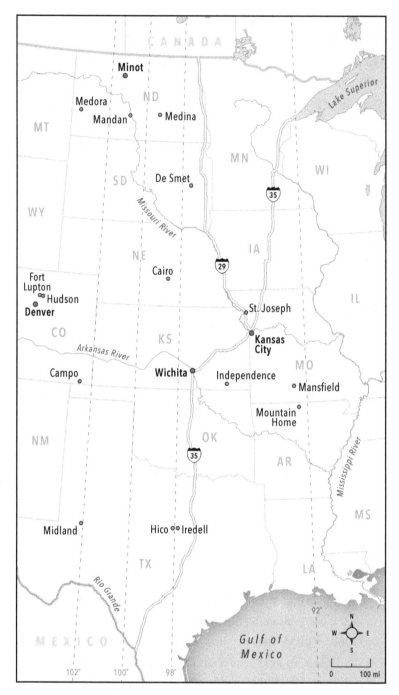

Readers' tendency to view the United States from east to west has obscured migration and movement from north to south and south to north on the Great Plains, where some have argued the West "begins." Erin Greb Cartography.

Elliott was working north to south, not west to east. From at least 1980, he identified articles in the *Primrose* as a product of NAPA, the National Agricultural Press Association, which he had founded. Beginning in December 1982, Elliott began selling memberships in NAPA. For twenty dollars, members received a certificate, a press card, and a car sticker. With his swag, Elliott headed up and down the Midwest, peddling packaged Posse-style lawsuits that he promised would void farmers' loans, all of which were accompanied by requests for donations and investment. He shared common Posse claims: banks and government were controlled by an international Jewish tribunal; no law enforcement higher than a sheriff was legitimate; farmers could declare their property a federal post and thereby deny entry to law enforcement. Elliott was probably working the I-35 corridor, completed in 1975, which wound from Laredo and San Antonio, Texas, through Wichita, Kansas, to Duluth, Minnesota. He may also have traveled I-29, which connected Pembina, North Dakota, with Kansas City, Missouri, and was completed in 1977, just as the AAM formed and the *Primrose* began publication. He appeared in Georgia and Colorado, but his focus seems to have been on the Midwest states of Kansas, Iowa, Wisconsin, Minnesota, and the Dakotas along the 92nd meridian: Wilder country.

That was where Kahl would die on June 3, 1983. After killing the federal marshals in North Dakota, Kahl fled and went into hiding south and just slightly east of Wilder's home in the Missouri Ozarks, in Mountain Home, Arkansas. There, after fatally shooting another FBI agent, Kahl was shot in the head, and the house where he had been hiding was burned to the ground. He became a martyr figure for the Posse movement. In May 1983 the *Primrose* had published Kahl's defense of his killings in North Dakota. In the same issue, it ran an advertisement from David Lane titled "The Death of the White Race," which insisted that readers' "FIRST LOYALTY MUST BE YOUR RACE WHICH IS YOUR NATION."[58] On June 15, 1983, less than two weeks after Kahl was killed, Alan Berg invited Roderick Elliott on air to spar.[59] A year later, Berg was dead, and Elliott was still working his circuit.

The Posse and NAPA gatherings that Elliott held were explicitly racist. The promotional announcement for NAPA included a full-page photo of a

Confederate flag. Elliott's speeches were laced with prejudiced rants against Jews, Cubans, and Mexicans. He called Japanese Americans "slant-eyed buggers." This was a far cry from the politics and rhetoric of Alan Simpson, who, just a few years later, cooperated with California congressional representative Norman Mineta, a Democrat, to further the Civil Liberties Act of 1988, which formally apologized for Japanese American incarceration and provided reparations. The two had met as boy scouts in Wyoming when Mineta was incarcerated at Heart Mountain and Simpson's troop visited the camp for a Boy Scout jamboree. They became lifelong friends.[60] In contrast, one watch organization veteran described NAPA as a "combination medicine show and fascist organizing project."[61] A Posse manifesto, called the "Posse Blue Book," likely modeled after the John Birch Society's, may have been passed around at such meetings.[62] Among those who may have picked one up alongside a copy of the *Primrose* was Arthur Kirk. Owing almost three hundred thousand dollars for his property and equipment, Kirk joined NAPA in 1984. As the Kansas Citian and *New Yorker* writer Calvin Trillin put it: he had problems.

Trillin, like Yegge and Bromley, had gone east for college, but like DeVoto, he stayed. His father had arrived in St. Joseph, Missouri, around the year 1909 from near Kyiv, then part of the Russian Empire. Trillin (whose family was called Trilinsky when they arrived in Missouri) would later describe his father's birthplace as "like one of those sorry, badly used farm towns which Midwestern cities sometime envelop as they expand."[63] Born in 1935, Trillin grew up paying close attention to his father's grocery business in Kansas City, attended Yale University, served in the US Army, and began writing for the *New Yorker* in 1963.

Like the dude rancher Larry Larom, Trillin and his family identified the East with Jewish life, but they did so positively, not negatively. "Looking back on it," Trillin wrote, "I assumed that the real Jews were in New York. In fact, New York was a code word for Jewish in Kansas City, in the way Lincoln was a code word for black—so that blacks went to the movies at the Lincoln and Jews bought bagels at the New York Bakery."[64] Like Larom, Trillin and his family were also aware of restrictions that barred Jews from opportunities. Inspired by the 1912 novel *Stover at Yale*, Trillin's father nurtured a dream that his son would attend the Ivy League school. When he first met with Yale representatives at Trillin's public high school college fair, he asked about quotas restricting Jewish admission. It was among Trillin's first introductions to antisemitism.

Trillin's background positioned him ideally to write about Arthur Kirk: he was from the region, his family's background predisposed him to sympathy for rural upheavals, his father's grocery business had introduced him to area farmers, he was invested in revealing the threats of antisemitism, and he was a well-published writer who understood the media landscape of the early 1980s. In his way, he recalled Struthers Burt's "educated Western man with a great deal of Eastern experience."

Beset by financial and family problems, Kirk represented struggling farmers better than most in 1984. Like Laura Ingalls, he had grown up poor on his family's farm. Even after World War II, his parents continued to farm with mules. Kirk clashed with his father over the purchase of irrigation and other equipment and left home to live in nearby Grand Island, where he went to work for the gas company. When he inherited the farm, he returned to it and borrowed extensively, with significant encouragement from federal and local agricultural agents, to purchase equipment and to farm additional land that he leased. Then the farm crisis hit. Just as credit became tighter, Kirk's son became more and more reckless, and his adult daughter died by suicide. Kirk had always been a gun enthusiast. Following a lecture from Elliott at a local Constitution study group, he tried to file one of the Posse legal complaints that he believed would void his loans. He began threatening loan officers, law enforcement, and neighbors. Trillin shared those observations from local law enforcement officers, who blamed Elliott and Posse Comitatus for leading farmers like Kirk to their ruin, but he also noted the contradictions that Nebraska farmers saw between the law's support for banks and its support for farmers. Like Kahl, Kirk became a local hero to some. Elliott appeared alongside Kirk's widow, Deloris, soon after his death, and she continued to support NAPA and publicly praised the organization for making her husband happier. One letter writer to the Cairo newspaper explained: "A large Chicago bank goes on the rocks. What happens? Several banks from around the world donate and the federal government comes with I forget how many billion dollars.... A farmer goes broke, they can't get to him to sell him out, so they kill him."[65] The *New Yorker* did not speak cow talk, but Trillin did understand the rural Midwest and its rhythms. He knew that Kirk was hardly alone in his problems.

Elliott continued his scam, but by the time of Kirk's death, he had problems of his own. NAPA members who had been defrauded of their money had begun complaining. In September 1984 the State of Colorado indicted Elliott and his wife, Karla, for theft and conspiracy.[66] Two months later, the Order's founder, Bob Matthews, was killed in a thirty-six-hour standoff on Whidbey Island in Washington State. Like Kahl and Kirk, he became a martyr to the white power cause. A joint task force—comprised of the FBI; the Secret Service; the Alcohol, Tobacco, Firearms and Explosives Bureau; the Internal Revenue Service; and the Bureau of Prisons—pursued Order members and ultimately apprehended Lane in North Carolina. In December 1985 Lane and other Order members were convicted of racketeering and conspiracy by a Seattle jury. In 1987 a federal district court in Denver indicted Lane and others involved in Berg's murder on charges of "interfering with a federally protected right resulting in a death." Prosecutors argued that the clash with Elliott on air had contributed to Berg's selection as a target. By then, Roderick and Karla Elliott had declared bankruptcy, and the *Primrose* had ceased publication. Elliott faded from the Posse, but the Posse itself and the white power groups with which it was affiliated did not. The standoff at Ruby Ridge, Idaho, in 1992; in Waco, Texas, in 1993; and the Oklahoma City bombing in 1995 showed white power's continued organization and strength. Media coverage of those events also made white power look like it emanated from the West.

Elliott knew better. If the 92nd meridian formed the Posse's eastern boundary of operations and the 99th its center, the 102nd was its western line. The AAM had formed in Campo, Colorado. Before returning to North Dakota, Gordon Kahl had worked oil fields in Midland, Texas. Head north of Midland through Campo, and one will arrive in Medora, North Dakota, two degrees west of the 100th meridian and of Mandan, the place, Era Bell Thompson had insisted, where the "real West begins." Like Thompson, Wallace Stegner had also placed the West beyond the 100th meridian. As the scholar Evelyn Schlatter has observed, Stegner saw "a gap between the reality of the West, which enforced cooperation 'even among outlaws' and the folklore of the West, which 'celebrated the dissidence of dissent.'"[67] But Stegner had left the Midwest behind. From Stegner's and DeVoto's perspective, the West was arid. The Midwest was not. When the rhetoric and the iconography of the West appeared there, it was mere folklore.[68] As for Thompson, North Dakota no longer beckoned. When she visited in 1977, friends from her Mandan days invited her to live with them in Minot. "Want me to leave Chicago and come live with them," she wrote in her notes on the trip. "No way."[69] The rural West could be a frightening place for a Black woman in the late 1970s, even one who credited her prairie upbringing for her career.

Like Thompson, like Stegner, like DeVoto, like the Udalls, Elliott looked beyond the hundredth meridian, but he looked east, not west. He took the Aryan Nations World Congress, the Sagebrush Rebellion, an enthusiasm for cowboy identity and prairie domesticity, a faith that Native peoples would vanish before colonization, and he tied it all to the fears and troubles of Great Plains farmers. He recognized that the center of the country represented one of the most marginalized of regions. He did not identify those of the Great Plains as fellow westerners. Rather, he understood that they, too, had crafted an East from the mythology of the frontier. And he knew that the American frontier, regardless of where one drew the line, ran from north to south.

Elliott encouraged readers to call the frontier home. Others built their homes, their perspectives, and their journeys from entirely different materials. They traveled the same highways with different aims. Their paths bring the story of back East to a close.

CHAPTER 6
BACK HERE, BACK HOME

Sitting in Tribes Café on the south side of Santa Fe in January 2023, the artist David Gaussoin recalled a summer internship that he had held in the Department of the Interior thirty years earlier. "It's funny. Whenever I would get homesick," he explained, he would go to the Bureau of Indian Affairs gift shop. "It was full of artwork from people we knew, from the Southwest.... I would look at the jewelry 'cause it reminded me of home. ... and the other place I would go to was the American History museum. ... they had a lowrider, and they had a feast day table with a bowl of chile. Oh, I wish I were home right now!" he would think. Sometimes he "would go upstairs to those murals by the late Alan Houser to have my lunch ... just to ground myself again ... I was just there all by myself. To me, those are our Picassos." Later David's younger brother, Wayne, who is also an artist, circled back to David's memory. "That's kind of weird. A gift shop and a history museum to remind you of home because that's their interpretation of us almost, you know."[1] Struggling with the ethnographer's imperative to listen, I suppress the desire to ask who "they" and "us" are.

David and Wayne, their mother, Connie, and Wayne's girlfriend, Olivia Amaya Ortiz, have agreed to talk with me about "back East" and allowed me to record our conversation. We are family. Connie married my mother's cousin over fifty years before we sat down for lunch at Plaza Café South and then retreated to the quieter Tribes to talk. Connie is Picuris Pueblo and Diné. I am not. She, her four children, and Ortiz are all artists. I am not. Our group shares an upbringing in the Southwest, but we have a lot of differences.[2]

I hear those differences in the course of our conversation. In the exchange between David and Wayne, I hear a little brotherly friction: they don't see everything the same way. I hear evidence of the passage of time. David's own art has been on display in the National Museum of the American Indian, a museum that did not even exist when he spent his homesick summer in Washington, DC, years ago. Today his and Wayne's younger sister, Tazbah, works there. I hear the unique pressures non-Native expectations impose on Indigenous creatives. As Wayne observes, Native artists present their own artistic subjectivity, but in the context of a museum or gift shop, they risk appearing as objects themselves.[3] I also hear the challenges of westerners navigating the pressures of back East—it beckons, and it repels. It can dictate, and it can stimulate.

I laugh a lot during our conversation. We joke about David and Wayne's older brother, Jerry, with whom I shared classes in high school. Jerry is recently retired from the army, and we are wondering whether he can adjust to the more relaxed pace of the New Mexico art world. I laugh because I am with family, and I am happy.

And also because I'm nervous. Intellectually, I'm groping. My request to interview the Gaussoins is my attempt to connect what I know of Native experience in the West with the role that the East might play in the American Indian regional imaginary. Other sources form a clearer path to the experiences of western Native writers in the East.[4] Emotionally, though, the conversation makes me feel like I'm on the right track. I am not Native, but listening to stories from family reminds me of how I first started thinking about back East to begin with. It reminds me of how an education back East compelled me to leave home.[5] It helps me to connect the dots among writers, universities, and the East.[6]

In addition to my effort to ground myself, I've asked David and his family to speak with me because I have a vague memory that David was recruited to attend Dartmouth College in New Hampshire in 1992. Although David and his family are not writers, Dartmouth is the alma mater of Louise Erdrich, an enrolled member of the Turtle Mountain Band of Chippewa and probably the most commercially successful living Native author in the United States. I'm curious how the recruitment of western

Native students to the Ivy League and the reception of Erdrich's work intersect.

Dartmouth has a long and complex relationship with Indigenous peoples in North America. Its eighteenth-century charter required that the school educate Native Americans, but that mandate largely fell by the wayside until the 1970s, when activist pressure, new leadership at the school, and Native students together pushed for the university to meet its founding commitments.[7] Although Dartmouth's charter writers had in mind Indigenous people of New England, most of the Native students whom Dartmouth recruited at the end of the twentieth century were from west of the Mississippi River. Erdrich's popularity, along with the experiences of Native students recruited to the school, reveal a different East than that imagined by most non-Native westerners.

Like Ricardo Sánchez, many western Native students saw schools like Dartmouth as vexed tools, potentially "alienating as hell."[8] The history of government and religious boarding schools that were designed to assimilate Indigenous peoples of Canada and the United States haunted late-twentieth-century Native students who pursued education in the East generations later.[9] Dartmouth and other elite universities tried to outgrow the condescending pressure that they had exerted against previous generations of Indigenous students, but individual, tribal, and institutional memory made the process uneven. Through their training, their connections, and their travel, students returned with educational knowledge for others like themselves. When they could dodge the assimilative pressures of the academy, the journey and the particular school were ancillary. The real destination was back home.

That meant that Native students formed their regional outlook around a narrative axis that stretched from their homes elsewhere. These lines did not always go eastward. Some Native students were easterners. Other Native students charted a north-south axis, as Sánchez often did, stretching across the United States–Mexico or United States–Canada borders to comprise Native nations that transcend US boundaries. International connections with both Indigenous and non-Indigenous peoples of other countries drove students too. Because storytelling is crucial in Native religious practice and for self-determination, these narrative axes operated in daily, professional, and political realms, even when students did not identify first as writers.[10]

Students who told the stories that situated themselves and their tribes as parts of journeys endeavored to share the insights of their homelands while building institutions that moved out from under eastern expectations. The murals of Chiricahua Apache artist Alan Houser, which David called "our Picassos," served this function, as did the lowrider in the American History museum. These elements of home, which sparked nostalgia and homesickness for David, educated audiences from outside the Southwest in the region's culture, but, as Wayne observed, they could also reinforce non-Native and non-western expectations of what Native people and the West are. In part to escape such expectations, Native students endeavored to build the museums, markets, bookstores, and schools that provided that education closer to the places that they called home and in environments in which they determined programming and curriculum. These places and efforts were sometimes products of colonialism themselves or marginal to mainstream cultural expression in the United States or marginalized some Native groups at the expense of others. Nonetheless, as they had for Sánchez, the margins could feel like home.

When western Native students encountered eastern Native communities, they moved away from outlooks that associated Indigeneity with the West and whiteness with the East. Instead, they acknowledged Indigenous independence amid multiple colonial forces across North America. As intra-tribal statements of independence grew, intertribal relationships created a different regional landscape for Indigenous America. Students learned that east was just one of many directions they could choose to go.

"It triggers a lot, back East." The day before I speak with Connie, David, Wayne, and Ortiz, I sit down with Regis Pecos, the former governor of Cochiti Pueblo, in Hotel Santa Fe, a hotel owned by Picuris Pueblo. The hotel is on the other side of town from Tribes Café, closer to downtown tourist centers, including Plaza Café, the parent restaurant to Plaza Café South and located on Santa Fe's first plaza, a center of Spanish colonialism. I am aware of how Hotel Santa Fe, steps from the city's popular farmers' market and what might be the city's fastest-growing tourist district, the Railyard, challenges a story of the Southwest's seamless incorporation into first the Spanish and then the US empires.[11] The hotel's presence and Native ownership denies conquest and the easy triumph of US industry.

Pecos and I are not family. We have talked previously about his lifelong efforts in the field of education, and I am seeking that grounding in our interview as well as information about his experience as a student at Princeton in the 1970s. He is in town to advocate for the education of Indigenous children in the state. He has spearheaded programs for education in Native languages and fought for a victory in the *Yazzie-Martinez* case, in which plaintiffs successfully argued that the New Mexico state constitution guarantees an adequate and culturally appropriate education for children.[12] We have been talking for almost an hour when I use the phrase *back East*. I think that he looks startled. "It's a reference . . . like with older people in our communities," he begins. "In the English translation, that reference . . . there's lots of connotations that come with that reference."[13] Pecos's reaction reminds me of Sánchez's poetry and the layers of language, memory, and history that rest within an imagined place, whether writers explore it in the center of the page or on the margins. *Back East* exists in multiple languages, and its translation affects its reception.[14] It can trigger a lot.

Before I use the phrase *back East*, I ask Pecos what his expectations of Princeton were. He remembers "one of those things that [was] among the most ridiculous and funniest" about his expectations was that he took his best clothing to school with him and then came to the "quick realization that students were coming to school in tennis shoes and torn jeans and T-shirts." He came to the conclusion that "it was no different than perhaps anywhere else in the country." Nonetheless, Pecos had observed that student behavior at Exeter and Princeton was different from what he was accustomed to among Cochiti elders and among teachers at his Albuquerque high school. He noted that he "used to be amazed at my peers and how they were never at a loss of an opinion on any issue and so often [I] would think as a freshman, 'How do these kids learn to be so opinionated?'" He came to the conclusion that families had prepared students to aggressively pursue elite educations and realized "that that's how families on the East

Coast consciously perpetuate . . . their lineage's access to financial and political power."[15] Memories of eastern elites and their pressure to pursue goals aggressively remained for Pecos.

Native students at Ivy League schools a generation later, in the 1990s, had similar experiences. In an effort to avoid scrutiny from classmates and teachers, they often favored T-shirts and jeans to look as much like other students as possible. At the same time, they worked to maintain behaviors that they considered consistent with their own Native identity. When an Anthropology instructor at one institution grossly misrepresented the social arrangement and Native language of a female student from a tribe in the Southwest, she did not challenge the professor. Anthropologist Bryan McKinley Jones Brayboy (Lumbee), who called the student "Debbie" in his 1999 study of Native students at elite schools, asked why. She paused, reflected, and responded: "I was always taught to respect my elders. He is my elder, and I must respect him. What he said is not right, but it is not my place to correct him. He will learn. . . . I could not say anything to him." Brayboy concluded that this was "a strategy Debbie employs for a larger cause: she and her elders recognize the power of a degree from an Ivy League university. They have made a choice for her to engage in schooling for the long-term good and not to get caught up in issues that may impact her psychically."[16] Debbie had "never been out East and never lived in a city." She chose to attend her school because she "wanted to try that and see what it was like" and because she "wanted to do something for her tribe." In class, Debbie refused the cultural norms of elite schooling. She refused to be, in Pecos's terms, "so opinionated." Her strategy allowed her to maintain her tribal identity and also her and her tribe's goal of gaining an education at an elite school back East.

Other Native students had similar encounters. In the foreword to a collection of Native students' memories of their experiences at Dartmouth, Louise Erdrich observed that "remarkable in a capitalist society, and yet perhaps not amazing given the sources, not a single narrative is about the wish to attain status, the ambition to make large amounts of money, or the desire to become famous. Instead, these students make a circular path, and even wind backwards down the generations, *come home.*" She credited her own success to her fellow Native students, the Native American Studies department, and the financial aid officers at Dartmouth who "got so many students through the next and the next month at Dartmouth." Rather than prestige, the goal of a Native education at Dartmouth for many was to make it through and return home to help family and tribe.[17]

Navigating such overlapping pressures could be difficult for a Native author like Erdrich. The critic, novelist, and founding editor of *Wičazo Ša Review*, Elizabeth Cook-Lynn (Dakota), explored these layers in depth beginning in the early 1990s. "Euro-American scholars throughout the ages," Cook-Lynn observed, "have been willing to forego the discussion concerning the connection between literary voice and geography and what that means to Indian nationhood." Cook-Lynn argued that Native independence, whether achieved through intertribal cooperation or a single tribe's activism, played a central role in the imagination of Native people and therefore the novel writing of Native authors. She praised Laguna author Leslie Marmon Silko for connecting her literary voice to geography and to Indian nationhood and called Silko's 1991 *Almanac of the Dead* "perhaps the most ambitious novel yet published by an American Indian fiction writer which fearlessly asserts a collective indigenous retrieval of the lands stolen through colonization."[18] *Almanac of the Dead* centers Tucson, Arizona, and imagines intertribal cooperation across Mexico and the United States to reclaim the Americas. Cook-Lynn praised it for engaging the imagination necessary for nationalist assertions among Indigenous peoples. Like some of Sánchez's poetry, the book attends to the ongoing colonial effects of Spanish presence in the Americas and therefore follows a trajectory that moves from south to north, rather than east to west.

In contrast, Cook-Lynn criticized Louise Erdrich for "unabashedly" saying in a 1992 interview, "I am probably an Easterner who mistakenly grew up in the Midwest."[19] Cook-Lynn queried, "How can one be a tribal nationalist and 'set the pace' if one claims no connection to the land either in one's personal life or in one's fiction?"[20] For me the criticism resonated with a memory of Pecos's, which he shared when describing his return to New Mexico after beginning his studies at Princeton. Pecos realized that for many of his former schoolmates, he was "the one from back East," and he felt compelled to "deal with, dismiss, minimize that perception." Identifying this challenge, his non-Native high school English teacher, who had recruited him to finish his secondary schooling at Exeter and then attend the Ivy League, invited him to speak to his former classmates. He asked if Pecos would be "a professional Indian." Later in our conversation, Pecos explained that "a professional Indian is what, in a subtle way, the East creates."[21]

In 1992 Erdrich may have appeared to some as a "professional Indian." Early in her career, she claimed more of a connection to geography than she did Indian nationhood in her personal life and in her fiction. Her comment regarding "mistakenly growing up in the Midwest" followed her observation of her work that "it has a lot to do with where I grew up [in North Dakota]. I set myself back in that pure, empty landscape whenever I am working on something . . . the place where everything comes from." While Erdrich described the landscape as "empty," she clarified further in terms that refuted frontier narratives familiar to non-Native readers: "People aren't 'lighting out for the territory.' The women in my books are lighting out for home.'" As Cook-Lynn observed, however, Erdrich herself appeared committed to remaining in the East. Erdrich followed her comment much like Bernard DeVoto may have: "I never felt very accepted or at home in my hometown. There are terrific people there but I found growing up there difficult because the emphasis is on conventionality. You have to conform."[22] Erdrich said that she would likely never return to the Midwest even though it provided her creative inspiration. While she rejected narratives that described people "lighting out for the territories," her own biographical narrative in 1992 moved along the same axis but from West to East, rather than East to West.

Born in 1954, Erdrich is the author or coauthor of seventeen novels for adults, one collection of short stories, and seven children's books. She is also the author of two works of nonfiction and three collections of poetry. Her first novel, *Love Medicine*, won the National Book Critics Circle Award in 1984. Her novel *The Last Report on the Miracles at Little No Horse* was a finalist for the National Book Award in 2001, and *The Plague of Doves* was a finalist for the Pulitzer Prize in 2009. Several of her novels follow interlocking generations of characters living on a fictional reservation in the northern plains. Her children's book *The Game of Silence* won the Scott O'Dell Award for Historical Fiction and forms part of a series chronicling the day-to-day life of an Anishinaabe girl living on Moningwanaykaning, the Island of the Golden-Breasted Woodpecker (also called Madeline Island), in Lake Superior. In addition to her successful career as a novelist, Erdrich's Twin Cities bookstore, Birchbark Books, recalls Ricardo Sánchez's Paperbacks . . . ¡y Más! and represents the kind of institution that Wallace Stegner celebrated when he saw that the West had created a literary culture to compete with that of the East.[23]

As an Indigenous woman who has contributed significantly to literature about the northern plains, Erdrich fits neatly into the category of the western writer, but her East was not formed by westernness. Erdrich came of age in a region that some, including herself, categorize as the Midwest. Her novels and her career have often centered rural and urban spaces that most would characterize as midwestern, not eastern or western. Like Hicks, Le Sueur, Thompson, Elliott, Trillin, and Sánchez, Erdrich indicates that midwesterners and westerners both constructed an East.

That East, as Cook-Lynn intimated, played an important role in Erdrich's development as a writer and a public figure. Erdrich arrived in the East in 1972, "a bewildered freshperson in red cowboy boots, a member of the first class of women and Native Americans," she remembered. "Four years after, I left wearing a pair of resurrected moccasins."[24] Although Dartmouth's 1769 founding charter dedicated the school to serving Native Americans, only about twenty had actually graduated by 1970, and most of those students had been subject to steady assimilative pressures and overt discrimination that included school celebrations of the "Dartmouth Indian" mascot.[25] In 1970 the university's new president, John Kemeny, asserted that Dartmouth would begin genuinely serving Native students. Erdrich was among the first to participate in Dartmouth's experiment.

Kemeny's effort corresponded with increased attention from the non-Native press to Native activism and Native artistic expression in the late 1960s and early 1970s. In 1961 the National Indian Youth Council formed in Gallup, New Mexico, and pressed for a greater Native voice and young Native influence in federal Indian policy.[26] In 1968 the American Indian Movement formed in Minneapolis, and in 1969 Native students who dubbed themselves "Indians of All Tribes," began an occupation of Alcatraz Island that lasted until 1971.[27] Also in 1969, Kiowa author N. Scott Momaday won the Pulitzer Prize for his novel *House Made of Dawn*, making him the first Native author to win a Pulitzer Prize for Fiction. These events formed the background for Kemeny's decision.

So also did an institutional assumption that Native people lived only in the West. When Kemeny announced his goal of enrolling sixty Native students in four years, he did so in regionalist terms. "As the Indians were pushed farther West, it just didn't seem practical for them to attend," he asserted. Dartmouth responded to Kemeny's announcement by recruiting heavily among midwestern and western tribes. Indeed, as the Dartmouth professor and historian Colin Calloway has concluded, "Few people today think of Dartmouth as a school in the heart of Indian country—quite the contrary: for many Indian students and their families in the West, Dartmouth is 'out there' in a remote northeastern corner of the country, far from the Indian communities they know—yet it is a school with a role in Indian country."[28] David Gaussoin expressed a similar sentiment when he spoke with me about his recruitment to the school in 1992: "Because I was Native they said, you need to apply. I had no idea what I was applying for. . . . Where the heck is this?"[29] By 1990 more than 125 Indigenous students, representing fifty-five different tribes, were enrolled at Dartmouth, but celebrations of the "Dartmouth Indian" continued, and for some western Native people, New England and Dartmouth appeared distant, unfamiliar, isolated, and hostile.

Nonetheless, as an Ivy League school with close proximity to Bread Loaf in Vermont, one of the nation's best-known writers' colonies, Dartmouth likely connoted a writer's life more readily than did most western colleges in 1972, when Erdrich arrived. Following her 1976 graduation, with majors in English literature and creative writing, Erdrich earned a master's degree from Johns Hopkins University in Baltimore and then went to work for *The Circle*, the Boston Indian Council newspaper. She worked for the program Poets in the Schools in North Dakota and returned to Fargo to write her first novel, *Love Medicine*. She did not participate in American Indian Movement protests such as the occupation of the Bureau of Indian Affairs in 1971, the occupation of Wounded Knee in 1973, or the Longest Walk, which arrived in Washington, DC, in 1978. In 1980 she became romantically involved with Michael Dorris, who identified himself as of Native descent. He served as the first director of Dartmouth's revived Native American Studies program and had been one of Erdrich's professors while she was a student. Dorris was a single father of three adopted Native children. Dorris and Erdrich married in 1981, and Erdrich became a writer-in-residence at Dartmouth. The spouses worked closely together on their literary projects. At the time of her 1992 interview, they had been widely recognized in the non-Native press for their literary work.[30]

A series of tragedies changed Erdrich's relationship with the East. In 1991 the couple's eldest child was killed in an auto accident. Ongoing friction with their other adopted children and Dorris's declining mental health, which may have included sexual abuse of his children, led to his separation from the family in 1996. In 1997 Dorris died by suicide. In 1999 Erdrich moved to Minnesota and opened Birchbark Books in 2001.[31]

Like Debbie's silence in class, Erdrich's move to Minnesota might have been a choice to work in and from the margins. Although Erdrich continued to publish with marquee publishers headquartered in New York City, her work centered the Upper Midwest and featured Native people and communities prominently. Independent bookstores are notoriously fickle enterprises, as Sánchez knew well, and the opening of Birchbark Books was a risk. As Regis Pecos observed when discussing school textbooks: "Who dictates? In education it's often those from the East, right? There is the perception that that's where the intellectualism is; that that's where people come from who are privileged and over time that's who controls academia and that's who controls the narrative and that's who controls the market of materials produced and in that is this narrative that now permeates all of our society . . . and we now succumb to that whole market system . . . but are marginalized within that framework."[32] In her pursuit of eastern educational and professional opportunities, Erdrich recognized the power that the East held over publishing and literature. At the same time, she recognized the voice and worldview that she could express from the Upper Midwest as both a writer and an independent bookstore owner. Like the students in Brayboy's study, she took what she needed from the East to further her region's and Native people's stories.

That did not mean that Erdrich abandoned attention to the East. Her 2004 novel, *The Painted Drum*, explores the separation from home that she may have felt during her years in New Hampshire. *The Painted Drum* begins with the story of a mother and daughter who descend from an Ojibwe woman who "was taken east and enrolled at Carlisle Indian School, in Pennsylvania. . . . The young teacher whom she married kept her in the east."[33] The two women live in a small New Hampshire town near a prestigious unnamed university in the late twentieth century. The East is not necessarily an exile in *The Painted Drum*, but it creates a distance between the mother and daughter and their relatives farther west. When observing her romantic partner, the daughter comments on her and her mother's liminal status among locals. "That is why we are not really Easterners," she concludes, "and partly why, I suspect, Krahe finds me interesting—he can't quite place exactly who I am."[34] *The Painted Drum* does not focus on the women's experiences as attenuated members of their tribe, but it does call attention to the distance that western Native people, including Erdrich herself, may have felt back East.

The passage in *The Painted Drum* reminds me of something that Regis Pecos and David Gaussoin described as well. Pecos remembered a series of narrower and narrower questions from his classmates at Exeter that began with the query "Where are you from?" David similarly observed that "going out East" for his internship made him "realize how Black and white America is . . . once I get out of the Southwest, I realize I'm brown . . . when I go out East I can feel the way that people look at me. . . . If you don't fit between those colors, you start getting this weird look, like, what are you? The long hair throws them off because they can't categorize you as Mexican. . . . When you're brown you can fit in a lot of places but it also throws people off; it's almost like they don't realize that Native Americans still exist."[35] Like David, Erdrich uses the phrase *out East* rather than *back East*.[36] The East is not a place to which they "returned" nor a region that "reclaimed" them. Rather, it is a foreign place with its own racial orders and codes, ones that do not always include Native peoples and the stories of their journeys.[37]

One of the challenges Erdrich has faced in her work is changing those orders and codes by anticipating or preempting the question: Where are you from? As Cook-Lynn's criticisms and Silko's novel suggested, that requires both challenges to US colonialism and the introduction of different narrative axes. As a result, the presence of Indigenous people does not consistently signal a western setting in Erdrich's novels as it did in Thompson's memoir, DeVoto's histories, Stegner's reveries, Cayton's and Miyamoto's academic studies, and Elliott's screeds. Erdrich's work has identified the east-to-west axis of US colonialism, and her own early biography trod that ground in reverse, but her fiction has also offered alternatives.

Erdrich's work has taken on colonialism and presented Indigenous survivance directly.[38] In its attention to domestic detail, her children's book series is similar to the Little House on the Prairie books by Laura Ingalls Wilder but intentionally challenges Wilder by presenting Native people as fully formed characters navigating competing pressures of settler colonialism rather than one-dimensional stereotypes. Like many of her books, the series also centers the Great Lakes as a region, rather than the West. *The Round House*, her 2012 novel, addresses sexual violence against Native women and the restrictions that the US federal government places on reservation justice systems.[39] Her fiction and her professional presentations locate Indigenous homelands throughout the United States, including the East, and in the present. In her 2009 Dartmouth College commencement keynote address, she acknowledged that the college sits on Abenaki land.[40] Via her inclusion of Michif and Métis characters and history, Erdrich has gestured toward those Native communities whose lands stretch across the US-Canada border and who understand their histories along north-south axes independent of US and Canadian settler colonialism that moved from east to west.[41] Increasingly, Erdrich's work has emphasized that *Indigenous* does not mean "western" and that the East has an Indigenous past, present, and future.[42]

That focus is apparent in her 2020 Pulitzer Prize–winning novel, *The*

Night Watchman, in which she constructs an East as an origin point of US colonialism. *The Night Watchman* differs from much of Erdrich's work in that it chronicles the changes of a real reservation and describes historical figures, including her grandfather Aunishenaubay, Patrick Gourneau, the chairman of the Turtle Mountain Band of Chippewa Advisory Committee during the mid-1950s. Gourneau's chairmanship overlapped with the US federal government's efforts to terminate reservations as Indigenous sovereign territory protected by nation-to-nation treaties, an effort that Erdrich, in her author's note, calls "a new front in the Indian Wars" and that Gourneau called "the worst thing for Indians to come down the pike."[43] Based on research that Erdrich conducted with the historian Brenda J. Child, *The Night Watchman* fictionalizes Gourneau's successful resistance to the federal government's termination efforts, efforts concentrated in the American East. The novel acts as a public correction to the archival record, which has often muffled and distorted Indigenous voices by presenting them only as representatives of the US state heard them.[44] In fact, Erdrich concludes her acknowledgments with the statement: "If you should ever doubt that a series of dry words in a government document can shatter spirits and demolish lives, let this book erase that doubt. Conversely, if you should be of the conviction that we are powerless to change those dry words, let this book give you heart."[45] The novel both questions and contributes to the archival record by bringing a broader history to a public audience in an accessible form that allows emotional reactions to the events of the past.[46]

Erdrich conveys an understanding of the East as an origin point of colonial power and influence that extends westward. That place first emerges in a conversation between Gourneau (called Thomas in *The Night Watchman*) and his father, Biboon, whom Thomas has sought out for advice about how to respond to the federal government's termination effort. Thomas's father suggests a strategy in which the tribe presents itself as an economically vital part of the region that would be lost if federal recognition of the tribe ended: "We're not nothing. People use our work. You got your teachers, nurses, doctors, horse-trading bureaucrats in the superintendent's office. You got your various superintendents. You got your land-office employees and records keepers." Erdrich explains that "all of these jobs and titles could be expressed in Chippewa. It was much better than English for invention, and irony could be added to any word with a simple twist." Biboon concludes: "Make the Washington DC's understand. We just started getting on our feet. Getting so we have some coins to jingle."[47] Erdrich's East, like the Udalls', is in Washington, DC.

Like many other westerners' Easts, Erdrich's East is intimidating. Overworked, sleep-deprived, and anxious, Thomas frets over the stakes of his plan to bring a delegation to Washington: "What on earth would a person do in Washington? How would they get there? Where would they stay? What if Arthur V. Watkins took him apart? The word was out on Watkins. He raked Indians to pieces with his words and his ways. What if Thomas failed? If he couldn't speak up? If he couldn't argue the case? If they got terminated and everyone lost their land and had to move to the Cities and he had to leave his home behind? What of his family? What of Biboon?"[48] Watkins, a key character in the termination effort, was a senator from Utah, but his westernness makes him no less "a Washington DC" in *The Night Watchman*.[49] As in DeVoto's New York or Sánchez's Yale, the East is a potential site of condescension and disempowerment.

Patrice, a fictional character, also draws a line around the East and the Washington DC's. She journeys with the delegation to talk about her work building jewel bearings for military watches and compasses, a task completed by real women from the reservation in the 1950s at the Turtle Mountain Ordnance Plant. Prior to delivering her testimony, Patrice sits in the Ladies' Chamber of Congress to acquaint herself with congressional proceedings. While there, she is an eyewitness to the 1954 Capitol shootings by Puerto Rican nationalists. Security guards take Patrice aside for questioning about one of the nationalists, and "it occurred to Patrice then that the woman with the dark hair could have been her sister." Patrice feels a kinship with the woman: "She realized that here in Washington she'd seen people shot, a thing she'd never seen before, not even on the reservation, a place considered savage by the rest of the country.... It was the woman in the pale brown suit she'd watched, her falcon eyes, her fearless cries, how she held the gun with both hands, how she had tried to unfurl a piece of cloth, red, white, and blue, to snap it out. And how awkward while holding the gun. How Patrice's impulse had been to say 'Here, let me help you.' To shake out the cloth for her. A flag, certainly a flag of her country."[50]

Patrice resolves to cleanse herself of violent thoughts and meditates on how she can support and protect her home without them. She identifies with the Puerto Rican nationalists, but she does so on the basis of politics, not regionalism, and she rejects violence as a means to her nation's sovereignty.[51] When she returns to the jewel-bearing plant after the delegation has successfully defended the Turtle Mountain Chippewa's land, a friend from the reservation asks, "Now you've been to Washington DC, are you too good to talk to me?"[52] The warm conversation that follows is an indication that Patrice still sees the reservation and its community as her source of pride and support. She still sees it as her place. What makes the East is not its location but its political relationship to her reservation.

In sum, *The Night Watchman* shows that Erdrich does not assume a US nation as a governing frame.[53] Speaking with an interviewer in 1988, just four years after the publication of *Love Medicine*, Erdrich reflected on the meaning of region in her work. The interviewer asked: "I grew up in the Southwest where there was virtually no such thing as a full-blooded Indian; everybody was mixed. Yet, as I grew older, I became aware that there were parts of the country where there was prejudice. Do you think it's a regional question?" Erdrich's answer suggested that she considered regions not as unbroken spaces on a map but from the perspective of human relationships, both political and racial, where borders could create threats for some but not others. "Yes," she said. "I think it is different in different parts of the country. Where Indian land impinges on valuable non-Indian land, or where non-Indians feel threatened, the prejudice is heightened, definitely. There's antagonism when people aren't safe from each other, when non-Indian people feel that something could be taken away."[54] What makes the East the East in *The Night Watchman* is not its place on the map but the desire of its most powerful white figures for Native land.

Erdrich's 1988 interviewer obscured deep prejudice against Native peoples in the Southwest. Residents of the region did not blithely accept that "everybody was mixed." Descendants of Spanish colonists worked hard to distinguish themselves from Native neighbors by identifying themselves as white rather than Native or Mexican or mestizo, a custom that Elliott had observed at *The Primrose* in his identification of "the Contessa." Among their efforts was an annual celebration, dubbed "Fiestas," a pageant in which a man of Spanish descent plays the role of Don Diego DeVargas, the Spanish colonist who led the 1692 reconquest of New Mexico following the 1680 Pueblo Revolt. For decades, Pueblo people had objected to the reenactment of their own conquest, and Pecos helped to negotiate between ardent supporters of the festival and its detractors for the elimination of the "entrada," a ceremony in which a DeVargas reenactor led a parade, with Native people at the rear, into the Santa Fe Plaza.[55]

Attuned to the pedagogical force of local festivals, Pecos argued that the event had erroneously instructed people in the region's history. Reconquest was not bloodless, as it is often portrayed, and Native people did not accept festival leaders' accounts of the event. Echoing some of the themes that Sánchez explored in his poetry, Pecos explains that "racism . . . and discrimination . . . is internalized and then people need to become [the] oppressor. . . . Internally you want to elevate yourself when race is part of a weaponized response to you." As a result, Pecos sees New Mexico as following "that colonial framework of reenacting conquest."[56] The result in daily life and in commemoration has been a tiered racial structure in New Mexico that places Mexican and Native people on the bottom and encourages people of Spanish descent to seek association with whites and whiteness.

White newcomers to New Mexico initiated Fiestas with aid from New Mexicans of Spanish descent. These local boosters imitated "frontier" celebrations elsewhere in the West such as the one that Micki Nellis of the *AAM News* helped run in Iredale, Texas, in the 1980s. Fiesta boosters endeavored to impress upon easterners and southerners that US independence from England was not the entirety of North American history. New Mexico's celebration emphasized Spanish influence in the Southwest instead and acted as a rejoinder of sorts to US conquest in the middle of the nineteenth century.[57]

As historical instruction, Fiestas have failed the region. Noting the complexity and diversity of the Southwest's history as well as the precious role that children play in traditional social structures, Pecos concluded that "we could be the example and the model of what education can be and should be in terms of children being valued . . . so that diversity is celebrated in the schools; we are celebrating the worst part of our history and that is conquest."[58] Pecos's observation reveals that tilting the narrative axis of historical investigation does not necessarily empower or liberate students of history in the Southwest. Charting Spanish conquest from south to north rather than US conquest from east to west can still result in a celebration of colonization.[59]

For David Gaussoin, tilting the narrative axis did not lessen the familial tension over the possibility that he attend Dartmouth either. My mother's cousin, David's father, wanted David to attend. He believed that the school would elevate David's standing and provide a firm financial foundation — the standards of success that contributed to New Mexico's tiered racial structure. As David explained, "I'm sure you had similar experiences with your parents, you know our dad came from the same family as you, and he had these very Americana ideas of what it was to be a man and what it was to be successful, and it was completely opposite of what we learned from our mom. . . . I was constantly dealing with that struggle . . . he used to say you can't make a living as an artist and to me that was always very discrediting to my mom . . . washing away her whole career, but I had to prove to him that, yes, I can be successful as an artist, and I can make a living. And be a hell of an artist!"[60] David credited his internship at the Department of the Interior for showing him what he did *not* want for his future. "I'm glad I received that training," he reflected. "It made me come back and realize I am an artist — this is who I was and who I was meant to be."[61] David narrated a struggle between white assimilative pressures and Indigenous cultural perseverance that played out as tension between his mother and father over his college decision and culminated with a fuller realization of himself.

More was at stake than familial well-being or his career. As David weighed the decision, he also drew on influences from his grandmother and his aunt, who had begun preparing him for traditional duties at Picuris Pueblo. "My dad was saying go, go, and they were saying stay, you need to stay home because you're the one who has to carry on ... and I'm glad they did because ... things would have been lost.... it *wouldn't* be good if I went out East." More was at play than David's career. As he concluded: "Because we are very based in our traditional teachings, I honored, respected their decisions and I realized the decision wasn't just mine only to make.... I don't regret it at all. If I had gone out there, who knows?" The traditions of Picuris Pueblo require presence at the pueblo. David could not pursue his training from a distance. David's younger brother, Wayne, clarified further: "It's a way of living, and *it has to be here*.... If you want to be committed to that, then *you have to be here*."[62] Connie emphasized the interconnections of family, faith, and place when she remembered: "They wanted someone who was truly interested in listening to them.... They saw it in him.... They saw something in David, and it's happened, it's happened in the past years, within our family, and David has followed through with what they wanted him to follow through with.... He's teaching our family, *our* family, who are interested in this.... It's a true serious religious thing there, that I'm not going to get into, but people who know will know what I mean. Thank you, David, *che, na, ho*." As Connie concludes, her gratitude to her mother, her sister, and her children affects all of us.

The depth of David's commitment and the intense meaning of home for him and his family makes our other conversation seem lighter. Wayne jokes that David chose the University of New Mexico, UNM, as "the university near mom," instead of Dartmouth. But there is no question that the decision meant more than proximity to family. As Wayne reflects at one point, "Our grandpa was encouraged to come to Santa Fe ... [he was compelled to] learn this American, white system," but, Wayne continued, "I don't know [why] you can't be successful in your own location." He recalls that our generation of Santa Feans were raised to "go out there to learn so you can bring back." Yet he wonders: "Bring back what?"[63]

I venture the opinion that Dartmouth might have provided the opportunity to meet people from other tribes. David is in agreement. He recalls that his own early schooling included little Indigenous education. The textbooks that marginalize Native people make it difficult for Native people to learn about tribes other than their own. David's time in Washington,

DC, introduced him to the Mashantucket Pequots and their history. He recalls that his boss at the Department of the Interior was Osage, a tribe with which his whole family was unfamiliar before his internship, even though Connie grew up on Osage Street in a neighborhood in which several streets had names drawn from tribes in North America. (We laugh about this too.) David also had an opportunity to meet Charles Blackwell of the Chickasaw Nation, the first ambassador of any Native American nation to the United States. "I had no idea what the Chickasaw Nation were!" David recalled. "So it was an introduction, not just out East but to other tribes. And to learn about their ways, and they're still alive, and it was cool."[64] It was perhaps such experiences at Dartmouth that led Erdrich to describe her arrival in cowboy boots and her departure in moccasins.

Connie insists that regional exchange is "a two-way street." As a teenager, she participated in the traveling entertainment group Up with People and developed a lifelong appreciation of travel as education. "I knew where I came from," she remembers. Not only did she disabuse host families of common misperceptions about Native peoples and share aspects of her own upbringing as Diné and Picuris Pueblo; she credits her travel with her knowledge of the Sami in Norway and the Kuna people of the San Blas Islands in Panama. Moreover, all three family members agree that connections to museums, galleries, and collectors back East and in Europe have aided their artistic careers and given them opportunities to learn about the artistic practices of other parts of the world. "If you're an Indigenous artist from here and you go out East," Wayne says, "you kind of almost have to do it because it does give you credit . . . to build your résumé, to build your career."[65] All of them see advantage and opportunity in travel, including travel back East.

Nonetheless, Wayne notes: "I think in the same light, there are a lot of Indigenous artists not from here that *come here* to kind of gain the same thing." David interjects, "Cred." "The Native art mecca is here," Wayne concludes. When I ask him if he's had opportunities to meet eastern Native artists, Wayne replies: "I did because it was here. . . . I was aware of other Indigenous cultures throughout the United States, but it was at IAIA [Institute for American Indian Arts] that I learned, that's where I learned a lot."[66] None of the Gaussoins are surprised to meet eastern Native artists today. Connie recalls that she "dated this one guy who was Mohawk" whom she met at IAIA in the 1960s and maintains contact on social media with other eastern Native friends she met in the same years. The Gaussoins' cosmopolitan education started in Santa Fe.

IAIA has its own connections back East. The school grew out of the Santa Fe Indian School "Studio," which trained area Native students in the arts. As a former Indian boarding school, IAIA began with strict rules regarding student behavior that mimicked the assimilationist agenda of such schools from the 1940s and 1950s. Artist Alfred Young Man recalls that when he arrived, the school's grounds were still designed to keep students from leaving.[67] Two of the school's directors had close ties with Arthur Watkins, the "Washington, DC," who "raked Indians to pieces" in *The Night Watchman* and spearheaded the termination policy.[68]

The school also operated under the aegis of the Department of the Interior. Among the school's exhibitions outside New Mexico was one held in the Interior Department gallery resurrected by Lee Udall. Udall subsequently hosted the American Indian Performing Arts Festival in Washington, DC, which included both an exhibition in the Interior Department gallery and a series of performances directed by IAIA's Cherokee art director, Lloyd New.[69] Udall also arranged "An Evening of American Indian Art," consistent with the cabinet's "An Evening with . . ." artists series, which included a performance by IAIA dancers for the president of Burkina Faso (then called Upper Volta). Other students were recruited to perform for international audiences in subsequent years and to further exchange with African youth and international audiences in Latin America. The gift shop that David visited on homesick afternoons descended from these gatherings.

IAIA was an exemplar for the "elite" beneficiaries of Indian education. When Lady Bird Johnson visited at Udall's invitation, she presented the school as a showcase for her husband's efforts to further democracy. "America is a country that puts high value on education," she stated. "Talents are not frustrated here. They unfold in an environment that nurtures the spark of genius that lies in every man. . . . Here . . . they find living expression in

Western Native students brought impressions of "out East" to peers and mentors following attendance at eastern colleges and universities and through diplomatic exchanges such as this IAIA student performance at the White House, 1965. IAIA Archives, RG 03, box18, Santa Fe, New Mexico.

the finest of traditional works, and the most imaginative of contemporary ventures."[70] Johnson foreshadowed the conclusions that Wayne would draw about the school decades later.

At the time of the school's founding, some local Pueblo and Diné peoples were skeptical. As the school opened, the governors of Cochiti Pueblo and Tesuque Pueblo, Joe Trujillo and Martin Vigil, respectively, objected that the transformation from studio program to independent institution meant that Pueblo children would no longer receive the vocational education that the Santa Fe Indian School and Bureau of Indian Affairs had originally promised Pueblo families. Speaking on behalf of the All-Pueblo Council, Vigil insisted that there was no need for a school for the "arts elite." Rather, he contended, "our greatest need is education." A reporter for the *Navajo Times* noted that the school was designed for "the cream of the crop" and that it was "making the unique Indian cultural and artistic heritage a strong and moving force in the business life of America."[71] Pueblo and Diné leaders cautioned that the non-Native arts and business leadership of Santa Fe Pueblo might dictate IAIA programming in the same way that they had that of Fiestas. So long as Native education rested in US government hands, the school risked sending colonialist messages. Back East had a way of showing up out West.

Native art instructors at the school insisted that they could move out from under colonialist expectations. Like Sánchez and Lorde had argued in their advocacy on their NEA panel, IAIA founder Lloyd New insisted that the arts themselves constituted education. He included poetry and theater in the arts. In response to a student anthology, he noted that "a back-up program is needed for these newly discovered student-writers, whose particular talents—as Indian writers—are likely to be nullified in the academic approaches of this country's standard institutions."[72] New had trained at the Art Institute of Chicago and, before establishing IAIA, taught Native student artists in Phoenix. He encouraged students to identify with their specific tribal background to foster their educational development.

David remembers from a conversation with New that the IAIA founder "wanted to get American Indian students excited about school. If [he] had to do it through art, so what."[73] Students pursuing the arts thrilled to the opportunities there. The poet Joy Harjo (Mvskoke Creek), who studied visual arts at the school and graduated in 1976, recalled that "the Indian school world was rife with paradox. Formerly run like a military camp by the Bureau of Indian Affairs, the school had been transformed into a unique school for native arts, like the New York City *Fame* school but for Indian students." Nonetheless, she remembers that "it was in the fires of creativity at the Institute of American Indian Arts that my spirit found a place to heal. I thrived with others who carried family and personal stories similar to my own. I belonged. Mine was no longer a solitary journey."[74] Harjo had previously considered attending Chilocco Indian School in Oklahoma, and IAIA teachers also reminded critics that Haskell Indian College in Kansas was available for students seeking a more traditional college education. There were alternatives for Native students pursuing higher education in the 1970s but only one school for Native students in the arts, and it was not back East.

Fifty-eight years after Robert Frost celebrated colonialism at John Kennedy's inauguration, Harjo became the first Native poet to serve as the US poet laureate. She met with Senator Tom Udall, Lee's son, as she toured the Library of Congress in her new role.[75] Two years later, Deb Haaland (Laguna Pueblo) became the first Native cabinet secretary when she became the secretary of the interior, the position Lee's husband, Stewart Udall, had held. Harjo and Haaland carried forward the tag team of culture and politics that had marked earlier generations of Native students who visited the US Capitol. Although Harjo described her writing instruction at IAIA as uneven, she is among many Native writers that the school has produced and supported since it refined and expanded its writing programs. Distance programming designed by instructors and administrators with an understanding of the limits of rural reservation schooling and the centrality of place for Native authors has allowed a vast network of Native peoples to participate in the writing program. In addition to Harjo, a partial list of notable instructors and graduates includes Esther Belin (Diné), Sherwin Bitsui (Diné), Chelsea Hicks (Osage/Wazhazhe), Oscar Hokeah (Cherokee Nation and Kiowa Tribe of Oklahoma), Layli Long Soldier (Oglala Lakota), Bojan Louis (Diné), Jake Skeets (Diné), David Treuer (Ojibwe), Toni Jensen (Métis), Tommy Orange (Cheyenne and Arapaho), Kelli Jo Ford (Cherokee), and Terese Marie Mailhot (Seabird Island Band).

Seven months after I visited with the Gaussoins and Regis Pecos, I met with Deborah Taffa (citizen Quechan Nation and Laguna Pueblo descent), the director of IAIA's MFA program in creative writing, which has produced many of the school's noted alumni. Like Connie, David, and Wayne, Taffa thrills to the cosmopolitanism of the school.[76] She glows as she tells me, "It's like a think tank of some of the greatest Indian intellectuals in the country."[77] She does not see the current vogue of Native artists as a peak in Native publishing. "I don't want to hear that this is a renaissance period," she told *Publisher's Weekly* in 2023. "*Renaissance* implies there will be a decline, when instead the publishing industry is waking up."[78] Alongside the school's writers, Taffa refers to the school's connections to political advocacy—one of the school's artists and deans, Charlene Teters (Spokane), led the I-Am-Not-Your-Mascot movement; several have connections to intertribal political organizations such as the National Congress of American Indians; and several attended or have family members who attended universities back East, such as Harvard.[79] The writers whom the school is currently producing appear to be the norm, not a renaissance.

Taffa is not averse to education or travel back East, but like Cook-Lynn and Silko and Sánchez and Pecos and the Gaussoins, she perceives a broader swath of Indigenous country that sweeps across the Americas. Her first trip East was to Maine in 1988 to work for the Audubon Society's efforts to protect the North Atlantic puffin. Three of her children attended Yale, and her own memoir—a contribution inspired by her father, who told her that the world needs Indigenous voices—was published by HarperCollins, one of the "big four" publishing houses headquartered in New York. Kwatsaan (Quechan) peoples were separated from one another in 1853 when the Gadsden Purchase redrew the US-Mexico border, a history that influences her viewpoint. "I think that a lot of my expectations of where Indian country is—I think of the entire continent North and South as being Indigenous in both heart and spirit," she says. She locates "those sort of strongholds of Indian Country" as "the Southwest, the Dakotas. . . . You see obviously that you're in Indian country. . . . I still feel Indigenous Indian country there [in Oklahoma]."[80]

Throughout Indian Country, whether in the Southwest, the Dakotas, the Penobscot Indian Nation in Maine, among the Lumbee tribe in North Carolina, in Oklahoma among the state's dozens of tribes, or north and south of US borders, Native writers trace journeys that head in all directions. Oklahoma particularly denies the easy application of any directional axes because forced removal brought tribes from the South, North, East, and West to the state when several tribes already called the region home. Just as Chicago did for Seattleites Cayton and Miyamoto in the 1930s and 1940s, Oklahoma can appear as the East in contemporary western Native author's work. In "By Alcatraz," a short story by Osage-Wazhazhe author Chelsea Hicks, a character describes herself as from "out East." She's from

Oklahoma.[81] When I asked Pecos if he thought that a time would come when Native students no longer felt compelled to go back East for school, as he had done, he replied, "I think the time is already here, and kids go all over."[82] The settler colonial narrative axis that moves east to west or, for many westerners, west to east, no longer applies for twenty-first-century Native students.

The emergence of Native intellectual centers such as IAIA and new narrative axes of inquiry can create differences and friction within Indian country. Pecos notes that students who have participated in programs that take them out East are sometimes surprised at the coloring among Native students in other parts of the country. When I asked if they are darker or lighter than Southwest Native students expect, Pecos replied, "Both!" He observed that "it's quite a pleasant surprise for our students from the West to learn of the continued existence of Indigenous people on the East Coast."[83] Differences of climate and culture affect Native representations of Indian Country too. Erdrich gently satirized Santa Fe in her 2021 novel, *The Sentence*. The headstrong stepdaughter of the novel's central character lives there after dropping out of IAIA. She waits tables, and her stepmother worries that pornographers will take advantage of her desire for an acting career when the city is "flooded with artists and collectors at Indian Market," an annual event with ties to Fiestas and at which the Gaussoins have exhibited their jewelry and fashion in the past. The stepdaughter "wants to live down there forever, or until the water runs out, at which time she plans to move up to Lake Superior." Her stepmother insists that she "won't be able to afford it, just the way you can't afford Santa Fe now."[84] Western Native ignorance of eastern Native experiences, climate change, gentrification, and the precarity of creative labor makes Santa Fe no Eden for Native artists, even though the presence of IAIA places the city at the center of Native creative endeavors, not in the margins.

The Gaussoins are well aware of these forces. Wayne laments how many gallery owners are from outside the region. Connie frets that the pattern of conquest and extraction that marked white settlement in previous centuries extends to artistic and intellectual labor in the present day. "The people from out East are coming here to get their knowledge and then they go over there to write about their knowledge," she says.[85] I am self-conscious about my own residence in St. Louis, east of Santa Fe, as well as my running recorder. Later, when I express my concern that maybe I have come to get knowledge and will go away to write about it, they remind me of my role. "When you're from an area, you're accountable to that area," David tells me. "You're from here, you're family . . . that's what makes you different . . . we know where you're from."[86]

It is perhaps this accountability that motivates Ortiz when she talks about her own relationship with the East. Following our conversation at Tribes, when I err by identifying her as Chicana, she gently corrects me. "I respectfully enter spaces by identifying myself as Chicana of Mescalero Apache descent." Originally from Tucson, Ortiz's narrative orientation stretches northward and southward from the US-Mexico border. "My mom's from literally on the border," she tells me. Like Taffa and the characters who appear in the books of IAIA-trained writers Tommy Orange and Oscar Hokeah, Ortiz perceives herself as part of a complex mix of Mexican and Indigenous culture in the Southwest.

Ortiz's visits East were sometimes tense. Before her first trip, her mom told her that she always felt "like a little bug in a mason jar" when she went East. The phrase reminded me of the "specimens" visited by eastern tourists in the Little Blue Books or the "marginal men" studied by University of Chicago sociologists. Ortiz was perplexed by the phrase, but once she arrived, she felt the same. In Tucson, she said, "you always look to the mountains to orient yourself. Whereas on the East Coast, I can't get my bearings." Ortiz traveled adventurously and lived for a while in Alaska, but climate and culture combined to bring her back to the Southwest. "At one point I was also encouraged to go out East and apply to schools there," she remembers, but she decided against it. "I feel good here," she says.

Accountability to a place breeds a certain kind of attachment. One can leave, as I have done, or begin one's quest from a different place: North, South, even out East, but the place you're from confers a responsibility. Learning the terrain, listening to the natural world, absorbing the lessons of family, revising one's knowledge of history and culture in conversation with one's community, apologizing for mistakes, making amends, and endeavoring to improve all take time and effort and require commitment. To travel does not lessen that responsibility or that attachment. Ortiz's conclusion applies regardless of where students begin or end their journeys seeking a creative life. "My idea of success is back here," she says, "back home."[87]

CONCLUSION
EASTWARD I GO ONLY BY FORCE

In the 1969 film *Easy Rider*, the film's leads ride motorcycles east across a bridge spanning the Colorado River. One, played by Peter Fonda, is bedecked with a helmet and jacket sporting the American flag. The other, played by Dennis Hopper, wears a cowboy hat. Steppenwolf's "Born to Be Wild" sounds over the opening credits. In a pre-credit sequence, Wyatt (also called "Captain America") has secreted a fortune in drug money in the gas tank of his motorcycle, which matches his outfit. With Billy he heads East to celebrate Mardi Gras in New Orleans and then retire in Florida. They never make it. After visiting with a white farmer and his Mexican family in Arizona, a white commune in New Mexico, and an alcoholic white lawyer whom they meet in a Texas jail cell, they have a bad LSD trip with a pair of white prostitutes in New Orleans and are shot and killed somewhere in the South by white men in a pickup who are hostile to counterculture hippies.[1] With its odyssey qualities, western iconography, and violent themes, *Easy Rider* has sometimes been called a "western."[2]

But what if it's an "eastern"? Like a counterculture Stegner and DeVoto, Wyatt and Billy attempt to carry the benefits they see in western counterculture eastward. When Wyatt explains to the Arizona farmer that they are from Los Angeles, the farmer reveals that he was headed to California himself but never made it. Wyatt assures him that he has made a living from the land. Fonda provides a characteristic cool lift of his chin in approval of the commune's efforts to support themselves. The film's high point is a scene with no dialogue but laughter as Wyatt and Billy frolic in a desert swimming hole with women from the commune. When Billy calls the alcoholic lawyer a "dude," the lawyer, played by Jack Nicholson, takes offense, but Wyatt explains that *dude* "means 'nice guy,' a regular sort of person." The film's heroes try to disabuse those they meet of calcified, outdated notions of what is acceptable behavior, notions that the film implies emanate from the East.

That the two travelers meet their demise in the South is not surprising. If the Northeast offers prestige and fulfillment in most westerners' narratives, the Southeast denies it. The East is a region in the western imagination, but the South is a racist, sexist, homophobic regime. It has almost always been where western creatives have located the nation's hostility to difference. Captain America and Billy might have an inflated sense of westerners' open-mindedness and influence, but whatever their motivation, they are unable to carry their vision to the Eastern Seaboard. The South stands in their way.

Western aficionados might remain unconvinced. *Easy Rider*, they might say, is an anti-western, that genre of western films that questions the individualism so often associated with traditional westerns. They might argue that Captain America and Billy's demise is a product of decadence, an overindulgence of their own will. When Billy and the lawyer lament the hostile stares and comments that they have received in a southern diner, the lawyer explains: "What you represent to them is freedom. . . . It's hard to be free when you're bought and sold in the marketplace." Maybe Wyatt and Billy are undone by their own appetites, or maybe they are just victims of an ever-present capitalism. If the counterculture of *Easy Rider* dodged the market through illegal drug trading, unorthodox fashion, back-to-the-land self-sufficiency, and liberated sexual encounters, it never escaped the inequalities that marked who bought and sold drugs, clothes, food, land, and sex. *Easy Rider* might be suggesting that it's hard to be free.

If so, then the West might be a regime of its own—a settler colonial one created by the East and revealed in a hitherto unmarked genre: the eastern. Consider Wyatt and Billy's journey. They acquire their drugs in a Spanish-speaking country, perhaps Mexico, given the film's quick transition to the Colorado River. The few Mexican American characters do not speak, although some Spanish-language graffiti appears on the walls of the Texas jail where Wyatt and Billy meet the lawyer. Mexican people appear as the white farmer's wife and children and as figures on the side of the road: boys riding horses bareback, men and women working fields. These figures on the margins become Black as the motorcycles cross into Louisiana. The sole Native face in the film is a mask in a Mardi Gras parade. The racial marginalization of back East is at play in *Easy Rider*, as are its economic patterns. White men can travel a narrative axis from west to east and believe they carry liberation with them, but that doesn't mean it's an open road for all. Farmers and back-to-the-landers can share what they've managed to accumulate, but that often means sending yet more wealth eastward with dubious emissaries. Indeed, it is hard to find a better metaphor for the apotheosis of settler colonial late capitalism than drug money concealed in a gas tank painted like the American flag.

If *Easy Rider* is an eastern, then it might have company. *Five Easy Pieces* (1970), which we might call a "regionalist eastern," since it never leaves the West, follows a Texas oil field worker northward to Washington State, where the lead, played by Jack Nicholson, is haunted by his own and his family's musical prowess demonstrated in a photo montage of their performances back East.[3] Or consider the handful of coming-of-age films that explore American identity through the western student's quest eastward. In *American Graffiti* (1973), a pair of young white men weigh the cost of leaving their California friends and cruising culture for a college like Middlebury in Vermont. The Chicana protagonist of *Real Women Have Curves* (2002) emerges from the New York subway after proving to Los Angeles family, neighbors, and friends that she deserves the opportunities of an eastern university education. In the 2017 film *Lady Bird*, the white hero from Sacramento seeks a school that's "like Yale, but not Yale" because she "probably can't get in there." And of course, many a New York City was created on Hollywood film sets.[4]

If the eastern film genre collapses too easily into Los Angeles and Hollywood, one could return to those people with connections to the writers who appear in this book. Although Wallace Stegner decried the counterculture, his student Ken Kesey had his own deep relationship with both the East and the counterculture. The phrase *back East* appears in Kesey's book *Sometimes a Great Notion* at least fifteen times, and an overlay of western masculine swagger and feminine eastern domestication serves as one of the book's themes, just as it does in some of Stegner's novels. Several figures attached to those who do appear in this book could tell different stories of back East. Possibilities might include Sanora Babb, who told the story of migrant laborers before John Steinbeck brought their plight to a national audience; Mari Sandoz, who dissected settlement and economic exploitation of the plains alongside Meridel Le Sueur; Arna Bontemps, whose characters and neighbors recalled Louisiana on the streets of Los Angeles; Yuriko Amemiya, who married Charles Kikuchi and danced with the Martha Graham Dance Company; Chet Olsen, who advocated for conservation in the halls of government with Bernard DeVoto's aid; Norman Maclean, who swaggered like Stegner in his relationships with eastern publishers; Frank Chin and Shaun Wong, who crossed paths with Ricardo Sánchez after battling S. I. Hayakawa when Hayakawa blocked the introduction of an ethnic studies program at San Francisco State University; Maxine Hong Kingston, who wrote Stegner about her experiences back East and battled with Chin over representations of Asian American gender roles; suffragist Nina Otero-Warren, who attended school in St. Louis and was the first New Mexico woman to serve in Congress; and Deb Haaland (Laguna Pueblo), the first Native secretary of the interior.[5]

If one wanted to expand into the genres of art and music and television, one could consider Missourian-turned-Montanan Charlie Russell, who used the margins of his letters to produce art that commented on eastern cities and fashion; Jackson Pollock, who credited Diné sand paintings for inspiring his own style; Mike Medicine Horse Zillioux (Akimel O'odham–Cheyenne–Pawnee), who commented in his work on Pollack's sloppy technique; Jaune Quick-to-See Smith (citizen, Confederated Salish & Kootenai Tribes), whose paintings frequently depict maps that query and mock settler colonialism; Seattleite Jimi Hendrix, whose most famous performance occurred at Woodstock in New York State; Nebraskan Laura Love, who comments on race relations from the plains; *The Fresh Prince of Bel-Air*, in which Philadelphia plays the role of authentic Black America; *The Bear*, in which a character relishes the statue of Ceres, the goddess of agriculture, atop the Chicago Board of Exchange as a "big fuck you to the East"; and *Reservation Dogs*, in which Native Dartmouth students condescend to Native high schoolers in an Oklahoma reservation community center and the character Rita dreams of smoking cigarettes on a fire escape in New York City.[6]

Back East is all over the place once you know how to look. Still other interpretive frames could yield new stories of the East. How did closeted queer westerners navigate the implications of the phrases *out West* and *back East*? What did it mean to be an out westerner? Or an out westerner back East? (Might Nicholson's character in *Easy Rider* fear the charge of effeminacy implied in the term *dude*? Or might he have signed onto a mission to bring a greater variety of sexual and gendered expression eastward and southward?)[7] The alternative realities and futurism of Octavia Butler and Ursula Le Guin offer possibilities for exploring back East in westerners' science fiction. Bill Gates, who spent a semester at Harvard and began Microsoft in a garage in Albuquerque before moving to Seattle, is another westerner who had back East on his mind. I think, too, of the regionalism of lifestyle magazines and foodways. *Sunset* magazine regularly used the East as a foil to sell the charms of western living. Charles Lummis's magazine *Out West* probably used the expression *back East* more than any other publication of the twentieth century. And I recall the Wyoming blacksmith who gave me his card. His motto: Get it hot and hit it! He remembered his teen years when his job for the Valley Ranch near Yellowstone included meeting a plane with food deliveries from New York City. "I am sure," he told me confidently, "that I am the first person born and bred in Cody, Wyoming, to eat a bagel."

Of course, other scholars undoubtedly could add to this list in ways that I have not considered. This is a book about western writers, and I identify as a western writer but as many other things besides: a cisgendered straight woman, a mother, a white person, and an able-bodied, middle-class, middle-aged academic. I am not a citizen of any tribal nation, and my status as a citizen of the United States is documented. My identity has undoubtedly shaped this book—from its embryonic stage during my college experience back East to my vexed reading of the news over the last two fretful decades.

I am aware of the privileges that my identity gives me, how they led me to write this book on Native land throughout the United States, and how they directed me to writers and archives and libraries and universities in my research. While doing this research, I regularly reminded myself that these institutions are often closed or hostile to those who do not share my identity and privileges. Despite those reminders, I am sure that I made some mistakes and that there are different stories about back East yet to be told.

Before you get carried away, though, let's consider the words *we* and *us*. When I used those words in this book, I did so to refer to readers. If we're persuaded that the East is a region, that westerners invented it, that liberalism shaped its contours, and that, as an invented region, the East shaped American culture in profound ways, then we might be tempted to chase some of the ideas I have charted in these pages. We might want to see what happens when we look for back East in film, art, television, music, and the work of a still wider cast of writers. We might be tempted to shut down liberal institutions—the archives, libraries, and universities that memorialized the work of some writers but not others and that squirreled away evidence of Native resistance to settler norms. We might question the value of democracy itself.

I encourage readers to navigate these temptations carefully. Writers may be the most mobile of creative artists, but they need archives and libraries and universities, and we do too. We need them even when they are unfair and even when they are underfunded and even when there are fewer and fewer of us. We need them for investigations of the conventional center and the unconventional margins. By revealing westerners' images of the East, this book calls attention to flaws of mid-twentieth-century liberalism: its capacity to marginalize in the name of inclusion and its lie that following the frontier's axis—whether pointed out West or back East—brings progress. How to maintain liberal institutions like libraries, archives, museums, and universities without swallowing such flaws? We need to imagine.

That means turning our gaze to those left on the side of the road in *Easy Rider*. This book shows how writers of the twentieth century navigated the presumption of settler colonialism and their own western regional upbringings in tandem. That negotiation reveals some of the flaws of liberalism, including its capacity to marginalize and its tendency to mask that marginalization under the promise of progress. It also reveals westerners not just as people from a place but as people with perspectives. What westerners saw and heard and smelled and felt and imagined has a history too. Western stories are not solely stories of settler colonialism nor stories of the West as a region.[8] Like archives, libraries, and museums, they are also expressions of subjectivity, and westerners bring diverse perspectives to the page. Easterners do not always write the script. The East does not always determine the axis along which westerners travel. Regardless of where they begin and end their stories, westerners' perspectives deserve telling too.

Liberalism requires compromise, and compromise favors the most powerful, and scholars of the American West have sacrificed too much by meeting scholars of the nation halfway. Replacing studies of the frontier with studies of the regional West and its relationship to the US nation can take us only so far. People move, and their imagination shapes what they see along the way.[9] Westerners need not pull up short at the Mississippi or the Missouri or the Rio Grande or the Columbia or the Colorado Rivers. They can cross every border that surrounds them. They have before. They can do it again. We just have to be willing to acknowledge their perspectives.

Libraries, archives, museums, and universities can show us the way. The People's College in Kansas and Union Graduate School in Ohio and IAIA in New Mexico moved out from under the expectations of an extractive, settler colonial framework when their administrations and faculty invested in the subjectivity of their own students. Students charted their own paths. With help from professors, librarians, curators, and independent booksellers, they read along the way. They challenged regimes. They did not always look back East or down South or up North or out West. They started from different conceptions of regions and of home and of themselves. We can follow their lead. We have imagined regions before.[10] We can imagine new ones now. In the words of yet another westerner who could be in this book but isn't, we can begin anywhere.[11]

ACKNOWLEDGMENTS

> You start thinking you're going to be Proust, and end happy if you've written a few pages you're not wholly unwilling your friends should see.
>
> —THEODORE MORRISON (paraphrasing Bernard DeVoto)
> to Wallace Stegner, September 19, 1945,
> Wallace Earle Stegner Papers

Serious research for this project began with a Saint Louis University (SLU) Provost Leave. Much thanks to Chris Pudlowski and Kelly Goersch, who, along with Provost Nancy Brickhouse, Phil Gavitt, and Hal Parker, made that research possible. A Summer Stipend from the National Endowment for the Humanities; a Resident Fellowship at the Buffalo Bill Center of the West, Cody, Wyoming; a Stolle grant from the SLU College of Arts and Sciences; and a sabbatical, approved by Provost Mike Lewis, allowed me to finish writing and to prepare the book for public reception. All errors, of course, are mine.

The interdisciplinary, community-minded frisson that is the SLU American Studies Department past and present gave me the freedom and the blueprint to write this book. Emily Lutenski, Heidi Ardizzone, Ben Looker, Kate Moran, Matt Mancini, Terri Foster, and Mark Cange, you all don't know how awesome you are.

My first efforts to get my thoughts on paper were inspired and nurtured by George Miles, Phoebe Hyde, John Liang, John Turci-Escobar, Andrea Campe, Silvana Siddali, Anne Hyde, Diana DiStefano, Laura Ferguson,

David Borgmeyer, and Christine Luebbert. Sarah Costello let me enjoy her beautiful home for a few days while I dipped into the archives at Reed College. Jim and Aleda Haug graciously hosted me on a visit, at the invitation of Kristen Buckles, to the Tucson Festival of Books held on the University of Arizona campus, where I was also able to conduct research in the Stewart Udall Papers. The festival is a brilliant and necessary celebration of the written word, and I'm so glad that I was able to attend and to work with the fabulous staff of the University of Arizona Libraries there just as this project began to germinate.

The Wallace Stegner Symposium held by the Ivan Doig Center at Montana State University in 2019 was a game changer for this book. The essay that I wrote for that gathering grew from the kind, generous, and brilliant assistance of Michael Lansing, Leisl Carr Childers, Michael Childers, Melody Graulich, Nancy Cook, Adam Sowards, Alexandra Hernandez, Bob Wilson, and Mark Fiege. Michael Lansing has been an indefatigable supporter of this book ever since and remains an ongoing source of inspiration. Thank you, Michael. My fellow Stegner symposium attendee Sara Gregg invited me to the University of Kansas to share portions of chapter 4 with her and other environmental historians, including Greg Cushman, Brian Frehner, and Joshua Nygren. Thank you, Sara.

A subsequent invitation from Alexander Finkelstein and Anne Hyde to a panel at the American Historical Association–Pacific Coast Branch conference and an accompanying edited collection on regionalism allowed me to refine my vision for the book as a whole and visit the Wallace Stegner Collection at the University of Utah's beautiful archives (and the Hell's Backbone Grill along the way—a truly magical trip). Thank you to the anonymous reviewers of that collection, whose feedback gave me a push when I needed it. Independent research from SLU alumna Nicole Madden allowed me to round out chapter 4 with details from daily life inside the beltway. My graduate students and undergraduates in the spring of 2021 allowed me to write alongside them in the American Studies Dissertation Colloquium and the History senior seminar. That work began to cohere at an SLU Women's and Gender Studies Brown Bag. Insights from Amanda Izzo, Jenni Semsar, Gretchen Arnold, Torrie Hester, Jennifer Popiel, Doug

Boin, and Lorri Glover led me to draft (finally!) an appropriately sized California interlude. Giuliana Piccione did the heavy lifting to prepare my bibliography and clarified much of my prose. She always worked with a smile. Thank you, Giuliana.

Librarians and archivists have been crucial to this project, just as they were to the lives of the people described in this book. Armed with my dim instructions and whatever one calls a Post-It note from 1919, Michelle Gachette at Harvard University Archives found exactly what I was seeking when I first published on this topic. SLU librarians Jamie Emery and Rebecca Hyde got me started on my Udall research. This project could not have been completed without Reed College Archives and Stanford University Special Collections. Gay Walker introduced me to the *Pacific Spectator* at Reed. Richard White told me I was on the right track when I first dived into the records at Stanford. Leif Anderson and Tim Oakes helped me with the Ricardo Sánchez Papers at Stanford when I returned, and Anneke Swinehart and Sean Kelly housed and entertained and educated me for a portion of that visit. Scott Daniels at the Oregon Historical Society made sure that more of Edith Green's experience in public service made it into published writing. Nathan Bender, Eric Rossborough, Ashlea Espinal, and Mack Frost gave me a friendly Wyoming welcome to the McCracken Library holdings at the Buffalo Bill Center. Gordon Ambrosino and Hunter Old Elk and, at SLU, Caitlin Stamm and my fall 2023 Native American and Indigenous Studies graduate seminar showed me how I might plant seeds for the future. One cold night, Beverly Cook at the Vivian Harsh Research Collection of the Chicago Public Library told me that I must learn about Era Bell Thompson. Now I can't imagine this book without her. Beth Loch and Cynthia Fife-Townsel followed up on every detail when I returned to the Woodson Branch of the Chicago Public Library. I can't think of a better argument for more funding for archives in public libraries than the Harsh Collection. Jori Johnson and Ann Sneesby-Koch at the Stephen H. Hart Research Center in the Colorado State Historical Society Library saved me weeks of travel and labor by digitizing records for me. Charles Taylor of Slough Press taught me much about the Texas poetry and bookstore scene. John McKiernan-Gonzalez just doesn't stop, and I'm grateful to him for inviting me to Texas State University (TSU) and to him and Sherri Turner-Herrmann for introducing me to the Wittliff Collection and to the work of Rolando Cortez and Penca Books in San Antonio. The TSU Center for the Southwest and the Clements Center at Southern Methodist University have allowed me to see Texas as a region rather than regime. Regions are better.

A fabulous discussion with Katherine Morrissey, Michael Lansing, Molly Rozum, Megan Birk, and Bryan Winston at the annual Western History Association conference in 2022 validated my thinking on the Midwest. Bryan's research for me on agrarian populism and his own research on the Mexican Midwest brought my first chapter and the "Texas Interlude" into focus. Annie Gilbert-Coleman and Peter Blodgett have been steady inspirations for this project. Peter also provided a reading of my proposal and used his deep knowledge of the Huntington Library's holdings to keep me on track. Mark Harvey knows everything about Bernard DeVoto and generously shared his knowledge with me. Discussion over good wine with Marsha Weisiger at multiple conferences let me better understand the Pacific Northwest and especially Oregon politicians. Ryan Carey responded to more than one archive-inspired text message with good humor. Leisl Carr Childers puzzled through the mysteries of local and national politics with me. On a bus ride to Las Vegas, Phil Deloria set me straight on American Indian students back East. Conversation on cutting-edge work in the field of western history with Nic Ramos, Beth Lew Williams, Joshua Garrett-Davis, Meg Frisbee, David Wrobel, Andy Kirk, and Kristen Buckles shaped this project in more ways than one. A double thank-you to Josh, who along with Gingy Scharff, Marni Sandweiss, Nancy Marie Mithlo, Anthony Macias, Emily Lutenski, and Steve Aron gave me a chance to think about the imagined East in light of the imagined West as we reconsidered the Imagined Wests galleries of the Autry Museum. Anthony provided inspiration and just the right reading recommendations on a subsequent visit to St. Louis. Sherry Smith and Rob Righter welcomed me to their Wyoming home and listened to my research finds with generous support. Louis Warren and Anne Hyde read multiple pitches for this book. Thomas Andrews, Katie Benton-Cohen, and Jenka Sokol provided a subtitle.

I'm grateful for the Western History Association, which has brought me together with so many brilliant thinkers. Among them are John Findlay and Jen Seltz. No part of this project could have been completed without John. He anticipated the idea of the mythic East before I had finished graduate school and with grace and generosity let me know. Jen introduced me to Jane Smiley's Century Trilogy, which influenced this book in numerous ways. I wouldn't have finished this book without Jen. She is hands down the best reader I've ever met.

This book had to be produced by a western press, and Mike Baccam and Andrew Berzanskis knew it before I did. Mike pointed me in the right direction with every gentle editorial nudge. Anonymous readers reports improved the manuscript enormously. Emily Feng got me organized with great patience. Joeth Zucco and Elizabeth Gratch provided elegant refinement. Much thanks to everyone at the press for preparing a beautiful book.

My gratitude to Jenny Price, Ellen Crowell, Juliana Chow, and Rachel Greenwald Smith for their example as writers, teachers, and thinkers.

Pam Sanfillippo and Diane Weber at the Gateway Arch National Park allowed me to present the Arch as the gateway to the East at a teacher training symposium in Indigenous history and culture. Much thanks to Craig Howe, Sarah O'Donnell, and Bob Moore for expanding my American Indian history knowledge at that event. The 2023 Counterpublic triennial and the 2022–23 STLr City/Indigenous St. Louis group, funded by the Mellon Foundation Divided City grant and wrangled by Gavin Kroeber and Charlie Boscoe, supported many of my back East musings. My gratitude to Pam Begay, Eric Pinto, Galen Gritts, and Rico Rose for deepening my knowledge of Indigenous studies; to Liz Childs and Tamara Schenkenberg for their determined commitment to art; to Alex Marr for expanding my art education and sharing his expertise on IAIA; and to Paige McGinley for her general awesomeness and for introducing me to Malinda Maynor Lowery, who encouraged me to bring my head and heart into alignment.

Ana Romero y Carver reminded me that this is a book about writers and artists and that creativity and imagination lie at its heart. Without Ana, there would be no stoop for my brother, and without my brother, there would be no stoop at all. Thank you, Ana. Thank you, Martin. Sharon

Ullman extended a helping hand to a homesick westerner back in the days of Stoopdude and never stopped believing in me.

A number of colleagues traded work with me as I drafted chapters or listened with open ears. Much thanks to Rob Good and Laura Westhoff for touching down in the flyover; to Fran Levine, Lisa Krassner, Hannah Nyala, and Robin Hoover, who reminded me that not everyone sees through westerners' eyes; to Leisl Carr Childers, Tori Herrera-Cannon, and Michael Karp, who reminded me that a lot of people do; to Enrique Dávila, who reminded me that Texas is different and Texans are varied; and to Natasha Howard, who reminded me of westerners' blinders and greatly enhanced my understanding of how geographers think. Nancy Bell guaranteed that I never forgot the South, and my NCFDD faculty success group cheered me on in the earliest stages of my writing. I am grateful to Gingy Scharff, Marni Sandweiss, Mary Madigan, Michael F. Brown, and the School for Advanced Research (SAR) for giving me the space and time to connect with colleagues, friends, and family in New Mexico as this project took root. My 2023 SAR summer course students provided more than one insight that I was able to incorporate into part 3. Thank you. My gratitude to Tarra Hassin and Brian Lax, who hosted me for some of my New Mexico musings, and to Maria Archuleta always for listening to my voice. Vanessa Fonseca-Chavez's excellent model taught me how to get started in oral history. Connie Gaussoin, David Gaussoin, Wayne Nez Gaussoin, Olivia Amaya Ortiz, Regis Pecos, and Deborah Taffa gave their time and energy to interviews with generosity. Thank you.

I come from a family of westerners and was lucky enough to marry someone from back East (well, Pittsburgh) who also came from a family of westerners. Thank you, my family, for understanding what I was up to all these years and for generously underwriting my research and my self-confidence.

This book has occupied my household for many years. Rusty and Tempo kept the beat. Kevin, my debunker, kept me honest. Pat held my hand. This book is for him.

NOTES

Preface

1. Gregory Lehane, dir., *Ghostwriters*, season 1, episode 14, "Into the Comics: Part 1," December 27, 1992, Children's Television Workshop, New York City.
2. Treatments of the frontier's dominance in scholarly interpretation include Cronon, "Trouble with Wilderness"; Grossman, *Frontier in American Culture*; Hyde, *American Vision*; Limerick, *Legacy of Conquest* and *Something in the Soil*; Marx, *Machine in the Garden*; Smith, *Virgin Land*; White, *Eastern Establishment and the Western Experience*; and Wrobel, *End of American Exceptionalism*. All respond to Turner, "Significance of the Frontier in American History."
3. Goetzmann and Goetzmann, *West of the Imagination*.
4. Kolodny, *Land before Her*; Hyde, *American Vision*; Miller, *Empire of the Eye*; and Sandweiss, *Print the Legend*.
5. Scofield, *Outriders*; Slotkin, *Gunfighter Nation*; and Warren, *Buffalo Bill's America*.
6. Pomeroy, *In Search of the Golden West*; Philpott, *Vacationland*; Rothman, *Devil's Bargains*; Wilson, *Myth of Santa Fe*; Wrobel, *Promised Lands*; and Wrobel and Long, *Seeing and Being Seen*.
7. National Museum of the American Indian, *Do All Indians Live in Tipis?*
8. O'Brien, *Firsting and Lasting*.
9. Deverell, *Whitewashed Adobe*; and Young, *California Vieja*.
10. Deloria, *Playing Indian*; Coleman, *Ski Style*; Findlay, *Magic Lands*; and Autry Museum of the American West, *Imagined Wests*.
11. Three critical exceptions that influence this book are Dorman, *Revolt of the Provinces*; Findlay, "Far Western Cityscapes"; and Limerick, *Something in the Soil*, "The American Landscape."

Introduction

1. Because I question liberal assumptions of homogeneity among democracy's citizens in this book, I use the terms *we* and *us* sparingly. I do, however, consider myself a part of a community of readers who imagine.
2. I relied on institutional archives to underscore my argument that the West has nurtured vibrant literary cultures that have been documented in forms readily available to scholars.
3. Burke, "Arrogance of the East."
4. Allmendinger, *Geographic Personas*; and Wrobel, *Promised Lands*.
5. Dorman, *Revolt of the Provinces* and *Hell of a Vision*; and Steiner, *Regionalists on the Left*.
6. Findlay, *Mobilized American West*.
7. Scholars typically focus on the florescence of regionalist thinking in the 1930s in the United States. See, for example, Steiner, "Regionalism in the Great Depression." This book focuses on the extension and complication of that thinking in the years following World War II.
8. For an explanation of the Midwest's disappearance that takes the frontier for granted, see Lauck, *From Warm Center to Ragged Edge* and *Lost Region*.
9. Findlay, *Mobilized American West*.
10. Hsu, "Literature and Regional Production"; and Morrissey, *Mental Territories*.
11. Wrobel and Steiner, *Many Wests*, preface, "Many Wests: Discovering a Dynamic Western Regionalism."
12. On the "fragmented, non-universalist ontologies" of late-twentieth-century western literature, see Comer, *Landscapes of the New West*, 5. On the West as third space, see Campbell, *Rhizomatic West*.
13. As literary critic Krista Comer has argued, "There can be no such thing as western authenticity." See Comer, *Landscapes*, 5.
14. The terms *cis-Mississippi* and *trans-Mississippi West*, common in the 1980s and 1990s among western historians, privilege a frontier narrative and split the Midwest in ways that can hinder regional analysis. I therefore do not use the terms here. Limerick calls attention to how frontier narratives privilege the cis-Mississippi West over the trans-Mississippi West in "The Case of the Premature Departure," *Something in the Soil*.
15. Rifkin, *Settler Common Sense*. On settler anxiety, see Slater, *Anxieties of Belonging in Settler Colonialism*. On the "settler uncanny," see Gelder and Jacobs, *Uncanny Australia*. On comparisons of the settler colonial environmental imagina-

tion in Australia and the American West, see Lynch, *Outback and Out West*. On distinctions between settler colonialism and colonialism, see Veracini, *Settler Colonialism*; and Wolfe, *Settler Colonialism and the Transformation of Anthropology*. On the importance of bringing discussions of the frontier into conversation with discussions of settler colonialism, see Young and Veracini, "If I Am Native to Anything."

16 At play in the boundaries of the Midwest is the adverbial form of the phrase *back East*, as defined by the *Oxford English Dictionary*: "In or to the eastern part of the United States or Canada (esp. the coastal regions) from the west." This book instead emphasizes the noun form of the phrase, *back East*, defined as "the eastern part of the United States or Canada (esp. the coastal regions), *as regarded by inhabitants of the west*" (emphasis mine). Because midwesterners participated in "regarding" the East, I include them here as inhabitants of the West.

17 Miller, *Empire of the Eye*; Sandweiss, *Print the Legend*; Scobey, "Looking West from the Empire City."

18 I do not address the states of Alaska and Hawaii in this book because their relationship to the regional imaginary was more in dialogue with the nation or the continent as a whole—as indicated in the phrases *the Lower 48* and *the mainland*—than it was with the American West as a region. On Alaska as imagined space, see Kollin, *Nature's State*. On Hawaii in the US settler colonial imaginary and Hawaiian resistance to settler views, see Silva, *Aloha Betrayed*. As both the locus of forcibly removed tribal communities in the United States and homeland to multiple Indigenous nations, Oklahoma has multiple "easts" and unique relationships with each. Dorman has well described the state's white literary regionalists. I address the state and some of its Indigenous writers lightly in chapter 6.

19 Lansing, "American Daughter in Africa"; Rozum, *Grasslands Grown*; Findlay, *Magic Lands*, "Stanford Industrial Park"; López, *Chicano Timespace*.

20 Steiner and Wrobel, *Many Wests*.

21 Olson, *Literature and Art in the Midwest Metropolis*.

22 I draw this insight from geographer Natasha Howard.

23 McWilliams, *Southern California*; and Roosevelt, *Address of President Roosevelt at Ventura*.

24 Of those writers who appear in this book, Ricardo Sánchez wrote most frequently in Spanish. Sánchez rarely questioned gender norms and found solidarity largely with other cisgendered, heterosexual, male Chicano poets. When he wrote in the 1970s and the 1980s, the masculine *o* ending stood for mixed communities of genders, and he did not use a gender-neutral term to refer to mixed communities

of men and women. Generally, he also privileged developments in the Spanish language vernacular over those in the academy. Therefore, in this book I use the terms *Latine* and *Chicane*, contemporary Spanish-language terms used to refer to a mixed community of men and women, rather than the contemporary terms *Chicanx* and *Chican@* or *Latinx* and *Latin@*, which have largely developed in the English language–dominated US academy (UW–Madison, for example, uses *Chican@* in the name of its Chican@ and Latin@ Studies program). While I suspect that Sánchez would have delighted in playing with the sounds of words ending in *x* and *@*, I choose to emphasize his insistence that Chicane poetry requires knowledge of Spanish. When quoting Sánchez or when emphasizing gender differences that Sánchez identified, I use the binary gendered terms *Chicano* and *Chicana*. When referencing gender nonconforming figures, I use *Chicanx*, a preferred term among trans communities. On the use of *Latine* and *Latinx*, see Melissa Ochoa, "Who Likes the Term Latinx?" YouTube, accessed January 4, 2024, https://www.youtube.com/watch?v=Zdug1JE-u28.

25 On the margins as sites of empowerment, see hooks, *Yearning*; Phelan, *Unmarked*. On the challenges of centering the margins, see Washington, "Disturbing the Peace."

26 I follow the lead of literary critics Jed Esty and Colleen Lye as well as Rosaura Sánchez and Beatrice Pita by investigating "peripheral standpoints." See Esty and Lye, "Peripheral Realisms Now"; and Sánchez and Pita, *Spatial and Discursive Violence in the US Southwest*, 23–24.

27 On liberalism broadly and racial liberalism specifically, see Brilliant, *Color of America Has Changed*; Brinkley, *Liberalism and Its Discontents*; Gerstle, "Protean Character of American Liberalism"; Gerstle, *American Crucible*; Jackson, *Gunnar Myrdal and America's Conscience*; Horton, *Race and the Making of American Liberalism*; Singh, *Black Is a Country*; Sugrue, *Sweet Land of Liberty*; and Wu, *Color of Success*.

28 Smith, *On Compromise*; Mouffe, *Democratic Paradox*.

29 Brilliant, *Color of America Has Changed*; Horton, *Race and the Making of American Liberalism*; Wu, *Color of Success*.

30 Ayers et al., *All Over the Map*; Burke, *Greenwich Village to Taos* and *Land Apart*; Coleman, *Ski Style*; Deverell, *Whitewashed Adobe*; Findlay, "Far Western Cityscapes" and *Magic Lands*; Hurt, *Big Empty*; Kropp, *California Vieja*; Lansing, "Creation as Erasure" in Fiege et al., *Wallace Stegner's Unsettled Country*; Limerick, *Legacy of Conquest* and *Something in the Soil*; Wrobel and Long, *Seeing and Being Seen*; Lutenski, *West of Harlem*; Morrissey, *Mental Territories*; Philpott,

Vacationland; Robbins, *Landscapes of Promise* and *Landscapes of Conflict*; Rothman, *Devil's Bargains*; Rozum, *Grasslands Grown*; Sandweiss, *Print the Legend*; Shoemaker, "Regions as Categories of Analysis"; Steiner, *Regionalists on the Left*; Wrobel and Steiner, *Many Wests*; Wilson, *Myth of Santa Fe*; Warren, *Buffalo Bill's America*; Zarsadiaz, *Resisting Change in Suburbia*.

PART 1 | SECOND CITY, FIRST DRAFT

1. "Going Home *(Burlington Route),*" in "The Aristocrat Service Directory Burlington Route," n.d., box 93, Advertising and promotional materials, 1932, Scrapbooks, 1862–1963, ser. 32.81, Chicago, Burlington & Quincy Railroad Company Records, Newberry Library, Chicago; hereafter cited as "CB&Q Scrapbooks."
2. Rozum, *Grasslands Grown*.
3. Allmendinger explores Cather's portrayal of marginal figures through reference to Bohemian people and Bohemian artists in *Geographic Personas*, 77–92.
4. Michael J. Lansing comments on this phenomenon in his review of Jon Lauck's *The Good Country*. See *Middle West Review* 10, no. 1 (Fall 2023).
5. Most scholars attribute the origin of the term *second city* to the *New Yorker* writer A. J. Liebling and the articles he compiled to form the 1952 book *Chicago: The Second City*.

Chapter 1. At the Other End of the Tracks

1. Hicks, *My Life with History*, 8.
2. *Middle West* began appearing on maps in the 1850s as the United States planned railroad lines extending from the East to the Pacific coast. See Lauck, "Formation of Midwestern Regional Identity," in Finkelstein and Hyde, *Reconsidering Regions*, 162.
3. Lauck, "Prairie Historians."
4. Hicks, *My Life with History*, 86.
5. Lauck, "Prairie Historians."
6. Hicks, *Populist Revolt*, vii.
7. Cather, *O Pioneers*, 66.
8. Faue, *Community of Suffering & Struggle*.
9. Hicks, *My Life with History*, 11.
10. Rodgers, *Atlantic Crossings*.
11. Canfield, "Bundle of Western Letters," 42.

12 Hicks, *Populist Revolt*, 452.
13 Hicks, *Populist Revolt*, 453.
14 Gleed, *Rand, McNally & Co.'s Overland Guide*.
15 Gleed, "Is New York More Civilized than Kansas?," 217.
16 Gleed, "Is New York More Civilized than Kansas?," 224.
17 Gleed, "Is New York More Civilized than Kansas?," 217.
18 Gleed, "Is New York More Civilized than Kansas?," 229.
19 Postel, *Populist Vision*; Lansing, *Insurgent Democracy*.
20 Hicks, "My Ten Years on the Wisconsin Faculty," 315.
21 Hicks, *My Life with History*, vii.
22 Goodwyn, *Populist Moment*; and Kantrowitz, "Ben Tillman and Hendrix McLane."
23 Hofstadter, *Age of Reform*; Postel, *Populist Vision*; Cantrell, *People's Revolt*; Kazin, *Populist Persuasion*.
24 For a midcentury critique of this trend that attributes its flaws to the consensus school, see Pollack, "Fear of Man," 66–67.
25 In referencing the southern agrarian literary critics, I attempt to follow the model of "promiscuous reading" offered by Kyla Wazana Tompkins, in "'You Make Me Feel Right Quare.'"
26 Deutsch, *Making a Modern US West*, 346–65; and Faue, *Community of Suffering & Struggle*. Hicks also published *The Populist Revolt* in 1931, before some of the more intense farmer-labor protests of the Depression.
27 Steiner, *Regionalists on the Left*; and Griffin, "Geographies of (In)Justice."
28 Mickenberg, "'Revolution Can Spring Up.'"
29 Dorman, *Revolt of the Provinces*; and Steiner, "'Regionalism in the Great Depression.'"
30 Dorman, *Revolt of the Provinces*; Mickenberg, "'Revolution Can Spring Up'"; Deutsch, *Making a Modern US West*; and Faue, *Community of Suffering & Struggle*.
31 Dorman, *Revolt of the Provinces*; Mickenberg, "'Revolution Can Spring Up'"; and Le Sueur, *North Star Country*, ix.
32 Mickenberg, "'Revolution Can Spring Up.'"
33 Le Sueur, *Crusaders*, 5.
34 Le Sueur, *Crusaders*, xv.
35 Le Sueur, *Crusaders*, 9.
36 Le Sueur, *Crusaders*, 9.
37 Le Sueur, *North Star Country*, 238, 237–40.

38 Le Sueur, "American Way," 6.
39 Le Sueur, *North Star Country*, 57, 68.
40 Le Sueur, *North Star Country*, 8–9, 59.
41 Tapes 14, 53, and 57, audio recordings, Meridel Le Sueur Papers, Minnesota Historical Society.
42 Le Sueur, *Crusaders*, xvi.
43 Graham, "Yours for the Revolution."
44 Allen, "'Dear Comrade,'" 123.
45 Le Sueur, *Crusaders*, xx–xxi.
46 Lee, *Publisher for the Masses*, 97.
47 L'Amour, *Education of a Wandering Man*, 9.
48 Julius Moritzen, *Literary Stars on the Scandinavian Firmament*, Little Blue Book No. 431, ed. E. Haldeman-Julius (Girard, KS: E. Haldeman-Julius, 1923), box 3, Little Blue Book Collection, Huntington Library, Art Collections, and Botanical Gardens, Rare Books Department; hereafter cited as "Little Blue Book Collection." Lloyd E. Smith, *How to Pronounce 4000 Proper Names*, Little Blue Book No. 696 (1925), box 4, Little Blue Collection. Arthur Shumway, *How Newspapers Deceive Their Readers*, Little Blue Book No. 1579 (1931); Maynard Shipley, *Origin of the Solar System*, Little Blue Book No. 1326 (1929); Leo Markun, *Your Intelligence and How to Test It*, Little Blue Book No. 1439 (1929); Leo Markun, *Great Dates in History*, Little Blue Book No. 1712 (193[?]), box 6, Little Blue Book Collection.
49 John Greenleaf Whittier, *Snow-Bound*, in Little Blue Book No. 146 (192[?]), box 1; and James Russell Lowell, "On a Certain Condescension in Foreigners," in Little Blue Book No. 225 (n.d.), box 2, both in Little Blue Book Collection.
50 "Low Vacation Fares Summer, from Various Western Points to: The East" 1938, box 94, CB&Q Scrapbooks.
51 Marguerite S. Shaffer describes a similar line between the urban effete and the rugged outdoorsman in *See America First*, 87–88.
52 Borne, *Dude Ranching*, 75–76, 165–66.
53 Johnson, "Romancing the Dude Ranch."
54 Borne, *Dude Ranching*, 165.
55 Randall, "Man Who Put the Dude in Dude Ranching," 29.
56 Borne, *Dude Ranching*, 47. Rodnitzky notes that snow cover made year-round ranching difficult or impossible and also attributes the rise of dude ranches to the financial collapse of the open range business in the 1880s. Rodnitzky, "Recapturing the American West," 112–13.
57 Borne, *Dude Ranching*, 72.

58 Kensel, *Dude Ranching in Yellowstone Country*.

59 Larry Larom to Paul Greever, June 20, 1936, from IHL (w/pc), 1936-06-20, item 14.9.04.05, MS 014 — Irving H. "Larry" Larom Collection, MS 014, McCracken Research Library, Buffalo Bill Center of the West; hereafter cited as "Larom Collection."

60 Johnson, "Romancing," 441.

61 Report from Member Ranches (5), March 22, 1957, 1957-03-22, item 14.15.1114, MS 014, Larom Collection.

62 "The West with a Capital 'W,'" *Dude Rancher* (November 1934): 19, Western History Collection, Denver Public Library.

63 "West with a Capital 'W.'"

64 "Dude Ranches Reached by Burlington Route in Wyoming and Montana" brochure, ordered March 1937, box 93, CB&Q Scrapbooks.

65 Max Big Man to Charles Asbury, February 19, 1931, National Archives at Denver, Record Group 75: Records of the Bureau of Indian Affairs, Correspondence Files 1910–58, 003, 1928–32, Custer Battlefield. https://catalog.archives.gov/id/23811900; hereafter cited as "NARA." On Big Man's travels, see White, "On the Road Again."

66 Clipping, *Chicago Daily News*, March 2, 1930, NARA, 003, 1928–32, Custer Battlefield (NAID 6984162).

67 *Dude Rancher Magazine*, 1933-06, 1933-10, 1935-11, folder MS41.01.79, box: MS41.01, folder: MS41.01.79, MS 041 — Mary Jester Allen — Original Buffalo Bill Museum Collection, MS 041; hereafter cited as "Original Buffalo Bill Museum Collection."

68 Chief Max Big Man, "The Buffalo Plunge, the Buffalo Roundup," *Dude Rancher* (June 1933): 1, 25, Western History Collection, Denver Public Library.

69 "West with a Capital 'W.'"

70 "Colorado: The Perfect Vacation Land," June 1937, box 93, Advertising and promotional materials, 1937, CB&Q Scrapbooks.

71 Rodnisky, "Recapturing the West," 111–12.

72 Raymond W. Thorp, "A Dudin' I Did Go," *Dude Rancher* (February 1935): 5, Denver Public Library, Western History Collection.

73 O'Brien, "Becoming Noncanonical."

74 Cather, *O Pioneers!*, 66. Allmendinger comments on Cather's ambivalence regarding the prairie's increasing international influence via economic production, in *Geographic Personas* (89–92).

75 Le Sueur, "Women on the Breadlines," 5.

76 Editorial note on Le Sueur, "Women on the Breadlines," 7.
77 Burt, *Dude Wrangler*, 49.

Chicago Interlude

1 Thompson, *American Daughter*, 193.
2 DeFreece-Wilson, "Era Bell Thompson," ix.
3 Lansing, "American Daughter in Africa."
4 Era Bell Thompson to Stanley Pargellis, book proposal, May 24, 1944, box 4, file 136, Office of the President, Record Group No. 03, Subgroup No. 05, Stanley McCrory Pargellis Papers, 1904–68, ser. 03, Administrative Subject File, 1942–62, Newberry Library, Chicago.
5 On the influence of childhood experiences with nature on western writers, see Rozum, *Grasslands Grown*.
6 Thompson, *American Daughter*, 113.
7 Thompson, *American Daughter*, 113.
8 On the South as regime rather than region, see Jennifer Ritterhouse, "Many Southerners, Many Souths: The New Beginnings of a Regional History," in Finkelstein and Hyde, *Reconsidering Regions in an Era of New Nationalism*.
9 Johnson, "This Strange White World."
10 Era Bell Thompson Papers, box 1, folders 1–3, Vivian G. Harsh Research Collection of Afro-American History and Literature, Chicago Public Library; hereafter cited as "Thompson Papers." The text reads "blacken fact" but is probably a typo.
11 Thompson, "Lots of Room for Negroes," 23–25.
12 Thompson Papers Scrapbooks, box 3, folders 1–3 and 5.
13 Thompson, *American Daughter*, 198.
14 Thompson, *American Daughter*, 240–41.
15 Thompson, "Negro Publications and the Writer," 304.
16 "Chicago Girl Singer a Hit in the East," Scrapbooks 1929–31, box 3, folder 4, Thompson Papers.
17 Russell Sanjek, director of Projects, Broadcast Music, Inc., to Era Bell Thompson, letter, February 18, 1952, box 10, folder 12, Thompson Papers.
18 Margo Jefferson wrestles with the ways in which Cather's work acted as both invitation and suppression of Black women's creativity, in *Constructing a Nervous System*, 101–31.
19 Thompson, *American Daughter*, 294.
20 Thompson, *American Daughter*, 296.

21 "Friends of the Middle Border to Hold Party," *Chicago Sunday Tribune,* July 7, 1946, clipping, box 54, folder 1, Thompson Papers.
22 Thompson, *American Daughter,* 276, 278.
23 Thompson, *American Daughter,* 279.
24 Thompson, *American Daughter,* 278–79.
25 Era Bell Thompson, "Bell's Lettres," December 1949, box 9, folder 9, Thompson Papers.
26 Era Bell Thompson, "Bell's Lettres," January 1950, box 9, folder 9, Thompson Papers.
27 Avis DeVoto to Era Bell Thompson, letter, November 3, 1949, box 20, folder 29, Thompson Papers.
28 Thompson, *Africa,* 16–17.
29 For example, Eslanda Good Robeson was called before Senator Joseph McCarthy's committee just after Thompson returned from her 1953 trip.
30 Thompson, *American Daughter,* 128.
31 Thompson, *American Daughter,* 145.
32 Thompson, "Japan's Rejected."

Chapter 2. The Marginal Man and the Marginal Midwest

1 Horace R. Cayton, "Robert Park: A Great Man Died, but Leaves Keen Observation on Our Democracy," *Pittsburgh Courier,* February 26, 1944, Horace R. Cayton Papers, box 3, folder 38, Vivian G. Harsh Research Collection of Afro-American History and Literature, Chicago Public Library; hereafter cited as "Cayton Papers."
2 Cayton, *Long Old Road*; and Hobbs, *Cayton Legacy.*
3 Drake and Cayton, *Black Metropolis*; and Bullard, *Black Metropolis in the Twenty-First Century.*
4 Jackson, *Gunnar Myrdal and America's Conscience.*
5 Jackson, *Gunnar Myrdal and America's Conscience.*
6 Yu, *Thinking Orientals.*
7 Park, "Human Migration and the Marginal Man"; and Yu, *Thinking Orientals,* chap. 5.
8 Asaka, *Seattle from the Margins.*
9 Wu, *Color of Success,* 153.
10 On the problematic nature of JERS, see Hirabayashi, *Politics of Fieldwork*; Ichioka, *Views from Within*; Feeley, *America's Concentration Camps during World War II.*

11 Cayton, *Long Old Road*, 3.
12 Flamming, *Bound for Freedom*; Taylor, *Forging of a Black Community*; and Sides, *LA City Limits*.
13 Cayton, *Long Old Road*, 20.
14 Cayton, *Long Old Road*, 20–21.
15 Cayton, "Bitter Crop," 174.
16 Cayton, *Long Old Road*, 62.
17 Cayton, "Bitter Crop," 181.
18 Cayton, *Long Old Road*, 153, 156.
19 Theresa McMahon to Cayton, letter, July 22–23, 1931, box 9, folder 50, Cayton Papers.
20 A. C. Senske, "Pasadena—A Charming City,—But," *Debunker* 14, no. 1 (December 1930): 27; "Debunking Rural Virtue," *Debunker* (May 1931): 34; and Fred DeArmond, "How the New York Yokels Do Their Stuff," *Debunker* (May 1931): 43.
21 E. C. Stewart, "If You Don't Like It Here, Go Back Where You Came From," *Debunker* 12, no. 2 (July 1929): 37, box 37, folder 15, Cayton Papers.
22 T. W. O. Rivers, "A Klown of the kkk Invades Kanada," *Debunker* 9, no. 2 (January 1929): 77, box 37, folder 9, Cayton Papers.
23 Cayton and Mitchell, *Black Workers and the New Unions*.
24 Drake and Cayton, *Black Metropolis*, v.
25 McCammack, *Landscapes of Hope*.
26 S. Frank Miyamoto, interview by Emiko and Chizuko Omori, September 28, 1992, Emiko and Chizuko Omori Collection, Densho Digital Repository, courtesy Emiko and Chizuko Omori, https://ddr.densho.org/interviews/ddr-densho-1002-1-1.
27 Miyamoto, "Introduction to the 1981 Edition," *Social Solidarity among the Japanese in Seattle*, vi.
28 Shotaro Frank Miyamoto, Sociology 310, October 7, 1939, box 171, folder 1, Ernest Burgess Papers, Hanna Holborn Gray Special Collections Research Center, University of Chicago Library; hereafter cited as "Burgess Papers."
29 Miyamoto, Sociology 310, October 7, 1939.
30 On the interrelationship of US internal and international race relations, see Von Eschen, *Race against Empire*; Dudziak, *Cold War Civil Rights*; Borstelmann, *Cold War and the Color Line*; Klein, *Cold War Orientalism*; Von Eschen, *Satchmo Blows Up the World*; Künnemann and Mayer, *Chinatowns in a Transnational World*; Hsu, "Disappearance of America's Cold War Chinese Refugees"; Oh, "From War Waif to Ideal Immigrant."

31 Miyamoto, interview by Emiko and Chizuko Omori.
32 Miyamoto, Sociology 310, October 7, 1939.
33 Miyamoto, Sociology 310, October 7, 1939.
34 Robinson, *Tragedy of Democracy*; Hayashi, *Democratizing the Enemy*; and Lyon, *Prisons and Patriots*.
35 Miyamoto, interview by Emiko and Chizuko Omori.
36 Ichioka, *Views from Within*, 8, 12, https://encyclopedia.densho.org/National_Japanese_American_Student_Relocation_Council.
37 "Resettlement in Chicago," *Densho Encyclopedia*, consulted January 25, 2023, https://encyclopedia.densho.org/Resettlement_in_Chicago.
38 "Setsuko Matsunaga Nishi," *Densho Encyclopedia*, consulted December 2, 2023, https://encyclopedia.densho.org/Setsuko_Matsunaga_Nishi.
39 Private recollection in possession of Ellen D. Wu, cited in Wu, *Color of Success*, 35.
40 Wu, *Color of Success*, 36–39.
41 "Charles Kikuchi," *Densho Encyclopedia*, consulted December 2, 2023, https://encyclopedia.densho.org/Charles_Kikuchi.
42 Thomas, Kikuchi, and Sakoda, *The Salvage*.
43 Ichioka, *Views from Within*, 22–23.
44 Thomas, Kikuchi, and Sakoda, *The Salvage*, 285, 340.
45 "Resettlement: Go East, Nisei, Bravely, Proudly," *Daily Tulean Dispatch*, January 9, 1943, 2–3; and Klee, "America's Food Army," 163.
46 See "Resettlement in Philadelphia," *Densho Encyclopedia*, consulted April 15, 2024; and Urban, "Digging Up the Backyard" and *Invisible Restraints*.
47 IHL to Mr. Ernest F. Shaw from (w/pc), letter, January 15, 1945, item 14.9.18.01, MS 014; IHL to Dr. C. H. Carpenter, letter, January 17, 1945 (w/pc), 1945-01-17, item 14.9.18.03, MS 014; IHL to Shaw, letter, January 23, 1945 (w/pc), 1945-01-23, item 14.9.18.05, MS 014, Irving H. "Larry" Larom Collection, MS 014, McCracken Research Library.
48 On the mixed emotions evoked by the natural world of Heart Mountain, see Chiang, *Nature behind Barbed Wire*, 3; on local prejudice, see 136.
49 Charles Kikuchi Diaries, May 15, 1945, Japanese American Evacuation and Resettlement Records, 1930–74, Bancroft Library, University of California, Berkeley, https://digicoll.lib.berkeley.edu/record/171787?ln=en.
50 Briones, *Jim and Jap Crow*, 224.
51 Ichioka, *Views from Within*.
52 Wu, *Color of Success*; and Brooks, "In the Twilight Zone between Black and White."

53 Wu, *Color of Success*, 6.
54 On the self-positioning of western Black writers, see Allmendinger, *Imagining the African American West*.
55 Cayton, "Bitter Crop," 189.
56 Cayton, "Bitter Crop," 189.
57 Cayton, "Liberals?" *Pittsburgh Courier*, July 14, 1945, box 3, folder 78, Cayton Papers.
58 Cayton, *Long Old Road*, 310, 270.
59 Segal, *Her First American*.
60 Miyamoto, interview by Emiko and Chizuko Omori.

PART 2 | THE EDUCATED OUTDOORSMAN

1 Stegner, *One Nation*, table of contents.
2 Fradkin, "Talented Teacher," *Wallace Stegner and the American West*.
3 Stegner, *One Nation*, 47.
4 Stegner, *One Nation*, 6.
5 Stegner, "West Coast," 41.
6 Comer, "Feminism, Women Writers, and the New Western Regionalism," 21.
7 John Darnton, "Udall, New Professor at Yale Puzzled by His Title," *New York Times*, October 3, 1969, 51.

Chapter 3. Exploits against the Effete

1 Mark Harvey addresses some of these flaws in "Bernard DeVoto and the Environmental History of the West."
2 Bernard DeVoto to Dean Briggs, Harvard, February 4, 1922 [transcribed from Harvard archives by Wallace Stegner, October 1968], box 5, M0242, Bernard Augustine DeVoto Papers, Department of Special Collections, Stanford University Libraries, Stanford, CA; hereafter cited as "DeVoto Papers."
3 DeVoto to Briggs, letter, February 4, 1922, M0242, DeVoto Papers.
4 Stegner, *Uneasy Chair*, 338.
5 DeVoto, "West: A Plundered Province," 359.
6 DeVoto, "Footnote on the West," 713–14.
7 DeVoto, "West: A Plundered Province," 359.
8 DeVoto, "West: A Plundered Province," 364.
9 DeVoto, *Mark Twain's America*.

10 DeVoto, *Year of Decision*; *Across the Wide Missouri*; *Course of Empire*.
11 DeVoto, *Mark Twain's America*; "West: A Plundered Province"; "West against Itself," 1–13; *Journals of Lewis and Clark*.
12 DeVoto to Stegner, letter, April 12, 1937, box 5, M0242, DeVoto Papers.
13 Theodore Morrison to Wallace Stegner, letter, November 8, [1945], Wallace Earle Stegner Papers, MS 676, box 18, Special Collections and Archives, University of Utah, J. Willard Marriott Library, Salt Lake City; hereafter cited as "Stegner Papers."
14 Fradkin, *Wallace Stegner and the American West*, 87.
15 Stegner, "Publishing in the Provinces."
16 Wallace Stegner, "Out Where the Sense of Place Is a Sense of Motion," *Los Angeles Times*, June 3, 1990, 15. Also see Wallace Stegner, address to the Western Literature Association, Ninth Annual Meeting, box 166, Stegner Collection. The lecture was reprinted in *Where the Bluebird Sings to the Lemonade Springs* as "Coming of Age: The End of the Beginning," 135–42.
17 Stegner, *Uneasy Chair*, 5, 12, 45.
18 Stegner, *Uneasy Chair*, 14, 70, 111, 280.
19 Stegner and Etulain, *Stegner*, 14. The *New York Times Magazine* article "Writers of the Purple Sage" (December 27, 1981) actually used the phrase "dean of Western American letters," but most subsequent articles, reviews, and obituaries used Stegner's paraphrase.
20 Berry, *What Are People For?*, 56–57.
21 Bain and Duffy, *Whose Woods These Are*, 13.
22 Morrison, *Bread Loaf Writers' Conference*, 98–99; Bain, "Bread Loaf at Sixty."
23 Stegner, *Uneasy Chair*, 122.
24 Fradkin, *Wallace Stegner and the American West*, 86.
25 Stegner and Etulain, *Conversations*, 98.
26 Stegner, *Uneasy Chair*, 194.
27 Homans, *Coming to My Senses*, 86.
28 DeVoto, *Mark Twain's America*; Brooks, *Ordeal of Mark Twain*.
29 Stegner, *Uneasy Chair*, 115.
30 Elizabeth Cook-Lynn notes Stegner's similar treatment of the term *savage* in *Why I Can't Read Wallace Stegner and Other Essays*, 32, 34–35.
31 Stegner, *Uneasy Chair*, 176.
32 Stegner's interviews and nonfiction writing contrast with some of his fictional explorations of gender and regionalism, particularly in *Angle of Repose*, in which the character of Susan, an eastern white woman, goes west and creates and rep-

resents a western literary tradition, a tradition actually created and represented by the character's historical model, Mary Hallock Foote. See Melody Graulich, "Book Learning: Angle of Repose as Literary History," in Radkin, *Wallace Stegner: Man and Writer*, 231–53. Paired, Stegner's fiction and nonfiction suggest that he did envision women as western writers, but his vision did not include the writers of northern New Mexico's Anglo art colonies.

33 Carr Childers, *Size of the Risk*, 32–34.
34 DeVoto to Arthur Schlesinger Jr., letter, August 3, 1946, cited in Brinkley and Limerick, *Western Paradox*, 22.
35 Merrill, *Public Lands and Political Meaning*, 201.
36 Larom's objections did not stop Ickes from offering him the directorship of the National Park Service, a position Larom declined. See October 12–November 22, 1939, correspondence between IHL, Milward Simpson, Joseph O'Mahoney, and John Spencer dealing in part with the Forest Service (7, w/pc), 1939-10-12, item 14.9.08.09; May 7, 1940, letter to Ickes from IHL, 1940-05-07, item 14.9.11.10; and August 11, 1940, to IHL from Mrs. C. R. Cooper (Gen) (3), 1940-08-11, item 14.9.12.09, Irving H. "Larry" Larom Collection, MS 014, McCracken Research Library, Buffalo Bill Center of the West.
37 Skillen, *Nation's Largest Landlord*, 14–20.
38 Merrill, *Public Lands and Political Meaning*, 196, 302.
39 DeVoto, "West against Itself," 3, 12.
40 DeVoto, "West against Itself," 2, 7.
41 DeVoto, "Anxious West," 483.
42 DeVoto, "Anxious West," 490.
43 DeVoto, "Anxious West," 485.
44 DeVoto, "Anxious West," 490.
45 Stegner, "Out Where the Sense of Place Is a Sense of Motion," *Los Angeles Times*, June 3, 1990, 15; Stegner, "Who Are the Westerners?," 38.
46 Stegner and Etulain, *Conversations*, 168; Thomas, *Country in the Mind*, 111–13.
47 Thomas, *Country in the Mind*, 125.
48 Era Bell Thompson, "BELL's Lettres," January 1950, box 9, folder 9, Thompson Papers.
49 See "California Interlude."
50 Stegner, *Uneasy Chair*, 305.
51 Struthers Burt to Wallace Stegner, letters, February 29 and June 16, 1948, box 12, Stegner Papers.
52 Burt, *Diary of a Dude-Wrangler*, 49. See chapter 1.

53 Struthers Burt to Wallace Stegner, letter, December 12, 1948, box 12, Stegner Papers.
54 Avis DeVoto to Wallace Stegner, letter, August 13, 1971, box 2, M0242, DeVoto Papers.
55 DeVoto, "Anxious West," 481.
56 DeVoto, "West against Itself," 8.
57 Robert Crichton, nonfiction editor of *Argosy: The Complete Man's Magazine*, to Carl Brandt, letter, October 4, 1953, box 2, M0242, DeVoto Papers.
58 Bernard DeVoto to [Julian] Heppler, letter, December 29, 1947, box 6, M0242, DeVoto Papers.
59 Bernard DeVoto to [L. R.] Beatty, letter, March 31, 1948, box 6, M0242, DeVoto Papers.
60 Bernard DeVoto to Carl Brandt, letter, September 12, 1953, M0242, DeVoto Papers.
61 Carr Childers, *Size of the Risk*, 41.
62 Robert Crichton to Bernard DeVoto, letter, May 7, 1954, box 2, M0242, DeVoto Papers.
63 Crichton to Brandt, letter, October 4, 1953.
64 Black, *Global Interior*.
65 Stegner, "Regionalism in Art," 4.
66 DeVoto, "Footnote on the West," 714.
67 DeVoto, "How Not to Write History."
68 DeVoto, "Regionalism or the Coterie Manifesto," 8.
69 DeVoto, "Anxious West," 490.
70 Adams, *Group of Their Own*, 132; "Lucia Mirrielees Finishes School Composition Text," *Montana Kaiman*, October 2, 1931, 1; and "Middlebury College Catalogue, 1926 Supplement," Middlebury, VT, accessed September 1, 2019, https://archive.org/stream/middleburyCourseCatalogs_a10-3_1926s/a10-3_1926s_djvu.txt.
71 Edith Mirrielees to DeVoto, letter, 1940, box 16, M001, DeVoto Papers.
72 Bernard DeVoto to Mirrielees, letter, May 20, 1947, box 1, Edith R. Mirrielees Papers (SC1028), Department of Special Collections, Stanford University Libraries, Stanford, CA.
73 See Black, *Global Interior*; and Kosek, *Understories*.
74 I choose to use *Nuevomexicane*, with the Spanish-language *e* ending, when referring to mixed-gender groups to underscore Ricardo Sánchez's emphasis on Spanish-language knowledge when exploring southwestern literature. I explore Sánchez's poetry in "Texas Interlude."

75 Stegner, *Uneasy Chair*, 321. Also see chapter 4.
76 Stegner, "The Geography of Hope," lecture delivered at University of Colorado at Boulder, October 19, 1988, 14; Stegner, "Out Where the Sense of Place Is a Sense of Motion," 15.
77 Stegner, "Who Are the Westerners?," 39.
78 Maxine Hong Kingston to Stegner, letter, August 24, 1990, box 17, Stegner Papers.
79 Jaramillo, *Romance of a Little Village Girl*; and Anzaldúa, *Borderlands / La Frontera*. Also see Stegner to Eliot Porter, letter, March 7, 1978, box 19, Stegner Papers, in which Stegner says that New Mexican villages were "overrun by tourists."
80 Stegner, "Out Where the Sense of Place Is a Sense of Motion," 15.
81 Stegner, "West Coast," 15–17, 47; *Pacific Spectator: A Journal of Interpretation*, 1947–56.

California Interlude

1 Mirrielees, "Shooting at Raeder."
2 Johnson, *Writing Kit Carson*, 5. As Johnson observes: "White men were the heroes of the frontier story, and trading on the imaginative overidentification of things western and things white and male brought rewards" (84–85). Also see Johnson, "'Memory Sweet to Soldiers.'"
3 Stegner, *Uneasy Chair*, 409–10 n. 12. Stegner misstates the year of Mirrielees's arrival as 1902 in *The Uneasy Chair*. I have altered the date in the body of the text to prevent confusion.
4 Abbott Lawrence Lowell to Horace Davis, February 6, 1915, box 71, Universities and Colleges—Leland Stanford, Records of the President of Harvard University, Abbott Lawrence Lowell, 1909–33, Harvard University Archives.
5 Jordan to Stanfords, as quoted in Mirrielees, *Stanford*, 42.
6 "Miss Mirrielees Retires after 25 Years at U," *Great Falls Tribune*, August 20, 1950, 51.
7 Mirrielees, "American University Training in English."
8 Adams, *Group of Their Own*, 30.
9 Wallace Stegner, John Dodds, and Robert Carver North, "Memorial Resolution," Stanford University Faculty Senate Records, accessed January 1, 2025, https://stacks.stanford.edu/file/druid:ym439ht5815/SC0193_MemorialResolution_MirieleesE.pdf; "Miss Mirrielees Retires after 25 Years at U," 51; and Mirrielees, *Story Writer*.

10   Stegner, *Uneasy Chair*, 120.
11   Stegner, *Uneasy Chair*, 132.
12   Bernard DeVoto to Edith Mirrielees, n.d., box 1, Edith R. Mirrielees Papers, 1870–1964, Stanford University Libraries Department of Special Collections, Palo Alto, CA, hereafter cited as "Mirrielees Papers."
13   Mirrielees, *Stanford*, 241.
14   Wallace Stegner to Ted Morrison, letter, January 3, 1945, as cited by Fradkin in "The New England Years," in *Wallace Stegner and the American West*.
15   "The Pacific Coast Committee for the Humanities," n.d., box 20, Reginald Francis Arragon Papers, Special Collections and Archives, Eric V. Hauser Memorial Library, Reed College, hereafter cited as "Arragon Papers."
16   Findlay, *Magic Lands*, 122.
17   Mirrielees, editorial statement, *Pacific Spectator*, 1.
18   Lewis, "Outlook for Western Publishing," 140.
19   William H. Honan, "Oscar Lewis, 99, an Early Writer on History of the American West," *New York Times*, July 15, 1992, sec. D, 19.
20   DeVoto, "Queen City of the Plains and Peaks," 38.
21   DeVoto, "Queen City of the Plains and Peaks," 42.
22   Rex Arragon to Hugh G. Dick, UCLA, December 9, 1946, box 20, Arragon Papers.
23   Rex Arragon to Edith Mirrielees, August 23, 1946, box 20, Arragon Papers.
24   Edith Mirrielees, editorial, *Pacific Spectator* 8, no. 1 (Winter 1954): 37.
25   Bisson, "Virgin Land versus Good Earth," 378.
26   Schweber, *This America of Ours*; and Stegner, *Uneasy Chair*, 348–63.
27   Schonberger, *Aftermath of War*; and Schonberger, "Thomas Arthur Bisson and the Limits of Reform."
28   Tani, "The Nisei since Pearl Harbor," 203; Griffith, "Who Are the Pachucos?" 352. On pachuco culture, see Macías, *Mexican American Mojo*; and McWilliams, *North from Mexico*.
29   Edith Mirrielees, "Editorial," *Pacific Spectator* 8, no. 3 (Summer 1954): 193.
30   On termination and relocation, see Fixico, *Termination and Relocation*; Miller, *Indians on the Move*; and Lobo and Peters, *American Indians and the Urban Experience*.
31   Mirrielees, "Cloud of Mistrust," 56, 57, 58–59. Mirrielees's article was cited by the Friends Committee on National Legislation (US). See *US Government Policy toward American Indians: A Few Basic Facts*, February 1, 1957 (Pasadena, CA: USGPO, 1957).

32 Mirrielees, "Cloud of Mistrust," 59.
33 Cooperrider, "No Longer a Minority," 168.
34 On *Sunset* magazine, see "*Sunset* Magazine: A History of Western Living," Stanford Library, Stanford University, accessed January 4, 2024, https://exhibits.stanford.edu/sunset.
35 Johnson, "What It Was Like to Be an African American Freshman."
36 Halaby, "Prelude for Public Service," 178.

Chapter 4. When Nature Became Culture

1 Finch, *Legacies of Camelot*, 7.
2 Finch, *Legacies of Camelot*, 16.
3 Tom Udall, "Foreword," in Finch, *Legacies of Camelot*, ix.
4 B. J. McFarland, "Udall Rides the Donkey," *Arizona Republic*, May 3, 1960, box 79, Stewart L. Udall Papers (AZ 372), Special Collections, University of Arizona Libraries; hereafter cited as "Stewart Udall Papers."
5 For similar developments in the National Forest Service, see Hirt, *Conspiracy of Optimism*.
6 Black, *Global Interior*.
7 Lee Udall, untitled manuscript, n.d., box 230, Stewart Udall Papers.
8 Smith, *Steward of the Land*, 77.
9 Krutch, "Things That Go Bump in the Night."
10 Krutch, *Desert Year*, 3–4.
11 Smith, *Steward of the Land*, 84; and Harvey, "Bernard DeVoto and the Environmental History of the West."
12 DeVoto, "Shall We Let Them Ruin Our National Parks," 42. Also see Thomas, *Country in the Mind*.
13 Wallace Stegner, "The Marks of Human Passage," in Stegner, *This Is Dinosaur*, 17.
14 Nash, *Wilderness and the American Mind*; and Pearson, *Still the Wild River Runs*. As historian Andrew Needham has argued, dam opponents benefited from a new power grid that drew most of its energy from coal, much of which was drawn from below the Navajo Nation, rather than hydroelectricity. See Needham, *Power Lines*. Stegner noted the contradictions as well in 1982. See Wallace Stegner, "The Artist as Environmental Advocate," an oral history conducted in 1982 by Ann Lage, Sierra Club History Series, Regional Oral History Office, Bancroft Library, University of California, Berkeley, 1983, 15–16. Dunaway, *Natural Visions*, 124–30.

15 Dunaway, *Natural Visions*, 124–30.
16 Smith, *Steward of the Land*, 87; and Dunaway, *Natural Visions*, 182–83.
17 Smith, *Steward of the Land*, 105–9; and Frank L. Thompson, January 13, 1955, Proquest Congressional, and "The Congress," *Newsweek*, February 4, 1957, box 226, Stewart Udall Papers. Udall expressed his frustration by criticizing the committee seniority system. Barden adopted his proposed revisions to the system.
18 Greenwald Smith, *On Compromise*.
19 Smith, "Robert Frost, Stewart Udall, and the 'Last Go-Down,'" 4.
20 Stewart Udall, "An Evening with Robert Frost," *Arizona Daily Star*, June 5, 1959, box 206, Stewart Udall Papers.
21 Finch, *Legacies of Camelot*, 18.
22 Office of the Historian, "Edith Starrett Green," 85–86.
23 Smith, "Robert Frost, Stewart Udall," 3
24 Smith, "Robert Frost, Stewart Udall," 4.
25 Frost, "Dedication," https://www.loc.gov/resource/mcc.088/?r=-0.063,0.074,1.201,0.638,0. *New York Times Magazine* reproduced the third line as "seems something artists ought to celebrate." Stewart L. Udall, "Frost's 'Unique Gift Outright,'" *New York Times Magazine*, March 27, 1961, 12, 98.
26 Frost, "Gift Outright."
27 Udall, "Frost's 'Unique Gift,'"
28 Black, *Global Interior*; and Rohrbough, *Land Office Business*, ix–xii.
29 In the *New York Times Magazine*, the passage appeared as: "For years Frost has believed that leaders who hold the levers of national power need the redeeming insights of men of art. To him poetry is not a fringe onlooker's musings, but a floodlight that adds graces to life and makes it truly creative. A poet, in Frost's view, should be deeply engaged at the very center of human affairs." *New York Times Magazine*, March 27, 1960, 12.
30 Edward Morgan, American Broadcasting Network, January 20, 1961, enclosed with note from Morgan to Udall, March 30, 1961, box 206, Stewart Udall Papers.
31 *New York Post*, December 9, 1960, clipping, box 242, Stewart Udall Papers.
32 Betty Beale, "Udall Leading Capital's Culture Kick, Interior Secretary Host for 'Evenings,'" *New York World Telegram and Sun*, March 31, 1962, box 149, Stewart Udall Papers.
33 Joseph Hearst, "WOMEN in Washington," *Chicago Tribune*, January 21, 1961, A1.
34 Dorothy McCardle, "White House Has No Line," *Baltimore Sun*, April 30, 1961, E7.
35 Dorothy McCardle, "Equality on the New Frontiers," Mirrors of Washington, *Baltimore Sun*, August 12, 1962, FA9.

36 Ansel Adams to Stewart Udall, letter, December 15, 1960, box 190, Stewart Udall Papers.
37 Dunaway, *Natural Visions*, 132–42.
38 Ansel Adams to Stewart Udall, letter, August 1, 1961, box 190, Stewart Udall Papers.
39 Ansel Adams to Stewart Udall, letter, June 28, 1962, box 190, Stewart Udall Papers.
40 Ansel Adams to Stewart Udall, letter, January 10, 1964, box 190, Stewart Udall Papers. In the same letter, Adams explained that he had intended to give a copy of "Moonrise over Hernandez, New Mexico" to Jackie Kennedy as a gift, but the president's assassination led him to forgo the offer because the photograph depicts a cemetery.
41 Wallace Stegner to David E. Pesonen, letter, December 3, 1960, reproduced at "Wallace Stegner," Wilderness Society, https://www.wilderness.org/articles/article/wallace-stegner.
42 Finch, *Legacies of Camelot*, 66; and Fradkin, *Wallace Stegner and the American West*.
43 Udall, *Quiet Crisis*, vii–viii.
44 Wallace Stegner to Stewart Udall, letter, October 23, 1961, box 190, Stewart Udall Papers.
45 Wallace Stegner, "Stegner Notes on a Film on the American Land," n.d., box 190, Stewart Udall Papers.
46 Lage and Stegner, "Artist as Environmental Advocate," 16.
47 Wendell Berry to Stegner, letter, May 23, 1989, box 12, MS 676, Wallace Earle Stegner Papers, Special Collections and Archives, University of Utah, J. Willard Marriott Library, Salt Lake City; hereafter cited as "Stegner Papers."
48 Wallace Stegner to Stewart Udall, letter, December 9, 1962, box 190, Stewart Udall Papers.
49 Finch, *Legacies of Camelot*, 67; and Smith, "Robert Frost, Stewart Udall, and the 'Last Go-Down,'" 29–30.
50 Black, *Global Interior*.
51 Lee Udall, "Indian Art Comes of Age," n.d., n.p., box 230, Stewart Udall Papers.
52 Needham, *Powerlines*, 213.
53 Fixico, *Indian Resilience and Rebuilding*, chap. 2.
54 Udall, "Indian Art Comes of Age."
55 Deloria, *Indians in Unexpected Places*. Finch reports that Lee was frustrated with the press's representation of Indian people and their use of offensive terms such as *savage* and *heap big*. Finch, *Legacies of Camelot*, 120.

56 Smith, "Robert Frost, Stewart Udall, and the 'Last Go-Down,'" 8.
57 "Lovely Images," *Washington Post*, October 8, 1964, A20, box 190, Stewart Udall Papers.
58 Wallace Stegner to Stewart Udall, letter, November 7, 1961, box 190, folder 21, Stewart Udall Papers.
59 "Udall and Frost Strolling through Dumbarton Oaks," May 11, 1962, box 102, Stewart Udall Papers.
60 Lyndon B. Johnson, "Remarks at the Signing of the Arts and Humanities Bill," September 29, 1965, at Office of the Presidency, https://www.presidency.ucsb.edu/documents/remarks-the-signing-the-arts-and-humanities-bill; and "How NEH Got Its Start," at NEH, https://www.neh.gov/about/history.
61 American Council of Learned Societies, *Report of the Commission on the Humanities*, iv.
62 Higham, "Schism in American Scholarship," 4; and Miller, *Excellence and Equity*, 20.
63 Glenway Wescott, president, National Institute of Arts and Letters, to Stewart Udall, letter, March 28, 1961, box 206, Stewart Udall Papers.
64 Kotz, "John Brademas."
65 Adams to Udall, letter, August 1, 1961.
66 "Frankie Hewitt," at NEH, https://www.neh.gov/about/awards/national-humanities-medals/frankie-hewitt.
67 Green, "Federal Role in Education," 11 and 26–27.
68 AP Wire photo, Wallace Stegner to Stewart Udall, letter, November 7, 1961, box 190, Stewart Udall Papers, https://speccoll.library.arizona.edu/online-exhibits/exhibits/show/stewart-lee-udall/item/1390.
69 See Review of Programs and Planning of the National Council on the Arts and the National Endowment for the Arts, 1965–67; National Endowment for the Humanities Fellowships Announced, February 1, 1967; National Endowment for the Arts Support for Arts Activities in Arizona, October 20, 1966; Review of the Scope and Exposure of Initial Programs of the National Council on the Arts, September 29, 1966; The National Endowment for the Humanities—Initial Programs, September 29, 1966, in Papers of Morris K. Udall, 1920–95, MS325, Special Collections, University of Arizona Libraries.
70 William Steiger, Congressional Record House, H 4733, June 14, 1973, Edith Green Papers, MS 1424, Oregon Historical Society Research Library, box 223; hereafter cited as "Edith Green Papers."
71 Lansing, *Insurgent Democracy*, 269–72.

72 Kammen, "Culture and the State in America," 804–5; Miller, *Excellence and Equity*, 38–59; and Higham, "Schism in American Scholarship," 5–10.
73 Baselice, "Wild All Around." Between 1995 and 2019 the Environmental Protection Agency also supported environmental humanities research through its Science to Achieve Results (STAR) Graduate Fellowship program. Consulted May 16, 2022, https://archive.epa.gov/epa/research-fellowships/science-achieve-results-star-graduate-fellowships.html.
74 Western Heritage Center to Wallace Stegner, letter, 1992, box 173, MS 676, Stegner Papers.
75 Thomas Youngblood to Edith Green, letter, July 17, 1964, box 101, Edith Green Papers.
76 Edith Green to Thomas Youngblood, letter, July 28, 1964, box 101, Edith Green Papers.

PART 3 | THE AXES

1 Ricardo Sánchez Papers, 1941–94, M0652, box 4, folder 4, Stanford University Libraries Department of Special Collections, Palo Alto, CA; hereafter cited as "Sánchez Papers." The full poem, "drizzling moments," later appeared in Sánchez, *Brown Bear Honey Madness*.
2 Sánchez's poetry resists simple translation. I have provided some, but I encourage readers to encounter his poems as he wanted, in a mixture of Spanish and English that demands more effort from non-Spanish-speaking readers. As I explain in the notes to the introduction, I choose to use *Chicane* to underscore Sánchez's preference for changes in Spanish-language vernacular over changes in the English language–dominated academy. When referencing trans or non-binary figures, I use the term *Chicanx*.
3 López, *Chicano Timespace*.
4 Audre Lorde to David Wilk and Mary McArthur, letter, November 1, 1980, box 30, folder 18, Sánchez Papers.
5 Sánchez to Mary McArthur, letter, March 3, 1984, box 31, folder 1, Sánchez Papers.

Texas Interlude

1 "Platicando con Ricardo Sanchez," *Rayas: Newsletter of Chicano Arts and Literature*, no. 2 (March–April 1978): 11, box 29, folder 40, Sánchez Papers.

2 Macías, *Mexican American Mojo*.

3 López, *Chicano Timespace*.

4 In expressing a Texas perspective, Sánchez echoed some of the frustrations of Américo Paredes, especially in his poem "Esquinita de mi Pueblo," discussed by Ramón Saldívar in "Américo Paredes," in Lyon, *Updating the Literary West*, 633–37. As noted earlier, I choose to use the term *Chicane* to refer to mixed-gender groups so as to highlight Sánchez's preference for developments in Spanish language vernacular over those in the US academy. When referring to trans or gender nonconforming people, I use *Chicanx*, a preferred term in trans communities.

5 Sánchez, "Flight: San Antonio, Houston, Atlanta, Richmond from El Paso . . . . . ," *Canto y Grito mi Liberación*, 57–58.

6 Sánchez, "Sojourns in Virginny . . . ," *Selected Poems*, 47.

7 Ricardo Sánchez, "Slums of Richmond, El Paso the Same," *Richmond Afro-American*, n.p., July 19, 1969, box 50, folder 6, Sánchez Papers.

8 Phillips, *Emerging Republican Majority*.

9 Sánchez, "Míctla: Long Road Home" (El Paso, Tejas: Míctla Publications, n.d.), 6, box 8, folder 24, Sánchez Papers.

10 Frank Adams, "Frederick Douglass Fellowships in Journalism," press release, n.d., box 40, folder 6, Sánchez Papers.

11 Essay fragment, n.d., box 40, folder 6, Sánchez Papers.

12 Sánchez, curriculum vitae, January 1972, box 50, folder 7, Sánchez Papers.

13 Sánchez, "Ayer, Ay, Ayer," *Selected Poems*, 49–50.

14 Jacqueline M. Hidalgo, "Why MEChA Burned Out after 50 Years," consulted January 6, 2025, https://latino-studies.williams.edu/articles/why-mecha-burned-out-after-50-years.

15 Anaya et al., *Aztlán*.

16 Sánchez rarely, if ever, explored Arizona in his poetry, and his travels during his graduate studies do not appear to have taken him to Arizona schools outside the Navajo Nation.

17 Sánchez, "A.M. bleakness, somewhere, el or sub or street," *Hechízospells*, 103.

18 Sánchez, "Mictla: Long Road Home."

19 Sánchez to COReS, letter, "9/30/78," box 21, folder 35, Sánchez Papers.

20 Sánchez, "migrant lament . . . ," July 28, 1970, box 7, folder 14, Sánchez Papers.

21 Sánchez, "Stream . . . ," *Canto y Grito*, 81.

22 Office of the Historian, "Edith Starett Green," https://history.house.gov/People/Detail/14080.

23 Anzaldúa, *Borderlands / La Frontera*.

24 Sánchez, "Mictla: Long Road Home."
25 "Platicando con Ricardo Sanchez," *Rayas: Newsletter of Chicano Arts and Literature*, no. 2 (March–April 1978), 11, box 29, folder 40, Sánchez Papers.
26 Sánchez, *Hechízospells*, xix.
27 "MAÑANA: Stanford U. Breakfast Blues," April 5, 1972, box 4, folder 24, Sánchez Papers.
28 Sánchez, "urgencia," *Amerikan Journeys: Jornadas Americanas*, 25.
29 Sánchez, "Old Man," October 8, 1972, *Selected Poems*, 55.
30 In this respect, Sánchez countered both frontier narratives and Mexican narratives of mestizaje. See Saldaña-Portillo, *Indian Given*, 6–15.
31 Sánchez, "San Antonio phantasmagoria," March 5, 1971, box 4, folder 24, Sánchez Papers.
32 Sánchez, "Progress Report," June 14, 1974, box 68, folder 22, Sánchez Papers.
33 On the murder of Santos Rodriguez, see Campney, "'Most Turbulent and Traumatic Years.'"
34 Sánchez, "Progress, Information & Communication Report," August 29, 1974, box 68, folder 22, Sánchez Papers.
35 Sánchez, "Communicación de viajes, progreso, etc.," November 13, 1974, box 68, folder 22, Sánchez Papers.
36 Sánchez, "Independent Studies Review," December 30, 1973, box 68, folder 21, Sánchez Papers.
37 "Union Graduate School," box 60, folder 21, Sánchez Papers.
38 Paperbacks Plus was renamed Little Dog Books in 2012; see https://www.luckydogbooks.com.
39 Rob Lewis, "Preface," in Sánchez, *Amerikan Journeys*, iii.
40 Yolanda Julia Broyles, "Bookstore Gathering to Feature Writer Pinero," *San Antonio Light*, March 17, 1985, box 64, folder 16; Musicanto: International Arts Fest, press release, March 1985, box 65, folder 1; and press release, December 20, 1987, box 65, folder 1, Sánchez Papers.
41 Lewis, "Preface," iv.
42 Sánchez to Javier Pacheco, letter, November 18, 1991, box 32, folder 2, Sánchez Papers.

Chapter 5. The Primrose Path

1 Estés, "The Ironies."
2 Belew, *Bring the War Home*, 132.

3 Coates, *Armed and Dangerous*, 6.
4 Steve Miletich, "A Man's Tale of Conversion to the Order," *Seattle Post-Intelligencer*, November 28, 1985, D5, James Aho Collection, box 13, folder 1, Idaho State University, Political Extremism and Radicalism Collection.
5 On the eastward migration of the 100th meridian, see Zoya Teirstein, "This GIF Shows How Far the 100th Meridian Has Shifted since 1980," *Grist*, January 7, 2019, https://grist.org/article/this-gif-shows-how-far-the-100th-meridian-has-shifted-since-1980.
6 Stock, *Nuclear Country*.
7 Stock, *Rural Radicals*, chap. 3.
8 Levitas, *Terrorist Next Door*, 225.
9 Of the three archives holding copies of the *Primrose and Cattlemen's Gazette*—Denver Public Library; the University of Kansas; and History Colorado, Steven H. Hart Research Center—no archive holds issues from before 1977, and no archive holds a full run of the paper thereafter. Levitas states that Elliott began publishing the newspaper "around 1974." Levitas, *Terrorist Next Door*, 225. Elliott published editorials in the *Primrose and Cattlemen's Gazette* on October 26, 1981, and September 13, 1982, both stating that the paper had begun publishing eight years earlier.
10 R. F. Elliott, "Without Consent, without Conscience," *Primrose and Cattlemen's Gazette* 7, no. 49, November 30, 1981, 1.
11 R. F. Elliott, "Working Blind—Working for Nothing," *Primrose and Cattlemen's Gazette* 7, no. 41, October 5, 1981, 1.
12 R. F. Elliott, "It Takes a Lot of Wind," *Primrose and Cattlemen's Gazette* 6, no. 14, March 31, 1980, 1.
13 Elliott, "It Takes a Lot of Wind," 1.
14 R. F. Elliott, "Horseflies, Feathers, and a Bull Whip," *Primrose and Cattlemen's Gazette* 6, no. 21, May 19, 1980, 1.
15 See "Frying Pan Follies: Egging on the Brass" and "Pizazz Meat Loaf," in The Woman's Touch, *Primrose and Cattlemen's Gazette* 6, no. 14, March 31, 1980, 8.
16 "Taxes Paid for Each Dollar of Federal Aid," *Primrose and Cattlemen's Gazette* 7, no. 45, November 2, 1981, 15.
17 "Simpson to Support Reagan," *Primrose and Cattlemen's Gazette* 6, no. 14, March 31, 1980, 5.
18 Al Simpson, "The Republican Majority, Part Two," Washington Update, *Primrose and Cattlemen's Gazette* 6, no. 46, November 26, 1980, 8.

19 Al Simpson, Washington Update, *Primrose and Cattlemen's Gazette* 6, no. 21, May 19, 1980, 2.
20 Al Simpson, Washington Update, *Primrose and Cattlemen's Gazette* 6, no. 39, October 6, 1980, 12.
21 Richard D. Lamm, "America Needs Fewer Immigrants. We Hate to Say 'No.' But . . . ," *New York Times*, July 12, 1981, E21; and "Few Issues as Important as Immigration," *Primrose and Cattlemen's Gazette* 7, no. 29, July 27, 1981, 1.
22 Childers, "Angry West."
23 "Spotlight on Your Legislators," *Primrose and Cattlemen's Gazette* 6, no. 21, May 19, 1980, 16.
24 Berry, *Cow Talk*.
25 *Primrose and Cattlemen's Gazette* 6, no. 14, March 31, 1980, 7; 6, no. 34–35, August 25–September 1, 1980, 2 and 3; 7, no. 28, July 20, 1981, 7; 7, no. 29, July 27, 1981, 5.
26 Lakenan Barnes, "The Pleasures of Reading," *Primrose and Cattlemen's Gazette*, 7, no. 51, December 14, 1981, 7.
27 *Primrose and Cattlemen's Gazette* 8, no. 16, April 12, 1982, 1.
28 *Primrose and Cattlemen's Gazette* 6, no. 29, July 14, 1980, 1.
29 Ranger Long, Riding along with Ranger Long, *Primrose and Cattlemen's Gazette* 6, no. 29, July 14, 1980, 2.
30 Nancy Landon Kassebaum, "Railroads: A Key Link between Field and Table," *Primrose and Cattlemen's Gazette* 10, no. 1, January 10, 1984, 22.
31 Levitas, *Terrorist Next Door*, 228.
32 *Primrose and Cattlemen's Gazette* 6, no. 45, November 19, 1980, 8.
33 *Primrose and Cattlemen's Gazette* 8, no. 19, May 10, 1982, 5.
34 R. F. Elliott, "I CAN'T ANSWER THAT!" *Primrose and Cattlemen's Gazette* 8, no. 39, October 4, 1982, 1.
35 R. F. Elliott, "We Must Thank President Carter," *Primrose and Cattlemen's Gazette* 6, no. 45, November 19, 1980, 1.
36 Belew, *Bring the War Home*, 6.
37 "Letter to the Publisher," *Primrose and Cattlemen's Gazette* 8, no. 43, October 25, 1982, 19.
38 *Primrose and Cattlemen's Gazette* 6, no. 21, May 19, 1980, 3.
39 Belew, *Bring the War Home*, 124.
40 Jay Pfeiffer, "Ex-DU Law Dean Is Accused of Propositioning Policeman," *Primrose and Cattlemen's Gazette* 6, no. 14, March 31, 1980, 12.

41 Chris Casey, "Professor John Bromley 'Made Quite a Mark,' Remembered for Generosity, Spirit," *Greely Tribune*, March 27, 2008, https://www.greeleytribune.com/2008/03/27/proffesor-john-bromley-made-quite-a-mark-remembered-for-generosity-spirit.
42 Levitas, *Terrorist Next Door*, 225.
43 On the divergent political paths occasioned by the farm crisis, see Devine and Vail, "Sustaining the Conversation."
44 Belew, *Bring the War Home*; Taylor, *Persistent Callings*.
45 Long, Riding along with Ranger Long, *Primrose and Cattlemen's Gazette* 8, no. 30, August 2, 1982, 4.
46 Fraser, *Prairie Fires*, 507.
47 Fraser, *Prairie Fires*, 477.
48 Wilson, "Burning Down the House"; and Kaye, "Little Squatter on the Osage Diminished Reserve."
49 On Wilder's observation of Native peoples who remained on the land, see Fatzinger, "Amid the Mockingbird's Laughter."
50 Robert Warrior, "Democratic Vistas of the Osage Constitutional Crisis," *People and the Word*.
51 Fraser, *Prairie Fires*, 458.
52 On the influence of Lane's travels on her presentation of national identity and westward migration, see Campbell, "Little House in Albania."
53 Fraser, *Prairie Fires*, 445.
54 Fraser, *Prairie Fires*, 452.
55 "Times of Change," *Little House on the Prairie*, season 4, episode 2, NBC Productions, aired September 19, 1977; and "The Stranger," season 4, episode 19, NBC Productions, aired February 20, 1978.
56 Self, *All in the Family*.
57 Fraser, *Prairie Fires*, 507.
58 "Direct from Gordon Kahl—Accused of Slaying Federal Marshalls in North Dakota," 8; and "The Death of the White Race," both in *Primrose and Cattlemen's Gazette* 9, no. 19, May 17, 1983, 19.
59 Levitas, *Terrorist Next Door*, 227.
60 Beck, "Two Boy Scouts Met in an Internment Camp."
61 Levitas, *Terrorist Next Door*, 227.
62 Schlatter, *Aryan Cowboys*, chap. 4.
63 Trillin, *Messages from My Father*, 8.
64 Trillin, *Messages from My Father*, 101.

65 Trillin, "I've Got Problems," 116.
66 People of the State of Colorado v. Roderick F. Elliott, Karla J. Elliott, and the National Agricultural Press Association.
67 Schlatter, *Aryan Cowboys*, chap. 4.
68 The line of aridity was moving eastward in these years. Climate scientists now place the effective line of aridity at the 98th meridian, rather than the 100th. It is tempting to ascribe farmers' problems and their accompanying violence in the early 1980s to climate change–induced aridity in places that had previously enjoyed higher rainfall. The social and political consequences of separating the Midwest from the West, however, are just as attendant if one draws the effective line of aridity at the 98th meridian as they are if one draws it at the 100th. The shortcomings in Stegner's and DeVoto's analysis were not a product of their attention to aridity but, rather, their treatment of the line of aridity as the frontier. As a result, they ignored the regional culture and economic pressures of the Midwest and Great Plains. A west-east orientation still obscured a south-north or north-south one.
69 "North Dakota," box 11, folder 10, Thompson Papers.

Chapter 6. Back Here, Back Home

1 Gaussoin family with Ortiz interview.
2 Clifford, *Predicament of Culture*, "On Ethnographic Authority," 21–54; and Madison, *Critical Ethnography*.
3 On museums as sites of Native expression and colonialism, see Lonetree, *Decolonizing Museums*; and Azoulay, *Potential History*. On museums as sites of diplomatic assemblage, see Horton, "Seeing the National Museum of the American Indian Anew."
4 A more traditionally historical chronology of western Native writers who went East for their education might include Gertrude Bonnin, Charles Eastman, Carlos Montezuma, Ada Deer, K. Tsianina Lomawaima, Anton and David Treuer, and members of the Deloria family, in addition to Louise Erdrich, whose journey eastward I describe later.
5 Following my own education back East, I was influenced by these works: Pratt, *Imperial Eyes*; and Grambell, *Women Intellectuals*.
6 Another possible route in this chapter would be tracing the relationship of the written word to Native sovereignty and citizenship. See Konkle, *Writing Indian Nations*; Pexa, *Translated Nation*; Lyons, "Rhetorical Sovereignty"; Lyons,

X-Marks; Brooks, *Common Pot*; O'Brien, *Dispossession by Degrees*; Piatote, *Domestic Subjects*; and Warrior, *People and the Word*.

7. Calloway, *Indian History of an American Institution*, 15.
8. Brayboy, "Hiding in the Ivy."
9. On the legacy of education within colonialism in North America, see Steineker, "'Fully Equal to That of Any Children'"; and Crandall, "Little Brother to Dartmouth Thetford Academy; Garrod, Kilkenny, and Taylor, *I Am Where I Come From*; Lomawaima, *They Called It Prairie Light*; and Child, *Boarding School Seasons*.
10. On the centrality of journeys to Native authors, see Cook-Lynn, "American Indian Fiction Writer." On stories as a part of theory, see Brayboy, "Toward a Tribal Critical Race Theory in Education."
11. Wilson, *Myth of Santa Fe*.
12. Greyeyes, Lee, and Martinez, *Yazzie Case*; and Child and Klopotek, *Indian Subjects*.
13. Pecos interview; also see Enos, "With Respect."
14. Still another possible route for this chapter would be an examination of Native writing and storytelling in Native languages and in translation, a route barred to me because I lack the necessary language skills. On the protection of Native lifeways within the English language and settler-dominated spaces, see Pexa, *Translated Nation*. On decolonization via literary expression, see Hernandez, *We Are the Stars*.
15. Pecos interview.
16. Brayboy, "Hiding in the Ivy," 133–34.
17. Erdrich, "Foreword," xi.
18. Cook-Lynn, "American Indian Fiction Writer," 32.
19. Pearlman, *Inter/View*, 145.
20. Cook-Lynn, "American Indian Fiction Writer," 28.
21. Pecos interview. On the pressure to perform an imagined Indian identity expected by non-Native people, see Berkhofer, *White Man's Indian*; Deloria, *Playing Indian*; Treuer, *Native American Fiction*; Vizenor, *Survivance*; and Owens, "As If an Indian Were Really an Indian"; and Shanley, "Indians America Loves to Love and Read," in Bataille, *Native American Representations*, 11–24, 26–49.
22. Pearlman, *Inter/View*, 145.
23. Erdrich, *Love Medicine*; *Plague of Doves*; *Birchbark House*.
24. Erdrich, "Foreword," ix.
25. Calloway, *Indian History of an American Institution*, 11 and 204.

26 Shreve, *Red Power Rising*.
27 Blansett, *Journey to Freedom*.
28 Calloway, *Indian History of an American Institution*, 19.
29 Gaussoin interview.
30 Dartmouth College Native American Alumni Reunion, October 4–7, 1990, Rauner Special Collections Library, Dartmouth College and Calloway, 223; Josh Getlin, "A Voice No Longer Ignored," *Los Angeles Times*, December 13, 1993; Halliday, "Louise Erdrich."
31 Some critics have speculated that Erdrich fictionalized Dorris's declining health and the unraveling of her marriage with him in the novel *Shadow Tag*. Leah Hager Cohen, "Cruel Love," *New York Times*, February 5, 2010; and Erdrich, *Shadow Tag*.
32 Pecos interview.
33 Erdrich, *Painted Drum*, 26.
34 Erdrich, *Painted Drum*, 26.
35 Gaussoin interview.
36 Erdrich, *Plague of Doves*.
37 Brayboy, "Transformational Resistance."
38 Vizenor, *Manifest Manners*.
39 Erdrich, *Round House*.
40 Erdrich, "Dartmouth Commencement 2009."
41 Erdrich, *Plague of Doves* and *The Sentence*.
42 On Indigenous futurism, see Estes, *Our History Is the Future*; and Gibson, *Indigenous Present*.
43 Erdrich, *Night Watchman*. On termination policy broadly, see Fixico, *Termination and Relocation*.
44 On the use of fiction in historical writing, see Miles, *Ties That Bind*.
45 Erdrich, *Night Watchman*, 451.
46 Miles, *Ties That Bind*.
47 Erdrich, *Night Watchman*, 119.
48 Erdrich, *Night Watchman*, 336.
49 On Watkins's use of Cold War–era rhetoric, including the terms *free* and *freedom* to describe termination efforts, see Rosier, "They Are Ancestral Homelands," 1301.
50 Erdrich, *Night Watchman*, 394–96.
51 On navigating Indigenous and US nationalist expressions, see Denetdale, "Securing Navajo National Boundaries," 131–48.

52. Erdrich, *Night Watchman*, 436.
53. In this respect, *Night Watchman* is similar in approach to Malinda Maynor Lowery's notion of a "nation of nations." See Lowery, "Are American Indians Part of a United States National History?"
54. Bonetti, "Interview," 88.
55. Wilson, *Myth of Santa Fe*; Horton, *Santa Fe Fiesta Reinvented*; Montgomery, *Spanish Redemption*; Nieto-Philips, *Language of Blood*; Burke, *Land Apart*; and Sanchez, *White Shell Water Place*.
56. Pecos interview.
57. Wilson, *Myth of Santa Fe*.
58. Pecos interview.
59. The effort to shift the axis of narrative inquiry among historians from one that moves along an east-west axis to one that moves along a south-north axis is a long-standing one. For a discussion of the historiography that connects Frederick Jackson Turner with such borderlands historians, see Weber, "John Francis Bannon and the Historiography of the Spanish Borderlands." Indigenous scholars of the American Southwest's Indigenous history, such as Maurice Crandall, have furthered this narrative axis of inquiry among historians. See Crandall, *These People Have Always Been a Republic*.
60. On the pressures of Native women artists, see Berlo, "Dreaming of Double Woman."
61. Gaussoin interview.
62. Silko, *Yellow Woman and a Beauty of the Spirit*, 14.
63. Gaussoin interview.
64. Gaussoin interview.
65. Gaussoin interview.
66. Gaussoin interview.
67. Fields, Lomahaftewa, Young Man, and Marr, "Artists in Conversation."
68. These were Hildegard Thompson, who directed the Navajo Special Education Program before her involvement in IAIA, and George Boyce, who was the superintendent of the Intermountain School before becoming IAIA's superintendent. See Gritton, *Institute of American Indian Arts*, 73.
69. Gritton, *Institute of American Indian Arts*, 110–11.
70. Gritton, *Institute of American Indian Arts*, 116–17, 135.
71. Gritton, *Institute of American Indian Arts*, 93.
72. New, "What Additional Things Should the Institute Be Doing."
73. Gaussoin interview.

74 Harjo, *Crazy Brave*, 87, 85.
75 "Summertime Is Laureate Time at the Library!" posted by Robert Casper, *Library of Congress Blogs*, July 31, 2019, https://blogs.loc.gov/catbird/2019/07/summertime-is-laureate-time-at-the-library.
76 On the role of artists and critics navigating the connections between the local and the global, see Hsu, "Literature and Regional Production."
77 Taffa interview.
78 Op de Beeck, "Committing to a Long Journey."
79 On the origins of the National Congress of the American Indians, see Cowger, *National Congress of American Indians*; and Allen, "Introduction." Also see Institute of American Indian Arts, "Academic Dean Charlene Teters Retires."
80 Taffa interview. On more expansive definitions of Indian Country, see Rosenthal, *Reimagining Indian Country*; and DeLucia, Kiel, Phillips, and Vigil, "Histories of Indigenous Sovereignty."
81 Hicks, *Calm and Normal Heart*, 39.
82 Pecos interview.
83 Pecos interview. Also see Coleman, *That the Blood Stay Pure*.
84 Erdrich, *The Sentence*, 52 and 82.
85 Cooper et al., "When Research Is Relational."
86 Gaussoin interview.
87 Gaussoin interview.

Conclusion

1 Hopper, *Easy Rider*. I have inferred these locations from the chronology of the film, the filming locations, and film dialogue.
2 The phrase *eastward I go only by force, westward I go free* appears in the essay "Walking" by Henry David Thoreau. Rifkin addresses, in *Settler Common Sense*, how Thoreau naturalizes the settler state in *Walden*.
3 Etulain, *Re-Imagining the Modern American West*.
4 Rafelson, *Five Easy Pieces*; Lucas, *American Graffiti*; Gerwig, *Lady Bird*; and Cardozo, *Real Women Have Curves*.
5 Kesey, *Sometimes a Great Notion*; Dearcopp and Smith, *Unknown No More*; Campbell, "Blowout Grass," in Steiner, *Regionalists on the Left*; Lutenski, *West of Harlem*; Choy, *What's Wrong with Frank Chin?*; Cahill, *Recasting the Vote*.
6 Taliaferro, *Charles M. Russell*; Flahive, "Mike Medicine Horse Zillioux," 126; Wadleigh, *Woodstock*; Washington, "Disturbing the Peace"; Storer, *The Bear*,

season 1, episode 6, "Ceres"; Borowitz and Borowitz, *Fresh Prince of Bel-Air*; Harjo and Waititi, *Reservation Dogs*, season 2, episode 6, "Decolonativization"; and season 2, episode 7, "Wide Net."

7 Boag, *Re-Dressing America's Frontier Past*.
8 Barker, *Sovereignty Matters*; and Blackhawk, "Iron Cage of Erasure."
9 Washington, "Disturbing the Peace," 15.
10 Wrobel, *Promised Lands*.
11 Cage, *Year from Monday*, 54.

BIBLIOGRAPHY

Archival collections that I consulted are listed here under "Archive and Manuscript Collections." I list as "Primary Sources" the interviews that I conducted and those published sources that I analyzed as firsthand representations of the idea of back East. I list as "Secondary Sources" the literary criticism that aided my close reading and the scholarship that contributed to my historiographical positioning or gave me wider historical understanding for the various eras that I address.

Archive and Manuscript Collections

Buffalo Bill Historical Center McCracken Library, Cody, WY
    Mary Jester Allen—Original Buffalo Bill Museum Collection, 1910–65
    Irving H. "Larry" Larom Collection, 1906–81
Chicago Public Library Vivian G. Harsh Research Collection of Afro-American History and Literature, Chicago
    Horace R. Cayton Papers, 1941–69
    Era Bell Thompson Papers, 1896–1986
Denver Public Library Western History Collection, Denver, CO
    Dude Rancher, 1933–38
    Primrose and Cattlemen's Gazette, 1977–84
Harvard University Archives, Cambridge
    Records of the President of Harvard University, Abbott Lawrence Lowell, 1909–33
History Colorado, Steven H. Hart Research Center, Denver
    Primrose and Cattlemen's Gazette, 1980–84
Huntington Library, Art Collections, Botanical Gardens, Rare Books Department San Marino, CA
    Little Blue Books Collection, 1921–43

Idaho State University, Political Extremism and Radicalism Collection
    James Aho Collection
Institute of American Indian Arts Archives (IAIA)
    IAIA History Reader
Minnesota Historical Society, Saint Paul, MN
    Meridel Le Sueur Papers, 1902-97
National Archives at Denver, Denver, CO
    Records of the Bureau of Indian Affairs, Correspondence Files, 1910-58
Newberry Library, Chicago
    Chicago, Burlington & Quincy Railroad Company Records, 1862-1963
    Stanley McCrory Pargellis Papers, 1904-68
Oregon Historical Society Research Library, Portland
    Edith Green Papers, 1955-75
Rauner Special Collections Library, Dartmouth College, Hanover, NH
    Dartmouth College Native American Alumni Reunion, October 4-7, 1990, DVD, pts. 1-4
Reed College Special Collections and Archives, Eric V. Hauser Memorial Library, Portland, OR
    Reginald Francis Arragon Papers, 1891-1986
Stanford University Libraries Department of Special Collections, Palo Alto, CA
    Bernard Augustine DeVoto Papers, 1885-1974
    De Voto (Bernard Augustine) Papers, 1918-55
    Edith R. Mirrielees Papers, 1870-1964
    Ricardo Sánchez Papers, 1941-94
University of Arizona Special Collections, Tucson
    Papers of Morris K. Udall, 1920-95
    Stewart L. Udall Papers, 1950-2010
University of California, Berkeley, Bancroft Library, Berkeley
    Japanese American Evacuation and Resettlement Records, 1930-74
    Sierra Club Oral Histories, 1974-2023
University of Chicago Library, Hanna Holborn Gray Special Collections Research Center, Chicago
    Ernest Burgess Papers, 1886-1966
University of Utah, J. Willard Marriott Library Special Collections and Archives, Salt Lake City
    Wallace Earle Stegner Papers, 1935-2004

Primary Sources

American Council of Learned Societies, Council of Graduate Schools in the United States, United Chapters of Phi Beta Kappa. *Report of the Commission on the Humanities*. New York: American Council of Learned Societies, 1964.

Anzaldúa, Gloria. *Borderlands / La Frontera: The New Mestiza*. San Francisco: Spinsters / Aunt Lute, 1987.

Baselice, Vyta. "The Wild All Around." *HUMANITIES* 41, no. 3 (Summer 2020). https://www.neh.gov/article/wild-all-around.

Bisson, T. A. "Virgin Land versus Good Earth." *Pacific Spectator* 4, no. 3 (Summer 1950): 370–80.

Bonetti, Kay. "An Interview with Louise Erdrich and Michael Dorris." *Missouri Review* 11, no. 2 (1988): 79–99.

Borowitz, Andy, and Susan Borowitz. *The Fresh Prince of Bel-Air*. TV series, September 10, 1990–May 20, 1996. Burbank, CA: Distributed by Warner Home Video, 2011.

Brooks, Van Wyck. *The Ordeal of Mark Twain*. New York: E. P. Dutton, 1920.

Burt, Maxwell Struthers. *The Diary of a Dude Wrangler*. 1924. Reprint, New York: Scribner, 1938.

Cage, John. *A Year from Monday*. Middletown, CT: Wesleyan University Press, 1967.

Canfield, James, et al. "A Bundle of Western Letters." *Review of Reviews* 10 (July 1894): 42–45.

Cardoso, Patricia, dir. *Real Women Have Curves*. New York: HBO Films, 2002.

Cather, Willa. *Death Comes for the Archbishop*. 1927. Reprint, New York: Vintage Books, 1990.

———. *My Ántonia*. 1918. Reprint, New York: Vintage Books, 1994.

———. *O Pioneers!* 1913. Reprint, Boston: Houghton Mifflin, 1988.

———. *The Professor's House*. 1925. Reprint, New York: Vintage Books, 1973.

———. *Song of the Lark*. 1915. Reprint, New York: Vintage Books, 1999.

Cayton, Horace R. "The Bitter Crop." In *Northwest Harvest: A Regional Stock-Taking*, edited by V. L. O. Chittick, 174–96. New York: Macmillan, 1948.

———. *Long Old Road: An Autobiography*. Seattle: University of Washington Press, 1963.

Cayton, Horace R., and George S. Mitchell. *Black Workers and the New Unions*. Chapel Hill: University of North Carolina Press, 1939.

Chittick, V. L. O., ed. *Northwest Harvest: A Regional Stock-Taking*. New York: Macmillan, 1948.

Coates, James. *Armed and Dangerous: The Rise of the Survivalist Right*. New York: Hill and Wang, 1995.

Cooperrider, Kenneth. "No Longer a Minority." In *Stanford Mosaic: Reminiscences of the First Seventy Years at Stanford University*, edited by Edith R. Mirrielees, 168. Stanford, CA: Stanford University Press, 1962.

Densho Encyclopedia. Live project. Accessed January 5, 2025. https://encyclopedia.densho.org.

DeVoto, Bernard. *Across the Wide Missouri*. Boston: Houghton Mifflin, 1947.

———. "The Anxious West." *Harper's Magazine*, December 1, 1946, 482–90.

———. *The Course of Empire*. Boston: Houghton Mifflin, 1952.

———. "The Easy Chair." *Harper's Magazine*, February 1, 1943, 333–36.

———. "Footnote on the West." *Harper's Magazine*, November 1, 1927, 713–22.

———. "How Not to Write History." *Harper's Magazine*, January 1934, 199–208.

———, ed. *The Journals of Lewis and Clark*. Boston: Houghton Mifflin, 1953.

———. *Mark Twain's America*. New York: Little, Brown, 1932.

———. "Page from a Primer." *Harper's Magazine*, September 1, 1937, 445–48.

———. "Queen City of the Plains and Peaks." *Pacific Spectator: A Journal of Interpretation* 1, no. 2 (Spring 1947): 132–44.

———. "Regionalism or the Coterie Manifesto." *Saturday Review of Literature*, November 28, 1936, 8.

———. "Shall We Let Them Ruin Our National Parks?" *Saturday Evening Post*, July 22, 1950, 17–18, 42–44, 46–47.

———. "The West: A Plundered Province." *Harper's Magazine*, August 1, 1934, 355–64.

———. "The West against Itself." *Harper's Magazine*, January 1947, 1–13.

———. *The Year of Decision, 1846*. New York: Little, Brown, 1943.

Drake, St. Clair, and Horace R. Cayton Jr., eds. *The Black Metropolis: A Study of Negro Life in a Northern City*. New York: Harcourt, Brace, 1947.

Environmental Protection Agency. "Science to Achieve Results (STAR) Graduate Fellowship Program." Environmental Protection Agency. Research Fellowships. Accessed May 16, 2022. https://archive.epa.gov/epa/research-fellowships/science-achieve-results-star-graduate-fellowships.html.

Erdrich, Louise. *The Birchbark House*. New York: HyperionBooks for Children, 1999.

———. "Dartmouth College Commencement Keynote, 2009: Keynote Address by Louise Erdrich." Dartmouth, Hanover, NH, June 16, 2009. YouTube video, 18:41. https://www.youtube.com/watch?v=4RqB98UxvZE.

———. "Foreword." In *First Person, First People: Native American College Graduates*

Tell Their Life Stories, edited by Andrew C. Garrod and Colleen Larimore, ix–xiii. Ithaca: Cornell University Press, 1997.

———. *Love Medicine*. New York: HarperPerennial, 1993.

———. *The Night Watchman*. New York: HarperCollins, 2020.

———. *The Painted Drum*. New York: HarperCollins, 2005.

———. *The Plague of Doves*. New York: HarperCollins, 2008.

———. *The Round House*. New York: Harper, 2012.

———. *The Sentence*. New York: Harper, 2021.

———. *Shadow Tag*. New York: Harper, 2010.

Estés, Clarissa Pinkola. "The Ironies: White Supremacist Convicted in Slaying of Alan Berg, Dies." *Moderate Voice*. https://web.archive.org/web/20071215063142/http://themoderatevoice.com/religion/judaism/jews/13149/the-ironies-man-convicted-of-slaying-alan-berg-dies.

Frost, Robert. "The Gift Outright." *The Poetry of Robert Frost*. New York: Henry Holt, 1969. Reprinted at Poetry Foundation. https://www.poetryfoundation.org/poems/53013/the-gift-outright.

"Frost Asks Congress to Declare Poets 'Equal to Big Business.'" *St. Louis Post-Dispatch*, May 6, 1960, 22.

Garrod, Andrew, Robert Kilkenny, and Melanie Benson Taylor, eds. *I Am Where I Come From: Native American College Students and Graduates Tell Their Life Stories*. Ithaca: Cornell University Press, 2017.

Gaussoin, Wayne, David Connie, and Olivia Amaya Ortiz. Interview with author, Santa Fe, NM, January 13, 2023. MS012, IAIA Oral History Collection. Courtesy of IAIA Archives, Santa Fe, NM.

Gerwig, Greta, dir. *Lady Bird*. New York: IAC Films, 2017.

Gleed, Charles S., ed. *Rand, McNally & Co.'s Overland Guide from the Missouri River to the Pacific Ocean via Kansas, Colorado, New Mexico, Arizona and California*. Rev. ed. Chicago: Rand, McNally, 1883.

Gleed, J. Willis. "Is New York More Civilized than Kansas?" *Forum* 17 (April 1894): 217–34.

Graham, John, ed. *"Yours for the Revolution": The Appeal to Reason, 1895–1922*. Lincoln: University of Nebraska Press, 1990.

Green, Edith. "The Federal Role in Education." In *Education and the Public Good*, edited by Edith Green and Walter Reuther. Cambridge: Harvard University Press, 1964.

Griffith, Beatrice. "Who Are the Pachucos?" *Pacific Spectator* 1, no. 3 (Summer 1947): 352–60.

Halaby, Najeeb E. "Prelude for Public Service." In *Stanford Mosaic: Reminiscences of the First Seventy Years at Stanford University*, edited by Edith R. Mirrielees, 178–79. Stanford, CA: Stanford University Press, 1962.

Halliday, Lisa. "Louise Erdrich: The Art of Fiction, No. 208." Interview. *Paris Review* 195 (Winter 2010): 132–66.

Harjo, Joy. *Crazy Brave: A Memoir*. New York: Norton, 2012.

Harjo, Sterlin, and Taika Waititi. *Reservation Dogs*. TV series. Los Angeles: FX Productions, August 9, 2021–September 27, 2023. Season 2, episode 6, "Decolonativization"; and season 2, episode 7, "Wide Net."

Hearst, Joseph. "WOMEN in Washington." *Chicago Tribune*, January 21, 1961, A7.

Hicks, Chelsea T. *A Calm and Normal Heart: Stories*. Los Angeles: Unnamed Press, 2022.

Hicks, John D. *My Life with History: An Autobiography*. Lincoln: University of Nebraska Press, 1968.

———. "My Ten Years on the Wisconsin Faculty." *Wisconsin Magazine of History* 48, no. 4 (Summer 1965): 303–16.

———. *The Populist Revolt: A History of the Farmers' Alliance and the People's Party*. 1931. Reprint, Lincoln: University of Nebraska Press, 1961.

Hofstadter, Richard. *The Age of Reform: From Bryan to FDR*. New York: Knopf, 1955.

Homans, George C. *Coming to My Senses: The Autobiography of a Sociologist*. Piscataway, NJ: Transactions Publishers, 1984.

Hopper, Dennis, dir. *Easy Rider*. Mountain View, CA: Raybert Productions and Pando, 1969.

Jaramillo, Cleofas M. *Romance of a Little Village Girl*. 1955. Reprint, Albuquerque: University of New Mexico Press, 2000.

Johnson, Lyndon B. "Remarks at the Signing of the Arts and Humanities Bill." *The American Presidency Project*. Reproduced online by Gerhard Peters and John T. Woolley. Accessed January 6, 2025. https://www.presidency.ucsb.edu/node/241335.

Johnson, Roy. "What It Was Like to Be an African American Freshman in 1962." *Stanford Magazine*, September 2017. https://stanfordmag.org/contents/what-it-was-like-to-be-an-african-american-freshman-in-1962.

Kesey, Ken. *Sometimes a Great Notion*. New York: Viking, 1964.

Kotz, Mary Lynn. "John Brademas: The Unquestioned Leader, the Energizer, the Touchstone of the Arts." *Art News*, September 1980, 90–96.

Krutch, Joseph Wood. *The Desert Year*. Iowa City: University of Iowa Press, 1952.

———. "Things That Go Bump in the Night." In *The Spectator Sampler*, edited by

Robert C. North and Edith R. Mirrielees, 25–31. Stanford: Stanford University Press, 1955.

L'Amour, Louis. *Education of a Wandering Man*. New York: Bantam, 1989.

Le Sueur, Meridel. "The American Way." *Midwest*, November 1936, 5–6.

———. *Crusaders: The Radical Legacy of Marian and Arthur Le Sueur*. With a new introduction by the author. St. Paul: Minnesota Historical Society Press, 1984.

———. *North Star Country*. 1945. Reprint, Minneapolis: University of Minnesota Press, 1998.

———. "Women on the Breadlines." *New Masses*, January 1932, 5–7.

Lewis, Oscar. "The Outlook for Western Publishing." *Pacific Spectator: A Journal of Interpretation* 1, no. 2 (Spring 1947): 138–43.

Liebling, A. J. *Chicago: The Second City*. Lincoln: Bison Books, University of Nebraska Press, 2004.

Lucas, George, dir. *American Graffiti*. Universal City: Universal Pictures, 1973.

"Micki Stout Nellis." Obituary. *Cleburne (TX) Times-Review*. Accessed January 6, 2025. https://obituaries.cleburnetimesreview.com/obituary/micki-nellis-887265062.

"Middlebury College Catalogue, 1926 Supplement." Accessed January 6, 2025. https://archive.org/details/blse_f7_1926_catalog.

Mirrielees, Edith Ronald. "The Cloud of Mistrust." *Atlantic*, February 1957, 55–59.

———. Editorial statement. *Pacific Spectator* 1, no. 1 (Winter 1947): 1

———. "The Shooting at Raeder." *McClure's Magazine* 39, no. 2 (June 1912): 187–96.

———. *Stanford: The Story of a University*. New York: Putnam, 1959.

———, ed. *Stanford Mosaic: Reminiscences of the First Seventy Years at Stanford University*. Stanford, CA: Stanford University Press, 1962.

———. *Story Writing*. Boston: The Writer, 1947. Previously published as *The Story Writer*, 1939.

Mirrielees, Lucia B. "American University Training in English of Prospective High School Teachers." PhD diss., Leland Stanford Junior University, 1924.

Miyamoto, S. Frank. Introduction to the 1981 edition of *Social Solidarity among the Japanese in Seattle*, v–viii. Seattle: University of Washington Press, 1984.

Morrison, Theodore. *Bread Loaf Writers' Conference: The First Thirty Years (1926–1955)*. Middlebury, CT: Middlebury College Press, 1976.

New, Lloyd H. "What Additional Things Should the Institute Be Doing if Time, Money, and Personnel Permitted." January 1969. RG-03, Institute of American Indian Arts. https://iaia.libguides.com/c.php?g=94372&p=612417.

Office of the Historian, US House of Representatives. "Edith Starrett Green." In *Women* in Congress, 1917–1990. Accessed March 21, 2025. https://history.house.gov/People/Detail/14080.

Park, Robert E. "Human Migration and the Marginal Man." *American Journal of Sociology* 33, no. 6 (May 1928): 881–93.

Pecos, Regis. Interview with author, Santa Fe, NM, January 12, 2023.

People of the State of Colorado v. Roderick F. Elliott, Karla J. Elliott, and the National Agricultural Press Association, Inc., District Court, Weld County, CO, case no. 84-CR-581, Division 4, September 17, 1984.

Rafelson, Bob, dir. *Five Easy Pieces*. Mountain View: BBS Productions, 1970.

Riechers, Maggie. "Frankie Hewitt: National Humanities Medal, 2002." National Endowment for the Humanities. Accessed January 7, 2025. https://www.neh.gov/about/awards/national-humanities-medals/frankie-hewitt.

Roosevelt, Theodore. *Address of President Roosevelt at Ventura, California, May 9, 1903*. Theodore Roosevelt Papers. Library of Congress Manuscript Division. https://www.theodorerooseveltcenter.org/Research/Digital-Library/Record?libID=o289808. Theodore Roosevelt Digital Library. Dickinson State University.

Sánchez, Ricardo. *Amerikan Journeys: Jornadas Americanas*. Edited by Rob Lewis. Iowa City: Rob Lewis, 1994.

———. *Brown Bear Honey Madnesses: Alaskan Cruising Poems*. Austin: Slough Press, 1981.

———. *Canto y Grito mi Liberación: The Liberation of a Chicano Mind Soul*. Pullman: Washington State University Press, 1995.

———. *Hechízospells*. Los Angeles: Chicano Studies Center–Publications, 1976.

———. *Selected Poems*. Houston: Arte Público Press, 1985.

Segal, Lore. *Her First American*. New York: Knopf, 1985.

Stegner, Wallace. *Crossing to Safety*. New York: Random House, 1987.

———. *One Nation*. Boston: Houghton Mifflin, 1945.

———. "Publishing in the Provinces." *Delphian Quarterly* 22, no. 3 (Summer 1939): n.p.

———. "Regionalism in Art." *Delphian Quarterly* 22, no. 1 (Winter 1939): 4.

———. *Second Growth*. Boston: Houghton Mifflin, 1947.

———, ed. *This Is Dinosaur: Echo Park Country and Its Magic Rivers*. New York: Knopf, 1955.

———. *The Uneasy Chair: A Biography of Bernard DeVoto*. Garden City, NY: Doubleday & Company, 1974.

———. "The West Coast: A Region with a View." *Saturday Review of Literature*, May 2, 1959, 15–17.

———. *Where the Bluebird Sings to the Lemonade Springs*. New York: Wings Books, 1992.
———. "Who Are the Westerners?" *American Heritage* 38, no. 8 (December 1987): 34–41.
———. "Wilderness Letter." Wallace Stegner to David E. Pesonen, December 3, 1960. Reproduced at "Wallace Stegner." Wilderness Society. https://www.wilderness.org/articles/article/wallace-stegner.
Stegner, Wallace, and Richard W. Etulain. *Stegner: Conversations on History and Literature*. Salt Lake City: University of Utah Press, 1990.
Storer, Christopher. *The Bear*. TV series. Season 1, episode 6, "Ceres." Los Angeles: FX Productions, 2022–.
Taffa, Deborah. Interview with author, St. Louis, MO, July 26, 2023. MS012, IAIA Oral History Collection. Courtesy of IAIA Archives, Santa Fe, NM.
Tani, Henry. "The Nisei since Pearl Harbor." *Pacific Spectator* 1, no. 2 (Spring 1947): 203–13.
Thomas, Dorothy Swaine, with the assistance of Charles Kikuchi and James Sakoda. *The Salvage: Japanese American Evacuation and Resettlement*. 1952. Reprint, Berkeley: University of California Press, 1975.
Thompson, Era Bell. *Africa: Land of My Fathers*. Garden City, NY: Doubleday, 1954.
———. *American Daughter*. 1946. Reprint, Chicago: University of Chicago Press, 1986.
———. "Japan's Rejected: Teen-Agers Fathered by Negro Soldiers Face a Bleak Future in a Hostile Land." *Ebony* (September 1967): 42–54.
———. "Lots of Room for Negroes." *Negro Digest* (March 1947): 23–25. Box 10, folder 58, Thompson Papers.
———. "Negro Publications and the Writer." *Phylon: The Atlanta University Review of Race & Culture* (1950): 304–6. Box 11, folder 7, Thompson Papers.
Thompson, Era Bell, and Herbert Nipson, eds. *White on Black: The Views of Twenty-Two White Americans on the Negro*. Chicago: Johnson Publishing Co., 1963.
Trillin, Calvin. "I've Got Problems." *New Yorker*, March 18, 1985, 109–18.
———. *Messages from My Father*. New York: Farrar, Straus and Giroux, 1996.
———. *Remembering Denny*. New York: Farrar, Straus and Giroux, 1993.
Udall, Stewart L. *The Quiet Crisis*. New York: Holt, Rinehart, and Winston, 1963.
Wadleigh, Michael, dir. *Woodstock*. Documentary film. Hollywood: Warner Brothers, 1970.
"The West with a Capital 'W.'" *Dude Rancher* (November 1934): 19.

Secondary Sources

Adams, Katherine H. *A Group of Their Own: College Writing Courses and American Women Writers*. Albany: SUNY Press, 2001.

Allen, Chadwick. "Introduction: Locating the Society of American Indians." *Studies in American Indian Literatures* 25, no. 2 (Summer 2013): 3–22.

Allen, Julia M. "'Dear Comrade': Marian Wharton of the People's College, Fort Scott, Kansas, 1914–1917." *Women's Studies Quarterly* 22, no. 1 (Spring–Summer 1994): 119–33.

Allmendinger, Blake. *Geographic Personas: Self-Transformation and Performance in the American West*. Lincoln: University of Nebraska Press, 2021.

———. *Imagining the African American West*. Lincoln: University of Nebraska Press, 2005.

Almaguer, Tomás. *Racial Fault Lines: The Historical Origins of White Supremacy in California*. Berkeley: University of California Press, 1994.

Anaya, Rudolfo A., Francisco A. Lomelí, and Enrique R. Lamadrid, eds. *Aztlán: Essays on the Chicano Homeland*. Albuquerque, NM: Academia / El Norte Publications, 1989.

Asaka, Megan. *Seattle from the Margins: Exclusion, Erasure, and the Making of a Pacific Coast City*. Seattle: University of Washington Press, 2022.

Autry Museum of the American West. *Imagined Wests*. Permanent exhibit. Los Angeles.

Ayers, Edward, et al. *All Over the Map: Rethinking American Regions*. Baltimore: Johns Hopkins University Press, 1996.

Azoulay, Ariella Aïsha. *Potential History: Unlearning Imperialism*. London: Verso Press, 2019.

Bain, David Haward. "Bread Loaf at Sixty: From 'Haphazard Experiment' to the Granddaddy of Writers' Conferences." *Middlebury College Magazine* (Spring 1985) n.p.

Bain, David Haward, and Mary Smyth Duffy, eds. *Whose Woods These Are: A History of the Bread Loaf Writers' Conference, 1926–1992*. Hopewell, NJ: Ecco Press, 1993.

Barker, Joanne Barker, ed. *Sovereignty Matters: Locations of Contestation and Possibility in Indigenous Struggles for Self-Determination*. Lincoln: University of Nebraska Press, 2005.

Bataille, Gretchen M., ed. *Native American Representations: First Encounters, Distorted Images, and Literary Appropriations*. Lincoln: University of Nebraska Press, 2001.

Beck, Julie. "Two Boy Scouts Met in an Internment Camp, and Grew Up to Work in Congress." *Atlantic*, May 17, 2019. https://www.theatlantic.com/family/archive/2019/05/congressmen-norm-mineta-alan-simpson-friendship-japanese-internment-camp/589603.

Beito, David T., and Linda Royster Beito. "Selling Laissez-Faire Antiracism to the Black Masses: Rose Wilder Lane and the 'Pittsburgh Courier.'" *Independent Review* 15, no. 2 (Fall 2010): 279–94.

Belew, Kathleen. *Bring the War Home: The White Power Movement and Paramilitary America*. Cambridge: Harvard University Press, 2018.

Berkhofer, Robert F. *The White Man's Indian*. New York: Vintage Books, 1979.

Berlo, Janet Catherine. "Dreaming of Double Woman: The Ambivalent Role of the Female Artist in North American Indian Myth." *American Indian Quarterly* 17, no. 1 (Winter 1993): 31–43.

Berry, Michelle. *Cow Talk: Work, Ecology, and Range Cattle Ranchers in the Postwar Mountain West*. Norman: University of Oklahoma Press, 2023.

Berry, Wendell. *What Are People For? Essays by Wendell Berry*. San Francisco: North Point Press, 1990.

Black, Megan. *The Global Interior: Mineral Frontiers and American Power*. Cambridge: Harvard University Press, 2018.

Blackhawk, Ned. "The Iron Cage of Erasure: American Indian Sovereignty in Jill Lepore's *These Truths*." *American Historian* 125 (December 2020): 1752–63.

Blansett, Kent. *A Journey to Freedom: Richard Oakes, Alcatraz, and the Red Power Movement*. New Haven: Yale University Press, 2018.

Boag, Peter. *Re-Dressing America's Frontier Past*. Berkeley: University of California Press, 2011.

Borne, Lawrence R. *Dude Ranching: A Complete History*. Albuquerque: University of New Mexico Press, 1983.

Borstelmann, Thomas. *The Cold War and the Color Line: American Race Relations in the Global Arena*. Cambridge: Harvard University Press, 2001.

Bracey, John H., Jr., August Meier, and Eliot Rudwick, eds. *The Black Sociologists: The First Half Century*. Belmont, CA: Wadsworth, 1971.

Braxton, Joanne M. *Black Women Writing Autobiography: A Tradition within a Tradition*. Philadelphia: Temple University Press, 1989.

Brayboy, Bryan McKinley Jones. "Hiding in the Ivy: American Indian Students and Visibility in Elite Educational Settings." *Harvard Educational Review* 74, no. 2 (Summer 2004): 125–52.

———. "Toward a Tribal Critical Race Theory in Education." *Urban Review* 37, no. 5 (December 2005): 425–46.

———. "Transformational Resistance and Social Justice: American Indians in Ivy League Universities." *Anthropology & Education Quarterly* 36, no. 3 (September 2005): 193–211.

Brilliant, Mark. *The Color of America Has Changed: How Racial Diversity Shaped Civil Rights Reform in California, 1941–1978*. New York: Oxford University Press, 2010.

Brinkley, Alan. *Liberalism and Its Discontents*. Cambridge: Harvard University Press, 1998.

Brinkley, Douglas, and Patricia Nelson Limerick, eds. *The Western Paradox: A Conservation Reader*. New Haven: Yale University Press, 2000.

Briones, Matthew M. *Jim and Jap Crow: A Cultural History of 1940s Interracial America*. Princeton: Princeton University Press, 2012.

Brooks, Charlotte. "In the Twilight Zone between Black and White: Japanese American Resettlement and Community in Chicago, 1942–1945." *Journal of American History* 86, no. 4 (March 2000): 1655–87.

Brooks, Lisa T. *The Common Pot: The Recovery of Native Space in the Northeast*. Minneapolis: University of Minnesota Press, 2008

Bullard, Robert D., ed. *The Black Metropolis in the Twenty-First Century: Race, Power and Politics of Place*. Lanham, MD: Rowman & Littlefield, 2007.

Burke, Flannery. "The Arrogance of the East: How Westerners Created a Region." *Western Historical Quarterly* 50, no. 4 (2019): 383–407.

———. *Greenwich Village to Taos: Primitivism and Place at Mabel Dodge Luhan's*. Lawrence: University Press of Kansas, 2008.

———. *A Land Apart: The Southwest and the Nation in the Twentieth Century*. Tucson: University of Arizona Press, 2017.

Cahill, Cathleen. *Recasting the Vote: How Women of Color Transformed the Suffrage Movement*. Chapel Hill: University of North Carolina Press, 2020.

Calloway, Colin G. *The Indian History of an American Institution: Native Americans and Dartmouth*. Hanover, NH: Dartmouth College Press, 2010.

Campbell, Donna. "Little House in Albania: Rose Wilder Lane and the Transnational Home." *Western American Literature* 53, no. 2 (2018): 205–25.

Campbell, Neil. *The Rhizomatic West: Representing the American West in a Transnational Global Media Age*. Lincoln: University of Nebraska Press, 2008.

Campney, Brent M. S. "'The Most Turbulent and Most Traumatic Years in Recent Mexican-American History': Police Violence and the Civil Rights Struggle in 1970s Texas." *Southwestern Historical Quarterly* 122, no. 1 (2018): 32–57.

Cantrell, Gregg. *The People's Revolt: Texas Populists and the Roots of American Liberalism*. New Haven: Yale University Press, 2020.

Carr Childers, Leisl. "The Angry West: Understanding the Sagebrush Rebellion in Rural Nevada." In *Bridging the Distance: Common Issues in the Rural West*, edited by David Danbom, 269–315. Salt Lake City: University of Utah Press, 2015.

———. *The Size of the Risk: Histories of Multiple Use in the Great Basin*. Norman: University of Oklahoma Press, 2015.

Casper, Robert. "Summertime Is Laureate Time at the Library!" *Library of Congress Blogs: From the Catbird Seat, Poetry at the Library of Congress*, July 31, 2019. https://blogs.loc.gov/catbird/2019/07/summertime-is-laureate-time-at-the-library.

Chiang, Connie. *Nature behind Barbed Wire: An Environmental History of the Japanese American Incarceration*. Oxford: Oxford University Press, 2018.

Child, Brenda. *Boarding School Seasons: American Indian Families, 1900–1940*. Lincoln: University of Nebraska Press, 1998.

Child, Brenda J., and Brian Klopotek, eds. *Indian Subjects: Hemispheric Perspectives on the History of Indigenous Education*. Santa Fe: SAR Press, 2014.

Choy, Curtis, dir. *What's Wrong with Frank Chin?* New York: FilmBuff, 2005.

Clifford, James. "On Ethnographic Authority." *The Predicament of Culture: Twentieth-Century Ethnography, Literature, and Art*, 21–54. Cambridge: Harvard University Press, 1988.

Coleman, Anne Gilbert. *Ski Style: Sport and Culture in the Rockies*. Lawrence: University Press of Kansas, 2004.

Coleman, Arica L. *That the Blood Stay Pure: African Americans, Native Americans, and the Predicament of Race and Identity in Virginia*. Bloomington: Indiana University Press, 2013.

Comer, Krista. "Feminism, Women Writers, and the New Western Regionalism: Revising Critical Paradigms." In *Updating the Literary West*, by Western Literature Association, edited by Thomas J. Lyon, 17–34. Fort Worth: Texas Christian University Press, 1997.

———. *Landscapes of the New West: Gender and Geography in Contemporary Women's Writing*. Chapel Hill: University of North Carolina Press, 1999.

Cook-Lynn, Elizabeth. "The American Indian Fiction Writer: 'Cosmopolitanism, Nationalism, the Third World, and First Nation Sovereignty.'" *Wičazo Ša Review* 9, no. 2 (Fall 1993): 26–36.

———. *Why I Can't Read Wallace Stegner and Other Essays: A Tribal Voice*. Madison: University of Wisconsin Press, 1996.

Cooper, Danielle Miriam, Tanya Ball, Michelle Nicole Boyer-Kelly, Anne Carr-Wiggin, Carrie Cornelius, J. Wendel Cox, Sarah Dupont, et al. "When Research Is Relational: Supporting the Research Practices of Indigenous

Studies Scholars." *Ithaka S+R.* Last modified April 11, 2019. https://doi.org/10.18665/sr.311240.

Cowger, Thomas W. *The National Congress of American Indians: The Founding Years.* Lincoln: University of Nebraska Press, 1999.

Crandall, Maurice S. "Little Brother to Dartmouth Thetford Academy, Colonialism, and Dispossession in New England." *New England Quarterly* 95, no. 1 (March 2022): 39–65.

———. *These People Have Always Been a Republic: Indigenous Electorates in the US-Mexico Borderlands, 1598–1912.* Chapel Hill: University of North Carolina Press, 2019.

Cronon, William. "The Trouble with Wilderness." In *Uncommon Ground: Rethinking the Human Place in Nature,* edited by William Cronon, 69–90. New York: Norton, 1985.

Cronon, William, George Miles, and Jay Gitlin. "Becoming West: Toward a New Meaning for Western History." In *Under an Open Sky: Rethinking America's Western Past,* edited by William Cronon, George Miles, and Jay Gitlin, 3–27. New York: Norton, 1992.

Dearcopp, Joanne, and Christine Hill Smith, eds. *Unknown No More: Recovering Sanora Babb.* Norman: University of Oklahoma Press, 2021.

DeFreece-Wilson, Eileen. "Era Bell Thompson: Chicago Renaissance Writer." PhD diss., Rutgers, State University of New Jersey, 2010.

Deloria, Philip J. *Indians in Unexpected Places.* Lawrence: University Press of Kansas, 2004.

———. *Playing Indian.* New Haven: Yale University Press, 1998.

DeLucia, Christine, Doug Kiel, Katrina Phillips, and Kiara Vigil. "Histories of Indigenous Sovereignty in Action: What Is It and Why Does It Matter?" *American Historian* 27 (March 2021): 20–33.

Denetdale, Jennifer Nez. "Securing Navajo National Boundaries: War, Patriotism, Tradition, and the Diné Marriage Act of 2005." *Wíčazo Ša Review* 24, no. 2 (Fall 2009): 131–48.

Deutsch, Sarah. *Making a Modern US West: The Contested Terrain of a Region and Its Borders, 1898–1940.* Lincoln: University of Nebraska Press, 2022.

Deverell, William. *Whitewashed Adobe: The Rise of Los Angeles and the Remaking of Its Mexican Past.* Berkeley: University of California Press, 2004.

Devine, Jenny Barker, and David D. Vail. "Sustaining the Conversation: The Farm Crisis in the Midwest." *Middle West Review* 2 (Fall 2015): 1–10.

Dorman, Robert L. *Hell of a Vision: Regionalism and the Modern American West.* Tucson: University of Arizona Press, 2012.

———. *Revolt of the Provinces: The Regionalist Movement in America, 1920-1945.* Chapel Hill: University of North Carolina Press, 1993.

Dudziak, Mary L. *Cold War Civil Rights: Race and the Image of American Democracy.* Princeton, NJ: Princeton University Press, 2000.

Dunaway, Finis. *Natural Visions: The Power of Images in American Environmental Reform.* Chicago: University of Chicago Press, 2005.

Enos, Anya Dozier. "With Respect. . . ." In *Indigenous Innovations in Higher Education: Local Knowledge and Critical Research,* edited by Elizabeth Sumida Huaman and Bryan McKinley Jones Brayboy. Rotterdam: Sense Publishers, 2017.

Estes, Nick. *Our History Is the Future: Standing Rock versus the Dakota Access Pipeline, and the Long Tradition of Indigenous Resistance.* London: Verso, 2019.

Esty, Jed, and Colleen Lye. "Peripheral Realisms Now." *Modern Language Quarterly* 73, no. 3 (2012): 269-88.

Etulain, Richard. "The American Literary West and Its Interpreters: The Rise of a New Historiography." *Pacific Historical Review* 45, no. 3 (August 1976): 311-48.

———. *Re-Imagining the Modern American West: A Century of Fiction, History, and Art.* Tucson: University of Arizona Press, 1996.

Fatzinger, Amy. "Amid the Mockingbird's Laughter: Non-Indian Removals in Laura Ingalls Wilder's Depression-Era Novels." *Western American Literature* 52, no. 2 (Summer 2017): 181-207.

Faue, Elizabeth. *Community of Suffering & Struggle: Women, Men, and the Labor Movement in Minneapolis, 1915-1945.* Chapel Hill: University of North Carolina Press, 1991.

Feeley, Francis McCollum. *America's Concentration Camps during World War II: Social Science and the Japanese American Internment.* New Orleans: University Press of the South, 1999.

Fiege, Mark, Michael J. Lansing, and Leisl Carr Childers. *Wallace Stegner's Unsettled Country: Ruin, Realism, and Possibility in the American West.* Lincoln: University of Nebraska Press, 2024.

Fields, Anita, Linda Lomahaftewa, Alfred Young Man, and Alexander Brier Marr. "Artists in Conversation: Action/Abstraction Redefined." Recorded lecture from June 23, 2023. St. Louis Art Museum. https://www.slam.org/adults/lectures-artist-talks-and-panel-conversations.

Finch, L. Boyd. *Legacies of Camelot: Stewart and Lee Udall, American Culture and the Arts*. Norman: University of Oklahoma Press, 2008.

Findlay, John M. "Far Western Cityscapes and American Culture since 1940." *Western Historical Quarterly* 22, no. 1 (February 1991): 19–43.

———. *Magic Lands: Western Cityscapes and American Culture after 1940*. Berkeley: University of California Press, 1992.

———. *The Mobilized American West, 1940-2000*. Lincoln: University of Nebraska Press, 2023.

Finkelstein, Alexander, and Anne Hyde, eds. *Reconsidering Regions in an Era of New Nationalism*. Lincoln: University of Nebraska Press, 2023.

Fixico, Donald. *Indian Resilience and Rebuilding: Indigenous Nations in the Modern American West*. Tucson: University of Arizona Press, 2013.

———. *Termination and Relocation, Federal Indian Policy, 1945-1960*. Albuquerque: University of New Mexico Press, 1990.

Flahive, Ryan S. "Mike Medicine Horse Zillioux." *Action/Abstraction Redefined: Modern Native Art, 1940s-1970s*. Santa Fe: IAIA, Museum of Contemporary Native Arts, 2018.

Flamming, Douglas. *Bound for Freedom: Black Los Angeles in Jim Crow America*. Berkeley: University of California Press, 2005.

Fradkin, Philip L. *Wallace Stegner and the American West*. New York: Knopf, 2008.

Fraser, Caroline. *Prairie Fires: The American Dreams of Laura Ingalls Wilder*. New York: Metropolitan Books, 2017.

Garrod, Andrew C., Robert Kilkenny, and Melanie Benson Taylor, eds. *I Am Where I Come From: Native American College Students and Graduates Tell Their Life Stories*. Ithaca: Cornell University Press, 2017.

Gelder, Ken, and Jane M. Jacobs. *Uncanny Australia: Sacredness and Identity in a Postcolonial Nation*. Melbourne: Melbourne University Press, 1988.

Gerstle, Gary. *American Crucible: Race and Nation in the Twentieth Century*. Princeton: Princeton University Press, 2001.

———. "The Protean Character of American Liberalism." *American Historical Review* 99, no. 4 (1994): 1043–73.

Gibson, Jeffrey, ed. *An Indigenous Present*. New York: DelMonico Books / DAP, 2023.

Glenn, Evelyn Nakano. *Unequal Freedom: How Race and Gender Shaped American Citizenship and Labor*. Cambridge: Harvard University Press, 2002.

Goetzmann, William H., and William N. Goetzmann. *The West of the Imagination*. New York: Norton, 1989.

Goodwyn, Lawrence. *Democratic Promise: The Populist Moment in America*. New York: Oxford University Press, 1976.

Grambell, Alice. *Women Intellectuals, Modernism and Difference: Transatlantic Culture, 1919-1945*. Cambridge: Cambridge University Press, 1997.

Graulich, Melody. "Cultural Criticism, circa 1974." *American Literary History* 16, no. 3 (Fall 2004): 536-42.

Greyeyes, Wendy S., Lloyd L. Lee, and Glenabah Martinez, eds. *The Yazzie Case: Building a Public Education System for Our Indigenous Future*. Albuquerque: University of New Mexico Press, 2023.

Griffin, Brent Garrett. "Geographies of (In)Justice: Radical Regionalism in the American Midwest." PhD diss., Northeastern University, 2013.

Gritton, Joy L. *The Institute of American Indian Arts: Modernism and US Indian Policy*. Albuquerque: University of New Mexico Press, 2000.

Grossman, James, ed. *The Frontier in American Culture: Essays by Richard White and Patricia Nelson Limerick*. Berkeley: University of California Press, 1994.

Harvey, Mark. "Bernard DeVoto and the Environmental History of the West." *Weber—The Contemporary West* 38, no. 1 (Fall 2021): 13-25.

Hayashi, Brian Masaru. *Democratizing the Enemy: The Japanese American Internment*. Princeton, NJ: Princeton University Press, 2004.

Hernandez, Sarah. *We Are the Stars: Colonizing and Decolonizing the Oceti Sakowin Literary Tradition*. Tucson: University of Arizona Press, 2023.

Hidalgo, Jacqueline M. "Why MEChA Burned Out after 50 Years." Williams College Latina/o Studies. Accessed January 6, 2025. https://latino-studies.williams.edu/articles/why-mecha-burned-out-after-50-years.

Higham, John. "The Schism in American Scholarship." *American Historical Review* 72, no. 1 (October 1966): 1-21.

Hirabayashi, Lane Ryo. *The Politics of Fieldwork: Research in an American Concentration Camp*. Tucson: University of Arizona Press, 1999.

Hirt, Paul W. *A Conspiracy of Optimism: Management of the National Forests since World War Two*. Lincoln: University of Nebraska Press, 1994.

Hobbs, Richard S. *The Cayton Legacy: An African American Family*. Pullman: Washington State University Press, 2002.

Holt, Thomas C. *The Problem of Race in the Twenty-First Century*. Cambridge: Harvard University Press, 2000.

hooks, bell. *Yearning, Race, Gender, and Cultural Politics*. Boston: South End Press, 1990.

Horton, Carol A. *Race and the Making of American Liberalism*. Oxford: Oxford University Press, 2005.

Horton, Jessica L. "Seeing the National Museum of the American Indian Anew, as a Diplomatic Assemblage." *American Art* 36, no. 3 (Fall 2022): 5–9.

Horton, Sarah Bronwen. *The Santa Fe Fiesta, Reinvented: Staking Ethno-Nationalist Claims to a Disappearing Homeland*. Santa Fe: SAR Press, 2010.

Hsu, Hsuan L. "Literature and Regional Production." *American Literary History* 17, no. 1 (Spring 2005): 36–69.

Hsu, Madeline Y. "The Disappearance of America's Cold War Chinese Refugees, 1948–1966." *Journal of American Ethnic History* 31, no. 4 (Summer 2012): 12–33.

Hurt, R. Douglas. *The Big Empty: The Great Plains in the Twentieth Century*. Tucson: University of Arizona Press, 2011.

Hyde, Anne F. *An American Vision: Far Western Landscape and American Culture, 1820–1920*. New York: New York University Press, 1991.

Ichioka, Yuji, ed. *Views from Within: The Japanese American Evacuation and Resettlement Study*. Los Angeles: University of California Press, 1989.

Institute of American Indian Arts. "Academic Dean Charlene Teters Retires." IAIA Happenings, October 2, 2020. https://iaia.edu/academic-dean-charlene-teters-retires.

Jackson, Walter A. *Gunnar Myrdal and America's Conscience: Social Engineering and Racial Liberalism, 1938–1987*. Chapel Hill: University of North Carolina Press, 1990.

Jefferson, Margo. *Constructing a Nervous System: A Memoir*. New York: Pantheon Books, 2022.

Johnson, Adrienne Rose. "Romancing the Dude Ranch, 1926–1947." *Western Historical Quarterly* 43, no. 4 (Winter 2012): 437–61.

Johnson, Michael K. "'This Strange White World': Race and Place in Era Bell Thompson's American Daughter." In *African Americans on the Great Plains: An Anthology*, edited by Bruce A. Glasrud and Charles A. Braithwaite, 184–203. Lincoln: University of Nebraska Press, 2009.

Johnson, Susan Lee. "'A Memory Sweet to Soldiers': The Significance of Gender in the History of the 'American West.'" *Western Historical Quarterly* 24, no. 4 (November 1993): 495–517.

———. *Writing Kit Carson: Fallen Heroes in a Changing West*. Chapel Hill: University of North Carolina Press in association with the William P. Clements Center for Southwest Studies, 2020.

Kammen, Michael. "Culture and the State in America." *Journal of American History* 83, no. 1 (December 1996): 791–814.

Kantrowitz, Stephen. "Ben Tillman and Hendrix McLane, Agrarian Rebels: White

Manhood, 'The Farmers,' and the Limits of Southern Populism." *Journal of Southern History* 66, no. 3 (August 2000): 497–524.

Kaye, Frances W. "Little Squatter on the Osage Diminished Reserve." *Great Plains Quarterly* 20, no. 2 (Spring 2000): 123–40.

Kazin, Michael. *The Populist Persuasion: An American History*. New York: Basic Books, 1995.

Kensel, W. Hudson. *Dude Ranching in Yellowstone Country: Larry Larom and Valley Ranch, 1915–1969*. Norman, OK: Arthur H. Clark, 2010.

Klee, Sam. "America's Food Army: Carceral Labor and Community Power during World War II." PhD diss., University of Oslo, 2024.

Klein, Christina. *Cold War Orientalism: Asia in the Middlebrow Imagination, 1945–1961*. Berkeley: University of California Press, 2003.

Kollin, Susan. *Nature's State: Imagining Alaska as the Last Frontier*. Chapel Hill: University of North Carolina Press, 2018.

Kolodny, Annette. *The Land before Her: Fantasy and Experience of the American Frontiers, 1630–1860*. Chapel Hill: University of North Carolina Press, 1984.

Konkle, Maureen. *Writing Indian Nations: Native Intellectuals and the Politics of Historiography, 1827–1863*. Chapel Hill: University of North Carolina Press, 2004.

Kosek, Jake. *Understories: The Political Life of Forests in Northern New Mexico*. Durham: Duke University Press, 2006.

Kropp, Phoebe S. *California Vieja: Culture and Memory in a Modern American Place*. Berkeley: University of California Press, 2006.

Künnemann, Vanessa, and Ruth Mayer, eds. *Chinatowns in a Transnational World: Myths and Realities of an Urban Phenomenon*. New York: Routledge, 2011.

Lansing, Michael J. "An American Daughter in Africa: Land of My Fathers; Era Bell Thompson's Midwestern Vision of the African Diaspora." *Middle West Review* 1, no. 2 (Spring 2015): 1–28.

———. *Insurgent Democracy: The Nonpartisan League in North American Politics*. Chicago: University of Chicago Press, 2015.

———. Review of *The Good Country: A History of the American Midwest, 1800–1900*, by Jon K. Lauck. *Middle West Review* 10, no. 1 (Fall 2023): 167–69.

Lauck, Jon K. *From Warm Center to Ragged Edge: The Erosion of Midwestern Literary and Historical Regionalism, 1920–1965*. Iowa City: University of Iowa Press, 2017.

———. *The Lost Region: Toward a Revival of Midwestern History*. Iowa City: University of Iowa Press, 2013.

———. "The Prairie Historians and the Foundations of Midwestern History." *Annals of Iowa* 71, no. 2 (Spring 2012): 137–73.

Lee, R. Alton. *Publisher for the Masses: Emanuel Haldeman-Julius*. Lincoln: University of Nebraska Press, 2018.

Levitas, Daniel. *The Terrorist Next Door: The Militia Movement and the Radical Right*. New York: Thomas Dunne Books / St. Martin's Press, 2002.

Limerick, Patricia Nelson. *Legacy of Conquest: The Unbroken Past of the American West*. New York: Norton, 1987.

———. *Something in the Soil: Legacies and Reckonings in the New West*. New York: Norton, 2000.

Lobo, Susan, and Kurt Peters, eds. *American Indians and the Urban Experience*. Walnut Creek, CA: Altamira Press, 2001.

Lomawaima, K. Tsianina. *They Called It Prairie Light: The Story of Chilocco Indian School*. Lincoln: University of Nebraska Press, 1994.

Lonetree, Amy. *Decolonizing Museums: Representing Native America in National and Tribal Museums*. Chapel Hill: University of North Carolina Press, 2012.

López, Miguel R. *Chicano Timespace: The Poetry and Politics of Ricardo Sánchez*. College Station: Texas A&M University Press, 2001.

Lowery, Malinda Maynor. "Are American Indians Part of a United States National History?" *Public Seminar*, May 7, 2019. https://publicseminar.org/essays/are-indians-part-of-a-united-states-national-history.

Lutenski, Emily. *West of Harlem: African American Writers and the Borderlands*. Lawrence: University Press of Kansas, 2015.

Lynch, Tom. *Outback and Out West: The Settler Colonial Environmental Imaginary*. Lincoln: University of Nebraska Press, 2022.

Lyon, Cherstin M. *Prisons and Patriots: Japanese American Wartime Citizenship, Civil Disobedience, and Historical Memory*. Philadelphia: Temple University Press, 2012.

Lyons, Scott Richard. "Rhetorical Sovereignty: What Do American Indians Want from Writing?" *College Composition and Communication* 51, no. 3 (February 2000): 447–68.

———. *X-Marks: Native Signatures of Assent*. Minneapolis: University of Minnesota Press, 2010.

Macías, Anthony. *Mexican American Mojo: Popular Music, Dance, and Urban Culture in Los Angeles, 1935–1968*. Durham: Duke University Press, 2008.

Madison, D. Soyini. *Critical Ethnography: Method, Ethics, and Performance*. Thousand Oaks, CA: Sage, 2005.

Marx, Leo. *The Machine in the Garden: Technology and the Pastoral Ideal in America*. Oxford: Oxford University Press, 1964.

Matsumoto, Valerie J., and Blake Allmendinger, eds. *Over the Edge: Remapping the American West*. Berkeley: University of California Press, 1999.

McCammack, Brian. *Landscapes of Hope: Nature and the Great Migration in Chicago*. Cambridge: Harvard University Press, 2017.

McWilliams, Carey. *North from Mexico: The Spanish-Speaking People of the United States*. Westport, CT: Praeger, 2016.

———. *Southern California: An Island on the Land*. Santa Barbara, CA: Peregrine Smith, 1973.

Merrill, Karen R. *Public Lands and Political Meaning: Ranchers, the Government, and the Property between Them*. Berkeley: University of California Press, 2002.

Mickenberg, Julia. "'Revolution Can Spring Up from the Windy Prairie as Naturally as Wheat': Meridel Le Sueur and the Making of a Radical Regional Tradition." In *Regionalists on the Left: Radical Voices from the American West*, edited by Michael Steiner, 25–46. Norman: University of Oklahoma Press, 2013.

Miles, Tiya. *Ties That Bind: The Story of an Afro-Cherokee Family in Slavery and Freedom*. Berkeley: University of California Press, 2015.

Miller, Angela. *The Empire of the Eye: Landscape Representation and American Cultural Politics, 1825–1875*. Ithaca: Cornell University Press, 1993.

Miller, Douglas. *Indians on the Move: Native American Mobility and Urbanization in the Twentieth Century*. Chapel Hill: University of North Carolina Press, 2019.

Miller, Stephen. *Excellence and Equity: The National Endowment for the Humanities*. Lexington: University Press of Kentucky, 1984.

Molina, Natalia. *How Race Is Made in America: Immigration, Citizenship, and the Historical Power of Racial Scripts*. Berkeley: University of California Press, 2014.

Montgomery, Charles H. *The Spanish Redemption: Heritage, Power, and Loss on New Mexico's Upper Rio Grande*. Berkeley: University of California Press, 2002.

Morrissey, Katherine G. *Mental Territories: Mapping the Inland Empire*. Ithaca: Cornell University Press, 1997.

Mouffe, Chantal. *The Democratic Paradox*. New York: Verso, 2000.

Mulloy, D. J. *The World of the John Birch Society: Conspiracy, Conservatism, and the Cold War*. Nashville: Vanderbilt University Press, 2014.

Nash, Roderick. *Wilderness and the American Mind*. Rev. ed. New Haven: Yale University Press, 2014.

National Endowment for the Humanities. "How NEH Got Its Start." NEH website. Accessed January 6, 2025. https://www.neh.gov/about/history.

National Museum of the American Indian. *Do All Indians Live in Tipis? Questions and Answers from the National Museum of the American Indian.* Rev. ed. Washington, DC: Smithsonian Books, 2018.

Needham, Andrew. *Power Lines: Phoenix and the Making of the Modern Southwest.* Princeton: Princeton University Press, 2014.

Ngai, Mae M. *Impossible Subjects: Illegal Aliens and the Making of Modern America.* Princeton: Princeton University Press, 2004.

Nieto-Phillips, John M. *The Language of Blood: The Making of Spanish-American Identity in New Mexico, 1880s-1930s.* Albuquerque: University of New Mexico Press, 2004.

O'Brien, Jean. *Dispossession by Degrees: Indian Land and Identity in Natick, Massachusetts, 1650-1790.* Cambridge: Cambridge University Press, 1997.

———. *Firsting and Lasting: Writing Indians Out of Existence in New England.* Minneapolis: University of Minnesota Press, 2010.

O'Brien, Sharon. "Becoming Noncanonical: The Case against Willa Cather." *American Quarterly* 40, no. 1 (March 1988): 110–26.

Ochoa, Melissa. "Who Likes the Term *Latinx*?" YouTube. Accessed January 4, 2024. https://www.youtube.com/watch?v=Zdug1JE-u28.

Oh, Arissa H. "From War Waif to Ideal Immigrant: The Cold War Transformation of the Korean Orphan." *Journal of American Ethnic History* 31, no. 4 (Summer 2012): 34–55.

Olson, Leisl. *Literature and Art in the Midwest Metropolis.* New Haven: Yale University Press, 2017.

Op de Beeck, Nathalie. "Committing to a Long Journey: Indigenous Voices in Publishing." *Publishers Weekly*, January 20, 2023. https://www.publishersweekly.com/pw/by-topic/industry-news/publisher-news/article/91340-committing-to-a-long-journey-indigenous-voices-in-publishing.html.

Pearlman, Mickey. *Inter/View: A Voice of One's Own: Conversations with America's Writing Women.* Boston: Houghton Mifflin, 1992.

Pearson, Byron E. *Still the Wild River Runs: Congress, the Sierra Club, and the Fight to Save Grand Canyon.* Tucson: University of Arizona Press, 2002.

Pexa, Christopher. *Translated Nation: Rewriting the Dakhóta Oyáte.* Minneapolis: University of Minnesota Press, 2019.

Phelan, Peggy. *Unmarked: The Politics of Performance.* New York: Routledge, 1995.

Phillips, Kevin. *The Emerging Republican Majority.* New Rochelle, NY: Arlington House, 1969.

Philpott, William. *Vacationland: Tourism and Environment in the Colorado High Country*. Seattle: University of Washington Press, 2013.

Piatote, Beth H. *Domestic Subjects: Gender, Citizenship, and Law in Native American Literature*. New Haven: Yale University Press, 2013.

Pollack, Norman. "Fear of Man: Populism, Authoritarianism, and the Historian." *Agricultural History* 39, no. 2 (April 1965): 59–67.

Pomeroy, Earl. *In Search of the Golden West: The Tourist in Western America*. Lincoln: University of Nebraska Press, 1957.

Postel, Charles. *The Populist Vision*. New York: Oxford University Press, 2007.

Powell, Miles A. *Vanishing America: Species Extinction, Racial Peril, and the Origins of Conservation*. Cambridge: Harvard University Press, 2016.

Pratt, Mary Louise. *Imperial Eyes: Travel Writing and Transculturation*. London: Routledge, 1992.

Radkin, Charles, ed. *Wallace Stegner: Man and Writer*. Albuquerque: University of New Mexico Press, 1996.

Randall, L. W. (Gay). "The Man Who Put the Dude in Dude Ranching: Dick Randall, Hunting Guide to Teddy Roosevelt, Became the Father of Dude Ranching in Montana." *Montana* 10, no. 3 (Summer 1960): 29–41.

Rifkin, Mark. *Settler Common Sense: Queerness and Everyday Colonialism in the American Renaissance*. Minneapolis: University of Minnesota Press, 2013.

Robbins, William G. *Landscapes of Conflict: The Oregon Story, 1940–2000*. Seattle: University of Washington Press, 2004.

———. *Landscapes of Promise: The Oregon Story, 1800–1940*. Seattle: University of Washington Press, 1997.

Robinson, Greg. *A Tragedy of Democracy: Japanese Confinement in North America*. New York: Columbia University Press, 2009.

Rochberg-Halton, Eugene. "Life, Literature, and Sociology in Turn-of-the-Century Chicago." In *Consuming Visions*, edited by Simon Bronner, 311–38. New York: Norton, 1989.

Rodgers, Daniel T. *Atlantic Crossings: Social Politics in a Progressive Age*. Cambridge: Harvard University Press, 1998.

Rodnitzky, Jerome L. "Recapturing the American West: The Dude Ranch in American Life." *Arizona and the West* 10, no. 2 (Summer 1968): 111–26.

Rohrbough, Malcolm J. *The Land Office Business: The Settlement and Administration of American Public Lands*. New York: Oxford University Press, 1968.

Rosenthal, Nicolas G. *Reimagining Indian Country: Native American Migration and*

Identity in Twentieth-Century Los Angeles. Chapel Hill: University of North Carolina Press, 2012.

Rosier, Paul. "'They Are Ancestral Homelands': Race, Place, and Politics in Cold War Native America, 1945-1961." *Journal of American History* 92, no. 4 (March 2006): 1300–1326.

Rothman, Hal K. *Devil's Bargains: Tourism in the Twentieth-Century American West*. Lawrence: University Press of Kansas, 1998.

Rozum, Molly P. *Grasslands Grown: Creating Place on the US Northern Plains and Canadian Prairies*. Lincoln: University of Nebraska Press, 2021.

Saldaña-Portillo, María Josefina. *Indian Given: Racial Geographies across Mexico and the United States*. Durham: Duke University Press, 2016.

Sanchez, F. Richard, ed. *White Shell Water Place: An Anthology of Native American Reflections on the 400th Anniversary of the Founding of Santa Fe, New Mexico*. Santa Fe: Sunstone Press, 2010.

Sánchez, Rosaura, and Beatrice Pita. *Spatial and Discursive Violence in the US Southwest*. Durham: Duke University Press, 2021.

Sandweiss, Martha A. *Print the Legend: Photography and the American West*. New Haven: Yale University Press, 2002.

Schlatter, Evelyn A. *Aryan Cowboys: White Supremacists and the Search for a New Frontier, 1970-2000*. Austin: University of Texas Press, 2006.

Schonberger, Howard B. *Aftermath of War: Americans and the Remaking of Japan, 1945-1952*. Kent, OH: Kent State University Press, 1989.

———. "Thomas Arthur Bisson and the Limits of Reform in Occupied Japan." *Bulletin of Concerned Asian Scholars* 12, no. 4 (December 1980): 26–37.

Schweber, Nate. *This America of Ours: Bernard and Avis DeVoto and the Forgotten Fight to Save the Wild*. Boston: Mariner Books, 2022.

Scobey, David. "Looking West from the Empire City: National Landscape and Visual Culture in Gilded-Age New York." In *New York: Art and Cultural Capital of the Gilded Age*, edited by Margaret R. Laster and Chelsea Bruner, 17–40. New York: Routledge, 2019.

Scofield, Rebecca. *Outriders: Rodeo at the Fringes of the American West*. Seattle: University of Washington Press, 2019.

Self, Robert O. *All in the Family: The Realignment of American Democracy since the 1960s*. New York: Hill and Wang, 2012.

Shaffer, Marguerite S. *See America First: Tourism and National Identity, 1880-1940*. Washington, DC: Smithsonian Institution Press, 2001.

Shanley, Kathryn. "The Indians America Loves to Love and Read: American Indian Identity and Cultural Appropriation." In *Native American Representations: First Encounters, Distorted Images, and Literary Appropriations*, edited by Gretchen M. Bataille, 26–49. Lincoln: University of Nebraska Press, 2001.

Shoemaker, Nancy. "Regions as Categories of Analysis." *Perspectives* 34 (November 1996): 7–8.

Shreve, Bradley. *Red Power Rising: The National Indian Youth Council and the Origins of Native Activism*. Albuquerque: University of New Mexico Press, 2011.

Sides, Josh. *LA City Limits: African American Los Angeles from the Great Depression to the Present*. Berkeley: University of California Press, 2003.

Silko, Leslie Marmon. *Yellow Woman and a Beauty of the Spirit: Essays on Native American Life Today*. New York: Simon & Schuster, 1996.

Silva, Noenoe K. *Aloha Betrayed: Native Hawaiian Resistance to American Colonialism*. Durham: Duke University Press, 2004.

Singh, Nikhil Pal. *Black Is a Country: Race and the Unfinished Struggle for Democracy*. Cambridge: Harvard University Press, 2004.

———. "Liberalism." In *Keywords in American Cultural Studies*, edited by Bruce Burgett and Glenn Hendler, 153–58. 2nd ed. New York: New York University Press, 2014.

Skillen, James R. *The Nation's Largest Landlord: The Bureau of Land Management in the American West*. Lawrence: University Press of Kansas, 2008.

Slater, Lisa. *Anxieties of Belonging in Settler Colonialism: Australia, Race and Place*. Abingdon, UK: Routledge, 2019.

Slotkin, Richard. *Gunfighter Nation: The Myth of the Frontier in Twentieth-Century America*. New York: Harper/Perennial, 1992.

Smith, Henry Nash. *Virgin Land: The American West as Symbol and Myth*. Cambridge: Harvard University Press, 1950.

Smith, Lawrence B. *Dude Ranches and Ponies*. New York: Coward-McCann, 1936.

Smith, Rachel Greenwald. *On Compromise: Art, Politics, and the Fate of an American Ideal*. Minneapolis: Graywolf Press, 2021.

Smith, Thomas G. "Robert Frost, Stewart Udall, and the 'Last Go-Down.'" *New England Quarterly* 70, no. 1 (March 1997): 3–32.

———. *Stewart L. Udall: Steward of the Land*. Albuquerque: University of New Mexico Press, 2017.

Steineker, Rowan Faye. "'Fully Equal to That of Any Children': Experimental Creek Education in the Antebellum Era." *History of Education Quarterly* 56, no. 2 (May 2016): 273–300.

Steiner, Michael C. "Regionalism in the Great Depression." *Geographical Review* 73, no. 4 (October 1983): 430–46.

———, ed. *Regionalists on the Left: Radical Voices from the American West*. Norman: University of Oklahoma Press, 2013.

Stock, Catherine McNicol. *Nuclear Country: The Origins of the Rural New Right*. Philadelphia: University of Pennsylvania Press, 2020.

———. *Rural Radicals: Righteous Rage in the American Grain*. Ithaca: Cornell University Press, 1996.

Sugrue, Thomas J. *Sweet Land of Liberty: The Forgotten Struggle for Civil Rights in the North*. New York: Random House, 2008.

Taliaferro, John. *Charles M. Russell: The Life and Legend of America's Cowboy Artist*. Norman: University of Oklahoma Press, 2003.

Taylor, Joseph. *Persistent Callings: Seasons of Work and Identity on the Oregon Coast*. Corvallis: Oregon State University Press, 2019.

Taylor, Quintard. *The Forging of a Black Community*. Seattle: University of Washington Press, 1994.

Thomas, John L. *A Country in the Mind: Wallace Stegner, Bernard DeVoto, History, and the American Land*. New York: Routledge, 2000.

Tompkins, Kyla Wazana. "'You Make Me Feel Right Quare': Promiscuous Reading, Minoritarian Critique, and White Sovereign Entrepreneurial Terror." *Social Text* 35, no. 4 (December 2017): 53–86.

Treuer, David. *Native American Fiction: A User's Manual*. Minneapolis: Graywolf Press, 2006.

Turner, Frederick Jackson. "The Significance of the Frontier in American History." *The Frontier in American History*. 1920. Reprint, Tucson: University of Arizona Press, 1986.

Urban, Andy. "Digging Up the Backyard: Seabrook Farms and the Importance of Critical Local Histories." *New Jersey Studies: An Interdisciplinary Journal* 3, no. 2 (Summer 2017): 257–68.

———, ed. *Invisible Restraints: Life and Labor at Seabrook Farms*. Digital exhibit. Rutgers. Accessed January 6, 2025. https://exhibits.libraries.rutgers.edu/seabrook_farms.

Veracini, Lorenzo. *Settler Colonialism: A Theoretical Overview*. New York: Palgrave Macmillan, 2010.

Vizenor, Gerald. *Manifest Manners: Narratives on Postindian Survivance*. Lincoln: University of Nebraska Press, 1999.

———, ed. *Survivance: Narratives of Native Presence*. Lincoln: University of Nebraska Press, 2008.

Von Eschen, Penny M. *Race against Empire: Black Americans and Anticolonialism, 1937-1957*. Ithaca, NY: Cornell University Press, 1997.

———. *Satchmo Blows Up the World: Jazz Ambassadors Play the Cold War*. Cambridge: Harvard University Press, 2004.

Warren, Louis S. *Buffalo Bill's America: William Cody and the Wild West Show*. New York: Knopf, 2005.

Warrior, Robert. *The People and the Word: Reading Native Nonfiction*. Minneapolis: University of Minnesota Press, 2005.

Washington, Mary Helen. "'Disturbing the Peace: What Happens to American Studies if You Put African American Studies at the Center?' Presidential Address to the American Studies Association, October 29, 1997." *American Quarterly* 50, no. 1 (1998): 1-23.

Weber, David J. "John Francis Bannon and the Historiography of the Spanish Borderlands: Retrospect and Prospect." *Journal of the Southwest* 29, no. 4 (Winter 1987): 331-63.

West, E. James. "Johnson Publishing Company and the Search for a White Audience." *American Journalism* 39, no. 3, July 19, 2022, 293-314.

White, Cody. "On the Road Again: Max Bigman's Lecture Career." *Text Message*. Accessed June 1, 2021. https://text-message.blogs.archives.gov/2021/06/01/on-the-road-again-max-bigmans-lecture-career.

White, G. Edward. *The Eastern Establishment and the Western Experience: The West of Frederic Remington, Theodore Roosevelt, and Owen Wister*. Austin: University of Texas Press, 1989.

Wilson, Chris. *The Myth of Santa Fe: Creating a Modern Regional Tradition*. Albuquerque: University of New Mexico Press, 1997.

Wilson, Waziyatawin Angela Cavender. "Burning Down the House: Laura Ingalls Wilder and American Colonialism." In *Unlearning the Language of Conquest: Scholars Expose Anti-Indianism in America*, edited by Four Arrows (Don Trent Jacobs), 66-80. Austin: University of Texas Press, 2006.

Wolfe, Patrick. *Settler Colonialism and the Transformation of Anthropology: The Politics and Poetics of an Ethnographic Event*. London: Continuum, 1998.

Wrobel, David M. *The End of American Exceptionalism: Frontier Anxiety from the Old West to the New Deal*. Lawrence: University Press of Kansas, 1993.

———. *Promised Lands: Promotion, Memory, and the Creation of the American West*. Lawrence: University Press of Kansas, 2002.

Wrobel, David M., and Patrick T. Long, eds. *Seeing and Being Seen: Tourism in the American West*. Lawrence: University Press of Kansas, 2001.

Wrobel, David. M., and Michael C. Steiner, eds. *Many Wests: Place, Culture, and Regional Identity*. Lawrence: University Press of Kansas, 1997.

Wu, Ellen D. *The Color of Success: Asian Americans and the Origins of the Model Minority*. Princeton: Princeton University Press, 2014.

Young, Alex Trimble, and Lorenzo Veracini. "'*If* I Am Native to Anything': Settler Colonial Studies and Western American Literature." *Western American Literature* 52, no. 1 (2017): 1–23.

Young, Phoebe S. K. *California Vieja: Culture and Memory in a Modern American Place*. Berkeley: University of California Press, 2006.

Yu, Henry. *Thinking Orientals: Migration, Contact, and Exoticism in Modern America*. Oxford: Oxford University Press, 2001.

Zarsadiaz, James. *Resisting Change in Suburbia: Asian Immigrants and Frontier Nostalgia in LA*. Berkeley: University of California Press, 2022.

INDEX

Italicized page numbers refer to figures.

Abbey, Edward, 142
Across the Wide Missouri (DeVoto), 89–90
Adams, Ansel: at Interior Department art gallery, 146; *Moonrise over Hernandez, New Mexico*, 143; photos provided by, 139; on preservation of land, 140
Adams, Frank T., Jr., 164–65
Africa: Land of My Fathers (Thompson), 42, 51
agrarian populism, 18, 22, 40, 181–82, 193
Almanac of the Dead (Silko), 210
Amemiya, Yuriko, 74, 235
American Academy of Arts and Letters, 147
American Agriculture Movement, 182, 191
American Council of Learned Societies, 76, 111, 116
American Daughter (Thompson), 41, 43–44, 46, 47, 52, 53
American Folkways (Caldwell), 24
American Indian Movement, 213
American Indian Performing Arts Festival, 224

American National Livestock Association, 98
American Rhythm (Austin), 106
Anderson, Marian, 134, 142
Anti-Alien Land Laws, 69
Anti-Defamation League, 189
antisemitism, Trillin's introduction to, 200–201. *See also* white supremacy
"Anxious West, The" (DeVoto), 98, 104, 107
Anzaldúa, Gloria, 169
Appeal to Reason (socialist newspaper), 27, 63
Armed and Dangerous (Coates), 179, 196–97
Arragon, Reginald "Rex," 116, 119–20, 125
artists/musicians, vision of back East, 5
Artists Series, Presidential Cabinet, 134, 142, 145
arts and humanities as leisure, perception of, 146
August, John. *See* DeVoto, Bernard
Austin, Mary: *American Rhythm*, 106

Babb, Sanora, 235
Barden, Graham, 132–33

Barrett, William, 97
Bell's Lettres (Thompson), 50
Berg, Alan: indictment for his death, 202; memorials to, 179; murder of, 178, 197, 199
Bernstein, Leonard, 134
Berry, Wendell, 94, 142
Beyond the Hundredth Meridian (Stegner), 101, 131
Big Man, Max, 3, 35–37, 54
Birchbark Books, 212, 214
"Bitter Crop, The" (Cayton), 76
Black Metropolis (Cayton and Drake), 56, 65, 77–78, 125
Black Workers and the New Unions (Cayton and Mitchell), 64
Blue Book, The (John Birch Society), 159, 188
boarding schools, 206
Bontemps, Arna, 235
Bookman (literary monthly), 94
Boone, Raymond H., 164
Borne, Lawrence, 33
Brademas, John, 133, 134, 147, 148
Branch, Bonnie, 62, 78–79
Brayboy, Bryan McKinley Jones, 209
Bread Loaf Writers' Conference: about, 2; attendees photo, 91; beginning of, 94; Cather at, 13, 94; DeVoto at, 87; Frost at, 94; Guthrie at, 103; Edith Mirrielees at, 7, 114–15; Lucia Mirrielees at, 114–15; setting for, 85; Stegner at, 90; Thompson at, 50, 51; the Udalls' integration into, 134
Brinegar, David, 132
Bromley, John, response to *The Hidden Tyranny*, 190–91

Brooks, Van Wyck, 89
Brooks, Winthrop, 34
Brower, David, 139
Burciaga, José Antonio, 170, *174*
Bureau of Land Management, 97
Burgess, Ernest, 69
Burlington Railroad: advertising of, 31, 35; and collaboration with dude ranches, 32
Burt, Struthers: as conservationist, 102–3; *Diary of a Dude Wrangler*, 102; on wranglers, 39

Caldwell, Erskine: *American Folkways*, 24
California, 83, 91, 114, 118, 121; city locations misstated by *New York Times*, 118–19
Calloway, Colin, 213
Canto al Pueblo (poetry festival), 175
Canto y Grito mi Liberación (Sánchez), 162
Cather, Willa: about, 5, 12–13; on agrarian populism, 18; as Bread Loaf faculty, 94; harsh judgment of, 38; Lou Bergson (fictional character), 18; prairie trilogy, 13, 19; Thea Kronberg (fictional character), 13; view of Midwest, 24–25
Cather, Willa, works of: *Death Comes for the Archbishop*, 13; "Going Home," 11–12, 15; *My Ántonia*, 13, 38, 46; *One of Ours*, 13; *O Pioneers!*, 13, 18, 38; *The Professor's House*, 13; *Song of the Lark*, 13, 38
Caxton Printers (Caldwell, ID), 91–92, 195

Cayton, Horace: background of, 55–56; and breadth of reading, 64; career of, 64–65; and funding from WPA, 65; and National Endowment for the Humanities grant, 79; Parkway Community House run by, 71; on persistent racism, 76; photo of, *67*; *Pittsburgh Courier* column, 64; on racism as a binary structure, 79; on racism in the West, 116–18; as sociology research assistant, 64

Cayton, Horace, works of: "The Bitter Crop," 76; *Black Metropolis*, 56, 65, 74–75, 77, 125; *Black Workers and the New Unions*, 64; "Childhood in the West," 60; "Liberals?," 78; *Long Old Road: Back to Black Metropolis*, 60, 61, 62

Chicago, as East, 12, 25, 77

Chicago Defender, 44–45

"Chicago School" of sociology: Park as co-creator of, 55; on race as binary, 58; Stegner and, 81

Chicane, choice of term, 248n24; 267n2; 268n4

Chicano presses, 169

"Childhood in the West" (Cayton), 60

Chin, Frank, 235

Civil Liberties Act of 1988, 200

Coates, James: *Armed and Dangerous*, 179, 196–97

colonialism: Erdrich's challenge to, 216; origin point of, 217; Spanish, 207–8, 210

Colorado River Storage Project, 131

Committee on Minority Groups of Chicago, Council of Social Agencies, 71

"Condescension in Foreigners" (Lowell), 29

conservation: Ansel Adams on, 140; economic arguments for, 141; legislation on, 109; Stegner on, 140; of western public lands, 90

conservationists: Burt as, 102–3; DeVoto as, 96, 101; Stegner as, 96, 101, 140

Cook-Lynn, Elizabeth, 210, 211, 212, 216, 228

Cooperrider, Kenneth: "No Longer a Minority," 124

Course of Empire, The (DeVoto), 89–90

Crow Nation, advocacy for, 36

Crusaders (Le Sueur), 26, 27

Dartmouth College: commencement address (2009), 216; Indigenous attendees of, 205, 206, 209–10, 212

Dasburg, Andrew, 108

Davis, William N., Jr., 21

Daughter of the Middle Border, A (Garland), 48

Death Comes for the Archbishop (Cather), 13

Debunker (magazine), 29, 63, 64

Desert Year, The (Krutch), 131

DeVoto, Avis: at Bread Loaf Writers' Conference, 51; and Communist sympathizer charges, 121; photo of, *88*

DeVoto, Bernard: about, 4; on absentee exploitation, 100–101; articles for the *Pacific Spectator*, 119; as Bread Loaf faculty, 50, 94; and Communist sympathizer charges, 121; as conservationist, 83, 96, 101; on dam in Dinosaur National Monument, 131; Frost on, 119;

DeVoto, Bernard (*continued*)
gendered language/views of, 96, 190; *Harper's* Easy Chair column of, 87, 95; New England vs. New York preference of, 95; on New York as extractive economy, 166; and opposition to privatization of public land, 98, 105; on outdoor recreation, 99; photo of, 88; Stegner's biography of, 92–93

DeVoto, Bernard, works of: *Across the Wide Missouri*, 89–90; "The Anxious West," 98, 104, 107; *The Course of Empire*, 89–90; "Footnote on the West," 106; *The Hour*, 95; *The Journals of Lewis and Clark*, 89–90; *Mark Twain's America*, 89–90, 93, 95; *Mountain Time*, 93; "Queen City of the Plains and Peaks," 119, 131; "The West: A Plundered Province," 87, 99; "The West against Itself," 98, 104; *The Year of Decision: 1846*, 89–90

Diary of a Dude Wrangler (Burt), 102

Discovery of Freedom, The (Lane), 195

Dorris, Michael, 214

Douglass fellowships, 164–65

Drake, Sandra, 125

Drake, St. Claire: *Black Metropolis*, 65, 125; and funding from WPA, 65

dude, definition/connotations of, 37

Dude Rancher (newsletter), 32, 34, 36–37

Dude Ranchers' Association, 32

dude ranches: about, 32–35; advertising for, 32, 37–38; clientele of, 34; photo of, 33

education: Green on, 149–50; of Indigenous children, 208; and Indigenous goals, 209

Education of a Wandering Man (L'Amour), 28–29

Elliott, Roderick: about, 4; and attack on Bromley, 190; bankruptcy of, 202; on Berg's show, 199; and blaming the East, 182–83; criminal record/imprisonment of, 182; discontent created by, 183–84; inaccuracy by, 184; and indictment for theft and conspiracy, 202; with Kirk's widow, 201–2; peddling NAPA memberships/false claims, 199; use of resentment targeting the East by, 180–81. See also *Primrose and Cattlemen's Gazette*

El Paso, Texas, 177

Emerging Republican Majority, The (Phillips), 163–64

environmental humanities: articulation of, 84, 134; role of, 152; support for, 150–51; Udall's sense of, 131

Environmental Protection Agency, 129

Erdrich, Louise: about, 4; Cook-Lynn on, 210, 211; Dartmouth commencement address (2009) by, 216; education of, 213; on Indigenous educational goals, 209; marriage of, 214; success of, 205; writing style of, 212

Erdrich, Louise, works by: *The Game of Silence*, 212; *The Last Report on the Miracles at Little No Horse*, 211; *Love Medicine*, 211, 214, 219; *The Night Watchman*, 216–19; *The Painted Drum*, 215; *The Plague of Doves*, 211; *The Round House*, 216; *The Sentence*, 229

Etulain, Richard: *Stegner: Conversations on History and Literature*, 93–94

Executive Order 9066, 71

farm crisis, 182, 192, 201
farmers: activism of, 182; challenges facing, 181; and land as collateral for loans, 181; as moderating excesses of eastern capitalists, 20–21; as symbol of democratic citizenship, 22; "tractorcades" by, 182, *183*
Farrar, John, 94, 115
filmmakers/television producers, vision of back East, 5
Fisher, Rudolph, 45
"Footnote on the West" (DeVoto), 106
frontier, viii–xi, 10, 15, 60, 89, 136, 180. *See also* settler colonialism
Friends of the Middle Border: region celebrated by, 56–57; Thompson's interaction with, 48, 53
Frost, Robert: and advocacy for property as National Monument, 142–43; in the Artists Series, 134; as Bread Loaf faculty, 94; on DeVoto, 119; at Dumbarton Oaks, 145–46; "The Gift Outright," 136, 147; as poetry consultant, 133; reading at Kennedy's inauguration, 134, 135–37; with the Udalls, *135*

Galicia, Homero, 170
Game of Silence, The (Erdrich), 212
Garland, Hamlin: about, 5; *A Daughter of the Middle Border*, 48; *A Son of the Middle Border*, 48
Gaussoin family, 204, 213, 215, 221–24
"Gift Outright, The" (Frost), 136, 147
Gleed, James Willis, 19–20

"Going Home" (Cather), 11–12, 15
Gonzalez, Corky: "I Am Joaquín," 167
Gonzalez, N. V. M., 125
Gourneau, Patrick (Aunishenaubay), 217
Green, Edith, 133, 134, 148, 149, 152–53
Greever, Paul, 34
Guthrie, A. B.: about, 102; career of, 103; *Shane* (screenplay), 103; *The Way West*, 103

Haaland, Deb, 227, 235
Halaby, Najeeb E., 125
Haldeman-Julius, Emanuel: *Appeal to Reason* (socialist newspaper), 27, 63; *Debunker* (magazine), 28; Little Blue Books, 28, *30*, 63, 64
Haldeman-Julius, Marcet: *Appeal to Reason* (socialist newspaper), 27; Little Blue Books, 28, *30*
Harjo, Joy: education of, 226; as US poet laureate, 227
Harvard University, 86, 95
Haworth, Leland, 146–47
Hayakawa, S. I., 235
Hayden, Carl, 124, 128
Hechízospells (Sánchez), 168
Her First American (Segal), 78
Hewitt, Frankie, 148
Hicks, John: about, 17; agrarian populism, 181–82; comparison with Thompson, 54; as faculty, 17, 21; Gleed as information source for, 19–20; *The Populist Revolt: The Farmers' Alliance and the People's Party*, 17–19; and view of Midwest, 24–25; views of, 31
Higham, John, 146
Hill, Jim, 24

Index 311

Hoover, Herbert, 124
Hopper, Dennis, 232
Hour, The (DeVoto), 95
House Made of Dawn (Momaday), 213
Houser, Alan, 207
Hughes, Langston, 45
humanities: Green on, 150; Stegner on, 150–51. *See also* arts and humanities; environmental humanities; National Endowment for the Arts and National Endowment for the Humanities
"Human Migration and the Marginal Man" (Park), 57

"I Am Joaquín" (Gonzalez), 167
I-Am-Not-Your-Mascot movement, 228
Ickes, Harold, 96–97, 142
Imamura, Fuji, 125
Immigration Act of 1924, 69
Indians of All Tribes, Alcatraz Island occupation by, 213
Indigenous art displays, 143–45, *144*
Institute for American Indian Arts: history of, 223–27; MFA in creative writing, 227; performance at the White House, 225; political advocacy as advocacy, 228
Interior Department: art gallery of, *144*, 146, 147, 224; extractive and exploitative stance of, 129–30; and jurisdiction over historic sites, 145; *The Quiet Crisis*, 140–41; responsibilities of, 137, 148

Japanese American Citizens League (JACL), 70–71
Japanese Americans: discrimination against, 73–74; incarceration and relocation of, 69–72, *73*, 81; as model minority, 75–76, 81–82; viewed as government informers, 70–71
Japanese Evacuation and Resettlement Study (JERS), 57–58
John Birch Society, 159, 188, 195–96
Johnson, Lady Bird, 224–25
Johnson, Lyndon, 128–29
Joint Livestock Committee on Public Lands, 98
Jordan, David Starr, 114
Journals of Lewis and Clark, The (DeVoto), 89–90

Kahl, Gordon, 197, 199
Kemeny, John, 212–13
Kennedy, John F.: Frost reading at inauguration of, 134; introduction to *The Quiet Crisis*, 140–41; Udall appointment by, 128
Kesey, Ken: *Sometimes a Great Notion*, 234–35
Kikuchi, Charles: and collection of life histories of relocated Japanese Americans, 71–72; marriage of, 74, 235; multiracial perspective of, 58–59; as psychiatric social worker, 74; and view on African American equality, 75
Kingston, Maxine Hong, 235
Kirk, Arthur, 197, 200, 201
Krutch, Joseph Wood: *The Desert Year*, 131; on value of solitude, 131
Ku Klux Klan, 180

Lamm, Richard, 185–86
L'Amour, Louis: *Education of a Wandering Man*, 28

Lane, David, 180, 202
Lane, Rose Wilder: about, 193–95; *The Discovery of Freedom*, 195; politics of, 195
Larom, Larry, *33*, 34, 73–74, 97
Last Report on the Miracles at Little No Horse, The (Erdrich), 211
law enforcement deaths, 197, 199
Lawrence, D. H., 106–7
Leopold, Aldo: *Sand County Almanac*, 131
Le Sueur, Meridel: about, 23–25, 235; and agrarian populism, 181–82; blacklisting of, 29, 63; comparison with Thompson, 54; *Crusaders*, 26, 27; *North Star Country*, 24, 25; parents of, 23, 26; and wealth extracted from Indigenous People/land, 26; "Women on the Breadlines," 38–39; and work involving Indigenous/Native Peoples, 27
Lewis, Oscar: *The Big Four*, 118
Lewis, Rob, 176
liberalism, 9–10, 77–78, 237–38
"Liberals?" (Cayton), 78
libertarianism, 195–96
Liberty Amendment, 195–96
Little Blue Books, 28, *30–31*, 63, 64, 192. See also Haldeman-Julius, Emanuel; Haldeman-Julius, Marcet
Little House on the Prairie series (Wilder), 193–94, 196, 197, 216
Lorde, Audre, 157–58
Love Medicine (Erdrich), 211, 214, 219
Lowell, Abbott Lawrence, 86, 114
Lowell, James Russell: "Condescension in Foreigners," 29
Luhan, Mabel Dodge, 106–7, 108

MacBride, Roger, 195–96
Maclean, Norman, 235
"MAÑANA: Stanford U. Breakfast Blues" (Sánchez), 170–71
"marginal man" thesis: as binary view of race, 58; development of, 56–57; shortcomings of, 59
Mark Twain's America (DeVoto), 89–90, 93, 95
Martinez, Maria, exhibit, 143
Martinez, Tom, 190
Matthews, Bob, 202
McCarren, Pat, 97
McCarthy, Eugene, 132
McCormick, Harold, 186
McGovern, George, 132
McGrath, Jim, *144*
McKay, Claude, 45
McMahon, Theresa, 63
McWilliams, Carey, 7
MEChA (Movimiento Estudiantil Chicano de Aztlán), 165
Medicine Horse Zillioux, Mike, 235
Metcalf, Lee, 132
"Míctla: Long Road Home" (Sánchez), 169
Midwest: definition of, 5; as regime, 53
Midwest Canto al Pueblo, 175
migration north-south, 197, *198*, 199
Mineta, Norman, 200
Mirrielees, Edith: about, 111; at Bread Loaf Writers' Conference, 107; career of, 107, 113–15; as editor of *Pacific Spectator*, 7, 118; photo of, *117*; "The Shooting at Raeder," 113; *Stanford: The Story of a University*, 114; *Stanford Mosaic*, 124, 125; Stegner as successor to, 83; *Story Writing*, 124

Index 313

Mirrielees, Lucia, 114–15
Mitchell, George S.: *Black Workers and the New Unions*, 64
Miyamoto, S. Frank: background of, 67–68; education of, 69; faculty position of, 79; incarceration of, 57–58, 70; on racism as a binary structure, 79; and role in JERS, 57–58; "Social Solidarity among the Japanese in Seattle," 67–68
Momaday, N. Scott: *House Made of Dawn*, 213
Moonrise over Hernandez, New Mexico (Adams), 143
Morgan, Edward P., 137
Morgan, Pierpont, 24
Morison, Samuel Eliot, 21
Morrison, Kay, 94, 133
Morrison, Ted: as Bread Loaf's director, 94; interaction with Udalls, 134; photo of, *117*
Mountain Time (DeVoto), 93
Movimiento Estudiantil Chicano de Aztlán (MEChA), 165
My Ántonia (Cather), 13, 38, 46

National Academy for the Arts, 147
National Agricultural Press Association (NAPA), 199–202
National Defense of Education Act, 134
National Endowment for the Arts and National Endowment for the Humanities, 1, 4, 84, 111, 129, 134, 142, 145, 150, 157
National Foundation for the Arts, 147, 150
National Foundation on the Arts and Humanities, 146

National Indian Youth Council, 212–13
National Institute of Arts and Letters, 147
National Museum of the American Indian, 205
National Wool Growers Association, 98
Nellis, Alden, 191–92
Nellis, Micki, 191–92
Neuberger, Maurine, 149
Neuberger, Richard, 148–49
New, Lloyd, 224, 226
new sectionalism, 19
New York City: as represented by westerners, 49, 94–95, 101, 165–66
Nightwatchman, The (Erdrich), 216–19
Nishi, Setsuko Matsunaga, 71
Nitobe, Inazo, 68
Nixon, Richard M., 128
Nonpartisan League, 23, 24, 41
Nordstrom, Ursula, 193–94
North Dakota Humanities Council, 151–52
Northern Pacific railway: collaboration with dude ranches, 32; merger with Great Northern railway, 24
North Star Country (Le Sueur), 24, 25
Northwest Harvest (Pacific Coast Committee for the Humanities), 76, 116–18, 119–20, 148–49
Northwest Railroad, land grants, 25

Oklahoma City bombing, 202
"Old Man" (Sánchez), 171–72
Olsen, Chet, 102, 235
One Nation (Stegner), 81–82
One of Ours (Cather), 13
O Pioneers! (Cather), 13, 18, 38

Order, the (white power): Berg's murder by, 178; and charges against members, 202; and founder's death in standoff, 202; as western organization, 180; white homeland as goal of, 179
Ortiz, Olivia Amaya, 204, 207, 230
Ota, Lillian, 75
Otero-Warren, Nina, 235

Pacheco, Javier, 170, 176–77
Pacific Coast Committee for the Humanities, 2, 76, 111, 116, 126
Pacific Northwest, anti-Black racism in, 61–62
Pacific Spectator: Asian writing in, 120; content of, 118–21; Indigenous policy (Indian policy) of, 122–24; Mirrielees as editor, 111; publication of, begun, 148–49; race and racism discussions in, 121–22; Red Scare articles in, 121; termination/demise of, 124
Painted Drum, The (Erdrich), 215
Paperbacks . . . ¡y Más! (bookstore): model for, 176; and Poets of Texas series, 176; Tiltons as supporters of, 176
Park, Robert E.: as Cayton's mentor, 55; dedication to, 65; "Human Migration and the Marginal Man," 57; and "marginal man" thesis, 56–57
Parkway Community House, 71, 77
Paterson, Isabel Mary, 195
Pecos, Regis, 207, 210–11, 214, 215, 220–21, 229
People's College (Fort Scott, KS): about, 27–28; vigilante destruction of, 29
People's Party, 24

Phillips, Kevin: *The Emerging Republican Majority*, 163–64
Picuris Pueblo, hotel ownership by, 207
Plague of Doves, The (Erdrich), 211
Pollock, Jackson, 235
Populist Revolt, The (Hicks), 17–19
Posse Blue Book, 200
Posse Comitatus, 159, 180, 197, 199
Powell, John Wesley, 101, 131
Presidential Cabinet Artists Series, 134, 142, 145
Primrose and Cattlemen's Gazette: and abdication of journalistic ethics, 191; acquisition of readers, 191–92; advertising in, 186–87; and alleged interview with Rosenthal, 190–91; anti-government editorials in, 188–89; antisemitism in, 187; audience of, 193; demise of, 202; as Elliott's platform, 180–84; and free copies for politicians, 184; and Fund to Restore an Educated Electorate, 188; gender stereotypes in, 196; *The Hidden Tyranny*, 190–91; immigration discussions in, 185–86; "New World Order Trilateral Commission," 188; publisher of, 180; Republican goals reflected in, 185; and resentment of the East, 180–81, 192–93; and Sagebrush Rebellion, 186, 203; and survivalism, 196–97
Professor's House, The (Cather), 13
public lands, privatization of, 97, 98, 100, 105, 186
Pueblo Revolt (1680) and reconquest, 220

"Queen City of the Plains and Peaks" (DeVoto), 119, 131

Quiet Crisis, The (Interior Department), 140–41

railroads: advertising by, 31–32; American Indian opposition to, 25; automobiles as competition, 32; Burlington line, 31, 32; economic critique of, 3; economic exploitation by, 14; Great Northern railway, 24; hoboes use of, 27; labor for, 25; and power in shaping regional boundaries, 31; and transcontinental completion, 25; as where the East began, 17. *See also* Northern Pacific railway; Union Pacific Railroad
Randall, Dick, 32–33
Reagan, Ronald: presidency of, 186; Simpson as advocate of, 179; views of, 179
Red Scare, 120–21
regional identity, 3, 4, 9–10
regional proletarianism, 23
regional word choices, vii
reservation termination efforts, 217–18
Revels, Hiram, 55, 60
Richmond Afro-American's Frederick Douglass Fellows program, 161–62
Roosevelt, Theodore, 7
Rosenthal, Harold, 190–91
Round House, The (Erdrich), 216
Ruby Ridge, Idaho, standoff, 202
Russell, Charlie, 235

Sagebrush Rebellion, 186, 203
Salvage, The (D. Thomas), 72
"San Antonio phantasmagoria" (Sánchez), 173

Sánchez, Ricardo: about, 4, 235; and Aztlán, 167; bookstore and press of, 162; and Canto al Pueblo (poetry festival), 175; doctorate and teaching positions of, 162; as faculty, 175, 176–77; and Ford Foundation Fellowship, 169–70; and Frederick Douglass fellowship, 161–62; imprisonment of, 157, 161; influences of, 161, 162; and Míctla Publishing, 169; on NEA Literature Advisory Panel, 158–59; and One World Poetry Festival, Amsterdam, 166; poetry by, 155–56, 162–63, 165, 166, 167–68, 170–71; portrait of, *174*; Pueblo ancestry of, 171; as supporter of Afro-Latines, 164; and timespace, 157, 158; at Union Graduate School, 169–70, 175; on white police brutality, 173; and work on behalf of migrant workers, 162. *See also* Paperbacks . . . ¡y Más!
Sánchez, Ricardo, works by: *Canto y Grito mi Liberación*, 162; *Hechízospells*, 168; "MAÑANA: Stanford U. Breakfast Blues," 170–71; "Míctla: Long Road Home," 169; "Old Man," 171–72; "San Antonio phantasmagoria," 173; "Slums of Richmond, El Paso the Same," 163
Sandburg, Carl, 134
Sand County Almanac (Leopold), 131
Sandoz, Mari, 235
Schlesinger, Arthur, Jr., 107
Seeger, Pete, 27
Segal, Lore: *Her First American*, 78
Sentence, The (Erdrich), 229
settler colonialism, 36, 52, 136. *See also* frontier

Shane (screenplay) (Guthrie), 103
"Shooting at Raeder, The " (Mirrielees), 113
Sierra Club: books produced by, 132; *This Is Dinosaur*, 131; *This Is the American Earth*, 139
Silko, Leslie Marmon: *Almanac of the Dead*, 210
Silva, María Teresa, 161
Simpson, Alan, 185–86, 200
Simpson, Milward, 97
"Slums of Richmond, El Paso the Same" (Sánchez), 163
Smith, Henry Nash: *Virgin Land*, 120
Smith, Jaune Quick-to-See, 235
Smith, Thomas, 131
"Social Solidarity among the Japanese in Seattle" (Miyamoto), 67–68
Sometimes a Great Notion (Kesey), 234–35
Song of the Lark (Cather), 13, 38
Son of the Middle Border, A (Garland), 48
South, as regime, 43, 60, 64
Stanford: The Story of a University (Mirrielees), 114
Stanford Mosaic (Mirrielees), 124, 125
Stanford University, 90–91, 114–16, 124–26, 170
state humanities councils, 151
Stegner, Wallace: *Beyond the Hundredth Meridian*, 101, 131; at Bread Loaf Writers' Conference, 94–95; as conservationist, 83, 96, 101; contributions to Interior Department by, 140–41; as "Dean of Western Writers," 93–94; as faculty, 90–91; on federal cultural policy, 145; gendered language/views of, 96, 190; and groundwork for environmentalism, 141–42; introduction to Sierra Club publication, 131–32; on literary culture in western states, 90–92; name misstated by *New York Times*, 93–94; New England vs. New York preference of, 95; *One Nation*, 81–82; and opposition to privatization of public land, 98, 105; racist dehumanizing language by, 95–96; on the Southwest, 106; on Stanford, 116; as successor to Mirrielees, 83; *The Uneasy Chair*, 92–93, 95, 102, 115; "Wilderness Letter," 140, 147–48
Steiger, William, 151
Steinbeck, John, 124
Story Writing (Mirrielees), 124
Stover at Yale (Johnson), 200–201
Sunbelt, 164
survivalism, 196–97

Taffa, Deborah, 4, 227–28
Taylor Grazing Act (1934), 96, 97–98
Terman, Frederick E., 116
Texas, 158, 162, 173, 176
Teters, Charlene, 228
textbooks, choices/control over, 214
This Is Dinosaur (Sierra Club), 131
This Is the American Earth (Sierra Club), 139
Thomas, Dorothy Swaine: field of study of, 70; *The Salvage*, 72
Thomas, John L., 101
Thomas, William I., 70, 72
Thompson, Era Bell: *Africa: Land of My Fathers*, 42, 51; African colonialism/

Thompson, Era Bell (*continued*)
independence movements, 52; *American Daughter*, 41, 43–44, 46, 47, 52, 53; Bell's Lettres, 50; at Bread Loaf Writers' Conference, 50; *Chicago Defender* articles by, 44–45; on DeVoto, 102; and friendship with Avis DeVoto, 51; Indigenous friendships of, 52–53; photo of, *67*; and Rockefeller Fellowship, 42; segregation experienced and witnessed by, 43–44; and support from Friends of the Middle Border, 48; travels of, 49–50, 51–52; and view of Chicago, 7, 42, 46–47, 54; and women's support groups, 51; writing as a career of, 44–45

Thompson, Frank, Jr., 132–33
"tractorcades," 182, *183*
Trillin, Calvin, 200–202
Trujillo, Joe, 225
Tsuneishi, Warren, 75
Turner, Frederick Jackson, 17
Twain, Mark (Samuel Langhorne Clemens), 89, 93

Udall, Lee: about, 4; art gallery managed by, *144*, 146, 147, 224; hosting Frost, 133–34, *135*, 224; managing husband's image, 143; media comments on, 137–38; on outdoor experiences, 83–84, 130, 143

Udall, Stewart: about, 4; and appreciation of the natural world, 83–84, 143; *Arizona Daily Star*, 133; on avoiding collisions with environmentalists, 132; and committee appointments, 130–31, 132; at Dumbarton Oaks, 145–46; as faculty, 84; favorite books of, 138; hosting Frost, 133–34, *135*; media comments on, 137–38; and support for dams, 132; and support for integration, 132; and support for strip mining, 143; and Stegner, 140

Udall, Tom, 128, 129, 227
Uneasy Chair, The (Stegner), 92–93, 95, 102, 115
Union Graduate School, 169–70
Union Pacific Railroad: collaboration with dude ranches, 32; midwesterners' relationship with, 17, 22

Vigil, Martin, 225
Virgin Land (Smith), 120

Waco, Texas, standoff, 202
Wall Street, as represented by westerners, 18, 99
War Relocation Authority, 70
Washington, Booker T.: skepticism of, 65; on universal presence of prejudice, 60–61
Washington, DC, as represented by westerners, 83, 100, 110, 127, 218
Washington State University, 176–77
Watt, James, 186
Way West, The (Guthrie), 103
"West, The: A Plundered Province" (DeVoto), 87, 99
"West against Itself, The" (DeVoto), 98, 104
Westcott, Glenway, 147
Westerners (organization), 48
white supremacy: *The Blue Book*, 159, 188; John Birch Society, 159, 188,

195–96; language of, 190; and NAPA, 199–200; and New World Order, 188; Posse Blue Book, 200; Posse Comitatus, 159, 180, 197, 199; robberies as funding source of, 178–79; violence generated by, 197 *See also* Order, the
Wicazo Ša Review, 210
Wilder, Laura Ingalls: about, 5; Little House on the Prairie series, 193–94, 196, 197, 216
Wilder, Thornton, 134
Wilderness Act, 152
"Wilderness Letter" (Stegner), 140, 147–48
Wister, Marina, 108
Wister, Owen, 101

"Women on the Breadlines" (Le Sueur), 38–39
Wong, Shaun, 235
Works Progress Administration: and funding for writers, 2; Idaho state guide from, 91–92; and New Deal effects on African Americans, 64; regionalism support from, 23
Wright, Richard, 65

Yale University: and Stewart Udall, 84; and Sánchez, 174–75
Yazzie-Martinez case, 208
Year of Decision, The: 1846 (DeVoto), 89–90
Young Man, Alfred, 224

www.ingramcontent.com/pod-product-compliance
Lightning Source LLC
Chambersburg PA
CBHW020557300725
30256CB00002B/4